Green Finance in the European Union

While global challenges continue to reshape the here and now, public and corporate finance management needs to adapt quickly to increase the efficiency of institutions, enterprises and policies to face our new reality. There are very few publications that offer a comprehensive approach to the financing of environmental protection activities by the European Union. This book explores this topic from various angles and levels, as well as highlighting the determinants that influence micro- and macro-level decisions in this area.

It presents an in-depth and unique analysis of the sources of funding for environmental measures implemented by European Union institutions, against the backdrop of national expenditure by Member States, and analyses the plausibility of the adopted targets in the run-up to 2050, in the context of the war in Ukraine and ad hoc energy policy solutions. This book is a voice in an ongoing discussion among the community of practitioners and theoreticians on sources of financing for the energy transition to achieve independence from Russian sources in the quickest possible timeframe. It demonstrates that environmental measures cannot occur without the financial participation of economic actors and financial institutions, particularly the capital market, and further underscores the scale of involvement in environmental projects, as measured by the value of green loans and green bonds covered by European financial institutions. The authors offer policy recommendations for financing activities related to environmental policy, notably energy transition.

This book will appeal to scholars, students and researchers of corporate finance, banking, strategic and public finance management as well as policy-makers and practitioners involved in green finance investments.

Marta Postuła is the head of the Finance and Accounting Department at the Faculty of Management, University of Warsaw, Warsaw, Poland.

Mariusz Lipski is an assistant professor at the Risk Management Unit in the Institute of Corporate Finance and Investment, Collegium of Business Administration, SGH Warsaw School of Economics, Warsaw, Poland.

Routledge International Studies in Money and Banking

International Banking in Global Perspective
Edited by Carmela D'Avino and Mimoza Shabani

Non-Fungible Tokens
Multidisciplinary Perspectives
Edited by Usman W. Chohan

Open Banking
Global Development and Regulation
Francesco De Pascalis and Alan Brener

Banking Reforms in Africa
Implications for Economic Welfare and Poverty Reduction
Agnes Olatokunbo Martins

Safe Assets in the Global Economy
Supply, Demand and Financial Stability
Joanna Bogołębska, Ewa FederSempach and Ewa StawaszGrabowska

Green Bonds and Sustainable Finance
The Evolution of Portfolio Management in Conventional Markets
Muhammad Saeed Meo and Marcin Staniewski

Strategy, Finance and Sustainable Value Creation
Claudio Scardovi

Green Finance in the European Union
Marta Postuła and Mariusz Lipski

For more information about this series, please visit: www.routledge.com/Routledge-International-Studies-in-Money-and-Banking/book-series/SE0403

Green Finance in the European Union

Marta Postuła and Mariusz Lipski

Routledge
Taylor & Francis Group
LONDON AND NEW YORK

First published 2025
by Routledge
4 Park Square, Milton Park, Abingdon, Oxon OX14 4RN

and by Routledge
605 Third Avenue, New York, NY 10158

Routledge is an imprint of the Taylor & Francis Group, an informa business

We would like to thank our translator Joanna Łuczak for helping us reach out to an English-speaking public.

British Library Cataloguing-in-Publication Data
A catalogue record for this book is available from the British Library

Library of Congress Cataloging-in-Publication Data
Names: Postuła, Marta, author. | Lipski, Mariusz, author.
Title: Green finance in the European Union / Marta Postuła and Mariusz Lipski.
Description: Abingdon, Oxon ; New York, NY : Routledge, 2025. |
Series: Routledge international studies in money and banking | Includes bibliographical references and index.
Identifiers: LCCN 2024018464 (print) | LCCN 2024018465 (ebook) |
ISBN 9781032562605 (hardback) | ISBN 9781032562612 (paperback) |
ISBN 9781003434689 (ebook)
Subjects: LCSH: European Union countries—Economic conditions. |
Sustainable development—European Union countries. | Environmental economics—European Union countries.
Classification: LCC HC240.9.E5 P68 2025 (print) | LCC HC240.9.E5 (ebook) | DDC 338.9/27094—dc23/eng/20240517
LC record available at https://lccn.loc.gov/2024018464
LC ebook record available at https://lccn.loc.gov/2024018465

ISBN: 978-1-032-56260-5 (hbk)
ISBN: 978-1-032-56261-2 (pbk)
ISBN: 978-1-003-43468-9 (ebk)

DOI: 10.4324/9781003434689

Typeset in Times New Roman
by codeMantra

Contents

Figures

Tables

Introduction

The complexity of the socio-economic phenomena associated with the sustainable development challenges and the geopolitical and demographic changes taking place in the world make it necessary to apply new institutional solutions and financial instruments to meet them. Efforts in that direction include research not only by economists looking for new concepts and models based on the changes they observe in the economy but also by sociologists and political scientists who prepare societies for those changes. Sustainable development, and the attendant process of bridging the gap between the poorest and the wealthiest regions, is currently one of the main challenges facing decision-makers not only in Europe but also worldwide. When work on this book started, this challenge seemed to be the main one, but over time, due to the geopolitical situation, another one surfaced, equally if not more important: ensuring Europe's external security in the context of Russia's actions. It is yet one more reason why all kinds of resources, both private and public, should be used effectively and efficiently to ensure meeting both these challenges and achieving the sustainable development goals in place.

It has become apparent that political and social demands focusing on sustainable development, financial stability and mitigation of economic and social vulnerability require new economic and social paradigms incorporating not only macro- and microeconomic aspects but also environmental elements, which have a significant impact on the former. The energy transition taking place before our eyes, made necessary on the one hand by the war in Ukraine and on the other by environmental concerns, is part of a wider global process of adapting to and mitigating the climate changes taking place. At the same time, it is related to macroeconomic circumstances of the ongoing geopolitical and demographic changes. According to one of the most quoted definitions from the UN report titled 'Our Common Future', also known as the Brundtland report, "…sustainable development is development that meets the needs of the present without compromising the ability of future generations to meet their own needs…" (UN, 1987). In practice, this means seeking to meet the needs of present and future generations while maintaining environmental, social and economic sustainability.

The major challenges facing modern society are captured in the Sustainable Development Goals developed by the United Nations in 2015. It is a set of 17 goals and 169 targets that aim to improve the quality of life of people and protect the

DOI: 10.4324/9781003434689-1

environment worldwide by 2030. The 2030 Agenda, which contains these goals, is the result of three years of negotiations between UN Member States, with a broad participation of private, scientific and social sectors. The Sustainable Development Goals reflect the three dimensions of sustainable development: economic, social and environmental. Their implementation is expected to contribute to eradicating poverty in all its forms, combating inequality and injustice, ensuring decent working conditions and economic growth, promoting health and education, protecting biodiversity and climate and building peace and partnerships for the common good. The McKinsey (2022) report emphasises the need to shape a more sustainable economy that takes into account environmental, social and governance (ESG) factors, rather than just focusing on the environmental dimension and limiting action only to reducing greenhouse gas emissions. If broadly defined society represented by the public and private sectors wishes to achieve these goals and comply with the relevant regulations, a fundamental shift in socio-economic development strategy is required.

Such complex and ambitious actions require transnational, global and international cooperation, innovation and public engagement to address these challenges and build a better future for all. The political consensus on the fact that the type of capitalism built over the last century does not meet the requirements of sustainable development as defined above has become the starting point for agreements at the international level to take action to put the economy back on a sustainable track. This, in turn, implies changes in the market environment, which its participants cannot ignore. Some attempts at supranational consensus are made annually at so-called climate summits, but there is no doubt that – whatever the ultimate level of global climate ambition – the bottom line is that a gigantic effort is required at public sector level, which determines macroeconomic conditions, and fundamental changes at the micro level.

The transition to a low-carbon economy is part and parcel of an integrated sustainable development strategy for the modern world and, despite the crisis, will remain a long-term priority for the public sector as a whole, but it will not succeed without private sector's support. It should be clear, however, that this process requires a major financial commitment, which often involves a change of investment focus and the use of hitherto non-standard tools. This was confirmed by conclusions of the discussions held in France and reflected in the 2015 Paris Agreement, which unequivocally stressed that the creation of frameworks and rules to enable climate finance is an integral part of climate action tools.

The financing of climate policy measures has been a relatively new topic in recent years, which is attracting increasing attention from academics as well as practitioners, as it cannot be ignored due to changes in the regulatory and economic environment. Indeed, the concept of sustainability is becoming a permanent feature of the business environment – an external determinant having a significant impact on the way business is conducted. Increasingly, studies are focusing on the efficiency and effectiveness of financing private and public investments in climate change adaptation and mitigation (Hong et al., 2020).

The public sector should support (through regulatory action and financial instruments) the private sector in the process of investing in sustainable and resilient sources of energy and food and remodel its offerings and supply chains to fit in with the overall efforts of governments and civil society, whose common goal is to ensure equitable access and distribution. In particular, there is no doubt that the world is facing an urgent need to reduce greenhouse gas emissions (including, for example, carbon dioxide and methane) to prevent catastrophic and irreversible impacts of climate change.

Another important source of information on the 'grand challenges' facing business today is the Global Risk Report (2023) produced by the World Economic Forum (WEF). This report, based on a survey of nearly 1,000 decision-makers from the public and private sector as well as from academia and civil society, identifies the contemporary world's most important risks (Cieslik et al., 2023). These risks are divided into a number of categories covering economic, environmental, geopolitical, social and technological issues.

In the context of the above-mentioned report and other academic discussions, yet another research area is identified, focusing on the implications climate change risks and their impacts have for economic and social decisions, for investors' approach to the investment decision-making process, as well as to hedging these risks in financial markets (Giglio et al., 2021). Environmental risks include threats related to climate change, biodiversity loss, air and water pollution and land degradation. These threats can undermine the planet's ability to sustain life and provide resources for humanity. Social risks, on the other hand, refer to threats related to inequality, poverty, migration, conflict, terrorism and human rights violations, which can undermine social cohesion, political stability and global peace.

In the European context, the narrative is grounded on the actions of the European Union and its ambitious plans to become a climate-neutral continent by 2050. These assumptions translate into actions required from the Member States, which are reflected in the ten-year national energy and climate plans. Combined with the planned changes resulting from the adoption of the European Green Deal and the Just Transition Fund, this means that Member States are faced with urgent challenges and expectations of profound changes in the financial market as well, without which it will simply not be possible to achieve the climate goals. National authorities, as part of their climate policies, can use a range of fiscal instruments, the most important of which are taxes and public expenditures that fit into the definition of green finance used throughout this monograph. Public transfers as part of fiscal policy aim to change the very structure of the production and distribution of gross domestic product. The assessment of the impact of public spending and taxation on economic growth and environmental protection is not easy and evolves in parallel with the economic and social thought (Gosh et al., 2009; Reinhart & Rogoff, 2009; Boston et al., 1991). The direction and consequences of income redistribution, and, accordingly, those of public spending, depend on the growth theory on which the analysis is based. The alleged effects of an increase in public spending (positive, neutral or negative) on the economic growth and climate vary across the schools of economic thought (new classical economics, neoclassical economics, neo-Keynesian economics or real business cycle theory). However, this does not solve the basic problem that is the impact of spending on growth and environmental indicators – programmes implemented with public spending may have a variety of positive effects on economic growth. Firstly, public goods are provided through public spending, and secondly, public spending produces products and services to correct market failures and improve market functioning. The sustainability effects of public spending are evaluated by analysing the effectiveness of government action's impact on environmental indicators through tax and spending instruments, taking into account the wealth of individual countries' societies.

Environmental taxation, on the other hand, is one of the many tools that can help us get closer to achieving environmental and climate goals. In the EU context, environmental taxation, and more specifically energy tax, is becoming an increasingly important issue as the European Green Deal aims to align energy taxation with climate goals. As noted by the European Court of Auditors (2022), this objective is particularly difficult because attractive carbon prices and non-discouraging energy taxes on fossil fuels result in higher costs for low-carbon technologies, delaying the green transition. European climate law has set a minimum target of a 55% reduction in net greenhouse gas emissions by 2030, and the EU has committed to becoming climate neutral by 2050 (European Commission). Environmental taxes are also a revenue-generating tool. In 2022, total revenues from environmental taxes in the EU amounted to almost €320 billion, equivalent to 2.2% of EU GDP and 5.4% of total EU government revenues from taxes and social contributions (Eurostat, 2023). Among environmental taxes, energy taxes accounted for more than 70% of total environmental tax revenues (77.2%), followed by taxes on transport (19.1%) and on pollution and natural resources (3.7%). However, there are other measurable benefits of environmental taxes. Pautrel (2008) showed the positive impact of environmental taxes on life expectancy through reduced pollution and thus a positive impact on public health. By appropriately steering environmental taxes, policy-makers aim to influence consumer choices through price incentives to direct consumers to other available products and services that are more sustainable, making environmentally harmful goods more expensive and consequently less attractive. At the same time, higher environmental taxes make the production process more expensive, encouraging producers to seek more environmentally friendly technological solutions (Kosonen, 2012). Finally, Li et al. (2021) showed that environmental taxes are more effective in reducing emissions compared to pollution discharge fee policies. However, regulatory spending and taxation measures taken by the public sector will not succeed without the involvement of the private sector, especially the financial market willing to finance a corporate-level shift towards sustainability.

Analyses show that, as has been the case to date, private companies and prosumers will play the greatest role, for example, in increasing the share of renewable energy sources or in changes in agriculture. It is therefore necessary to show where the funding for these challenges will come from and what measures need to be taken to ensure that public funding complements private expenditure as efficiently as possible to implement environmental measures. The financial environment, which has a significant impact on the pace and scale of change in the energy field, also plays an extremely important role in this process.

Therefore, the aim of this monograph is to indicate areas of companies' activity in which climate transition can have a significant impact on their further development but also on the feasibility of the goals defined, for example, in the Green Deal. Private sector's contribution to efforts to reduce greenhouse gas emissions is necessary to achieve the goals of the Paris Agreement and this is a process that has been ongoing for years. For example, according to the European Environment Agency, industry is the sector that has reduced its energy intensity the most since 2005.

It is vitally important that companies understand and accept the need to operate in line with the concept of sustainability. This awareness is growing rapidly, as evidenced by the consistent message of key economic reports.

New business models will go beyond optimising the carbon footprint alone. Already today, globally operating companies must consider not only their own added value but also the entire value chain, from suppliers to consumers, and the externalities generated by their activities. The monograph also points to the increasing pressure on business. On the one hand, companies have to comply with increasingly stringent regulatory requirements, such as the EU Green Deal or the plastic tax. On the other hand, they can gain competitive advantage and customer loyalty if they offer products and services in line with social expectations and environmental awareness. Hence, in order to do so, companies need to define their sustainability goals and strategies themselves and find the right tools and partners to implement them. Interestingly, however, this effort can lead to identifying new opportunities and thus, for companies making this effort, can contribute to building a competitive advantage within the future modern and sustainable economy. Therefore, business sector needs to accelerate its low-carbon transition and foster innovation and collaboration in the green economy.

Sustainability requires managers, but to a large extent also funding entities, to consider not only the short-term financial benefits but also the long-term environmental and social impacts of their decisions. It also involves looking for innovative solutions that can benefit not only enterprises and their shareholders but also their stakeholders. It is not only an ethical and legal obligation but also an opportunity to gain a competitive advantage and improve a company's reputation in the market.

Sustainability also poses many challenges for investors. Some of these are the lack of uniform standards and criteria for assessing sustainable investments. From this perspective, it is important to know the rules of efficient investment in economic, infrastructural and environmental projects, taking account of sustainability principles, and to be able to apply financial modelling tools tailored to the specificities of the projects implemented. Other necessary areas of competence include sustainable investment strategies, ESG frameworks and metrics, methods for assessing the efficiency of investment projects, taking account of financial and non-financial benefits, methods for making investment decisions and tools for identifying and quantifying risks associated with implementing a project that meets sustainability requirements.

This book presents a comprehensive and empirically verified knowledge on ways to evaluate the efficiency of institutional solutions used by the public sector but also by the financial sector, in the implementation of Sustainable Development

Goals in EU countries. The publication focuses on green finance the focus of which is to achieve sustainable development goals. It draws attention to the need to take into account ESG aspects in the decision-making process of fiscal and investment policy-making. This is of particular importance to employees of financial institutions, such as banks, investment funds and insurance companies, which play a key role not only in financing investment projects but also to politicians and decision-makers who shape the socio-economic development of a community that is the European Union but also the Member States' policies at the national level.

Chapter 1 presents the scale of financial support for ongoing climate policy at the European level between 2001 and 2021. In the European context, the environmental policy narrative is grounded on the actions of the European Union and its ambitious plans to become a climate-neutral continent by 2050, which may unfortunately change due to the armed conflict in Ukraine. The documents presented indicate a vision of how the European Union's environmental policy to 2050 should work and what financial resources are needed to make it realistic. The chapter also identifies and analyses the linkages between the environment, the economy and society, which are essential for effective systemic decisions to build sustainable solutions. Efforts to accurately interpret and assess environment's contribution to different dimensions of human functioning are among the key tasks carried out as part of sustainability policy that can count on financial support from the EU institutions, as further presented and discussed in this chapter.

Chapter 2 outlines the scale of public funding and its effectiveness for national-level environmental measures. National measures represent a large part of COFOG classification subcategories where national authorities should retain full competence for public policy-making and developing the process for financing such measures and implementing a specified catalogue of tasks. European authorities may have an important impact – in line with their competences described in Chapter 1 – on European policies in the specified areas and develop a relevant coordination and control procedure. However, national policy is of great significance so it is important to present the financial flows coming from the national level. The Authors came to conclusion that the efficiency of implementation and management of relevant measures is linked to a given country's development model (the economic school followed by those in power) adopted by the democratically elected authorities. Research confirms that it is possible to obtain good results by implementing them even at the national level, which the Authors tried to present and prove in this part of the monograph.

Chapter 3 outlines the scale of financial market involvement in meeting environmental targets. The last few years have seen positive trends in renewable energy investments in Europe. However, according to the European Commission's experts, annual investment in renewable energy alone must double by 2050 in order to meet the climate targets in place. Making an investment of this scale involves committing sufficient capital to accelerate the world's transition to a low-carbon economy. However, it should be borne in mind that in many cases these investments come in addition to companies' own planned growth investments. In this context, policy-makers, investors and financial institutions need to develop a set of financing solutions for companies to use, and it should not be forgotten that owners and investors are looking at return on equity and enterprise value. Therefore, a compromise needs to be struck between environmental objectives and these parameters. It is these dilemmas and proposed solutions that will be discussed.

Chapter 4 presents Authors' own research and a review of the literature on the impact of respective forms of environmental funding on environmental quality indicators, and in particular on air and water quality. These specific indicators will be analysed in comparison with indices used by the European Commission. In this part of the monograph, recommendations will also be made on how to finance activities related to environmental policy, in particular energy transition.

This monograph is a contribution to the discussion on the efficiency of public and private sector financing and implementing sustainable development goals at the EU level and that of individual Member States. It is also an attempt to assess, based on past experience, the tools used in the European Union to effectively and efficiently implement sustainable development goals, bearing in mind the limited resources, including financial ones. The ongoing economic and political processes require an in-depth theoretical discussion and sensible solutions in practice in order to cope with the changes taking place at the macro- and microeconomic level. The Authors hope that this book will inspire readers to reflect further on these issues.

1 Implementation of the European climate goals as an economic challenge to the public and private sector

1.1 Economic circumstances of the climate policy as a challenge to the contemporary social and economic policies

The climate crisis phenomenon has laid bare the imperfection of the existing economic concepts and, consequently, of the way they translate into the economic and social policy in place. It has turned out that with political and social expectations oriented to sustainable development, financial stability and mitigating economic and social instability, some new economic paradigms and efficient national and international institutions need to be developed to support this process (Postuła, 2015, 2022). Preventive legislation that marks out an effective course of governmental action and helps avert crises, including the sustainability crisis, as well as modified economic proposals and social expectations as to the way the government and public services should function became the subject-matter and the organising feature of the political science. This issue was already presented over 50 years ago by Donella H. Meadows, Dennis L. Meadows, J. Randers and William W. Behrens III in their book titled *Limits to Growth* (1972, Polish edition in 1973). The book demonstrates, based on a dynamic simulation model where companies and households take short-sighted decisions regardless of the long-term consequences of the short-term production and consumption, that the depletion of natural resources and environmental degradation might lead to an irreversible decline of the global economy as soon as in the 21st century. Amid the dynamic changes unfolding in the social, economic and geopolitical environment, virtually every country today is facing the challenge of undertaking green transition or building the foundations of growth based on low-emission economy. Such action involves far-reaching implications and expectations as regards land management, planning, infrastructure, investments, technologies, jobs and building social justice, which, in turn, directly translates into economic phenomena at the global, regional and national levels alike.

The climate policy has also attracted the interest not only of international bodies, e.g. the Global Commission on the Economy and Climate (2014), inspiring research at the national level, but also that of multilateral economic organisations (OECD, WB, IM, UNDP), resulting in impacts to the social and economic policy and practices in place in some developing countries (IPCC, 2014; Bailey & Compston, 2012) as well as in developed countries (The White House). All these measures

DOI: 10.4324/9781003434689-2

have contributed to extending the international climate cooperation, as exemplified by the emergence of new coalitions supporting initiatives to foster common development and climate action. One good example would be G7 communiqué of June 2015 on Climate and Clean Air Coalition (Leaders' Declaration. G7, 2015) or a joint U.S.-China statement on climate change issued by President Barack Obama and President Xi Jinping in November 2014, strongly highlighting the cooperation on energy innovation, seeing it as a guarantee of a more sustainable growth in the future. Such international initiatives have a potential of broadly impacting actions taken by other countries, provided that countries (and sub-national level entities) understand that quickly embarking on decarbonising their economies serves their best interests, in which case it will be possible to achieve major progress in this respect. While identifying climate challenges as a global issue, international cooperation in this respect focuses more on coordination, joint actions and experience sharing as well as accelerating and supporting a beneficial internal transition. At the same time, it should be borne in mind that developed countries act faster and have at their disposal bigger funds for the necessary technologies and for other forms of transition support in developing countries.

Challenges related to combating climate change, to the extent no other issue does, can be described by the metaphor of communicating vessels, with unilateral and one-off action bringing little outcome. This is why resources should be committed to climate protection both at the micro- and macroeconomic levels. In the classical theory of impact on climate change, economics points to:

- optimal rate of extraction of natural resources (Hotelling's rule);
- optimal tax policy (Pigouvian theory).

Meanwhile, over the last decades, the climate economics has been discussing how to address the need to limit greenhouse gas emissions (GHGs) and to mitigate climate change with actions that are effective and anchored in the foundations of the economic phenomena taking place. Economists realise that climate change will dominate the contemporary thinking on social and economic development (Tol, 2014), calling for well-thought-out action in that regard. It is true that the limit to natural resources and the related economic challenges have been addressed by various theories; however, these issues have never been in the main stream of the scientific discourse. However, considering contemporary challenges, i.e. growing CO_2 emissions, rising sea level, intensifying extreme weather events and negative health impacts of climate change which pose a threat to human beings and the economy alike, a comprehensive economic approach is increasingly becoming a must. It is hard to contest the view that climate change requires a global and interdisciplinary approach as part of the research undertaken and theories proposed, through adequate governmental decisions because the threats of climate change involve varying aspects, including:

- technology (Karakosta et al., 2010; Gans, 2012),
- health (Deschênes et al., 2009; Jones, 2019; Barreca & Schaller, 2020),

- well-being (Kelly & Adger, 2000; Barnetta, 2003; Pecl et al., 2017),
- energy (Karl & Trenberth, 2003; Davis et al., 2010; Spence et al., 2011).

All of these elements require investing new financial resources or changing the redistribution of those currently at the disposal of the public sector and private money, hence the discussion of green finance presented in this monograph. In other words, turning to varied scientific disciplines and extensive international cooperation and striking the balance between a given discipline and interdisciplinary cooperation is of key importance to the contemporary economics. In addition, considering that new significant factors often emerge in the climate economics with phenomena such as technological innovation, globalisation, new political programmes and new social/environmental problems, identifying the key challenges and opportunities that can contribute to the emergence of new ones is a major challenge in the context of the economic processes taking place. In view of the above, a complementary understanding of the interrelation between climate, growth and development is increasingly becoming the subject of research in disciplines such as economics (Stern, 2015; Aghion & Roulet, 2014; Urge-Vorsatz et al., 2014), international relations (Stewart et al., 2013), game theory (Hannam et al., 2015; Heal & Kunreuther, 2012) and climate ethics (Shue, 2015; Caney, 2012).

Climate change is not only a threat to the life as we know it; on the one hand, it is an opportunity to reorganise the global economy, and on the other hand, it can deepen the existing gap between poor and rich countries. Research results emphasise that in the near future, climate change will cause a yet greater income disparity across households, sectors and regions, making it necessary to adjust prices on energy markets, increasing the inflation volatility, impacting the functioning of the financial markets, boosting innovation, causing a surge of migration and public debt. Though these interrelations abound, these challenges might be properly leveraged by EU Member States. This is specifically realistic in the scenario of an early and orderly climate transition (ECB, 2023) where adequate financial tools are selected to carry it out, as will be discussed in more detail further in the monograph. This part of the monograph attempts to showcase selected studies from the literature touching on the key issues related to climate change and the attempts to prevent its intensification in the context of long-term economic outcomes of those phenomena.

One of the trends in the research conducted as part of economic analyses accompanying the discussion of climate policy involves the issues of the deepening disproportion between global economies and the wealth level in connection with the ongoing climate change. Why are some countries wealthier or poorer than others? This is the question underlying the development economics and one that is also directly linked to climate circumstances. Is the European Union (EU) as a community capable of proposing and implementing, through its action, the tools to enhance the competitiveness of this European 'family'? Before an attempt is made to answer these questions, it is worth reflecting on what this it hinges on. An extensive literature on the subject attempts to identify the 'major determinants' which best explain the social and economic development in the long term as these phenomena cannot be reliably assessed in a short term. This search increasingly boils down to recognising the importance of the geographical situation, which directly implicates the kind of climate challenges involved and the effectiveness of institutions in charge of the social and economic policy. A country's geographical situation has an impact on its economy by means of a number of economic interrelations, including the one related to agriculture performance, disease vectors and proximity of markets. A given country's institutions defined here as the principles and norms governing a society – including those imposed by external actors – influence the stimuli met by individuals to engage, personally or collectively, in the manufacturing activity. Which of those two factors is dominant cannot be empirically settled in a definite way so it is partly a matter of opinion. Nevertheless, the opinion of the majority and the historical research conducted in recent years both speak in favour of efficient institutions as the key condition for properly addressing the current challenges. Can climate change shift the scale of impact towards geography? The recent research focusing especially on the impact of climate change on average temperatures points to such a possibility, which is why it is important to look at these phenomena from the point of view of economics. It has been established that temperature impacts income through agricultural crops, employees' physical and cognitive performance, energy demand as well as the prevalence of crime, social unrest and conflicts (Aghion et al., 2022). Based on earlier research in that domain, in the second half of the 20th century, an average 1°C temperature increase in a given country in a given year caused income per capita to drop by 1.4% on average. (…) Importantly, this effect persisted once the temperature shock was over, which, over time, affected this country's economic results. Further research revealed that the relationship between temperature changes and income is non-linear. (…) Therefore, while global warming may mean increased productivity in countries where average annual temperatures are low, the increase in temperatures foreshadows increasingly dramatic decline in productivity in countries whose climate is already warm (…) (Missirian & Schlenker, 2017). This research suggests that future analyses of deep determinants of economic results may play a greater role in terms of the impact of geographic situation on development, these factors turning out to be of special importance in defining respective countries' economic goals in the current and future era of climate change. Furthermore, it also indicates that the economic prospects for countries that are poorer today will disproportionately deteriorate as these countries, on average, function in higher temperatures and are expected to record especially high temperature increases. Hardly something to be seen as a positive thing as it means deepening of the disparities in population's disposable income, it is an important argument in the discussion on the imperative of climate protection from a strictly economic point of view rather than due to some vague, unidentified future consequences.

When reviewing research results estimating the total cost of damages or the impact of climate change (disaggregated in various sectors) in various world regions, it is hard to compare those results and identify clear trends. As mentioned above, CO_2 emissions are the basic parameter taken into account when assessing climate change and scientists predominantly focus on examining the impact of this very parameter on the economy and population (see Pearce et al., 1996, see Fankhauser and Tol, 1996; Fankhauser et al., 1997). Results are difficult to compare because different studies provide for different climate scenarios, make different assumptions as to adaptation and consumption as well as a different regional disaggregation (....). They also include different climate parameters, which is why some of those presented date back also to the 20th century. Of course, all research results are there to polemicise with but none can be omitted in a discussion on the economic circumstances of climate change.

Despite the inability to make such simple comparisons, the negative impact of climate change on economic growth is corroborated both by theoretical and empirical evidence. Firstly, the environmental degradation caused by depletion, floods, droughts, extinction of rare taxa and mortality caused by extreme weather conditions has long-term implications for the economic growth. Secondly, the use of funds necessary to mitigate the consequences of climate change may reduce investment capabilities with respect to financial and physical infrastructure alike, research and development and intellectual capital, thus slowing down development (Pindyck, 2011; Ali et al., 2012). Theoretically, this relationship could be described based on the macroeconomic and microeconomic characteristics. The macroeconomic consequences involve the impact on the agricultural output and a country's propensity for economic development (e.g. by changing investments or institutions in favour of those that foster economic production development) (Dell et al., 2012). The interaction between the elements of microeconomic analysis and the multiple variables such as physical and mental performance, conflicts and well-being may have an impact on the economy (Gallup et al., 1999). Due to the inherent uncertainty as to how the climate will change, it is hard to accurately assess the costs to expect from the climate change. This is mainly due to the fact that this requires making assumptions about future events. These costs will also, to a great extent, depend on how well economies are able to mitigate the consequences of global warning, how we can adapt to it, what climate change management policies will be implemented and how effective these will be. Bearing this uncertainty in mind, we can, however, predict that the cost of climate change will be significant and unevenly distributed among countries and regions.

Despite those limitations, there is a fast growing literature regarding the economic and financial consequences of climate change. In their research conducted already a quarter century ago, Nordhaus and Boyer (1999) forecasted a very strong if not catastrophic impact of climate change in the economic growth. In turn, research results of Mendelsohn et al. (1999) and Tol (2002a) had more optimistic assumptions related to the adaptability to the change unfolding and to the mitigation of its economic consequences. In Tol, the assumed basic developmental trends predominantly result in positive outcomes. In their publications, Tol et al. (1998) argue that 7%–24% of the damages will result from the adaptation costs, the rest being actual damages. Tol's estimates (2002a) probably still fail to appreciate the true scale of the threat, for example they gloss over some serious climate change consequences and scenarios (Cf. Nordhaus, 1994; Tol, 1995, 1999, 2004). For his work on climate economics, Nordhaus was awarded the Sveriges Riksbank Prize in Economic

Sciences in memory of Alfred Nobel in 2018. Meanwhile, Downing et al. (1996) point to a much greater range of uncertainty, from nearly zero impact to nearly 40% of the global gross domestic product (GDP), reflecting a much broader scope of assumptions than those commonly taken into account. Generally speaking, the way aggregated estimates are currently generated, the actual cost of climate change may be understated because the analyses conducted have a tendency to ignore extreme weather events and underestimate or ignore the compound effect of multiple stress (see Schneider et al., 2003). Meanwhile, Nordhaus, who pioneered the analysis of the economic consequences of climate change, and Moffat conducted research whose results indicate that, on the global scale, the consequences of climate damages would be equivalent to a permanent reduction of global GDP by 2%. In turn, IPCC reports that it is reasonable to expect damages in the order of 1%–5% of the global GDP in the event of the global average temperature rising by 4°C (IPCC, 2007). It should be also pointed out that estimates from both of those studies are obviously subject to a certain error. The values provided are relatively low at first sight but it would be a mistake to come to such a conclusion. First of all, 2% of the current global GDP is a significant number. Secondly, these costs will certainly not be evenly distributed but will hit specific regions especially hard. For example, Burke et al. (2015) show that in 2100, should climate change mitigation efforts fail, GDP per capita in Sub-Saharan Africa will be 80% lower while in Europe it will be 70% higher. Similarly, the impact of climate change on the GDP growth rate seems impossible to ignore and concentrates in the world's poorest regions. Dell et al. (2009) use historic temperature oscillations in countries to establish their impact on the overall results. They find that there is a large negative impact of higher temperatures on growth but only in the poor countries, to be more specific, a 1 degree increase in temperature slows down the economic growth rate in that year by 1.3 percentage point. Such a situation does not occur in rich countries, where temperature changes do not have an observable impact on growth. Last but not least, Colacito et al. (2019) reached an opposite result, indicating a negative impact of higher temperatures on the growth rate in the United States.

The main difficulty in impact assessment is the still incomplete understanding of the very essence of climate change, among other things its regional effects (Mahlman, 1997; Wigley & Harvey, 2003). Local effects particularly involve weather changeability and extreme phenomena. The current research into the impact of climate change on the economic processes use the differences in space and time that are too limited to capture many significant details to help define the expected results. Short-term damages most probably are a greater concern for decision-makers (and would be discounted to a lesser extent than long-term penalties) and are less susceptible to failure to adapt. Social and economic factors and institutions such as the ones listed above have an impact not only on the adaptation of performance but also on the exposure and vulnerability to climate threats. Exposure is often believed to be a static factor which contributes to susceptibility rather than being in itself shaped by a range of political, socio-economic and demographic processes. Changes in the number and spatial distribution of people through population increase or decrease and through processes such as seasonal or international migrations and urbanisation may significantly change the population's exposure. The availability of natural, human, social and financial resources as well as policies that support and plan mobility or try to limit it or fail to plan the coming demographic changes in advance are key determinants of where people live. Poorer social groups are forced to live in more vulnerable areas, for example on steep slopes or river banks as they cannot afford to live in safer locations. Also political, economic and management factors such as lack of employment and poor wage-earning opportunities, no social services or a social conflict cause them to migrate to urban areas. Similarly, a high dependence on natural resources, being a key indicator of vulnerability, is related to and shaped by economic and social structures. Ownership principles, agriculture, land ownership, urban planning and many other factors may increase or decrease respective individuals' capacity to change their livelihood to one less sensitive to climate change. In summary, the most vulnerable to climate change are usually poor people with precarious living conditions, who run farms on degraded land, are poorly educated, have little control over the decision-making process, work in precarious conditions and/or live in countries and regions with low-quality healthcare systems, use limited resources and sometimes have no choice but to rely on poor management systems. Their social, cultural or political circumstances, characterised by inequalities and discriminatory practices, deprive them of fundamental goods, rights and institutional support needed for sustenance and well-being even in normal conditions, to say nothing of being able to meet the increased and additional challenges caused by climate change. These factors, not linked directly to climate, and the socio-economic context in which they are embedded at the time climate problems arise, will be probably of equal if not greater importance than threats related to climate change itself.

Gaps in the understanding of the impact of climate change on economic growth can be found in the impact analysis, in particular with respect to data for regions or individual countries. Despite the growing number of analyses conducted on the national level (e.g. U.S. Country Studies Program, 1999), the knowledge of local impacts is still too incomplete to enable a detailed comparison between regions, while there are methodological problems even for the best-assessed locations (Hahnemann, this volume). Moreover, frequent differences in assumptions make it difficult to compare case studies from different countries. Only a handful of studies attempt to ensure cohesion of the big picture based on uniform set of assumptions. Instead, many such global impact assessment studies seem to be based on limited-scope case studies, often undertaken in the United States, and then extrapolated to other regions. For example, a global assessment of impacts on water resources conducted by Fankhauser (1995) is based on a single case study in northern California; earlier studies, such as by Cline (1992) and Nordhaus (1991), are even more limited, some of the later studies such as Mendelsohn et al. (1998) not being significantly better, either. Such an extrapolation is difficult – even between northern and southern California – and will be only possible if taking due account of regional circumstances including differences in geography, level of development, value systems and adaptability.

While the understanding of developed countries' circumstances is improving – at least when it comes to the market impact – there is still a shortage of information on developing countries. Non-market damages, indirect effects (e.g. the impact of changes in agricultural output on the food processing industry), horizontal interlinkages (e.g. interplay between water supply and agriculture, or the way the loss of ecosystem function will impact GDP) and the socio-political implications of change are also still poorly understood (Newell et al., 2021). The uncertainty, transient effects (the impact of a changing rather than changed and static climate) and the impact of changes on climate variability are some other factors that deserve more attention in terms of assessment of their impact. Another key problem is adaptation (see Callaway, 2003; Klein et al., 2004; Yohe, 2004).

A macroeconomic identification of the impact of annual changes in climate conditions is a tough empirical task – Gallup et al. (1999), Nordhaus (2007) and Dell et al. (2012) note that higher temperatures cause a major limitation of economic growth in developing countries. Burke et al. (2015) confirm these findings and point out that higher temperatures would have brought greater damage in countries located in geographical areas with warmer climate, hence the aforementioned importance of geography. Analysing further, Acevedo et al. (2018), Burke and Tanutama (2019), Kahn et al. (2021) and Akyapi et al. (2022) use big data sets to show that a long-term economic impact of weather anomalies such as persistent temperature changes above or below historic norm is not homogenous in all countries and that the economic growth features a non-linear response to extreme temperatures. Moreover, Cevik and Jalles (2023) found that the increase in susceptibility to climate change is correlated to the growing income disparity, especially in the developing countries, mainly due to a poorer capability to adapt to climate change and to mitigate its effects. It is also well documented that the growing frequency and severity of natural phenomena related to negative climate change has an impact on the economic development (Loayza et al., 2012; Noy, 2009; Raddatz, 2009; Skidmore & Toya, 2002; Rasmussen & Conway, 2004), limits the human capital accumulation (Cuaresma, 2010) and upsets the external balance (Gassebner et al., 2010). Recently Cevik and Jalles (2020, 2021, 2022) pointed out in their research that the susceptibility to climate change has a growing impact on the government bond yields and spreads, the likelihood of sovereign debt default and sovereign credit ratings, especially in developing countries. Bansal et al. (2016) and IMF (2020a and 2020b) concluded the risk related to climate change – caused by temperature increase – has a negative impact on asset valuations while Bernstein et al. (2019) show that real estate exposed to the risk of sea level rising is valued below similar unexposed houses. In economic models, shocks related to climate change and carbon policy act as adverse productivity shocks (Känzig, 2021). Climate change 'destroys' a factor's productivity: a smaller output can be manufactured for a given amount of labour, capital and land – maybe upon reaching a critical point a much lower quantity is produced. Extreme weather events may act as very large adverse productivity shocks while a stable global temperature growth means smaller productivity shocks. Extreme weather events may also directly destroy capital and land, and diminish the labour supply, and the decline in supply of this kind of means for production has consequences for the economy that resemble adverse productivity shocks (Breckenfelder et al., 2023).

Remedies in this regard can also have a negative impact. CO_2 emission tax (or an equivalent climate change mitigation policy) acts as something adverse, causing a temporary productivity shock, diminishing the economy's overall production capacity for some time, while companies and households will move away from fossil energy sources to non-fossil fuel. Adverse productivity shocks increase the marginal cost of production, triggering inflation. As climate change and CO_2 emission policy act as negative productivity shocks, by raising the marginal cost of production – they can be expected to exert a certain inflationary pressure in the economy. Likewise, extreme weather events, which reduce the availability of inputs, exert inflationary pressure. As global temperature rises, very big inflationary shocks related to climate may occur more often. Inflationary consequences of climate change may be referred to as 'climate inflation'. Direct inflationary effects of the higher price of carbon energy are called 'fossilflation'. The process of companies adapting to the switch from carbon energy to non-carbon energy or green investment may cause 'green inflation'. Climate change and shocks related to CO_2 emission policy will certainly have varied impacts on respective sectors of economy, induced by changes in relative prices. For example, climate change may have a disproportionate impact on agriculture whereas CO_2 emission taxation involves sectors that to a great extent are based on carbon energy as input. Since climate change and CO_2 emission allowance prices have a different impact on various sectors, they can be expected to induce relative price changes in the economy. Such relative price changes can be very long-lasting and will take place over time irrespective of the aggregate inflation rate, whether inflation rate stands at a level corresponding to, above or below the central bank inflation target. Some argue that the central bank, when faced with a change of relative prices, should tolerate an increase in headline inflation rate, as long as the core inflation rate remains at the target level. Therefore, aside from different less or more optimistic discussions of the subject, climate change and carbon policy shocks may increase the medium- and long-term inflationary expectations and create a risk of a very persistent inflation. When households and companies have no certainty about the medium- and long-term inflation rate, they revise their outlooks based on observations of the actual inflationary effects. In this process, natural persons may relatively well rely on regular purchases of energy and food, for example. That is why an inflationary shock may increase the medium- and long-term inflation expectations and create a risk of inflation rate hovering above stable price levels. The likelihood of de-anchoring increases if the direct inflationary impact of the shock is big (e.g. a serious climate disaster, major raise of the CO_2 emission tax), if it is followed by a series of significant shocks resulting in the inflation rate initially exceeding the central bank target or if the deflationary effect of expenses is restrained by fiscal policy (e.g. households, green investment policy for public sector, private sector or both). The risk of persistent inflation is a reason to tighten monetary policy in response to climate disturbances or carbon policy. Monetary policy has a delayed impact on inflation so the optimum central bank's response to shocks is to be guided by inflation forecast rather than by current inflation. After a shock period, time is needed to adequately assess its consequences for the aggregate economy. Moreover, if the central bank decides to change its policy in response to the shock, this changed policy will impact, in a delayed manner, the total expenditure, output and inflation. That is why the optimum response of the monetary policy is to follow inflation forecasts rather than current inflation targets. The central bank develops conditional inflation projections and other significant variables on a medium-term basis, taking account of alternative monetary policy options and chooses a preferred projection. This is the general argument which also holds true for shocks caused by climate change or climate policy. Following climate change or a carbon policy shock, a projection resulting from unchanged monetary policy will most likely show a period of above-target inflation. The same projection may also point to a major risk of above-target inflation continuing in the medium and long terms. On the other hand, projections resulting from monetary policy tightening will probably demonstrate yet greater damage to the real economy than the shock itself. Importantly, projections will depend on the expected political fiscal measures undertaken to address the climate shock or measures accompanying the CO_2 emission allowance prices, such as budget transfers to support low-income households and subsidies or direct expenditure on environmental projects. Such measures can be expected to reduce the shrinking total expenditure.

Evidence suggests an ambiguous impact of carbon policy on the real economy in the EU. Some studies have demonstrated a major contractionary effect from climate policy. For example, Känzig (2021) argues that the EU carbon policy has had a significant and durable effect. According to that study, euro zone GDP, aggregate investment, aggregate consumption and unemployment follow hump-shaped paths relative to a baseline of the Emissions Trading System (ETS) CO_2 emission price increase caused by EU CO_2 emission policy. In response to climate policy intervention, HICP energy price index increase normalises around 1%, with aggregate consumption down by 0.5% in year two and starting to return to zero only in year four. The effect of the unemployment rate reaches its peak of ca. 0.2–0.4 percentage point in year two, remaining at least 0.1 percentage point above the baseline four years after the shock occurred. Other studies revealed, however, that the real impact of climate is close to nil or even positive. Similar findings can be seen in OECD research (2015), which states a similar number, that of ca. 2%. This research further proves that should temperature increase reach 4°C, then the costs could amount to as much as 10% of GDP. Weitzman (2009) argues that the costs of climate change are much higher, if disasters are taken into consideration. It should be noted that these costs are usually expressed in GDP percentage, as a way to make calculation easier, though the costs might just as well be expressed in dollars. For example, McKibbin et al. (2021) document the negative impact of domestic carbon policies in the euro zone on GDP, but this effect disappears once the authors control for country and time. Metcalf and Stock (2020) even observed a mild-to-moderate positive citizen impact on EU CO_2 emission policies in relation to GDP and total employment growth indices. In the same vein, Estrada and Santabárbara (2021) argue that a well-designed carbon policy can stimulate economic activity in the region in the mid-term, as long as the income is used to reduce other, more distortionary taxes. The real effect of climate policy greatly depends on the response of technology. The faster climate-friendly technologies are developed as a result of more stringent climate policy, the more positive medium-term impact on production and productivity will be. In summary, it can be stated beyond any doubt that climate change is uncertain when it comes to impact on the total economic growth while a decline potentially causes a major outcome.

Generally speaking, the empirical analysis presented by IMF (2023) indicates that climate-induced natural disasters have different and opposite effect on inflation and growth through multiple channels such as (i) increasing or reducing farming products' and food prices, (ii) dampening economic activity and lowering work performance, (iii) decreasing wealth and income and thus consumption and investment, (iv) influencing the transport infrastructure and distribution costs. Moreover, these transmission channels greatly vary depending on respective countries' level of economic development and diversification, as discussed above.

However, these and other similar studies could have also overlooked a certain positive outcome of climate change and have not sufficiently explained how development may reduce the impact of climate change. Separate publications could be entirely devoted to the impact of climate change on economic processes alone. A perfect collation of the above-mentioned results is provided by Tol (2022), as presented in Table 1.1.

Table 1.1 Estimates of the comparative static impact on global economic welfare

Study	*warming*	*impact*	*st. dev.*	*min*	*max*	*method*	*Scc*
d'Arge (1979)	−1.0	*−0.6*				enum	*92*
Nordhaus (1982)	2.5	−3.0		−12.0	5.0	enum	74
Nordhaus (1991)	3.0	−1.0				enum	17
Nordhaus (1994b)	3.0	−1.3				enum	23
Nordhaus (1994a)	3.0	−3.6		−21.0	0.0	elicit	62
	6.0	−6.7					29
Fankhauser (199)	2.5	−1.4				enum	35
Berz	25	−1.5				enum	37
Schauer (1995)	2.5	−5.22	8.44			elicit	129
Tol (1995)	2.5	−1.9				enum	47
Nordhaus and Yang (1996)	2.5	−1.4				enum	35
Plambeck and Hope (1996)	2.5	−2.9		−13.1	−0.5	enum	71
Mendelsohn et al. (2000)	2.5	0.03	0.05			ectric	0.7
	2.5	0.10	0.01				−2.5
	4.0	−0.01					0.1
	4.0	−0.04					0.4
	5.2	−0.01					0.1
	5.2	−0.13					0.7
Nordhaus and Boyer (2000)	2.5	−1.5				enum	37

Table 1.1 (Continued)

Study	*warming*	*impact*	*st. dev.*	*min*	*max*	*method*	*Scc*
Tol (2002)	1.0	2.3	1.0			enum	−355
Maddison (2003)	2.5	0.0				ectric	−0.8
Rehdanz and Maddison (2005)	0.6	−0.2				ectric	77
	1.0	−0.3					48
Hope (2006)	2.5	−1.0		−3.0	0.0	enum	24
Nordhaus (2006)	3.0	−0.9	0.1			ectric	16
	3.0	−1.1	0.1				18
Nordhaus (2008)	3.0	−2.5				enum	43
Horowitz (2009)	1.0	3.8		−4.2	−2.7	ectric	587
Eboli et al. (2010)	3.0	−1.35				CGE	23
Hope (2011)	3.0	−0.7		−1.8	−0.3	enum	12
Maddison and Rehdanz (2011)	3.2	−5.1				ectric	77
Ng and Zhao (2011)	1.0	−1.35				ectric	209
	1.0	−1.61					249
Bosello et al. (2012)	1.9	−0.5				CGE	21
Roson and van der Mensbrugghe (2012)	2.9	−1.8				CGE	33
	5.4	−4.6					24
McCallum et al. (2013)	2	−0.7				CGE	27
	4	−1.8					17
Nordhaus (2013)	2.9	−2.0				enum	37
Desmet and Rossi-Hansberg (2015)	4.6	5.1				ectric	−37
	9.3	−4.9					9
	13.6	−24.1					20
	16.7	−78.9					44
Sartori and Roson (2016)	3.0	−0.7				CGE	12
Kompas et al. (2018)	1.0	−0.5				CGE	72
	2.0	−1.1					41
	3.0	−1.8					32
	4.0	−2.8					27
Dellink et al. (2019)	2.5	−2.0				CGE	49
Takakura et al. (2019)	2.0	−1.1	0.1			CGE	43
	4.0	−3.9	0.4				37
	6.0	−9.1	1.6				39
Howard and Sylvan (2020-09)	3.0	−9.2	10.3	−20	−2	elicit	158
Kalkuhl and Wenz (2020)	1	−2.3	1.32			ectric	355
Conte et al. (2021)	3.7	−3.7				ectric	42
Cruz and Rossi-Hansberg (2021)	7.2	−5.0				ectric	15
Howard and Sylvan (2021-07)	1.2	−2.2	2.9			elicit	236
	3.0	−8.5	6.7				146
	5.0	−16.1	13.3				100
	7.0	−25.0	20.7				79
Newell et al. (2021)	4.3	5.63				ectric	−47
	4.3	3.61					−30
	4.3	−1.71					14
	4.3	−1.63					14

(*Continued*)

Table 1.1 (Continued)

Study	*warming*	*impact*	*st. dev.*	*min*	*max*	*method*	*Scc*
	4.3	−2.17					18
	4.3	−0.64					5
	4.3	−1.82					15
	4.3	−1.75					15
	4.3	−2.16					18

Valuation methods are enumerative, elicitation, econometric, and computable general equilibrium.
The social cost of carbon, in 2010 US dollar per metric tonne of carbon, is for emissions in the year 2015, the SSP2 scenario, a pure rate of time preference of 1% and a rate of risk aversion of 1; impacts are proportional to temperature squared.

Source: Richard S. J. Tol. (2022). A Meta-analysis of the total economic impact of climate change. *CESifo Working Paper Series* 9919, CESifo.

Results of research by various economists also illustrate demographic and structural difference as well as poorer fiscal and institutional capability of respective regions and countries to adapt to climate shocks and to mitigate their effects (Stern & Stiglitz, 2021). Consequently, a number of important implications follow for the social and economic policy in place as a consequence of the accelerating climate change. These phenomena may cause inflation and growth rate to be more volatile, which may lead to a feedback loop in all sectors of the economy. Another economic effect is that different responses of inflation patterns and growth to climate shocks cause a greater heterogeneity in the inflation and income levels experienced by various segments of the society in a given country. In other words, households with a consumer basket consisting of goods and services that are more likely to experience inflation increase and lack of income as a consequence of natural disasters will be more affected compared to households whose consumption contains proportionally fewer of such products and whose income is not subject to negative shock (IMF, 2023). Looking forward, it is also important for decision-makers to acknowledge that even though moving away from fossil fuels to alternative energy sources is a vital element of efforts to mitigate climate change, still, such an approach will certainly impact inflation and growth rate. All these economic interrelations will be undoubtedly observed and felt in the near and remote future alike, but it is important to counteract the changes that are within our control and adapt to those that are beyond it as they were overlooked in the past.

After counteraction, adaptation is the second most significant area and line of action as it reduces negative social and economic effects and may strengthen the positive ones. Adaptation will entail complex behavioural, technological and institutional adjustments across all social strata but not all population groups will adapt at the same pace (Downing et al., 1997). Adaptation is treated differently in different studies, but in all approaches, it is either underestimated or, on the contrary, its effectiveness and costs are overestimated. Impact studies are to a great extent limited to autonomous adaptation, meaning an adaptation which happens without clear intervention from the government. Such studies overlook planned adaptation. However, in many cases, governments will also start to implement adaptive policies to avert certain climate change effects and they may launch these policies much earlier before a critical climate change occurs (Cf. Fankhauser et al., 1999) – for example by linking climate change adaptation to other actions for development and global change,

Considering the heterogeneous results of research aimed to determine the impact of economic growth on quality KPIs related to climate policy, a decision has been made to conduct own research in this respect based on data from EU Member States. Now a question arises: what is the desirable effect of the social and economic policy pursued by the government: is it economic growth or cumulative quality of life index reflected, for example by metrics such as Human Development Index (HDI), Better Life Index, Inequality-Adjusted Human Development Index (IAHDI) or maybe environmental quality improvement regardless of the short-term economic costs. This monograph is using HDI, widely used to measure living standards and calculated based on three indicators: life expectancy as a measure of longevity, level of education representing knowledge, and the real GDP.

Bearing the above in mind, it has been decided to include in the model to what extent GDP growth and HDI level influence selected environmental parameters, i.e. CO_2 and NH_3 emissions. Since the parameters taken into account in the analysis may have impacts on the condition of the environment in the coming years, a further decision has been made to take account of the delayed effect of the impacts under analysis in the upcoming periods i.e. n + 1, n + 2, n + 3.

Taking account of the diversity of EU Member States, Table 1.2 presents fixed effects coefficients for all countries; these are usually treated as variables of which all values analysed are represented in a data set and can be used in assessment, also with respect to a given country.

Table 1.2 Fixed effects coefficients for the variables analysed

Dep	*Country*	*GDP*			*HDI*		
		n + 1	*n + 2*	*n + 3*	*n + 1*	*n + 2*	*n + 3*
CO_2	Austria	14.622	13.653	13.743	17.098	16.162	15.537
	Belgium	14.262	13.274	13.363	16.794	15.844	15.209
	Bulgaria	4.803	6.201	6.198	5.599	5.505	5.501
	Croatia	4.584	6.126	6.141	5.477	5.379	5.376
	Cyprus	1.399	3.111	3.170	2.399	2.297	2.292
	Czechia	5.571	7.182	7.210	6.485	6.380	6.376
	Denmark	9.142	6.323	6.310	10.621	9.775	9.139
	Estonia	3.728	5.306	5.326	4.621	4.518	4.514

(*Continued*)

Table 1.2 (Continued)

Dep	*Country*	*GDP*			*HDI*		
		n + 1	*n + 2*	*n + 3*	*n + 1*	*n + 2*	*n + 3*
	Finland	14.056	13.092	13.184	16.608	15.647	15.009
	France	18.499	17.495	17.582	20.913	20.017	19.405
	Germany	18.244	17.249	17.336	20.832	19.870	19.228
	Greece	5.195	6.857	6.903	6.152	6.047	6.041
	Hungary	5.103	6.647	6.662	5.997	5.897	5.893
	Ireland	12.670	11.730	11.792	15.159	14.211	13.578
	Italy	6.579	8.344	8.423	7.600	7.492	7.485
	Latvia	3.893	5.420	5.432	4.768	4.670	4.667
	Lithuania	3.844	5.376	5.388	4.713	4.613	4.610
	Luxembourg	6.958	4.181	4.151	8.171	7.342	6.719
	Malta	1.107	2.766	2.806	2.066	1.964	1.961
	Netherlands	14.799	13.853	13.946	17.366	16.402	15.757
	Poland	6.878	8.396	8.407	7.734	7.632	7.627
	Portugal	4.675	6.325	6.365	5.650	5.549	5.544
	Romania	5.884	7.341	7.349	6.714	6.634	6.639
	Slovakia	4.832	6.392	6.411	5.734	5.635	5.631
	Slovenia	3.650	5.309	5.351	4.586	4.478	4.473
	Spain	6.214	7.933	7.995	7.209	7.103	7.098
	Sweden	13.923	12.987	13.091	16.465	15.498	14.860
NH_3	Austria	11.115	11.272	11.367	3.174	3.450	6.385
	Belgium	11.511	11.653	11.737	3.462	3.746	6.714
	Bulgaria	5.266	5.271	5.271	3.277	3.096	3.191
	Croatia	4.512	4.534	4.546	2.471	2.281	2.383
	Cyprus	3.066	3.133	3.168	1.054	0.855	0.960
	Czechia	5.738	5.778	5.799	3.622	3.418	3.524
	Denmark	5.406	5.474	5.527	−0.651	−0.131	2.782
	Estonia	3.886	3.921	3.939	1.773	1.574	1.682
	Finland	10.858	11.012	11.111	2.760	3.044	6.033
	France	14.788	14.907	14.975	7.065	7.327	10.193
	Germany	15.175	15.314	15.396	6.986	7.277	10.296
	Greece	6.071	6.119	6.145	3.996	3.792	3.895
	Hungary	5.285	5.309	5.321	3.240	3.047	3.146
	Ireland	10.203	10.411	10.538	2.303	2.615	5.586
	Italy	6.966	7.050	7.096	4.951	4.740	4.840
	Latvia	4.033	4.057	4.068	1.974	1.786	1.891
	Lithuania	4.389	4.415	4.427	2.300	2.108	2.215
	Luxembourg	3.947	4.102	4.223	−1.946	−1.436	1.417
	Malta	2.197	2.251	2.280	0.141	−0.053	0.056
	Netherlands	12.196	12.366	12.473	4.095	4.375	7.371
	Poland	6.982	7.002	7.011	4.876	4.679	4.782
	Portugal	5.557	5.604	5.629	3.560	3.365	3.464
	Romania	5.936	5.949	5.953	3.938	3.757	3.855
	Slovakia	4.684	4.714	4.729	2.641	2.449	2.552
	Slovenia	4.005	4.057	4.084	1.865	1.657	1.765
	Spain	7.044	7.113	7.150	5.004	4.799	4.903
	Sweden	10.658	10.836	10.953	2.564	2.838	5.834

Source: Own elaboration.

The analysis uses the fixed effects exponential model for data from 2002 to 2022. The choice of model mostly stems from the nature of the data; the estimation related to the change over time of characteristics shared by selected European countries.

The exponential model is as follows (1.1):

$$y(t,x)_{ij} = A_j \bullet e^{(a_1 t + a_2 x)} \bullet \epsilon_{ij}, \tag{1.1}$$

where A_j – fixed effect; absolute term specific for each j-th country, t – time variable (year 2002 = 1), a_1 – parameter for time variable t, x – dependent variable (GDP pc or NOx), a_2 – dependent variable parameter, ϵ_{ij} – random term.

A_{ij} shows the hypothetical value of a characteristic y in period zero (2001 in this case) with characteristic x equal to zero. For the parameter to make economic sense, the A_{ij} exponent must be calculated. Structural parameters a_1 and a_2 indicate how the value of the y characteristic will change in percentage terms if the value of t or x characteristics increases by one unit.

The Equation (1.1) can be transformed to (1.2):

$$\ln\left(y(t,x)_{ij}\right) = a_1 t + a_2 x + A_j + \epsilon_{ij} \tag{1.2}$$

Then the parameters indicate how, on average, the natural logarithm of the y characteristic will change if the value of a given independent variable increases by one unit.

In addition, also considering the earlier presented conclusions as to a greater environmental impact depending on a country's wealth, a decision has been made to split EU Member States into two groups in terms of GDP per capita. The results of the analysis conducted are presented in Table 1.3.

The results obtained are quite interesting; firstly, an increased HDI level can be observed in the EU countries where above-average GDP per capita is coupled with decreased CO_2 emissions starting from the next year for the next three years. This means that the climate factor is an important parameter, which has an impact on the assessment of the quality of life in wealthier European countries. The same cannot be said of poorer countries (i.e. below average GDP per capita) because in their case, an increased HDI level is also coupled with higher CO_2 emissions, which confirms the argument put forward earlier on whereby environmental aspects will deepen the disparity between wealthier and poorer regions. In EU countries with lower GDP per capita, climate issues often play second fiddle, and changes related to environmental protection, with adequate resources earmarked thereto, are much more difficult to implement, both from social and political point of view. Meanwhile, what is surprising is the results related to the impact of GDP growth on CO_2 emissions as the model has shown that it is only in the n + 1 period that there is any real interrelation between these parameters, while in other periods, it stands at 0. Also in this case one can observe differences between higher and lower GDP per capita, i.e. in the former, each one-unit increase in GDP is coupled with a 0.287 unit drop in CO_2 emissions while in the latter, each one-unit increase in GDP is coupled with 0.174 unit increase in CO_2 emissions.

Table 1.3 Research results on the impact of GDP and HDI on CO_2 and NH_3 emissions taking account of time

Group	Dependent	Indep	Shift	*t*						*Independent*						*R2*
				Estimate	*LB*	*UB*	*Std. Error*	*t-value*	*Pr(>|t|)*	*Estimate*	*LB*	*UB*	*Std. Error*	*t-value*	*Pr(>|t|)*	
Above-average PKB per capital EU	CO	GDP	n + 1	−0.034	0.962	0.971	0.003	−13.316	0.000	−0.287	0.637	0.884	0.083	−3.443	0.001	0.901
			n + 2	−0.033	0.963	0.972	0.002	−15.004	0.000	0.000	1.000	1.000	0.000	−4.730	0.000	0.908
			n + 3	−0.033	0.963	0.971	0.002	−15.154	0.000	0.000	1.000	1.000	0.000	−4.480	0.000	0.906
		HDI	n + 1	−0.026	0.967	0.981	0.004	−7.080	0.000	−5.018	0.001	0.062	1.141	−4.397	0.000	0.906
			n + 2	−0.028	0.964	0.980	0.004	−6.689	0.000	−4.091	0.001	0.188	1.234	−3.314	0.001	0.900
			n + 3	−0.030	0.963	0.977	0.004	−7.826	0.000	−3.386	0.004	0.303	1.118	−3.030	0.003	0.898
	NOx	GDP	n + 1	−0.050	0.946	0.957	0.003	−16.900	0.000	0.000	1.000	1.000	0.000	0.579	0.564	0.872
			n + 2	−0.046	0.949	0.960	0.003	−15.226	0.000	0.000	1.000	1.000	0.000	−0.800	0.425	0.872
			n + 3	−0.043	0.952	0.962	0.003	−14.537	0.000	0.000	1.000	1.000	0.000	−1.970	0.051	0.875
		HDI	n + 1	−0.069	0.925	0.942	0.005	−14.821	0.000	6.836	55.495	15600.570	1.438	4.752	0.000	0.891
			n + 2	−0.069	0.924	0.943	0.005	−13.047	0.000	6.287	26.212	11020.709	1.541	4.079	0.000	0.887
			n + 3	−0.058	0.934	0.953	0.005	−11.503	0.000	3.008	1.176	348.395	1.452	2.071	0.040	0.876
Above-average PKB per capital EU	CO	GDP	n + 1	−0.043	0.955	0.961	0.002	−25.477	0.000	0.174	1.117	1.268	0.033	5.355	0.000	0.780
			n + 2	−0.034	0.962	0.970	0.002	−16.458	0.000	0.000	1.000	1.000	0.000	−0.863	0.388	0.767
			n + 3	−0.033	0.964	0.972	0.002	−15.092	0.000	0.000	1.000	1.000	0.000	−1.869	0.062	0.770
		HDI	n + 1	−0.039	0.956	0.967	0.003	−12.898	0.000	0.812	0.589	8.623	0.685	1.186	0.236	0.764
			n + 2	−0.040	0.954	0.967	0.003	−12.535	0.000	0.951	0.693	9.669	0.672	1.415	0.158	0.768
			n + 3	−0.041	0.954	0.966	0.003	−12.622	0.000	0.968	0.755	9.184	0.638	1.518	0.130	0.769
	NOx	GDP	n + 1	−0.042	0.956	0.962	0.002	−26.825	0.000	0.000	1.000	1.000	0.000	3.832	0.000	0.848
			n + 2	−0.040	0.958	0.964	0.002	−24.043	0.000	0.000	1.000	1.000	0.000	2.348	0.019	0.844
			n + 3	−0.039	0.958	0.965	0.002	−22.469	0.000	0.000	1.000	1.000	0.000	1.536	0.125	0.841
		HDI	n + 1	−0.048	0.949	0.958	0.002	−20.386	0.000	2.687	5.202	41.466	0.530	5.074	0.000	0.852
			n + 2	−0.050	0.946	0.956	0.002	−20.186	0.000	2.963	6.995	53.565	0.519	5.706	0.000	0.854
			n + 3	−0.050	0.946	0.955	0.002	−20.206	0.000	2.862	6.654	45.967	0.493	5.804	0.000	0.854

Source: Own elaboration.

An analysis of the impact of GDP and HDI on NH_3 emissions has demonstrated a lack of interrelation between the economic growth and this parameter regardless of how wealthy a given EU Member State is. For HDI, the model has shown than each one-unit increase in the index causes NH_3 emissions to rise by 6.84 in n + 1, by 6.29 in n + 2, by 3.00 in n + 3, respectively, in countries with an above-average GDP per capita. Meanwhile, in the other group, that of poorer countries, this interrelation is similar, the impact being less significant, i.e. 2.69 in n + 1, 2.96 in n + 2, and 2.86 in n + 3, respectively.

It should be noted that the understanding of the impact of climate on human well-being is gradually increasing. One can observe, though, that as time goes by, the latest insights point to the naivete of the earlier research on the impact of climate on the social and economic development. Nevertheless, one thing that is certain is that the consequences of climate change will not be evenly distributed. Some will lose, while others will benefit from climate change; some will lose or benefit only slightly, with others losing or benefiting quite a lot. This depends on when, where and what actions are being analysed. Another sure thing is that the poor will lose the most, at least in terms of their income. The poor are the most vulnerable as their adaptability is lower. If vulnerabilities are not the same, caution should be exercised when aggregating estimates of the impact for respective countries, economy sectors and income classes. A good solution could be capital weights, e.g. acknowledging the weight of moral choices. If susceptibility to threats is not equal in respective countries and sectors, it will change over time. Research into the dynamics of susceptibility has only started, but the first results are already showing that results are complex and important for both moral and economic factors. Though it can be said with a high degree of certainty that economic growth would decrease the susceptibility to threats, it cannot be said that accelerating the economic growth, which, considering the current characteristics of the global economy, would result in continued GHGs, would necessarily decrease the impacts; nor limiting GHGs, and consequently slowing down the economic growth, would necessarily reduce the climate change effects. Neither can it be established whether or not the current economic development policy is exactly what is needed to reduce the susceptibility to climate change or whether these policies require slight or major adjustments. The impact of climate change is significant but also subtle and further research is necessary to manage mitigation policy in an adaptive manner that corresponds both to the scope and complexity of the problem. Any future research should take account of a more comprehensive concept of adaptability which has recently come to light and should be based on a more extensive and varied set of social and economic scenarios, taking account of the susceptibility to threats, economic development and emissions. Such research will not only provide a better insight into who is susceptible to threats but also into how to minimise them. Ways to measure the (in)justice of climate change effects should be developed and presented. Inequalities related to climate change effects should be compared to inequalities in terms of GHG reduction. With the current state-of-the-art in the understanding of susceptibility and adaptation, it is hardly likely for loss reduction optimisation to be empirically founded, anchored in well-understood processes or reflecting a consensus on ethical issues (Taconet et al., 2020).

When pointing to the significance and high impact of climate change on the social and economic policy, it is worth emphasising that the way to address this change is not always enthusiastically received. Taking that into account, it would be useful to go back to one of the aspects already mentioned here, namely how the climate change will impact the pursuit of economic growth in poor countries. The consequences of that change go far beyond those countries and global development, triggering a sense of injustice when climate change winners and losers are set up against one another. This can include the re-emergence of the Non-Aligned Movement and of the Group of 77 as prominent factions in the multilateral system. There is a growing importance of failed states, which, as a result of climate change, have been declared incapable of development and as such resistant to foreign investment. Failed states act as an overlapping source of global instability with climate change (Ginglinger & Moreau, 2019). The spheres of global risk are more clearly defined by geographic situation. Risk management strategies will need to respond accordingly, placing a greater emphasis on weather patterns and linkages across country borders as well as taking account of instability of the economies whose exports are dominated by fossil fuels. It is to be expected that green transition in those countries is causing economic, political and social shocks whose consequences will potentially reverberate beyond their borders. Power will be derived to a lesser extent from controlling natural resources and potentially more from controlling transmission routes of renewable energy and intellectual property of green technologies (Gielen, Zwiers, 2018). Norms related to the use of green intellectual property are not immutable and will decide on whether or not such power will be manifested. A more regular distribution of national and international security forces will be needed to help communities affected by crises. The normalisation of post-disaster reconstruction, along with humanitarian aid operations, will place greater demands on security forces and make their work more visible to civilians. Methods and tools borrowed from the domain of security (such as scenario planning and risk management) will be increasingly applied to economic planning and global development. This promises a better alignment between the two policy communities.

A balance between disciplinary perfection and interdisciplinary cooperation is of key importance to climate economics. In addition, new topics often emerge in climate economics following technological innovation (Postuła et. al., 2021), globalisation, new political programmes and new social/environmental issues, identifying the key challenges and opportunities that could contribute to yet new challenges.

Literature on the subject abounds in a number of critical views on the impact of climate change on economic processes and on decisions taken as part of them, which indicate the significance of the challenge facing the world and the multitude of questions that cannot be reliably answered as of today in this area. Therefore, it can be clearly stated that climate change as well as the social and economic policy aimed to avert it will continue to shape the world and redefine or correct the economic phenomena taking place globally and the global competitiveness. The Nobel Prize winning economist Amartya K. Sen wrote in his book titled *Development as Freedom* that the path to improving human prosperity will be paved by extending the scope of choices and opportunities. While a policy promoting sustainable development may lead in a short term to (a certain but not unlimited) economic growth, an opposite outcome is hard to achieve. Hence, achieving sustainable development will also require strengthening actions by the state and by communities such as the EU, which clearly need to include environmental and social goals as the fundamental and self-sufficient dimension of development (Sen, 1999). Having that in mind, those very issues are examined in greater detail further in the monograph.

1.2 European climate goals – origin, evolution and evaluation

The climate policy, as presented and emphasised in the previous subchapter, is a major factor shaping economic processes, broadly defined competitiveness of a region and its residents' quality of life. Hence, no wonder that these days it is also a significant if not the most significant challenge the European Community is facing in its efforts. From the EU's point of view, this means running policies intended to combat climate change and adapt to the new conditions as well as to strive to be a global leader of such actions. This is important because the area of rational environmental policy requires support from all participants of the ongoing economic processes (government, market, world and financial markets) as environment protection requires reconciling the interests of economic operations, social welfare and the needs of future generations, as presented by Donella H. Meadows, Dennis L. Meadows, Jørgen Randers and William W. Behrens III in the already mentioned 'Limits to Growth' (1972). To highlight the horizontal dimension of the environmental policy and the need to place it in a global context, it is also worth citing here the results of public opinion poll conducted among EU residents. According to the last survey (Special Eurobarometer, 468) held in 2020, 74% of respondents concluded that environmental protection decisions should be taken jointly at the EU level, while 32% of those polled were in favour of taking such decisions at the Member State level. Though the result means that most of respondents find it suitable to have environmental problems solved at the EU level, it should be noted that their percentage has fallen compared to 2008. According to the survey held back then (Special Eurobarometer, 295), the share of individuals identifying the EU as the competent level for environmental action was 78%, so in twelve years it went down 4% (Postuła, 2022). Such a situation may be due to the lack of social awareness of the measures taken at the EU level and, consequently, a belief that EU-level measures are ineffective, as well as due to new challenges being identified, perceived by the public as local problems. A good example of the latter case would be urban pollution, where the society naturally considers local or national authorities to be the competent entity to take action. Nevertheless, as demonstrated before, failure to identify global goals or standards also with respect to problems occurring locally (noise, urban pollution) will make it impossible to achieve the right outcomes. This means that it is necessary to take measures to better publicise and increase the social awareness of the scope and principles of the common environmental policy.

The above measures are gaining a special significance in the light of other results relating to the social perception of environmental protection issues. A survey conducted in 1976 (The Perception of Poverty in Europe, March 1977) revealed that for 94% of the people environmental protection and limiting air pollution is important (63% very important, 31% important). Recent survey in this respect, conducted in 2017 (Special Eurobarometer, 468), indicates that the result remains similar, i.e. 95% of those polled believe environmental protection to be important (53% very important, 42% important). Also when asked whether regulations to foster environmental protection in respective Member States should be developed at the EU level, a great majority of those polled – 77% – answered affirmatively.

It is often assumed in macroeconomic climate change mitigation modelling that the emission reduction entails transitioning to a lower-emission business model with higher input-output coefficients and costs, bringing about both short-term losses in domestic production and limited consumption due to cost increase, and consequently a reduced production and consumption in the long term, because low-emission substitutes are more expensive. Social sciences studies into international cooperation on climate change predominantly suppose that mitigating climate change consequences is costly for every participating country, while bringing only global effects, incalculable benefits, meaning that an action ostensibly seems contrary to the country's interest, which is why it is referred to as a prisoner's dilemma and the 'tragedy of the commons'. Likewise, most research in applied moral and political philosophy, also called 'climate ethics', is based on this assumption and tries to develop the principles of ethical distribution of emission fees, rights and allowances. Both national and international climate policies have undoubtedly been developed under the influence of all those scientific disciplines and based on the assumptions presented.

The EU is but one of the players implementing actions to protect our climate, which is a relative latecomer to the discussion on the subject. Historically speaking, climate problems were already on the agenda at the 1972 'Only One Earth' Stockholm conference, which marked the turning point in the development of the international environmental policy. Then, 1979 saw the first international meeting on climate, which led to the creation of the World Climate Programme. Another phase was establishing in 1988 the Intergovernmental Panel on Climate Change (IPCC), an intergovernmental scientific organisation under the UN auspices whose purpose is to provide the international community with information on the current state of scientific knowledge on climate change and its potential environmental, economic and social impact. To date, IPCC has published several dozen reports on climate threats, and its report recommendations are the basis for binding decisions, including the Paris Agreement in 2015. Another important step was the 'United Nations Conference on Environment and Development' held in 1992 in Rio de Janeiro and featuring heads and representatives of 162 states and international organisations, often referred to as the 'Earth Summit'. It is believed that it was there the ecodevelopment era started from adopting important documents including the Rio Declaration on Environment and Development. It also adopted Agenda 21, the so-called comprehensive plan of action, and the United Nations Framework Convention on Climate Change (UNFCCC), intended to protect climate and reduce global GHGs. Collective action led to the first Conference of the Parties (COP1) in 1995 in Berlin (UN, 1995), which concluded that UNFCCC's climate commitments were incommensurate with the earlier defined goals, and to signing the 1997 Kyoto Protocol. The Protocol was the first global greenhouse gas reduction treaty and it obliged developed countries to reduce gas emissions by an average of ca. 5% by 2012 compared to 1990 emissions.

Presently, key climate change conferences are held by the UN, in particular COP, which supervises the Convention implementation by national entities as well as drafts new regulations in the form of decisions. In 2005, a new important climate policy tool came to being: the EU emissions trading system (EU ETS) launched to reduce CO_2 emissions from the industry by applying strict financial instruments. It covers more than 11,000 power stations and factories all over the EU, which are obliged to hold an emission allowance per each ton of CO_2.

The first climate policy discussions at the European Council, Commission and its bodies were spurred by the publication of the first summary report of the IPCC in 1990. That was the point climate change was discussed for the first time by the European Council as part of preparations to the coming negotiations on the United Nations Framework Climate Change Convention (UNFCCC). As a consequence of those talks, EU leaders agreed to maintain the European Community's 1990 GHG level by 2000. Unfortunately, it was not specified at that point what action would be taken to achieve such an emission goal, which triggered a discussion on joint and coordinated initiatives in that respect and the source of funds to be earmarked for their implementation. At an early stage of the climate policy-making, three main areas and solutions were identified, which serve as a basis for the actions taken: GHG emissions reduction, promoting renewable energy sources (RES) and improving energy efficiency. It should be borne in mind that despite the indisputable impact of climate change on the economic growth among Member States, in the face of the current problems, it was hard to find enthusiasm for fast and joint action. The first renewable energy and energy performance instruments were agreed upon. To solve the GHG emission problem, a motion relating to the European CO_2 Programme in the context of energy tax was discussed in 1992. There was no consensus, however, within the Community as to the need to introduce such a tax and as to its amount, and a group of Member States led by the United Kingdom prevented the introduction of the proposed solutions. Despite the lack of success with CO_2 tax, softer instruments in the area of energy performance and renewable energy had already been agreed upon. 1991 saw the implementation of the 'Special Action Programme for Vigorous Energy Efficiency' (SAVE), a programme intended to promote and facilitate the implementation of energy performance policies and programmes, and to optimise the process to the extent possible. Except for voluntary emission reduction agreements with car manufacturers in 1998 pursuant to Directive 1999/31/EC on the landfill of waste to reduce the amount of methane in 1999, no concrete progress was made in the late 1990s when it comes to European climate goals. In addition, biofuel and energy performance regulations were adopted. This 1992 programme involved joint standards to be met in Member States by heating boilers, electric refrigerators, freezers and other electrical appliances and the energy labelling scheme for household appliances to enable comparison of electricity consumption between different monitoring systems. In turn, 1993 saw the adoption of the SAVE Directive, which imposed on Member States the obligation to reduce GHG emissions through further measures such as energy audits for energy-intensive companies, building certification or thermal insulation for new buildings. Actions taken in that period were of great significance as they showed the mind-set and pointed to problems humanity would need to tackle. Nevertheless, no quantitative targets were indicated and the policy implementation could be designed by a Member State. In 1993, with the ALTENER programme, EU introduced a Community-wide indicative target to promote renewable energy and Member States' active engagement in its implementation also at the national level. It was expected RES would account for 8% of energy supplies in 2005 and biofuels, for 5% of the road fuel market. Moreover, ALTENER provided funding for measures to facilitate renewable energy development, including research, monitoring activities and promotional and pilot campaigns. Using the monitoring mechanism established by the decision 93/389/EEC, the Community was able to assess the development of national GHG reduction programmes (there were no targets set for Member States) and monitor the progress against the 2000 target. Though emissions were falling in the early 1990s, this was mainly due to Germany unification and lower demand for gas in the United Kingdom and not so much to an effective climate policy. At the same time, the European Environment Agency was established to monitor performance against climate goals and to ensure objective, reliable and comparable information on the condition, pressures and vulnerabilities of the environment in the EU and its surroundings. One of the ways EEA shares this information is by publishing 'State of Environment' reports, of which there have been dozens to date but to better understand the evolution in mentality taking place back then at the EU level, it is worth mentioning the first three:

- Europe's Environment: The Dobris Assessment (1995);
- Environment in the European Union – 1995 – Report for the Review of the Fifth Environmental Action Programme (1995);
- Europe's Environment: The Second Assessment (1998).

These reports were aimed to provide strategic support for environmental planning and involved major steps in the EU (or European) policy. Another comprehensive publication by this institution, i.e. 'Environment in the European Union at the Turn of the Century', caused quite a stir, showing the direction climate change was heading and how many challenges the EU was facing in that regard.

The inevitability of changes to the social and economic policies in place due to the advancing climate change, also with an active participation of the United Union, was also the topic of discussion at international forums, e.g. at the climate summit in Kyoto in December 1997, where industrialised countries agreed on a set of quantitative targets for GHG emissions, with the European Community committing to a 8% reduction for a basket of six GHG in the commitment period of 2008–2012 (compared to 1990 levels). It was the Kyoto Protocol that established market-based mechanisms for meeting reduction targets, i.e. Emissions Trading,

Clean Development Mechanism and Joint Implementation. These assumptions in particular influenced the design and wording of the existing multilateral climate treaties, i.e. UNFCCC and Kyoto Protocol. The climate change mitigation model from Kyoto Protocol aimed to put in place an emission reduction regime through targets for developed countries (and post-Soviet economies in transition) based on the principles of 'burden sharing' in accordance with 'common but differentiated responsibilities' and attempted to make these countries comply with their commitments by making those legally binding and enforceable on the global arena. Discussion on the equity of burden sharing continually led to divisions; meanwhile, the implementation of the Protocol mechanism was very poor and in any case it was possible to circumvent it through non-participation (as was the case of the USA) or withdrawal from the agreement (the case of Canada) – such is the nature of the international public law in the sovereign state system. However, it being necessary to define the goal implementation strategy, the Community entered the phase of more dynamic climate policy goal-setting in the beginning of the new millennium. In 2000, the European Climate Change Programme (ECCP) was launched to examine a wide range of policy sectors and instruments with a potential to reduce GHG emissions, as a result of which common and coordinated strategies to achieve Kyoto goals were developed. This led to ETS being introduced by Europeans, with national GHG caps for energy and industry sectors in each Member State, as well as proposals and communications regarding areas such as energy labelling and promoting combined heat and power generation and biofuels (Bekkhus, 2007). Moreover, the Renewable Energy Directive (RED) introduced indicative renewable energy share targets for each Member State.

Policies and measures aimed to comply with the Kyoto Protocol's first commitment period targets were discussed and implemented in the social and economic policies in place between 1998 and 2006 and were meant to achieve them by introducing reductions for 2008–2012. Table 1.2 contains an overview of policies implemented pre-Kyoto, post-Kyoto, in the late 1990s and in the early 21st century in the first commitment period, as well as in 2007–2010 as part of preparations for 2020 targets. The overview shows that the European climate policy was from the outset oriented to deal with the main pillars of climate policy, namely GHG, RES and energy efficiency measures. Even though agreement was not reached to introduce CO_2 tax as a way to combat GHG emissions in the early 1990s, further periods saw the introduction of various instruments in that area.

The Climate and Energy Package was a follow-up to the three-pronged political approach. In March 2007, EU heads of state agreed on a set of three goals referred to as '20-20-20 by 2020', including GHG emission, renewable energy and energy performance targets. To ensure implementation of the new goals, the European Commission introduced the 'Climate and Energy Package' in 2008. This programme involved four main parts: the amended ETS Directive with one EU-wide cap for the third allocation period (2013–2020), the Effort Sharing Decision (ESD) introducing national emission reduction targets for non-ETS sectors in all Member States, RED laying down national targets for heating/cooling and transport energy consumption and Carbon Capture and Storage Directive (CCS Directive). Moreover, fuel quality and CO_2 emission standards were adopted with the Climate and

Energy Package. It is also worth emphasising that energy efficiency is not directly addressed in the package with specific measures but is implemented by means of a sector-wide approach using tax measures, standards and information tools. Since 2012, the Energy Efficiency Directive (EED) has been in effect as a common framework of actions to promote energy efficiency (see Table 1.4 for an overview of policies implemented in that time interval).

Another milestone was the signing, in Paris in 2015, of the first ever international agreement where the signatories committed to keep the average global temperature increase well below 2°C compared to the pre-industrial era and to continue efforts to limit global warming to 1.5°C above the pre-industrial era. What the countries signing the agreement wished to achieve is to slow down GHG emission increase as fast as possible and balance emissions and absorption in the second half of the century. The agreement stresses the need to reduce CO_2 concentration in the atmosphere as fast and effectively as possible to improve water and air quality and to stop desertification and loss of biological diversity. The agreement stipulates that actions to reduce CO_2 concentration will be considered by all parties, with full respect of their specifics and socio-economic capabilities. The Paris Agreement

Table 1.4 Development of key EU climate policy instruments by policy objective

	Pre-Kyoto (1990–1997) *aimed at 2000*	**European Climate Change Programme** *and additional legislation* **(1990–2006)** *aimed at 2010 (or 2008–2012)*	*Climate and Energy Package and additional legislation (2007–2010) aimed at 2020*
GHGs	No European policy (discussion on CO_2 tax, which was not adopted) Mainly national polices	EU ETS (2003)	EU ETS review (2008, 2009) (One EU-wide ETS target / including aviation) ESD (National non-ETS targets)
		Fluorinated Gases Regulation	Fluorinated Gases Regulation review
		Mobile Air-Conditioning Systems Directive	Further implementation
		Voluntary agreement with car manufacturers (1998/1999)	Mandatory standards for cars and vans
RES	ALTENER	Renewable Electricity Directive (2001)	RED & Fuel Quality Directive
		Biofuels Directive	
EEff	SAVE	Energy Services Directive	EED
		Combined Heat and Power Directive	
		Ecodesign of Energy Using Products Directive	Further Implementation
		Energy Labelling Framework Directive	Energy Labelling Framework Directive review
		Energy Performance of Buildings Directive	Energy Performance of Buildings Directive review

Source: Ecologic Institute 2015, https://climatepolicyinfohub.eu/european-climate-policy-history-and-state-play.html (12.10.2023).

also provides that in this period, a balance between GHGs and absorption should be reached, for example through forests.

The EU was also an active participant in the process of developing the UN Agenda 2030. As interpreted by the European Commission, the adopted Sustainable Development Goals (SDGs) were mirrored by the already existing *Europe 2020 Strategy* and the Juncker Commission's ten priorities. As noted by the European Court of Auditors (ECA, 2019), the consequence was that no additional strategic framework was introduced, which meant that, except for climate and energy goals, the assumptions already in place were subject to monitoring until 2020 rather than until 2030.

Once the political guidelines for the new Commission (2019/2024) were defined and the same was appointed (December 2019), Sustainable Development Goals became the centrepiece of the newly created strategy. The guidelines of the European Green Deal fit squarely into the philosophy of Agenda 2030 and are aimed at transforming the EU into an area that manages its resources efficiently and on a climate-neutral basis. Sustainable Development Goals were also embedded in the European Semester procedure, starting from publishing the Annual Sustainable Growth Strategy in 2020 (and reflected in national reports prepared as part of that process. What has and still does pose a huge challenge is introducing SDGs and the related measures into the budgeting process. Since 2017, the European Commission has provided information, in descriptive terms, how a given programme contributes to their achievement, but it has been done by means of communications rather than reports.

Table 1.5 also shows that legal instruments of the EU climate policy have developed over time as new challenges emerged.

Table 1.5 Overview of main energy efficiency policy initiatives taken at the EU level over the last 50 years

Type of policy	*Description*
Resolutions	Council Resolution 75/C 153/2 of 17 December 1974 concerning Community energy policy objectives for 1985 Council Resolution 80/C 149/1 of 9 June 1980 concerning Community energy policy objectives for 1990 and convergence of the policies of the Member States Council Resolution 86/C 241/01 of 16 September 1986 on new Community energy policy objectives for 1995 and convergence of the policies of the Member States
Regulations	Regulation 305/2011/EU of the European Parliament and of the Council of 9 March 2011 laying down harmonised conditions for the marketing of construction products and repealing Council Directive 89/106/EEC
Directives	Council Directive 1978/170/EEC of 13 February 1978 on the performance of heat generators for space heating and the production of hot water in new or existing non– industrial buildings and on the insulation of heat and domestic hot-water distribution in new non-industrial buildings

(*Continued*)

Table 1.5 (Continued)

Type of policy	*Description*
	Council Directive 1989/106/EEC of 21 December 1988 on the approximation of laws, regulations and administrative provisions of the Member States relating to construction products
	Council Directive 1992/42/EEC of 21 May 1992 on efficiency requirements for new hot-water boilers fired with liquid or gaseous fuels
	Council Directive 1992/75/EEC of 22 September 1992 on the indication by labelling and standard product information of the consumption of energy and other resources by household appliances
	Council Directive 1993/76/EEC of 13 September 1993 to limit carbon dioxide emissions by improving energy efficiency (SAVE)
	Directive 1996/57/EC of 3 September 1996 on energy efficiency requirements for household electric refrigerators, freezers and combinations thereof
	Directive 2000/55/EC of 18 September 2000 on energy efficiency requirements for ballasts for fluorescent lighting
	Directive 2002/91/EC of 16 December 2002 on the energy performance of buildings
	Directive 2005/32/EC of 6 July 2005 establishing a framework for the setting of eco-design requirements for energy-using products and amending Council Directive 92/42/EEC and Directives 96/57/EC and 2000/55/EC of the European Parliament and of the Council
	Directive 2006/32/EC of 5 April 2006 on Energy End-use Efficiency and Energy Services and Repealing Council Directive 93/76/EEC
	Directive 2009/125/EC of 21 October 2009 establishing a framework for the setting of ecodesign requirements for energy-related products
	Directive 2010/31/EU of 19 May 2010 on the Energy Performance of Buildings (recast)
	Directive 2012/27/EU of 14 November 2012 on Energy Efficiency, Amending Directives 2009/125/EC and 2010/30/EU and Repealing Directives 2004/8/EC and 2006/32/EC
	Directive 2018/844/EU of 30 May 2018 amending Directive 2010/31/EU on the energy performance of buildings and Directive 2012/27/EU on energy efficiency
	Directive 2018/2002/EU of 11 December 2018 amending Directive 2012/27/EU on energy efficiency
Communications	EC, 1987. Towards a continuing policy for energy efficiency in the European Community. COM (1987) 223 final. Brussels, 13.05.1987
	EC, 1998. Energy Efficiency in the European Community - Towards a Strategy for the Rational Use of Energy. COM (1998) 246 final. Brussels, 29.04.
	EC, 2000. EU policies and measures to reduce GHGs: towards an ECCP. COM (2000) 88 final. Brussels, 08.03.2000
	EC, 2000. Action Plan to Improve Energy Efficiency in the European Community. COM (2000) 247 final. Brussels, 26.04.2000

(*Continued*)

Table 1.5 (Continued)

Type of policy	*Description*
	EC, 2000. Green Paper on Towards a European Strategy for Energy Supply. COM (2000) 769 final. Brussels, 29.11.2000
	EC, 2005. Green Paper on Energy Efficiency or Doing More with Less. COM (2005) 265 final. Brussels, 22.06.2005
	EC, 2006. Communication from the Commission - Action Plan for Energy Efficiency: Realising the Potential. Brussels, 19.10.2006
	EC, 2007. An energy policy for Europe. COM (2007) 1 final. Brussels, 10.1.2007
	EC, 2011. A Roadmap for moving to a competitive low carbon economy in 2050. COM (2011) 112 final. Brussels, 8.3.2011
	EC, 2015. Energy Union Package: A Framework Strategy for a Resilient Energy Union with a Forward-Looking Climate Change Policy. COM (2015) 80 final. Brussels, 25.2.2015
	EC, 2019. The European Green Deal. COM (2019) 640 final. Brussels, 11.12.2019
Recommendations	Council Recommendation of 4 May 1976 on the rational use of energy in the heating system of existing buildings
	Council Recommendation of 4 May 1976 on the rational use of energy for electrical household appliances
	Council Recommendation of 4 May 1976 on the rational use of energy by promoting the thermal insulation of buildings
	Council Recommendation of 25 October 1977 on the regulation of space heating, domestic hot water production and the metering of heat in new buildings
	Council Recommendation of 5 February 1979 on the reduction of energy requirements for buildings in the Community

Source: M. Economidou, V. Todeschi, P. Bertoldi, D. D'Agostino, P. Zangheri, L. Castellazzi, Review of 50 years of EU energy efficiency policies for buildings, *Energy and Buildings*, Volume 225, 2020, 110322, https://doi.org/10.1016/j.enbuild.2020.110322.

Some elements have evolved and come to being based on experience with previous elements which were transformed and further developed as new data came in and new solutions were worked out. Requirements of some interest groups also actively shaped and impacted the design of climate policies. When it comes to GHG, EU ETS evolved from a national emissions cap for each Member State towards an EU-wide cap, thus taking over a certain control over some economy sectors from Member States. A good example for renewable energy is the Electricity Directive (indicative Member States' renewable energy targets) and Biofuel Directive, the two combined as part of the Climate and Energy Package in the RED Directive. Moreover, RED was introduced into binding national renewable energy targets as a share in the final energy consumption, and thus the directive raised the legal status of instruments and included renewable heating and cooling. The target framework for 2030 shows, however, that the policy development should not necessarily aim for more stringent solutions. Solutions binding only at the EU level will be introduced as a renewable energy goal for 2030, and the stringency of the directive for red points should be adapted to those, with Member

States allowed to choose their own indicative targets. Until 2013, each installation would receive a free emissions allowance as part of caps that were set locally and approved at the EU level for a given country. Since 2013, the allowance allocation system has significantly changed. Each year the number of allowance is reduced by 1.74%. A list of energy-intensive industries has been compiled, to include 177 sectors (sectors at risk of relocation outside of the EU, which would generate carbon leakage), to which free emissions allowance were allocated until 2020. Some countries, including Poland, are additionally able to negotiate a transfer of free allowances for the energy sector. In the EU as a whole, free allowances in 2020 should represent 30% of the total. The remaining allowances necessary to maintain the production level can be purchased by companies at the stock exchange. As of now (August 2023), allowance prices are around EUR 24 per 1 ton of CO_2 emissions, this price continually going up since 2014. For each industrial plant in the EU that emits CO_2, this means costs of several million (Hengge et al., 2023). Either a plant carries out a costly modernisation to increase its combustion efficiency, thereby reducing CO2 emissions, or, otherwise, it will have to spend considerable amounts to buy additional CO_2 emissions allowance at the stock exchange. That is why even if the EU does not formally prohibit using coal in combustion processes in the energy sector, the CO_2 ETS is still very cumbersome. In the late 2017, EU countries agreed to deregulate energy prices on the European market and create a so-called power market. The aim was to improve competitiveness and decrease prices. As an example in the Polish context, the power market was supposed to support coal-based energy sector and yield benefits from support mechanisms until 2030. The emissions cap for energy entities eligible for public support was set at 550 g/kWh.

In May 2022, the Commission adopted REPowerEU, a plan aimed to reduce the EU dependence on Russian fossil fuels. The plan suggested to further increase energy efficiency by 2030 – from 39% to 42% – as well as the target share of renewables in the energy consumption by 2030 – from 40% to 45%. On 30 March 2023, negotiators of the European Council and of the Parliament reached a preliminary political agreement to increase, by 2030, the share of renewable energy to 42.5%, or even – thanks to an additional commitment at an indicative level of 2.5%–45%. In April 2023, negotiations continued between the European Council and the Parliament about the motion to increase energy efficiency goals for 2030. The current status of the four legislative motions included in REPowerEU is available for review at the European Parliament's website.

To sum up, as time goes by, the EU has set for itself increasingly ambitious climate and energy goals, as emphasised by the European Court of Auditors in its opinions. These include goals for 2020 and 2030 as regards:

- reducing GHG emissions compared to 1990 emissions (see Figure 1.1);
- increasing the share of renewable energy in the energy consumption (see Figure 1.2);
- promoting energy efficiency, i.e. reducing energy consumption (see Figure 1.3).

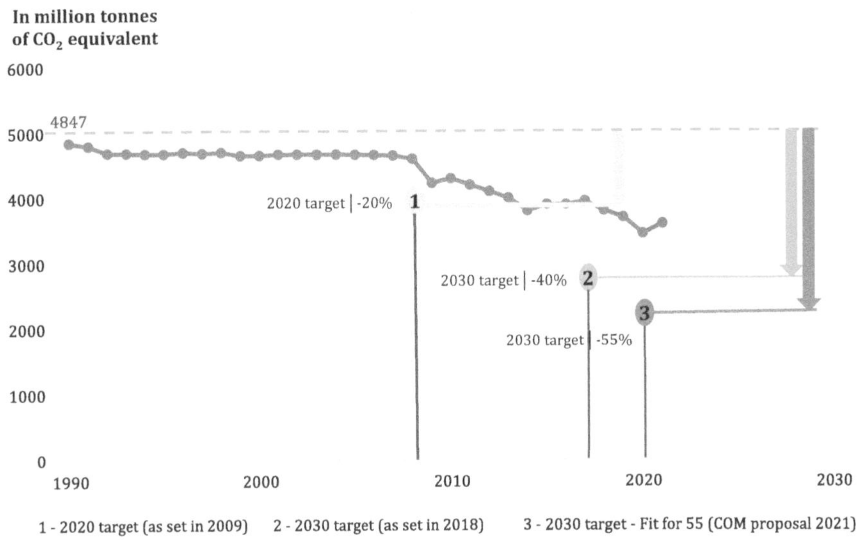

Figure 1.1 Reducing GHG emissions compared to 1990 emissions

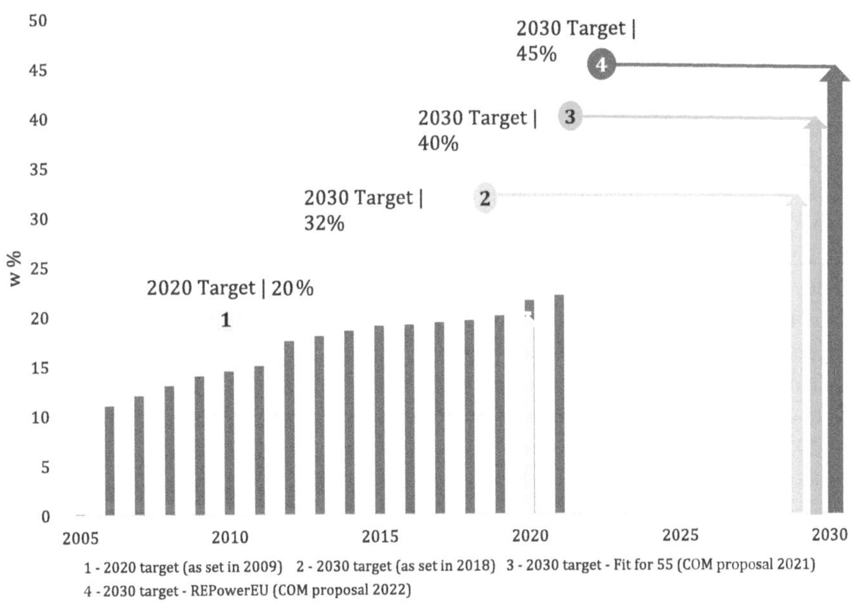

Figure 1.2 Increasing the share of renewable energy in the energy consumption

This discussion of the goals of the EU but also of the world as a whole has referred to the energy sector as the focal point for their implementation. However, it is worth pointing out that there is yet another very significant European economic sector which has a major impact on climate change, namely agriculture. It is known from

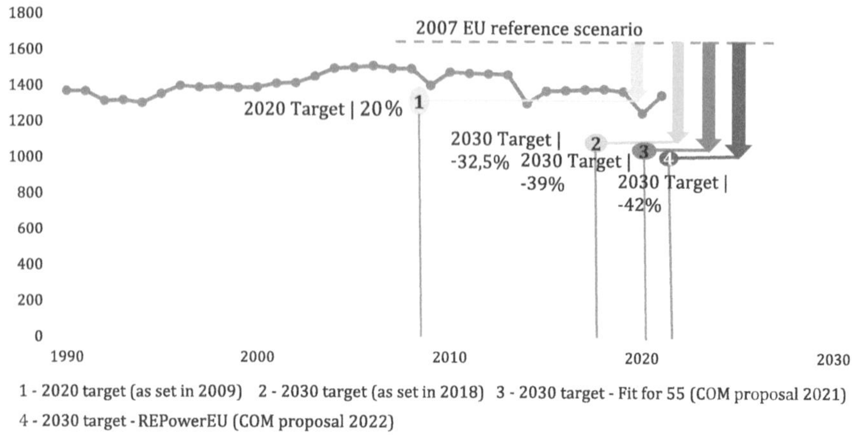

Figure 1.3 Promoting energy efficiency, i.e. reducing energy consumption

research that the interrelations between the abundance of natural resources and agricultural practices are very complex (Arora, 2019; Bennett et al., 2017; Webb et al., 2017). Even though agriculture is one of the sectors to be the most vulnerable to climate change, it is also among the most important areas having impact on climate change (Agovino et al., 2019). Nevertheless, agriculture may improve mitigating actions by reducing GHG production but also through balanced ecosystem and green infrastructure management (Webb et al., 2017). Agriculture maintains precious habitats all over Europe, but intensive farming operations and inadequate practices may deplete natural resources and have a negative impact on ecosystem services and further aggravate the impact of climate change (Bosco & Simeoni, 2018). In this context, the EU has demonstrated a strong commitment to the COP21 Paris Agreement and to the priorities indicated by the Chilean presidency at COP 25. In particular, energy and climate goals for 2030 set an ambitious level of 40% CO_2 emission reduction by that time for all sectors of economy (Horowitz, 2016), which will also require changes in agriculture. Climate action is also at the core of the European Green Deal which includes EU Strategy on climate change adaptation to make Europe a community of climate-resilient societies by 2050 (European Commission, 2019). The European Commission is also of one mind when it comes to the UN SDGs regarding Climate Action and Life on Land, implementing regional efforts to improve climate change mitigation as well as improve and support climate action through sustainable farming practices (Kastrinos & Weber, 2020). The data gathered points to increasingly difficult climate conditions facing the farming community, loss of biodiversity of European soils and a threat of price volatility the sector may be exposed to (de Graaff et al., 2019). The concept of consolidating the climate adaptation and mitigation policy with environmental protection and improvement has enjoyed a great interest from the European Commission. These goals have been recently strengthened by the European Green Deal (European Commission, 2019), by the Common Agricultural Policy

(CAP) and the post-2020 reform aimed to increase environmental ambitions and climate action, and to contribute to the achievement of the EU's environmental and climate goals (Jongeneel et al., 2019). The proposed regulation contains a specific reference to climate management and the attendant risk, defined in terms of direct losses and disasters attributed to agriculture. The Commission's recommendations on the Italian CAP strategic plan also highlight the need: to increase the production sustainability combined with climate change mitigation and reduction in GHG emissions and air pollution; to foster climate action through adaptation and increasing resilience as part of encouraging sustainable management of arable and woodland; and to halt and reverse the loss of biodiversity. While the implementation of agricultural policy support systems such as green infrastructure and eco-schemes may greatly contribute to the mitigation action (Calliari et al., 2019; Panagopoulos & Dimitriou, 2020), limitations in the way environmental and climate policies are monitored may limit the effective assessment of farming practices and thus their progress and efficiency, handicapping the European agriculture in its fight against climate change. It was only recently that the EU approved the use of Copernicus satellite data and information as an official way to monitor the CAP implementation and to make payments to farmers. Moreover, future CAP regulations provide for introducing an area monitoring system: Copernicus Sentinels satellite data will enable a regular and systematic observation, tracking and assessment of farming practices and of their current status. In fact, many studies emphasise the positive opportunities arising from the use of Earth Observation (EO) data in drought monitoring (Arun Kumar et al., 2021; Crocetti et al., 2021); classification of different crop types (Bargiel, 2017; Hao et al., 2015; Piedelobo et al., 2019; Rousi et al., 2021); irrigation management (Brocca et al., 2018; Foster et al., 2020; Vanino et al., 2015); identification of various soil tillage practices (Azzari et al., 2019; Hively et al., 2018) and in ecosystem services and biodiversity conservation (Braun et al., 2018; Dantas de Paula et al., 2021; Hill et al., 2019). Among the many available sources of data, Europe has also provided a series of free-of-charge and open satellite data through the Copernicus programme and has gradually linked the implementation of EU policies to the use of such resources (Campos-Taberner et al., 2020; Sarvia et al., 2021). According to the rules set out in the new approach to CAP monitoring, the eligibility for the aid requested may be verified not only through on-site checks but also using Sentinels data and Copernicus EO missions to ensure continuous, regular and systematic monitoring of the whole country (European Commission, 2018a). As the use of EO data in monitoring agro-environmental goals has been lagging behind, the use of a complex administrative procedure for farmers has been given a high priority to ensure legal compliance and proper distribution of agricultural payments (Mack et al., 2021; Pe'er et al., 2020). Currently, the large-scale use of remote sensing data is limited by financial, legislative and budgetary constraints as well as by experience, skills and need to hold relevant training. Part of the problem lies in the way technical specifications and agro-environmental services are developed. In fact, the EO sector has become dominated by technology determinants rather than by the users' needs while both are of importance to stimulate innovation in this area (Toth & Concini, 2019). In that survey, those polled argued that the so-called 'market pull' approach where mission details are driven by users' needs would not only optimise the use of EO data but also improve the monitoring of agro-environmental goals for the long-term sustainable growth of the European agriculture. This assumption is also demonstrated using an interactive approach adapted from Taramella et al. (2020), focusing in particular on the potential of the free and open market of Copernicus, EU's EO programme. A solid technical and operational analysis of user requirements would bring benefits to the expansion of its services in the European space, but user needs in this domain have been analysed only as part of limited research (Geraldini et al., 2021; Gomarasca et al., 2020; Taramelli et al., 2020).

The climate policy goals presented in this sub-chapter show how complex and complementary they are and how they are impacted by ongoing external phenomena, e.g. the COVID-19 pandemic, war in Ukraine etc., which is why they should be systematically assessed. The climate policy literature provides a strong case for arguing that this assessment should be participatory in nature as climate management is based on incomplete and uncertain information. Moreover, the achievement of the goals set is influenced by behaviours of many independent stakeholders (e.g. Moberg & Galaz, 2005; Pielke, 2007). Stakeholders that should be involved include ordinary citizens, politicians and other decision-makers, private companies and local executive officials, etc. (see Vedung, 2005). Irrespective of those limitations, the process of evaluating climate goals is systematically carried out. Research shows that both scientists and climate policy practitioners are increasingly interested in evaluating the results of the existing policies (Haug et al. 2010). In the climate management literature, lack of reflection is regularly indicated as something to be avoided (see Hischemöller & Hoppe, 1995; Pahl-Wostl, 2009; Huitema et al., 2009, among others). This literature certainly emphasises the need for reflective evaluation practice (see Russel et al., 2010, for example), which means that goals should be openly called into question rather than being taken for granted. Interestingly, the idea behind it is that 'shallower' levels of evaluation may ultimately lead to deeper and more durable learning methods, which is underappreciated. Consequently, when it comes to climate goals, it is worth discussing their viability and executability, pointing to the impossibility to achieve them within the timeframe planned without drastically impacting citizens' economic life.

Evaluations have focused on the environmental impact and economic costs of the measures and these have been taken into account in nearly all of the evaluations. These criteria have been assessed in quantitative terms, except for one Swedish ex-post evaluation (Nordisk Komunikation, 2007), where the environmental impact was evaluated only in qualitative terms. Some criteria have been evaluated in both quantitative and qualitative terms, e.g. the impact on the air quality (five quantitative evaluations and two qualitative evaluations), the impact on distribution (three quantitative and one qualitative), interactions with other policies (one quantitative and three qualitative), acidification (two quantitative and one qualitative) and eutrophication (one quantitative and one qualitative). The criteria evaluated only in qualitative terms, each taken into account in only one or two evaluations, included the impact on energy poverty, energy security, successes and limitations, competitiveness, organisational matters, innovation and research, stakeholders' views and behaviours, SMEs, awareness raising, biodiversity, smell and nuisance of a degraded environment. The criteria were rather evenly distributed between ex-ante and ex-post evaluations and there were no clear patterns to suggest that quantitative or qualitative criteria were more often applied. Most evaluations used a combination of quantitative and qualitative methods. The MARKAL model, a general equilibrium model for modelling energy consumption and energy costs, was used in one British (DECC, 2009) and two Swedish studies. A British evaluation was used, namely the MARKAL model, for which the UK Department for Environment, Food & Rural Affairs (Defra) commissioned an extension quantifying air quality benefits achieved thanks to energy system changes resulting from climate policy. Since 2003, the model has also been updated to include more detailed information and assumptions on technological costs and processes. UK MARKAL is a dynamic energy optimisation model that provides insights into technological options and costs of coal until 2050. Scenarios with different CO_2 emission limitations were compared to the reference case, where the energy system and CO_2 emissions were calibrated to the current UK situation. In Sweden, MARKAL-NORDIC was used, which includes not only the energy sector in Sweden but also in the neighbouring countries (Denmark, Finland and Norway). The model was launched for two major scenarios: one involving 1990 policy measures which were extended for the entire modelling period and one involving the present policy measures (at the time of evaluation). Demand for energy, development of alternative energy technologies, fuel prices etc. were assumed at the same level in both scenarios. The Danish ex-ante evaluation (Klimakomissionen, 2010) modelled the economic impacts of phasing out fossil fuels using different models. A spreadsheet-based model STREAM was used to model energy consumption for four sectors and also includes modules for calculating energy system's operating costs. Another model applied was Balmorel, an optimisation model that includes the Scandinavian and German energy markets. It was run at five-year intervals to find the most profitable energy system structure from now to 2050. The consequences of the Danish economy's transition from fossil fuels were modelled using ADAM, a macroeconomic, demand-driven Keynesian model that includes 20 different sectors. Another macroeconomic model, one developed specifically for this evaluation by DREAM group, was used to evaluate future trade balances and tax distortion effects, among other things. Two Swedish ex-ante evaluations of the Climate Investment Programme (KLIMP) (Naturvårdsverket, 2004, 2009) did not include modelling exercise. The evaluations were based on the database of KLIMP projects, which includes, for example project reports. This data was used to calculate the cost-efficiency with respect to how much money was to be earmarked for each kilogram of CO_2 saved. Qualitative methods such as questionnaires and document analysis were also used to evaluate, for example interactions with other policy instruments or the impact on employment and competition, and other environmental targets. Finnish ex-ante evaluations related to Finland's long-term climate and energy strategy (Council of State, 2008). One evaluation was contained in the strategy itself, with another conducted separately, focusing on different environmental impacts of the strategy (Hildén et al., 2014). The strategy presents two scenarios: the baseline one, corresponding to the current measures and developments, and the target one, corresponding to meeting EU and national targets. Strategy impacts were then calculated for both scenarios. When it comes to impacts on the national economy, direct costs of the strategy were first assessed using an economic energy model of the Technical Research Center of Finland (VTT), and the results were used in further calculations with the national economy model of the Government Institute for Economic Research (VATT). The environmental impact assessment (Hildén et al., 2014) used life cycle assessment to estimate various impacts of energy production and consumption, production being conducted partly outside of Finland. The evaluation was conducted with ReCiP method, commonly used for life cycle assessments (Sleeswijk et al., 2008). Particle emissions were evaluated using the Finnish regional emission scenario model (Karvosenoja, 2008). Two of the four ex-post evaluations used exclusively qualitative methods such as document analysis, interviews, questionnaires and stakeholder seminars. One of them evaluated the Swedish efforts to develop local climate strategy (Naturvårdsverket, 2010) and the other addressed information as a steering instrument as part of the Swedish Climate Investment Programme (KLIMP) (Nordisk Komunikation, 2007). The evaluations focused on organisational matters, stakeholders' experiences as well as factors that fostered or hindered the effectiveness of instruments.

Pursuant to the Decision concerning the mechanism for monitoring Community GHGs and for implementing the Kyoto Protocol (Decision 280/2004/EC of the European Parliament and of the Council), EU Member States are obliged to draft a biannual report containing information on national policies and on the measures implemented in the reporting period to limit GHG emissions. Article 3(2) of Decision 280/2004/EC is of general nature and defines the requirements for reporting policies and measures to the EU (EC, 2004). The biannual reports are a source of information on what climate policies and measures have been implemented in respective EU countries. To be able to design cost-efficient policies and measures to combat climate change, it is necessary to know whether the existing measures have met their objectives in a cost-efficient manner. Policy assessments play a vital role here and may provide valuable information to decision-makers. Huitema et al. (2011) presented an overview of climate policy evaluations in EU countries, analysing, among others, the methods and criteria used in evaluations, whether they included elements of participation and what bodies carried out evaluations. According to Huitema et al. (2011), the number of climate policy evaluations has increased eight times in 2000–2005. There are, however, significant differences between countries in terms of the number of evaluations conducted. Between 1990 and 2019, GHG emissions fell by 1% per year. Between 2007 and 2019, the pace accelerated to nearly 2% per year. The 2030 target requires decarbonisation rate to double again, up to nearly 4% per year. The 2050 target is even more ambitious, but there are more problems with that.

In 2023, the European Court of Auditors published a report titled 'EU climate and energy targets' containing the results of an audit examining whether to achieve the energy and climate targets for 2030 the EU relied on measures that had already yielded positive outcomes before. The auditors checked whether upon achieving the 2020 targets the right conclusions were drawn to help the EU meet the yet more ambitious 2030 targets. The Court established that the EU 2020 targets were indeed met but external factors partly contributed to that achievement. The Commission did not evaluate to what extent this was due to the progress in policy implementation, and to what extent, it was helped by external factors such as the financial crisis in 2009 and the COVID-19 pandemic in 2020. ECA also found that in terms of GHG emissions reduction, the EU had performed well compared to other developed countries. However, EU GHG emissions figures for 2020 are not inclusive of the emissions resulting from trade, carbon leakage (it is estimated that, if accounted for, they would increase the total emissions level by ca. 8%) and emissions from international air and maritime transport (3.4% and 3.6% respectively).

1.3 Green finance – basic assumptions for sources of financing climate goals in the EU

Rational climate protection policy calls for large-scale financial resources to be mobilised by all participants of the economic processes taking place (government, market, world and financial markets) because being investment intensive, it requires reconciling the interests of business operations, social welfare and the needs of future generations. Public sector support is therefore essential for a different perspective on this process.

Of great importance to environmental measures is the financial environment that significantly impacts the pace and scale of changes in the area of investment activities without which the process would not have been possible. In the European context, the narrative is anchored in the EU measures and ambitious plans to become a climate-neutral continent by 2050. Over the last couple of years, positive renewable energy investment trends have been observed in Europe. However, according to the European Commission's experts, annual investment in renewable energy alone must double by 2050 to achieve the expected climate targets. Conducting projects of that scale would entail investing adequate capital to speed up EU Member States' transition to low-emission economy. It must be borne in mind, however, that in many cases, these development investments come on top of those planned by governments and companies. These assumptions translate into measures required from Member States, which are reflected in ten-year national energy and climate plans. Combined with the planned changes resulting from the adoption of the European Green Deal and of the Fair Transition Fund, this means that Member States must reckon with urgent challenges and expectations of deep changes in the structure of central and local public expenditure and with the need for active involvement of capital market institutions as well, without which it will be simply impossible to reach the climate targets.

In this context, decision-makers, investors and financial investors must develop a set of financial solutions available for use by central and local governments and companies. It should not be overlooked that owners and investors look at the return on equity and goodwill, while the public sector has a number of fiscal rules to comply with. Therefore, a certain middle ground must be negotiated between environmental goals and those parameters.

National-level challenges require action from all entities operating within the market and regulatory context. The process of climate transition, and thus energy transition as well, may not take place without an active participation of the central and local public sector because what matters in the process is the scale of engagement of all players taking part in economic activities on all levels. This has already been highlighted here but is undoubtedly worth reiterating, given the importance of this point. Therefore, climate transition may have a significant impact on further social and economic development and the quality of life of people in local communities. Demonstrating the significance of energy efficiency, environmental, social and governance (ESG) reporting and non-financial reporting on issues related to green finance are milestones of such discussions. This chapter will elaborate on one of those elements, namely green finance.

The concept of green finance has no clear-cut, precise and generally accepted definition, and the problem with defining it starts already from the word 'green' as it could be replaced with environmental or climate. This issue was addressed by the UN Environmental Programme (UNEP), as part of which a guidebook was prepared to help distinguish between terms such as 'low-emission', 'climate', 'green' and 'sustainable', and the discussions and definitions provided there can be applied to financial products. For example, investments considered to be carried out using 'sustainable financing' and 'sustainable financial products' meet a number of environmental, social, economic and corporate governance criteria. In accordance with these discussions, a 'green' investment should reflect in its essence the environmental criteria based on climate protection (including adaptation to climate change) and other priorities such as conservation of water resources and biodiversity. Despite such a wider scope of 'green finance', this term often refers to a narrower perspective related to financing energy-saving and climate-friendly assets, and to related financial products which are entirely linked to the fight against climate change without taking account of the remaining criteria. One of the reasons for the inaccurate use of this term may be that it is used in international climate negotiations, though the most often used term is 'climate finance', in the sense of supplying capital and funds for climate change mitigation or adaptation (programmes, projects), i.e. those provided by industrialised countries to emerging and developing countries (Fernando, 2020). This term is strictly linked to international negotiations on climate change. Climate finance is also defined by UNFCCC Standing Committee on Finance as finance that aims at reducing emissions, and enhancing sinks of greenhouse gases and aims at reducing vulnerability of, and maintaining and increasing the resilience of, human and ecological systems to negative climate change impacts (UNFCCC Standing Committee on Finance, 2014). Meanwhile, the EU uses a definition of 'sustainable finance' with environmental issues among its aspects. As a matter of fact, in the context of the EU policy, sustainable finance is understood as finance that supports economic growth while reducing pressure on natural environment and taking account of social aspects. Sustainable finance also includes transparency about the risks related to ESG factors, which may have an impact on the financial system, and mitigating those risks through adequate management of financial and corporate entities. Meanwhile, in China, 'climate finance' emphasises the financial needs related to counteracting climate change and is treated as an important element of 'green finance'. It must be pointed out, however, that climate action is one of the many objectives of green finance such as combatting air pollution or waste management, among others, which has not been highlighted as part of the term 'green finance' (Buchner et al., 2021). For the purposes of this publication, a broader definition of environmental impact will be applicable to the term 'green finance', taking also account of conservation of biodiversity, preventing pollution and circular economy. What matters is that, regardless of the source of finance, environmental projects carried out by central or local authorities, or by business entities, should have clear and reliable principles of verifying non-financial benefits. These elements make it possible to manage the expected environmental outcomes at various levels of their implementation.

Green financial instruments are very similar to traditional financial instruments, the main difference in their definition being the need to identify specific purposes for which the funds acquired can be used, and the measurable environmental effects to be achieved this way. The key distinctive feature of green finance is how it can be demonstrated that an investment project is bringing the expected environmental benefits, and some products may be liable to fines where such verification has not been ensured. Green finance can also involve more stringent requirements as regards decarbonising measures and the ambitions of the suppliers responsible for project execution. From the point of view of public task execution, such an approach is highly beneficial as it helps account for efficiency and effectiveness of a given investment project, not only a public one, but also a private one, and determine its environmental impact. Green finance includes non-repayable aid in the form of subsidies awarded for the execution of environmental protection projects, or capital participation through ownership (buying shares) or debt (green bonds) in the execution of such projects.

In the case of EU Member States, the non-repayable aid predominantly comes from the European budget and is supported by national ecological and environmental funds especially created with such measures in mind, or directly from national central or local government budgets. It is worth emphasising that the EU and its Member States contribute the most to the international public financing of measures related to climate change, and since 2013, they have nearly doubled their contribution to financing such measures to support developing countries. The Council has called on other donors to intensify their efforts and expects that the collective target of mobilising USD 100 billion annually will be achieved by 2023.

The basis for awarding subsidies from the EU budget is the Multiannual Financial Framework currently adopted and approved by Member States in the amount of EUR 1,074 billion, i.e. ca. 1.10% of GNI between 2021 and 2027, representing a major source of non-repayable aid for 2021–2027. In the current EU financial perspective, the proposed Cohesion Policy funds are supplemented as part of MFF for 2021–2027 by the Just Transition Fund (JTF), which is part of the European Green Deal and the 1st pillar of the Just Transition Mechanism. The purpose of JTF is to mitigate social and economic impacts of the energy transition. The European Council has increased the overall climate expenditure target from 25% to 30% of the MFF+NGEU total expenditure excluding loans, combined with the introduction of the principle of doing 'no harm'. The total MFF+NGEU expenditure in the final package adopted by the European Parliament was higher than in the Commission's motion, and it required higher climate expenditure also in absolute value (EUR 439 billion vs. EUR 400 billion).

From the point of view of the public sector, to additionally support the most vulnerable high-emission regions in the transition to climate-neutral economy, a new fund called JTF has been created. It receives financing both from the next long-term budget and from the EU recovery instrument (as part of *NextGenerationEU*). Looking for further forms of support for environmental measures, the International Renewable Energy Agency published in 2020 a series of financial reports regarding renewable energy, analysing solutions to enable increasing the uptake of RES. The above-mentioned analyses conclude that innovative ways to finance renewable energy include green bonds, which can help attract considerable global capital to renewable energy and other green assets. The importance of this instrument is attested by the fact that in her first State of the EU address (16.09.2020) the President of the European Commission Ursula von der Leyen mentioned as one of the goals of her presidency to raise 30% of the 750 billion NextGenerationEU's lending through green bonds. Green bonds are the preferred vector of financing energy transition and are increasingly becoming the subject of regulatory efforts at the EU level (Glinka et al., 2021). The incipient green bond market requires tackling the factors affecting its development, such as the scale of emissions, the liquidity of the market for such securities, and monitoring the actual pro-environmental impact to avoid *greenwashing* (European Court of Auditors, 2021a). Therefore, it is an instrument that combines all the characteristics of financial products and the elements of non-financial reporting, as discussed above.

The non-repayable support system, both the historical one and the one planned for the coming years, is therefore impressive and represents a vital tool in implementing environmental protection policies. In addition, as mentioned above, it is important for local government sector that the most vulnerable high-emission regions are supported in their transition to climate-neutral economy by the newly created JTF. Sustainable development issues have for many years been financed from the EU budget, though not always being a top priority of the strategies implemented by the EU. The most evident EU policy-making measures, also related to SDGs, include but are not limited to the European Green Deal. With the political commitment to earmark no less than 30% of the EU budget to climate measures and the adoption of the European Green Deal in 2020, EU and all of the 27 Member States presented proposals for transforming Europe in the first climate-neutral continent by 2050, with at least 55% medium-term emissions reduction target ('Fit 55') by 2030 compared to 1990 levels. Especially with respect to energy and climate: SDG 7 ('Ensure access to affordable, reliable, sustainable and modern energy for all') and SDG 13 ('Take urgent action to combat climate change and its impacts'), EU has committed to adopt ambitious 2030 targets when it comes to

GHG emissions reduction, improving energy efficiency and increasing the share of renewable energy. The European Green Deal also includes a variety of measures related to other Sustainable Development Goals such as SDG 6 (Clean water and sanitation), SDG 14 (Life below water) and SDG 15 (Life on land), and addresses transition, or issues related to SDG 10 (Reduced inequalities). In this context, Eurostat has been urged to regularly monitor and assess the progress against SDGs in Europe. The EU statistical office has developed a set of EU SDG indicators and currently prepares regular reports to monitor progress towards achieving SDGs. Consequently, European Semester country reports contain an analysis of respective Member States and their progress in the SDG achievement as well as the scale of financial commitment to SDGs.

When analysing the EU budget expenditure structure, it can be seen to have been mostly allocated to Lisbon Strategy's major goals such as employment increase, research and development, climate change and energy, education and sustainable development. It is worth pointing out that the EU Strategy for Sustainable Development adopted in 2006 and the Lisbon Strategy for growth and jobs complement each other (Dall'Erba, Fang, 2017). The Strategy for Sustainable Development mostly deals with quality of life, intra- and intergenerational justice and cohesion of all policy areas, including its external aspects. It appreciates the role of economic development, recognising that it facilitates transition to a developed society. Meanwhile, Lisbon Strategy essentially helps achieve the overriding goal of sustainable development as it predominantly deals with measures and means aimed to boost competitiveness, accelerate economic growth and mobilise the creation of new jobs. Meanwhile, the natural resources conservation and management represented, between 2007 and 2011, the largest share of EU budgetary expenditure (even though a decline from 48% in 2007 to 40% in 2013 was recorded). An analysis of the cost trend in natural resources conservation and management measures revealed a stable level until 2011. In 2011, sustainable growth expenditure exceeded natural resources conservation and management expenditure, among others, specifically due to the implementation of the sustainable growth strategy (Wilkin, 2013, 2016). The 'Europe 2020 Strategy' included three interrelated priorities:

- Smart growth: developing an economy based on knowledge and innovation;
- Sustainable growth: promoting a more resource efficient, greener and more competitive economy;
- Inclusive growth: fostering a high-employment economy delivering social and territorial cohesion.

'Europe 2020' also adopted a more customised, and thus, as it would seem a more realistic approach to its implementation by respective countries. Indeed, an opportunity was offered to each Member State to adapt 'Europe 2020 Strategy' to its specific situation, meaning that the aforementioned measurable EU goals were translated into national goals and methods of operation. At the same time, the aforementioned detailed goals fit squarely into the implementation of the said three general priorities – smart, sustainable and inclusive growth. It was also announced that the list of programme instruments of this new strategy was open-ended and efforts towards its implementation should be more comprehensive, meaning that they should not involve only national and EU level but also the international one as these spheres have some overlaps.

An analysis of expenditure structure as part of budgetary measures revealed that between 2014 and 2016, smart and inclusive growth had the largest share of expenditure (earlier it was sustainable growth). This means the policy lines set in the Lisbon Strategy were consistently continued and further developed in the newly introduced 'Europe 2020 strategy' and EU Strategy for Sustainable Development, especially when it comes to agriculture (Milea et al., 2015). Consequently, a stable increase in expenditure for sustainable and smart economic growth can be observed in the period under analysis as well as continued predominance of this direction of allocation. Expenditure on sustainable growth, like at the end of the previous period, represented as much as ca. 45% of the EU budgetary expenditure and remained at this level throughout the period under analysis. Other expenses stood at levels similar to previous years, though being of less significance compared to strategic expenditure on smart and sustainable growth. Between 2014 and 2020, EUR 221 billion or 20.6% of the EU budget was allocated to fighting climate change. Even this synthetic information shows that the EU earmarks considerable funds to finance projects as part of measures to support sustainable development, which may benefit both private and public sectors. Data for 2019 confirm that the EU remains the largest contributor of public climate finance to developing countries, having provided ca. EUR 22 billion in 2019 and more than doubled its contributions since 2013. In 2020 alone, the EU and its Member States allocated EUR 23.39 billion to finance climate change measures to support developing countries in reducing GHG emissions and adapting to climate change impacts. In 2021, the EU and its Member States earmarked EUR 23.04 billion from public sources for the same purpose.

At the same time, in its communication of 2022, the European Council quite strongly urged other market players to intensify efforts, expecting to achieve in 2023 the collective goal of mobilising funds in the amount of USD 100 billion annually.

The need for a yet greater investment of public funds in the implementation is confirmed by various analyses and reports, for example reports of the European Court of Auditors published in September 2018 and 2021, which reveal that the EU's measures undertaken to protect human health against air pollution did not bring the expected results. Each year ca. 400,000 EU residents die prematurely as a consequence of air pollution, and the attendant external health costs amount to hundreds of billions of euros. The scale of the phenomenon suggests the need to take coordinated prevention measures of global nature. When confronting those impacts with financial data, it is hard to conclude the results of those measures are good or at least satisfactory. In addition to supranational measures, active financial action at the national level is undoubtedly of significance. The EU committed to allocate at least 20% of its budget for 2014–2020 to climate measures. Meanwhile, in the EU budget for 2021–2027, the value increased to 30%, i.e. ca. EUR 87 billion annually.

This amount, however, represents less than 10% of the total investments necessary to achieve 2030 goals, which investments are estimated at ca. EUR 1 trillion. It is expected that the remaining part of investments will be financed from national and private funds (ECA, 2023).

At the same time, starting from 2018, the EU has supported the process of green finance development not only through expenditure but also through legislation. The European Commission presents legislative motions related to sustainable finance. In May 2018, it presented a package of proposed measures aimed to (EC, 2023):

- establish a unified EU-wide system for economic activity classification ('taxonomy');
- fine-tune the requirements regarding the disclosure of how institutional investors integrate ESG factors in their risk processes;
- create a new benchmark category to help investors compare carbon footprint of their investment.

In addition, those regulations were followed in 2019 by introducing obligations to disclose information on how financial companies account for ESG in their investment decisions and a proposal was presented to create a new category of financial reference indices aimed to provide more information on a given investment portfolio's carbon footprint (Berg et al., 2021). Such a solution would intensify financial sector's commitment to financing green projects as the European Commission is perfectly aware of the fact that without this sector the concept of sustainable development stands no chance of succeeding. Moreover, in 2002, the European Council agreed on a position on European Green Bonds, one of the chief instruments to finance investments in green technologies, energy efficiency, efficient resource management, sustainable transport infrastructure and research infrastructure. An EU regulation lays down uniform requirements for bond issuers who wish to use the name 'European Green Bond' or 'EuGB' for their environmentally sustainable bonds made available to investors in the EU and establishes a registration system and governance framework for external reviewers of European Green Bonds.

The taxonomy will enable investor to re-orient their investments towards more sustainable technologies and companies. This will be of key importance to the EU becoming climate neutral by 2050 and achieving the goals of the Paris Agreement for 2030. These include reducing GHG emissions by 40%, for which the Commission estimates that the EU must close the investment gap of ca. EUR 180 billion annually. At the same time, the European Council urged financial institutions to increase financing of climate measures.

Central and local government expenditure on environmental protection for all EU countries jointly (UE-27) between 2012 and 2021 followed an upward trend in absolute numbers, and as a share of GDP, it stood at the same level in most years, i.e. it grows at the same pace as GDP (unfortunately not faster). The expenditure in question has grown from EUR 69,239.5 million in 2012 to EUR 80,335.1 million in 2020. Its share of GDP in that period stood at ca. 0.6%. A slight fall of both values could be observed in late 2016 and early 2017. In the period discussed

France, Italy and Germany were invariably in the lead of European countries whose central and local institutional sectors spent the largest amounts on environmental protection both in figures and as a share of GDP. An analysis of Eurostat data reveals, however, the already mentioned discrepancies in the scale of environmental expenditure by respective EU Member States' public sector. This can stem from a variety of factors, for example from differences in public awareness of the necessity of such expenditure, however, according to the authors hereof, this was, to a greater extent, due to differences in respective countries' social and economic development.

When it comes to debt instruments and capital investments, these include finance subsidies, preferential finance or a system of government guarantees for the projects financed. Public authorities act through the banking system, environmental funds or specialised institutions that are development banks (DBs). The reason why government gets involved through such instruments is that, considering the inherent uncertainty as to future returns on investment, especially when investing in new missions/sectors/projects/companies that need financing, private banks and capital markets often do not offer financing or its scale is insufficient (especially for long-term debt finance), even if the financial system in a given country is fully developed. Taken the above into account, such measures should be considered highly welcome. Due to the economic and social situation as well as to the large number of challenges facing a country's sustainable development, the aforementioned measures are more and more often taken by DBs specifically established to play such a role. The functioning of such institutions is highly desirable as there are sectors and project investments that need to have their future structural transition and economic development (e.g. energy and heating) financed while their future and success is quite uncertain (Mazzucato, 2013; Mazzucato & Penna, 2018; Griffith-Jones et al., 2020b). For this reason, they may fail to meet the requirements discussed in greater detail further in this monograph as regards financing by private financial system, which prefers sectors or investment projects whose return on investment is more predictable and faster. Therefore, DBs are the source of capital for the most complex and capital-intensive sectors/projects/missions that require advanced expertise, which offer positive outcomes for the economy as a whole (positive external impacts, for example climate change mitigation through lower CO_2 emissions as is the case of renewable energy) and/or where the benefits of social nature outweigh private benefits.

The scale of activities of the several existing national DBs (NDB) is already very large so they have a significant impact nationally and globally, especially when it comes to respective countries' catch-up efforts and structural transition. Put together, all public development banks (PDB) (including multilateral, regional and national banks, the latter being the largest in scale) represent cumulative assets worth over USD 11.4 trillion, approximately corresponding to 70% assets of the entire US banking sector. Moreover, in 2019, all DBs made annual commitments worth USD 2.3 trillion, equivalent to 10% of cumulative capital (Griffith-Jones et al., 2020a based on AFD/INSE database). Ever since the financial crisis of 2007–2009, and even more so since the COVID-19 crisis and energy crisis resulting from

Russia's aggression on Ukraine, DBs have been enjoying a true revival and a growing recognition of their important role, among other things, in ensuring counter-cyclical finance in 'bad' times and in ensuring long-term finance at all times to help finance a significant structural transition and catch-up growth, which are urgently needed to achieve a more dynamic, inclusive and low-emission economy. DBs play an especially important role in financing investment in nascent economic sectors and in innovative projects that help expand existing sectors/missions/companies, where private banking sector would not invest due to the excessive risk. In such cases, DBs can provide the vision – and part of the resources – to do things that at present are not done at all (Keynes, 1926; Mazzucato, 2013). To do so, those entities need to have the expertise and a strategic vision of financing new sectors and technologies. This is facilitated by the fact DBs can grant long-term loans as well as demand lower returns. Moreover, these institutions can also gather their own expertise, which they can share with investors and borrowers to promote sustainability of key operations through finance. This way DBs may pool together their financial resources with private financial sector and help bridge the gaps in knowledge and in resources alike. This is probably one of the most valuable roles these entities have to play also when it comes to support for sustainable development. In addition, as mentioned before, they play a counter-cyclical role, which is of key importance to sustaining investment, innovation, job creation and economic growth over long-term periods, in which private lending declines or, worse yet, runs dry. The uncertainty of finance, accompanied by lower demand, may be a serious deterrent for private investments, unnecessarily extending the period of stagnation or low growth. DBs are there to help in both cases.

It is worth bearing in mind that PDBs can lend money for an extended period and at affordable prices, thus having a counter-cyclical effect and easing the pressure to finance sustainable projects. These institutions get public support and can cheaply finance their operations and pass this advantage on to their borrowers by way of lower interest rates as well as longer maturity periods. A good example in this context would be 40-year corporate loans which could be useful in development of nuclear power stations. DBs often combine financial support and technical assistance when it comes to projects and sectors that help fight the climate change and contribute to progress towards SDGs. Also, their systems have better risk-absorption and risk-management capabilities and greater potential for counter-cyclical effect. It is estimated that PDBs finance ca. 10% of investment projects worldwide, while not exhausting their full capacity. In the light of the large unmet financial needs related to the pursuit of SDGs, their role can be further strengthened in respect of scale of lending, lending terms and their cooperation as a 'DB system'. Commercial finance is a significant source of finance for sustainable projects in a growing number of developing countries, but government support will be necessary in case of such serious challenges. Commercial finance can be also a costly and unstable element of the finance structure. As a matter of fact, lending terms depend on the macroeconomic base and other factors, such as political risk, climate risk and disasters, but also on the global financial cycle. Having that in mind, to make sure the broadly defined financial sector can play its role as a source of stable and long-term finance to counter impacts of climate change on sustainable development, efforts need to be taken to:

- reduce the (actual and perceived) risk, both nationally and globally;
- expand the information ecosystem to enable long-term and sustainable investment projects; and
- share the risk between public and private entities (e.g. through mixed financial mechanism) for investment projects that are a shared priority.

To sum up, public sector involvement and efficient use of the resources mobilised by it helps support sustainable development measures and is one of the sources of finance for the necessary investment projects. Whether the best possible outcomes are achieved with the public capital invested depends on how well the support instruments selected match their purpose, and how effectively the risk involved in such investment is managed. However, when considering public funds as a source of finance for SDGs, it should be noted that they are limited. Undoubtedly, a just and sustainable growth mobilises public income, but it is also financed through public debt. One should be cautious not to fall into the related trap, i.e. higher GDP growth rates also improve the public debt trend (i.e. lower it) – if growth rates exceed interest rates, public debt becomes sustainable. Hence, financing projects through issuance of public debt may contribute to economic growth but this is not an unconditional situation as fast accumulation of public debt often leads to crises. Consequently, public sector undoubtedly takes part in financing SDGs or even achieves them itself, but there are limits to the scale of such involvement.

In view of the above, in order to meet the challenges of sustainable development policy implementation, it is necessary to mobilise public sector (central and local government), banking sector and capital markets to finance such investment projects. Speaking of broadly defined green finance, whichever source the invested funds come from, what matters is choosing the most efficient and effective solutions to maximise the likelihood of achieving environmental goals. On the one hand, one would expect that with more than half a century of experience behind them, policy-makers are able to apply adequate tools, but unfortunately, the complexity of economic phenomena and the external factors having impact on energy phenomena (e.g. war in Ukraine) make it necessary to keep searching for new instruments the society could make use of. The following chapters will analyse in detail what measures are effective in EU countries, and in which areas new financial support instruments still need to be sought.

2 Efficiency of environmental taxes and of the EU countries' public spending on climate action

2.1 Environmental taxes as a tool for implementing climate policy in the European Union – origin, evolution and effectiveness assessment

Chapter 1 of the monograph describes the scope of EU involvement in climate policy-making, mentioning the two models applied by the Community: additional tax burden model and 'positive' incentive model, i.e. subsidies, tax reliefs or grant-aided funding of environmental projects. This part of the publication will provide a detailed discussion of environmental taxes applied based on the 'polluter pays' principle, which is among the key principles underlying the EU environmental policy. In practice, this means that the polluters cover the costs of the pollution they cause, including the costs of measures used to prevent and control such pollution as well as costs incurred by the society in connection with this pollution. The implementation of this principle provides an incentive for polluters to avoid causing environmental damage and makes it possible to hold them accountable for the pollution introduced to the environment. Though this is the general rule, reality often deviates from theory and its application differs depending on the place where such a situation occurs. In one of the studies conducted for the European Commission, it was estimated that gaps in the implementation of EU environmental regulations generate costs and lost opportunity in the amount of ca. EUR 55 billion annually (European Commission, 2019). The research shows that fiscal authorities must take account of the specific effect of time dimension and the type of fiscal instruments in taking decisions affecting the volume and structure of environmental taxes, otherwise the effectiveness of such measures being greatly limited. The growing concerns over the costs of the green transition require a special approach such that the solutions proposed should bring the best climate impacts while not impeding social and economic development. Attention should be paid to the impact of environmental factors on the distribution and competitiveness of taxes and alternative compensatory solutions aimed to mitigate them. When analysing the choice of instruments to support climate policy, it should be emphasised that the advantage of environmental taxes over other regulatory solutions is that they generate revenues for the society that can be used to compensate those affected for the damage sustained (Pizer & Sexton, 2019). These compensations can be implemented

DOI: 10.4324/9781003434689-3

by modifying the tax structure used in some cases (exclusions etc.) or through targeted and limited transfers to specific sectors or social and economic groups, which would certainly bring better outcomes by introducing the desirable incentive effect.

When browsing scientific literature and reports of international organisations for a definition of environmental tax, it can be concluded that a great majority of the wording used puts emphasis on the effect of a given tax when it comes to its impact on the costs of activities and the prices of products that have a negative environmental impact. Meanwhile, the definition adopted by the European Commission focuses on the tax base, so an environmental tax is a tax whose tax base is a physical unit of something that has a specific negative impact on the environment. Hence, in line with the principle, the polluter is subject to a payment in the form of tax on negative environmental impact. The term 'environmental taxes' can be interpreted as referring to taxes that are environmentally rather than fiscally motivated. The purpose is not part of the definition used in environment tax statistics, while it should be taken into account and consequently one could argue that the term 'environmentally related taxes' (ERT) is more adequate and to a greater extent reflects the nature of this public charge. It is the term used in Regulation (EU) No 691/2011 and is preferred, e.g. by OECD. Being more linguistically convenient, the term 'environmental taxes' is in common use, also in the United Nations System of Environmental-Economic Accounting (SEEA, 2012) adopted in 2012 as the so-called international statistical standard. Experience over the years has shown that several interpretations of the concept of environmental tax may co-exist, which could be observed even in the divergent approach of OECD and the Commission on that issue. Due to the scope of this monograph, the European Commission's definition will be used here in further analyses.

When discussing environmental taxes, it is worth noting a number of dilemmas related to using them, especially to their effectiveness and the possibility to implement them in the existing tax systems. As regards effectiveness, one should answer the question: what is the tax base and how is it measured? Firstly, environmental taxes directly based on measured emissions may be, as a rule, very precisely targeted to environmental purposes. When the emissions of regulated chemical compounds go up, so does the tax base and the polluter pays an additional direct tax that is directly proportional to the emission increase. In such a model, it is up to the polluter to take any measures available to reduce its tax obligations by reducing the emissions of environmentally harmful substances. From the entrepreneur's point of view, the levies it pays represent an additional expense that does nothing to boost its competitiveness or strengthen its market position, so it is not worth incurring as an investment, quite the contrary. A good practical example of such a situation would be the Swedish tax on nitrogen oxide emissions (Millock et al., 2004) or water pollution fees in the Netherlands (Bressers & Lulofs, 2004). In the mid-term perspective, entrepreneurs who have invested in environmental solutions will be able to offer better and cheaper products to customers as they will not have to pay additional taxes. It should be also noted that environmental taxes can be a financial incentive for natural persons and entrepreneurs to switch from sources such as fossil fuels and other polluting substances to clean energy (Ambhore & Ofori, 2023;

Gyamf et al., 2022; Ofori et al., 2023; Adebayo et al., 2022; Steve et al., 2022; Bamidele et al., 2022). On the other hand, implementing environmental taxes may also involve challenges and compromises such as potentially increasing consumer energy prices and the need to develop and implement a policy to ensure that the goals of the taxes implemented are effectively met.

Questions arise in this context as to whether applying environmental taxes has an impact on consumption or serves as an investment impulse, considering their specificity. To try and find an answer to those question, Authors have conducted analyses for 2004–2021 using linear models, whose results are presented in Table 2.1. The parameter values presented show how much, on average, the value of a dependent variable will change, if the value of an independent variable increases by one unit. If a value in the *p* column is greater than 0.05, it means that the parameter does not significantly differ from zero. The LB-UB interval is a 95% confidence interval that covers the true unknown value of the parameter in the whole population. The parameter in the *estimate* column is always in the middle of that interval, with each value being equally likely to be the true unknown value. The research has been conducted and broken down into two groups of EU Member States based on a given country's GDP per capita and taking account of the time lag due to the fact that the impacts of environmental taxes may be felt in the upcoming years.

The results obtained indicate that environmental taxes, regardless of the country's wealth, have no negative impact on the consumption and inflation levels. As environmental tax revenue increases, consumption level increases accordingly, ceteris paribus, in the following way: a one-unit increase in the period n + 1 causes consumption to increase by 6.5 units, in n + 2 by 7.6 units and in n + 3 by 8.9 units. Environmental taxpayers do not pass on these additional charges directly to prices as analyses have demonstrated a very minor but actually opposite impact of the increase in environmental taxes on CPI.

On the other hand, when it comes to the impact of environmental taxes on the investment level, the situation is slightly more diverse and determined by a given country's wealth measured in GDP per capita.

Meanwhile, when discussing the micro-scale costs and benefits of using environmental taxes in climate policy-making, there is also the question of the costs of measuring individual emissions, which may discourage a universal use of environmental taxes, except in situations where a small number of emission sources are involved or if it is important to link the incentive to the amount of pollution emitted rather than basing the tax on other, easier-to-measure emission indicators. An alternative to direct taxation of emissions is to set or modify a generally applicable indirect tax rate (excise tax, sales tax or value-added tax) or to introduce an environmental tax linked to the sale of polluting goods or means of production. Goods and services involving environmental damage at the stage of production or consumption may be subject to higher taxation (e.g. tax on batteries and fertilisers). It is believed that goods that bring environmental benefits may be taxed at a lower rate than their substitutes as is the case of a lower tax on lead-free petrol (Hammar & Löfgren, 2004). Environmental taxes of that kind may generate lower administrative costs than taxes based on measured emissions. In some cases, it may

Table 2.1 Impact of environmental taxes on selected macroeconomic indicators

Group shift	*Independent variable*		*LB*	*estimate*	*UB*	*std. er.*	*p*	*R2*
Countries above-average GDP per capita	Consumption	n + 1	6.5498877	10.1076454	13.6654031	1.8152158	0.0000001	0.9879639
			4219.1775571	5710.9807177	7202.7838783	761.1380476	0.0000000	0.9879639
		n + 2	7.5541382	11.1434910	14.7328438	1.8313361	0.0000000	0.9882859
			3795.9594562	5307.8674633	6819.7754704	771.3958109	0.0000000	0.9882859
		n + 3	8.9424576	12.8160570	16.6896564	1.9763625	0.0000000	0.9885418
			3428.0752339	4959.3315937	6490.5879535	781.2676008	0.0000000	0.9885418
	CPI	n + 1	−0.0000764	−0.0000054	0.0000656	0.0000362	0.8819859	0.1239932
			−0.0796980	−0.0499324	−0.0201669	0.0151868	0.0012048	0.1239932
		n + 2	−0.0000504	0.0000221	0.0000946	0.0000370	0.5511721	0.1255485
			−0.0869637	−0.0564124	−0.0258611	0.0155877	0.0003800	0.1255485
		n + 3	−0.0000503	0.0000288	0.0001079	0.0000404	0.4768085	0.1262521
			−0.0891664	−0.0578931	−0.0266198	0.0159561	0.0003675	0.1262521
	Investments	n + 1	2.7587675	5.0646271	7.3704866	1.1764806	0.0000269	0.9689207
			3004.3057275	3971.1755638	4938.0454000	493.3100015	0.0000000	0.9689207
		n + 2	4.0430738	6.3423782	8.6416825	1.1731360	0.0000002	0.9704510
			2619.4699212	3587.9834181	4556.4969150	494.1486193	0.0000000	0.9704510
		n + 3	4.8536493	7.3382270	9.8228047	1.2676650	0.0000000	0.9710221
			2397.1344449	3379.3024479	4361.4704510	501.1153321	0.0000000	0.9710221
Countries below-average GDP per capita	Consumption	n + 1	8.6678737	10.0873758	11.5068779	0.7242491	0.0000000	0.9936291
			936.8987097	1380.5656372	1824.2325646	226.3648368	0.0000000	0.9936291
		n + 2	8.3444847	9.7249956	11.1055064	0.7043552	0.0000000	0.9935872
			866.5735942	1316.8909822	1767.2083701	229.7579912	0.0000000	0.9935872
		n + 3	8.1185085	9.5448442	10.9711799	0.7277357	0.0000000	0.9933452
			926.8532351	1384.4560626	1842.0588901	233.4751205	0.0000000	0.9933452

CPI	n + 1	−0.0001306	0.0000229	0.0001764	0.0000783	0.7702748	0.3272935
		−0.2381044	−0.1901280	−0.1421516	0.0244782	0.0000000	0.3272935
	n + 2	−0.0000906	0.0000581	0.0002068	0.0000759	0.4441162	0.3283429
		−0.2448314	−0.1963328	−0.1478342	0.0247447	0.0000000	0.3283429
	n + 3	−0.0000768	0.0000739	0.0002246	0.0000769	0.3370782	0.3290464
		−0.2470541	−0.1987006	−0.1503472	0.0246706	0.0000000	0.3290464
Investments	n + 1	−1.8324105	−0.8826718	0.0670669	0.4845695	0.0694526	0.9746650
		179.5590294	476.4009001	773.2427708	151.4527170	0.0018130	0.9746650
	n + 2	−1.0713222	−0.1460802	0.7791619	0.4720710	0.7571836	0.9744108
		61.6853524	363.4957959	665.3062393	153.9877497	0.0188455	0.9744108
	n + 3	−0.8279574	0.1105151	1.0489875	0.4788213	0.8176122	0.9744074
		19.7143648	320.7989174	621.8834701	153.6173905	0.0375587	0.9744074

Source: Own elaboration.

be also possible to use the already existing taxes (for example by means of VAT differentiation), which can prove less costly than developing and implementing a totally new administrative apparatus and procedure. Even if there is no possibility to use existing solutions, a separate environmental tax charged on the transaction value may have lower administrative costs than a tax levied on measured emissions, especially if it can be operated in a manner compatible with the existing tax base definitions. The disadvantage of such taxes is that they target emissions less precisely than measured-emissions taxes, so they may encourage inefficient polluters' responses (Sandmo, 1976), i.e. the latter may seek to pay lower taxes without engaging in bona fide pro-environmental measures. The use of tax on a proxy for emissions may, therefore, help save on administrative costs related to the direct emission measurement but there is a risk it will trigger behavioural responses which do not always favour achieving the most effective patterns of pollution abatement. In some cases, what could be more effective is a tax solution oriented to achieving environmental goals through a shrewd combination of indirect and direct taxes and subsidy support, meaning a so-called 'multi-part instrument' would be then created. To quote an example of such a measure – a tax directly based on emissions from motor vehicles may be impossible to implement, but the next best thing would be combining instruments such as petrol tax, subsidy for new car purchases, tax on older cars and tax chargeable on fuel consumption and emission rates (Fullerton & West, 2002). Likewise, incentives to reduce consumption of products that generate much waste and to properly dispose of waste can be equally effective as a tax that directly addresses these aspects, which is, however, unfeasible. It could be difficult to implement a targeted emissions tax if emissions cannot be measured, especially that the tax does not relate to a market transaction. The same effects can be achieved, however, by combining a tax on the company's output and a subsidy to purchase pollution abatement means and technologies. As both the sale of output and the purchase of clean inputs are market transactions, administration costs of those two instruments combined may be lower than for one emission tax.

The existence of administrative costs may contribute to the optimum structure and level of environmental taxes (Polinsky & Shavell, 2000; Cremer & Gahvari, 2002). It is, however, hardly likely that environmental taxes integrated into the existing tax systems such as VAT would be totally cost-free. Crawford et al. (2008) indicate that the administrative complexity of multiple-rate VAT systems is a strong case for minimising the VAT rate differentiation. A model example of such a measure would be a simple recyclable deposit for glass bottles, but the idea can have a much wider use. It can even apply to industrial pollution. One of many forms of environmental tax may be appropriate under specific circumstances and the choice should take account of administrative costs of different tax options as well as the extent to which respective tax designs can effectively target environmental incentive.

When reviewing economic literature, it can be observed that environmental taxes were proposed as early as in the beginning of the 12th century among the main instruments to mitigate environmental problems such as pollution and climate change (e.g. Pigou, 1920). Some researchers from that period were of the opinion that this type of fiscal tool can be classified as an incentive mechanism as it is believed that tax system can create appropriate incentives for its payers to refrain from causing pollution above the 'socially acceptable level', while, according to another approach, it can be seen as a generator of so-called 'external costs'. Of course, this is just one of the many perspectives on environmental taxes, which is not recognised by everybody and a debate on that subject is definitely more complex. Firstly, a question arises: how high the 'price' for polluting environment should be? In other words, how to determine the most efficient tax rate to ensure, on the one hand, it does not hinder economic growth or contribute to the spread of informal economy, and on the other, it promotes the achievement of the environmental goal (e.g. Parry & Small, 2004; Newberry, 2004). These are not merely theoretical debates as there are numerous studies pointing to negative consequences of implementing environmental taxes. Wier et al. (2005), for example, conclude that environmental taxes in Denmark have undesirable consequences in terms of distribution of outcomes as it has been demonstrated that these taxes are regressive in nature. Similar research conclusions have been reached and presented in publications by Br ännlund and Nordstrom (2004) as well as by West and Williams III (2004) for Sweden and the United States.

In scientific literature and reports of international institutions, the most often analysed relationship for assessing the effective climate impact of environmental taxes is the impact the CO_2 emissions tax levied on fossil fuels and other products has on CO_2 emissions abatement. Studies focus on establishing if such a relationship exists, and if so, on quantifying this impact as well as that of GHG, e.g. Filipović and Golušin (2015), Freire-González (2018), Aydin and Esen (2018), Timilsina (2018), He et al. (2019), Shahzad et al. (2020). Research conducted by Morley (2012), Miller and Vela (2013) and Haites (2018) indicate, for example, that energy taxes may reduce GHG emissions and energy consumption. Similar relationships have been observed by Sen and Vollebergh (2018) in OECD countries. The authors demonstrated that an increase of energy taxes by EUR 1 causes CO_2 emissions from fossil fuel consumption to fall by 0.73%. Those results were corroborated by Hashmi and Alam (2019), who pointed out that an increase in environment tax revenues per capita (by 1%) contributes to reducing CO_2 emissions (by 0.033%). Lin and Li (2011) apply the difference in differences (DID) approach to analyse the impact taxes on CO_2 emissions have on CO_2 emissions per capita. Authors note a significant effect in CO_2 emissions reduction in Finland and a negative but insignificant coefficient for the Netherlands, Denmark and Sweden. For Norway, the effect was quite the opposite: an increase in CO_2 emissions per capita, explained by an increase in the consumption of energy products. Even though many studies confirm the fact that environmental taxes are effective in reducing CO_2 and GHG emissions, still, overall research results are inconclusive. The discrepancies in the results have been pointed out, among others, by Gerlagh and Lise (2005), Loganathan et al. (2014), and Radulescu et al. (2017). Liobikienė et al. (2019) analysed the relationship between the energy tax and GHG emissions, consumption of renewable energy, consumption of fossil energy and energy intensity for 28 EU countries between 1995 and 2012, pointing out in the end that energy taxes did not contribute to a reduction in GHG emissions. On the other hand, the results of studies conducted by González-Sánchez and Martín-Ortega (2020) proved that since 2008, GHG emissions in EU-28 countries have declined, but other types of carbon mitigation policy have contributed more to that reduction. For example, Gerlagh and van der Zwaan (2006) use a top-down energy demand model to analyse various instruments, including carbon tax. The authors conclude that the portfolio standard of limiting the CO_2 emissions intensity with carbon taxes is a cheaper climate change mitigation than subsidies to produce non-fossil energy. Bruvoll and Larsen (2004) used general equilibrium simulation model to analyse the impact of carbon taxes on emissions changes in Norway. They discovered that CO_2 emissions taxes have little impact on CO_2 emissions reduction, contributing only to a 2% fall. However, emissions reduction per unit of GDP is significant, the main outcome being a reduction in energy intensity and process emissions. The main argument shared by some studies is a zero impact of CO_2 emissions taxes, when these are coupled with tax exemptions for energy-intensive industries and if these taxes are charged in highly inelastic demand sectors. Liang et al. (2007) come to the same conclusion, having applied a CGE model to assess the impact of various carbon tax scenarios for China. In a scenario where energy and trade-intensive sectors are fully exempt and where all non-exempt sectors are subsidised, the mitigating effects are very weak, while in the exempt sector CO_2 emissions increase. On the other hand, in this scenario, the negative impacts of CO_2 tax on GDP, employment rate and consumption are reduced, while trade-intensive manufacturing and export sectors are insensitive to this type of tax. In a prognostic study of the impact of energy and CO_2 emissions tax on Japan's energy system, Nakata and Lamont (2000) share the view that these taxes are the right instrument to reduce CO_2 emissions. Wissema and Dellink (2007) research Ireland's case and conclude that a 25% reduction compared to 1998 CO_2 level could be reached with a carbon tax amounting to EUR 10–15 per ton of CO_2. Di Cosmo and Hyland (2013), also taking account of Ireland's case, use a different approach to tax scenarios to analyse the impact on energy demand and CO_2 emissions. For a scenario where CO_2 emissions increase from EUR 21.50 in 2012 to EUR 41 in 2025, the authors concluded that CO_2 emissions will be reduced by 861,000 tons compared to the zero CO_2 tax scenario. Some experiences were negatively impacted by incorrect tax exemptions and badly designed reimbursement schemes. Vehmas (2005) analyses Finland's experience with environmental tax on energy and comes to the conclusion that a fiscally motivated departure from perfect environmental tax undermined the true purpose of that tax. At the same time, as pointed out earlier, some authors emphasise the significance of fossil fuel taxes. For instance, Sterner (2007) shows a positive long-term effect of fossil fuel tax in Europe when it comes to decreasing demand for fuels, which entailed reduced CO_2 emissions. The author explains that CO_2 emissions will be more than halved with high fuel taxes introduced, and the carbon content in the atmosphere will be reduced by over 1 ppm. In the same way, Yan and Crookes (2009) explain the significance of the scenario with fuel taxes reduced to meet fast growth in demand for vehicles and energy in China. This scenario leads to a potential 16.3% reduction in demand for energy, 18.5%

reduction in demand for crude oil and 16.2% reduction in GHG emissions until 2030 compared to the unchanged scenario. Concrete empirical evidence has demonstrated effectiveness of the plastic bag fees introduced in Ireland in 2002. One of the main outcomes is an over 90% reduction in plastic bag use at retailers with annual receipts from this tax amounting to ca. EUR 13 million. Deyle and Bretschneider (1995), upon analysing waste tax in the United States, in particular tax on land pollution, conclude that higher taxes decrease the quantity of waste directed to landfills compared to other forms of waste management.

Environmental taxes are clearly linked to political costs, which complicates their implementation. Nevertheless, some countries have introduced taxes which work similarly to an environmental tax, even though they were not established for environmental reasons. Some of the best known and most often implemented ERTs are taxes on fuel consumption, such as petrol and diesel fuel, whose general adoption is explained by their capacity to generate a large increase in fiscal receipts. The effectiveness and distributional consequences of these taxes have been examined in a number of studies. Irrespective of those discussions, however, environmental taxes would be a constant limiting factor in the economy, which could have impact on the consumption of fossil fuels and other heavy contaminants. Relatively few studies have dealt with the effectiveness of those taxes in this respect.

Taking account of the inconclusive views on the environmental tax effectiveness as identified in the literature review undertaken for the purposes of the discussions presented in this monograph, a decision has been made to conduct own analysis of the structure and level of environmental taxes in the European Union and the impact of their respective categories on the achievement of climate goals.

Environmental tax revenues come from four types of tax: energy taxes (which represent ca. 75% of the total amount), transport taxes (ca. 20% of the total) and taxes on pollution and natural resources (ca. 4% of the total).

Between 2004 and 2021, the environmental tax revenues as a share of total tax revenues in EU-27 ranged from 6.71% in 2004 to 5.52% in 2021. The general downward trend in the participation of environmental tax revenues in total tax revenues in the EU-27 is presented in Figure 2.1.

Data point to a drop in environmental tax revenues as a share of total tax revenues between 2004 and 2008. Then, a stable level of environmental tax revenues is observed until 2016, followed by another noticeable drop in revenues until 2021. Figure 2.2 also presents environmental tax revenues as a share of total tax revenues as a % of GDP. Also in this case an overall downward trend can be observed, though the drop is less marked, with the values ranging from 2.57% in 2004 to 2.24% in 2021.

In 2004, the highest environmental tax revenues as a share of total tax revenues were recorded in Cyprus (12.32%), Denmark (10.75%) and the Netherlands (9.84%), and the lowest in France (4.9%), Spain (5.74%) and Belgium (5.77%). In 2021, it was different countries' turn to record the highest and lowest environmental tax revenues as a share of total tax revenues. The highest share was recorded in Greece (9.98%), Bulgaria (9.06%) and Latvia (8.97%) and the lowest in Luxembourg (3.76%), Germany (4.38%) and Sweden (4.43%).

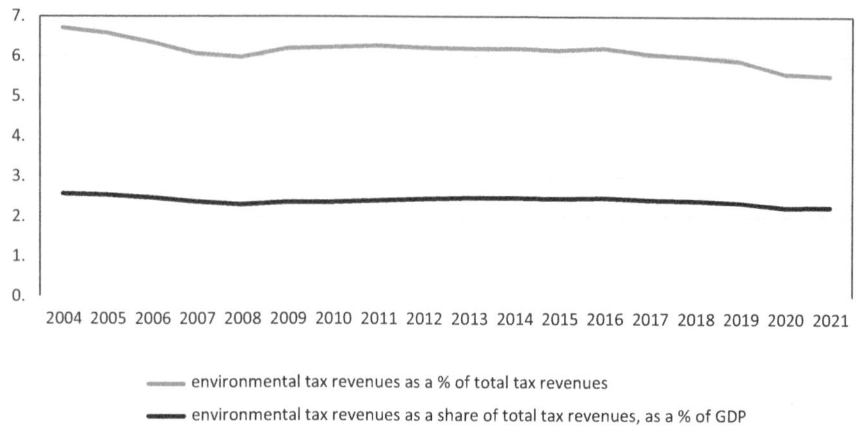

Figure 2.1 Environmental tax revenues as a share of total tax revenues and as a % of GDP from 2004 to 2021

Source: Own elaboration based on Eurostat data.

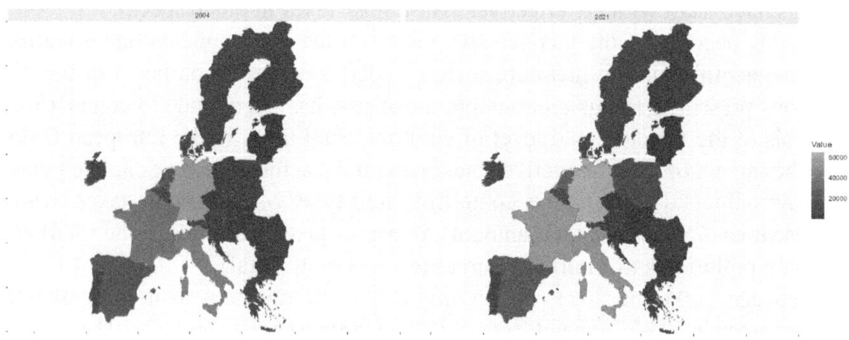

Figure 2.2 Environmental tax revenues in million euro in EU countries in 2004 and in 2021

Source: Own elaboration based on Eurostat data.

The general downward trend as presented in Figure 2.2 is confirmed by drops in the environmental tax revenues as a share of total tax revenues in respective EU countries between 2004 and 2021. The highest drops compared to 2004 and 2021 were recorded in Cyprus (5.82 p.p.), Denmark (4.75 p.p.) and Luxembourg (4.41 p.p.). It should be mentioned, however, that in three EU Member States the value has increased – in Greece (by 3.01 p.p.), Estonia (by 0.08 p.p.) and Latvia (by 0.07 p.p.).

As a next step, the intention was to establish whether there is any relationship between environmental tax revenues and environmental indicators. The research uses linear fixed effects model. The choice of the model was mostly motivated by the nature of data – it was changes over time in characteristics shared by selected EU countries that were assessed. The use of fixed effects for countries made it possible to observe and control for time-constant heterogeneity between research units in the periods analysed. In practice, this means that each of the countries is characterised by a different constant in the time series, a deterministic parameter that differs for respective countries.

The linear fixed effects model is expressed by the following formula:

$$y_{it} = x'_{it}\beta + \sum_{j=1}^{N} \alpha_j d_{ij} + \varepsilon_{it},$$

Where – explained variable – vector of explaining variables, – intercept for *j*th variant of random effects variable, – binary variable that takes the value 1 for $i = j$ (if the unit belongs to *j*th group) and otherwise 0, – random component. Model parameters are estimated using the least squares method adapted to the existence of (artificial) binary variables. Such an estimator is referred to as the *least squares dummy variables* (LSDV).

Including an intercept for each fixed effects, domain makes it impossible to estimate the equilibrium constant for the whole equation as if there was a time constant for each unit, this would result in strict collinearity with variables and make it impossible to identify the model.

The model assumes a zero expected value and a random component variance as well as no autocorrelation. The results obtained are presented in Table 2.2 and point to a positive climate impact of environmental taxes on CO_2, NOx and GHG emissions in the EU countries, in particular those with a higher GDP per capita. Using just a few identifiable relationships, research has confirmed that an increase in environmental tax revenues by one unit leads to CO_2 emissions in EU countries with above-average GDP decreasing in the next periods by 0.13 units in n + 1, 0.13 in n + 2, 0.14 in n + 3, respectively, while in EU countries with below-average GDP per capita, the environmental impact is definitely less marked: 0.073 unit in n + 1, 0.071 in n + 2, 0.069 in n + 3, respectively. Similar relationships, with only slightly different impacts, have been confirmed for NOx and other greenhouse gases.

Such a clear relationship cannot be found for the impact of environmental taxes on the share of energy from renewable sources. Analyses have demonstrated that environmental taxes can, albeit to a very little extent, have a negative impact on the share of RES, but it is a minimal and statistically negligible relationship so it could be concluded these are neutral, irrespectively of a country's wealth.

Environmental taxes are divided into several categories, especially in terms of their tax base, such a classification representing the most widely used method of identification for research purposes and for presentation in international comparisons. Other possible classification criteria for environmental taxes include:

- the purpose identified by the tax legislator,
- tax name,
- environmental purposes the revenues are allocated to.

However, classifications based on the above-mentioned criteria are less appropriate according to many experts and more difficult to use in practice.

Table 2.2 Impact of environmental taxes in million euro on basic environmental monitoring indicators under climate policy

Group shift	*Dependent variable*		*LB*	*estimate*	*UB*	*std. er.*	*p*	*R2*
Countries above-average GDP per capita	CO	n + 1	−0.1338486	−0.1188789	−0.1039092	0.0076377	0.0000000	0.9715570
			−13.6676164	−6.2067867	1.2540430	3.8066157	0.1046645	0.9715570
		n + 2	−0.1324998	−0.1170216	−0.1015433	0.0078972	0.0000000	0.9699740
			−11.9768675	−4.0745289	3.8278096	4.0318795	0.3135173	0.9699740
		n + 3	−0.1386508	−0.1214716	−0.1042925	0.0087650	0.0000000	0.9678003
			−11.4782480	−3.0987279	5.2807923	4.2753439	0.4694818	0.9678003
	Greenhouse gases	n + 1	−0.0057736	−0.0043683	−0.0029631	0.0007170	0.0000000	0.9930101
			−2.6548324	−1.9544592	−1.2540860	0.3573398	0.0000001	0.9930101
		n + 2	−0.0063111	−0.0049336	−0.0035562	0.0007028	0.0000000	0.9933683
			−2.3754157	−1.6721580	−0.9689004	0.3588115	0.0000060	0.9933683
		n + 3	−0.0072674	−0.0058337	−0.0044000	0.0007315	0.0000000	0.9937458
			−2.1036763	−1.4043584	−0.7050404	0.3568014	0.0001166	0.9937458
	NOx	n + 1	−0.0329949	−0.0290434	−0.0250919	0.0020161	0.0000000	0.9823757
			−8.0126923	−6.0432898	−4.0738874	1.0048156	0.0000000	0.9823757
		n + 2	−0.0341553	−0.0303552	−0.0265551	0.0019388	0.0000000	0.9839055
			−6.8941155	−4.9540142	−3.0139128	0.9898658	0.0000013	0.9839055
		n + 3	−0.0361012	−0.0319322	−0.0277632	0.0021271	0.0000000	0.9831365
			−6.5999339	−4.5664217	−2.5329096	1.0375253	0.0000180	0.9831365
	Renewable share	n + 1	−0.0003239	−0.0002035	−0.0000831	0.0000614	0.0011272	0.9866281
			0.7961305	0.8583607	0.9205910	0.0317507	0.0000000	0.9866281
		n + 2	−0.0003222	−0.0002013	−0.0000805	0.0000617	0.0013268	0.9866041
			0.7985856	0.8626489	0.9267122	0.0326860	0.0000000	0.9866041
		n + 3	−0.0003407	−0.0002105	−0.0000804	0.0000664	0.0018106	0.9865582
			0.7989215	0.8644022	0.9298828	0.0334091	0.0000000	0.9865582

Countries below-average GDP per capita	CO	n + 1	−0.0735170	−0.0676948	−0.0618726	0.0029706	0.0000000	0.9891152
			−9.4035998	−7.3329263	−5.2622529	1.0564855	0.0000000	0.9891152
		n + 2	−0.0717858	−0.0663922	−0.0609987	0.0027518	0.0000000	0.9898717
			−8.5099285	−6.4886265	−4.4673244	1.0312955	0.0000000	0.9898717
		n + 3	−0.0699412	−0.0641346	−0.0583279	0.0029627	0.0000000	0.9884163
			−9.2098567	−7.0508166	−4.8917765	1.1015713	0.0000000	0.9884163
	Greenhouse gases	n + 1	−0.0082990	−0.0074467	−0.0065944	0.0004348	0.0000000	0.9912228
			−0.9218439	−0.6187305	−0.3156172	0.1546525	0.0000784	0.9912228
		n + 2	−0.0083545	−0.0075840	−0.0068136	0.0003931	0.0000000	0.9922224
			−0.7618598	−0.4731165	−0.1843732	0.1473207	0.0014543	0.9922224
		n + 3	−0.0083686	−0.0075874	−0.0068062	0.0003986	0.0000000	0.9921106
			−0.7792608	−0.4888010	−0.1983411	0.1481965	0.0010818	0.9921106
	NOx	n + 1	−0.0349815	−0.0313369	−0.0276923	0.0018595	0.0000000	0.9663436
			−5.6294963	−4.3332923	−3.0370883	0.6613407	0.0000000	0.9663436
		n + 2	−0.0349465	−0.0316101	−0.0282738	0.0017022	0.0000000	0.9694189
			−5.0281338	−3.7777941	−2.5274545	0.6379401	0.0000000	0.9694189
		n + 3	−0.0350343	−0.0316570	−0.0282797	0.0017232	0.0000000	0.9690790
			−5.0928178	−3.8370684	−2.5813190	0.6407002	0.0000000	0.9690790
	Renewable share	n + 1	−0.0000678	0.0000401	0.0001479	0.0000550	0.4672750	0.9678513
			0.6496134	0.6891948	0.7287762	0.0201950	0.0000000	0.9678513
		n + 2	−0.0000811	0.0000221	0.0001254	0.0000527	0.6749120	0.9678117
			0.6515974	0.6917649	0.7319325	0.0204940	0.0000000	0.9678117
		n + 3	−0.0000827	0.0000197	0.0001221	0.0000522	0.7067239	0.9678079
			0.6520087	0.6921857	0.7323627	0.0204989	0.0000000	0.9678079

Sources: Own elaboration.

When analysing the reasons why authorities use environmental taxes, a major one that can be identified is to nudge behaviours by making a product more expensive in use and reducing its economic utility due to additional fiscal burden. As the environmental impact of the tax is mainly linked to its impact on relative prices, for example a petrol tax introduced for fiscal reasons will have the same impact as the one whose declared goal is only to reduce emissions. Consequently, this is one of the arguments in favour of the claim that environmental taxes should be identified based on tax base. In some cases, the tax base is measured or estimated with the volume of pollutant emissions, such as CO_2 or NOx, which can be difficult and costly to measure directly, though, hence many taxes are based on emissions indicators, for example heating oil consumption. In international statistics, also those applied by Eurostat for EU Member States, environmental protection taxes are divided into three main categories, i.e.

- energy taxes
- taxes on pollution/resources,
- transport taxes.

Obviously, in some situations, taxes represent borderline cases and it is better to leave it up to tax authorities to assess them on a case-by-case basis and decide whether they really represent environmental taxes and if so, which tax category they can be classified to. In such situations, an individual assessment should be conducted for each case, which should be based on analysing the tax base(s) and tax regulations.

Some statistics also include a further division into taxes on pollution and taxes on resources, making it a total of four subcategories. For the purposes of discussions undertaken in this monograph, the former division will be used, i.e. into three types of environmental taxes. In most countries, of greatest importance to the climate policy implementation and in terms of the amount of funds collected, are two categories: energy and transport.

The first of the categories identified as part of environmental taxes is that of energy taxes (including on transport fuel), which involves taxes on energy production and on energy products used both in the transport industry and in other sectors of the economy as well as by individual buyers. Major energy products for transport are petrol and diesel oil, while those meant for stationary use include heating oil, natural gas, coal and electricity. Biofuel taxes and taxes on all other forms of renewable energy and on energy-saving products are also included in this category of environmental taxes. CO_2 taxes are part of the energy tax category rather than taxes on pollution, as could be expected. There are a couple of reasons for why it is the case. The first one is that it is often impossible to separate CO_2 emissions taxes in statistical data as they are integrated with energy taxes, for example with tax rates for mineral oil being differentiated according to the fuel's carbon content. Furthermore, in many countries, other tax categories are introduced which depend on electricity consumption, and revenues from these taxes can be very high compared to revenues from tax on pollution. This means that including CO_2 emissions

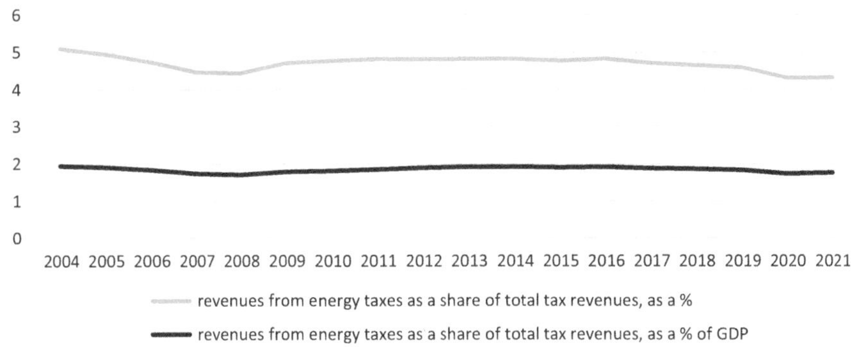

Figure 2.3 Energy taxes as a share of total taxes and as a GDP % in 2004–2021

Source: Own compilation based on Eurostat data.

taxes in the category of taxes on pollution rather than energy taxes would distort the situation both for national statistics and for international comparisons. Of course where CO_2 emissions taxes are identifiable, these are presented as separate categories. Energy taxes also take account of revenues from GHG taxes, and consequently the emissions-trading allowances. The government's receipts from auctioning emission allowances are treated as tax revenues in national accounts. The most important system of that kind is the EU Emissions Trading System (EU ETS) related to GHG emissions. The related revenues are also disclosed in national accounts and should be recognised in the energy tax category.

As mentioned before, energy taxes are one of the three tax categories making up environmental taxes, representing ca. 75% of the value of this group of tax revenues. Below is examined the evolution of energy taxes as a share of environmental taxes between 2004 and 2021.

From 2004 to 2021, energy taxes as a share of total tax revenues in EU-27 countries ranged from 5.10% in 2004 to 4.32% in 2021. An overall downward trend in energy taxes as a share of total tax revenues in EU-27 countries in the period analysed is presented in Figure 2.3.

Seeing as energy taxes represent a great majority (ca. 75%) of environmental taxes, the trends shown in Figure 2.3 are a natural replication of the trends shown in Figure 2.4, though with smaller numbers. Data presented in Figure 2.4 point to a decline in revenues from energy taxes as a share of total tax revenues from 2004 to 2008 in EU-27 countries. Then a stable level can be observed until 2016, followed again by a decline in those revenues as a share of total tax revenues until 2021. The above figure also illustrates energy taxes as a share of all tax revenues, calculated as a percentage of GDP. In this case, too, an overall downward trend can be observed, though the decline in itself is less marked, with the values ranging from 1.95% in 2004 to 1.76% in 2021. A similar situation was true for all environmental taxes as a share of overall tax revenues.

In 2004, energy tax revenues represented the highest percentage share of total tax revenues in Bulgaria (8.35%), Luxembourg (7.87%) and Romania (7.85%),

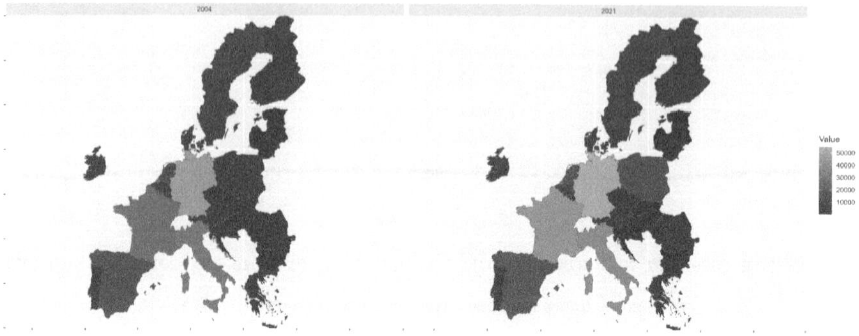

Figure 2.4 Revenues from energy tax in million euro in EU Member States in 2004 and 2021

Source: Own elaboration based on Eurostat data.

and the lowest in Belgium (3.42%), France (3.97%) and Malta (3.86%). By 2021, this ranking had already changed, with different countries recording the highest and lowest values of energy tax as a share of overall tax revenues. The highest shares were recorded in Bulgaria (7.98%), Greece (7.76%) and Latvia (7.34%), and the lowest in Austria (3.02%), Denmark (3.23%) and Sweden (3.31%).

The overall downward trend presented in Figure 2.4 is also confirmed by declines in energy tax revenues as a share of overall tax revenues in respective EU countries in 2004–2021. The highest drops were recorded in Luxembourg (by 4.39 p.p.), Denmark (2.73 p.p.) and Germany (2.08 p.p.). It is also worth noting that in 6 of EU Member Countries, this value increased between 2004 and 2021: in Greece (by 3.65 p.p.), Belgium (by 0.63 p.p.), Estonia (by 0.55 p.p.), Croatia (by 0.25 p.p.), Poland (by 0.19 p.p.) and France (by 0.06 p.p.).

When analysing the impact of energy taxes on environmental indicators presented in Table 2.3, significant statistical relationships can be observed between these parameters.

Model studies have revealed that in the event of a one-unit increase in energy tax revenues, a decrease in CO_2 emissions can be observed, irrespective of a country's wealth, beginning from the year after the increase occurred. Interestingly, though, the scale of CO_2 emissions reduction is quite varied, i.e. there is a faster positive impact for wealthier countries, i.e. 0.14 unit in the year n + 1, 0.14 unit in n + 2, 0.15 unit in n + 3 while for countries with lower GDP per capita a reduction in CO_2 emissions stands at 0.08 unit in each of the following years beginning from n + 1.

As regards NOx and GHG emissions, a positive impact on emissions reduction is recorded but only to a limited extent so it is hard to consider this tool effective in that case.

Meanwhile, when it comes to enhancing the availability of renewable energy sources, no positive impact of energy taxes on this category is recorded, irrespective of a given EU Member State's wealth; admittedly, there is a relationship but only a slight one and not a positive one. One could argue that this happens because

Table 2.3 Impact of energy taxes in million euro on basic environmental monitoring indicators under climate policy

Group shift	*Dependent variable*		*LB*	*Estimate*	*UB*	*std. er.*	*p*	*R2*
Country above-average GDP per capita	CO	n + 1	−0.1409125	−0.1224320	−0.1039516	0.0094290	0.0000000	0.9656820
			−22.1392720	−14.3902427	−6.6412134	3.9536590	0.0003526	0.9656820
		n + 2	−0.1404279	−0.1209738	−0.1015197	0.0099257	0.0000000	0.9636367
			−21.0467295	−12.8522754	−4.6578212	4.1809208	0.0024262	0.9636367
		n + 3	−0.1498605	−0.1281564	−0.1064522	0.0110738	0.0000000	0.9619864
			−20.2258449	−11.6460627	−3.0662806	4.3775203	0.0084786	0.9619864
	Greenhouse gases	n + 1	−0.0058182	−0.0041974	−0.0025766	0.0008269	0.0000009	0.9926388
			−3.0021318	−2.3225264	−1.6429211	0.3467438	0.0000000	0.9926388
		n + 2	−0.0064026	−0.0047722	−0.0031417	0.0008319	0.0000000	0.9928768
			−2.8073754	−2.1205908	−1.4338061	0.3504068	0.0000000	0.9928768
		n + 3	−0.0075294	−0.0057873	−0.0040452	0.0008888	0.0000000	0.9931701
			−2.5898010	−1.9011336	−1.2124662	0.3513674	0.0000002	0.9931701
	NOx	n + 1	−0.0346312	−0.0297990	−0.0249669	0.0024654	0.0000000	0.9791347
			−10.0938961	−8.0677171	−6.0415381	1.0337838	0.0000000	0.9791347
		n + 2	−0.0360226	−0.0311705	−0.0263185	0.0024756	0.0000000	0.9798842
			−9.3248530	−7.2810657	−5.2372784	1.0427678	0.0000000	0.9798842
		n + 3	−0.0386841	−0.0332976	−0.0279111	0.0027483	0.0000000	0.9791786
			−9.0346759	−6.9053597	−4.7760435	1.0864058	0.0000000	0.9791786
	Renewable share	n + 1	−0.0003394	−0.0002077	−0.0000760	0.0000672	0.0023375	0.9865205
			0.7863546	0.8459072	0.9054597	0.0303845	0.0000000	0.9865205
		n + 2	−0.0003361	−0.0002007	−0.0000652	0.0000691	0.0041857	0.9864348
			0.7858759	0.8468935	0.9079111	0.0311320	0.0000000	0.9864348
		n + 3	−0.0003573	−0.0002071	−0.0000569	0.0000766	0.0075843	0.9863477
			0.7842794	0.8466282	0.9089770	0.0318112	0.0000000	0.9863477

(*Continued*)

Table 2.3 (Continued)

Group shift	*Dependent variable*		*LB*	*Estimate*	*UB*	*std. er.*	*p*	*R2*
Country below-average GDP per capita	CO	n + 1	−0.0835692	−0.0767354	−0.0699017	0.0034867	0.0000000	0.9886426
			−9.1508330	−7.0149262	−4.8790194	1.0897684	0.0000000	0.9886426
		n + 2	−0.0821312	−0.0756857	−0.0692402	0.0032886	0.0000000	0.9892477
			−8.3461458	−6.2436522	−4.1411586	1.0727205	0.0000000	0.9892477
		n + 3	−0.0791409	−0.0719824	−0.0648238	0.0036524	0.0000000	0.9871067
			−9.4439271	−7.1472923	−4.8506574	1.1717740	0.0000000	0.9871067
	Greenhouse gases	n + 1	−0.0096661	−0.0087023	−0.0077384	0.0004918	0.0000000	0.9914978
			−0.8443436	−0.5430887	−0.2418337	0.1537043	0.0004706	0.9914978
		n + 2	−0.0097408	−0.0088540	−0.0079672	0.0004524	0.0000000	0.9923410
			−0.6993776	−0.4101117	−0.1208459	0.1475873	0.0057778	0.9923410
		n + 3	−0.0097275	−0.0088080	−0.0078884	0.0004692	0.0000000	0.9919942
			−0.7472675	−0.4522566	−0.1572457	0.1505185	0.0028681	0.9919942
	NOx	n + 1	−0.0405730	−0.0364289	−0.0322847	0.0021144	0.0000000	0.9670432
			−5.3401050	−4.0448504	−2.7495959	0.6608563	0.0000000	0.9670432
		n + 2	−0.0405637	−0.0366980	−0.0328324	0.0019723	0.0000000	0.9694816
			−4.8106632	−3.5496954	−2.2887277	0.6433627	0.0000001	0.9694816
		n + 3	−0.0404010	−0.0363879	−0.0323748	0.0020475	0.0000000	0.9680258
			−5.0314740	−3.7439696	−2.4564652	0.6569021	0.0000000	0.9680258
	Renewable/ share	n + 1	−0.0000688	0.0000532	0.0001752	0.0000622	0.3932241	0.9678738
			0.6476943	0.6876570	0.7276197	0.0203895	0.0000000	0.9678738
		n + 2	−0.0000897	0.0000282	0.0001461	0.0000601	0.6397092	0.9678166
			0.6505084	0.6910848	0.7316611	0.0207026	0.0000000	0.9678166
		n + 3	−0.0000936	0.0000240	0.0001416	0.0000600	0.6894323	0.9678099
			0.6512240	0.6917917	0.7323595	0.0206982	0.0000000	0.9678099

Source: Own elaboration.

increasing taxation without a possibility to increase product prices puts a damper on investment; however, a statistical analysis has demonstrated relationships at the level of the third decimal digit so one that is difficult to interpret reliably and to put forward recommendations based thereon.

The second of the large subcategories of environmental taxes are transport taxes, which mainly include taxes related to owning and using vehicles with an internal combustion engine. In addition, taxes on means of transport (e.g. aircrafts, boats or railway rolling stock) as well as on related transport services (e.g. customs duty on charter flights or scheduled flights) are also included if they meet the general definition of environmental taxes. This type of taxes may be one-off in nature, for example in case of importing or selling given equipment, or periodical, such as annual road tax. All taxes on means of transport should be taken into consideration, even on those that are significantly more environmentally friendly, such as railway rolling stock and public transport in general. A differentiation in terms of environmentally-friendliness is reflected in the tax rate charged on the tax base. Tax on electric cars should also be included in this category. What could be interesting to a person unfamiliar with the field of tax policy is that taxes on vehicle insurance also should be included in environmental transport taxes provided that these are specifically vehicle insurance taxes rather than general insurance taxes levied on all sorts of framework insurance contracts. As mentioned before, taxes on petrol, diesel oil and other transport fuels are not included in this category but instead in that of energy taxes. In many countries, taxes on CO_2 emissions specific for transport vehicles have also been introduced – these are one-off registration or import taxes or annual taxes on vehicles. These taxes are not related to the actual use of vehicles or the emissions actually generated. The tax base is the vehicle technical properties, e.g. average CO_2 emissions per 100 km or average fuel consumption per 100 km, often jointly with other technical properties such as vehicle's weight or engine power. Another form of taxation classified as environmental transport taxes is congestion charges (charges for entering the inner city or city charges). The charges seem to greatly vary in terms of their characteristics from country to country, and from city to city in respective countries. These charges are differently treated in national accounts of the countries where they have been implemented (e.g. some of such charges are treated as service charges, others as taxes). If a city charge is treated as a tax in national accounts, it should be recognised as a transport tax.

Transport taxes represent ca. 20% of the value of environmental taxes. From 2004 to 2021, revenues from transport taxes as a share of overall tax revenues in EU-27 countries ranged from 1.38% in 2004 to 1.00% in 2021. The stable downward trend in the revenues from transport taxes as a share of overall tax revenues in EU-27 countries is presented in Figure 2.5.

Data presented in Figure 2.5 indicate quite a uniform decline in transport tax revenues as a share of overall tax revenues from 2004 to 2021 in EU-27 countries (Figure 2.6). The above figures also show transport tax revenues as a share of overall tax revenues calculated as a percentage of GDP. In this case, the general downward trend can be also seen to be replicated for these revenues, with values ranging from 0.54% in 2004 to 0.41% in 2021.

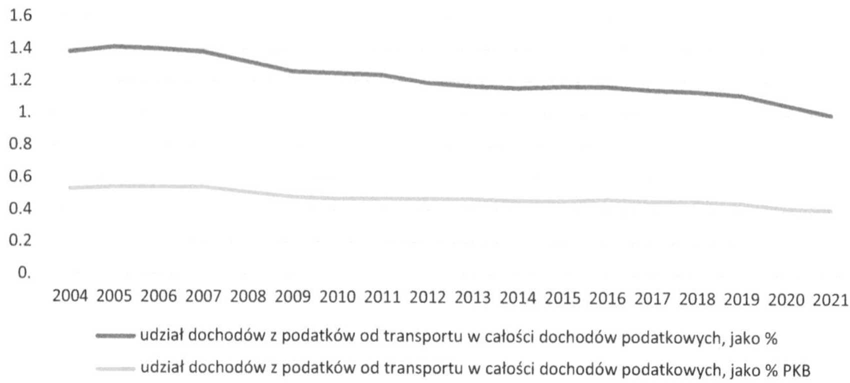

Figure 2.5 Revenues from transport taxes as a share of overall tax revenues and as a percentage of GDP in 2004–2021

Source: Own elaboration based on Eurostat data.

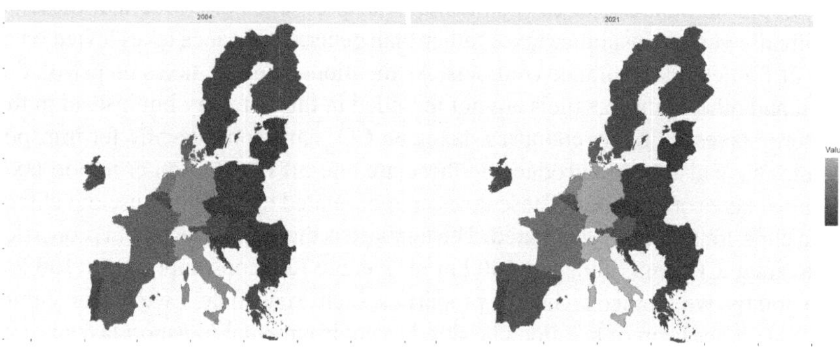

Figure 2.6 Revenues from transport taxes in million euro in EU Member States in 2004 and 2021

Source: Own elaboration based on Eurostat data.

In 2004, the transport tax revenues represented the highest share of overall tax revenues in Cyprus (5.88%), Malta (5.50%) and Denmark (4.13%), and the lowest in Estonia (0.23%), Romania (0.23%) and Luxembourg (0.30%). In 2021, the Netherlands (2.23%), Denmark (2.43%) and Malta (2.43%) (similarly to 2004) came in the lead of countries with the highest revenues from transport taxes as a share of total tax revenues. Nevertheless, it should be noted that in 2004, the share of those three countries hovered around 5%, while in 2021, it stood at ca. 2%. Meanwhile, the lowest revenues from transport taxes as a share of total tax revenues can be found in Estonia (0.12%), Luxembourg (0.25%) and Czechia (0.27%).

The downward trend presented in Figure 2.5 is confirmed by declines in revenues from transport taxes as a share of total tax revenues in respective EU Member States in 2004–2021, the highest ones being recorded in Cyprus (down by

4.56 p.p.), Malta (3.07 p.p.) and Lithuania (2.32 p.p.). Nevertheless, there are four EU countries where this value rose between 2004 and 2021, namely growth was recorded in Latvia (up by 0.09 p.p.), Sweden (up by 0.28 p.p.), Bulgaria (up by 0.31 p.p.) and Romania (up by 0.36 p.p.).

When assessing the effectiveness of transport taxes in the climate policy implementation, one could rely on at least several relationships, presented in greater detail in Table 2.4.

Analyses have revealed that transport taxes have a significant impact on CO_2 emissions reduction, its scale depending on EU Member State's wealth. For countries with above-average GDP per capita, there is a CO_2 reduction in every year starting from n + 1 by an average of 0.5 unit when revenues from transport taxes are increased by one unit. Meanwhile, in countries with below-average GDP per capita, the reduction amounts to 0.3 unit.

A positive impact of transport taxes was also recorded for NOx reductions, which go down by ca. 0.13–0.14 unit irrespective of EU Member State's wealth as well as for GHG emissions, going down by ca. 0.03 unit.

Moreover, similarly as in the case of other environmental tax categories, also in this case no statistically significant positive impact on the amount of energy from renewables was found.

The last subcategory identified in the breakdown of environmental taxes in EU statistics is taxes on pollution and natural resources, which includes:

- taxes on measured or estimated emissions to air and water except taxes on CO_2 emissions;
- taxes on noise;
- taxes on solid waste management;
- taxes related to mineral extraction or use of natural resources such as water, forests, wild flora and fauna.

In addition to the aforementioned categories, it is debatable whether lubricating oils are rightly included in the group, and it should be analysed in detail. Lubricating oils are not used for energy purposes and probably they would be best included within the scope of pollution taxes. The main environmental impacts may include soil or water pollution in the event of lubricating oil spillage. However, with lubricating oils included in the mineral oil tax, it may be impossible to identify the tax impacts related to lubricating oils specifically. All taxes intended to capture the resource rent from the extraction of natural resources should be excluded. Most taxes on land are real estate taxes and belong to the category of income taxes. However, in some countries, there are specific taxes to be paid for landscape conversion (e.g. deforestation), which should be included in this group.

Taxes on pollution and natural resources represent ca. 4% of the total value of this tax revenue group.

In 2004–2021, revenues from taxes on pollution and natural resources as a share of total tax revenues in EU-27 ranged from 0.22% in 2004 to 0.19% in 2021. The overall downward trend in this value is presented in Figure 2.7.

Table 2.4 Impact of transport taxes in million euro on basic environmental monitoring indicators under climate policy

Group	*Dependent variable*		*LB*	*Estimate*	*UB*	*std. er.*	*p*	*R2*
Countries above-average GDP per capita	CO	n + 1	−0.5286491	−0.4351606	−0.3416720	0.0476991	0.0000000	0.9548801
			−22.8133254	−13.0967274	−3.3801294	4.9575390	0.0089417	0.9548801
		n + 2	−0.5488553	−0.4600954	−0.3713356	0.0452865	0.0000000	0.9579770
			−18.0751548	−8.3749140	1.3253268	4.9491934	0.0922688	0.9579770
		n + 3	−0.5148600	−0.4217907	−0.3287213	0.0474852	0.0000000	0.9541481
			−21.7533972	11.680899	−1.6084017	5.1391239	0.0241612	0.9541481
	Greenhouse gases	n + 1	−0.0299737	−0.0231010	−0.0162282	0.0035066	0.0000000	0.9931998
			−2.4538419	−1.7395336	−1.0252253	0.3644497	0.0000036	0.9931998
		n + 2	−0.0333725	−0.0269348	−0.0204970	0.0032846	0.0000000	0.9938350
			−2.0103781	−1.3068210	−0.6032640	0.3589643	0.0003516	0.9938350
		n + 3	−0.0348600	−0.0285301	−0.0222003	0.0032296	0.0000000	0.9940852
			−1.9118696	−1.2268185	−0.5417674	0.3495223	0.0005609	0.9940852
	NOx	n + 1	−0.1325233	−0.1087304	−0.0849375	0.0121395	0.0000000	0.9740110
			−10.0404125	−7.5675285	−5.0946444	1.2616987	0.0000000	0.9740110
		n + 2	−0.1446181	−0.1228641	−0.1011101	0.0110992	0.0000000	0.9775523
			−8.1919237	−5.8145107	−3.4370977	1.2129881	0.0000033	0.9775523
		n + 3	−0.1390286	−0.1164305	−0.0938325	0.0115298	0.0000000	0.9759603
			−8.8725183	−6.4268272	−3.9811361	1.2478245	0.0000007	0.9759603
	Renewable share	n + 1	−0.0010579	−0.0004024	0.0002532	0.0003345	0.2306788	0.9858757
			0.7573148	0.8218930	0.8864712	0.0329487	0.0000000	0.9858757
		n + 2	−0.0011632	−0.0005580	0.0000473	0.0003088	0.0725605	0.9860257
			0.7702530	0.8369352	0.9036174	0.0340222	0.0000000	0.9860257
		n + 3	−0.0012010	−0.0006144	−0.0000278	0.0002993	0.0416261	0.9861027
			0.7755762	0.8422300	0.9088839	0.0340077	0.0000000	0.9861027

Countries below-average GDP per capita	CO	n + 1	−0.3724386	−0.3276553	−0.2828721	0.0228490	0.0000000	0.9826318
			−17.7499065	−15.4087889	−13.0676712	1.1944697	0.0000000	0.9826318
		n + 2	−0.3694820	−0.3307323	−0.2919825	0.0197707	0.0000000	0.9847768
			−16.3486771	−14.1311047	−11.9135324	1.1314353	0.0000000	0.9847768
		n + 3	−0.3649686	−0.3300063	−0.2950440	0.0178382	0.0000000	0.9862092
			−15.6819578	−13.5625401	−11.4431225	1.0813554	0.0000000	0.9862092
	Greenhouse gases	n + 1	−0.0308231	−0.0241477	−0.0174724	0.0034059	0.0000000	0.9854780
			−1.9851780	−1.6362112	−1.2872443	0.1780476	0.0000000	0.9854780
		n + 2	−0.0344753	−0.0286257	−0.0227760	0.0029846	0.0000000	0.9869452
			−1.8146769	−1.4799149	−1.1451530	0.1708001	0.0000000	0.9869452
		n + 3	−0.0350344	−0.0296452	−0.0242559	0.0027497	0.0000000	0.9876691
			−1.7396826	−1.4129855	−1.0862884	0.1666853	0.0000000	0.9876691
	NOx	n − 1	−0.1265607	−0.0980436	−0.0695266	0.0145498	0.0000000	0.9444280
			−10.1445912	−8.6538152	−7.1630393	0.7606139	0.0000000	0.9444280
		n + 2	−0.1423103	−0.1172421	−0.0921739	0.0127901	0.0000000	0.9497268
			−9.4389601	−8.0043579	−6.5697557	0.7319533	0.0000000	0.9497268
		n + 3	−0.1487926	−0.1259289	−0.1030651	0.0116654	0.0000000	0.9534619
			−9.0423902	−7.6563858	−6.2703813	0.7071581	0.0000000	0.9534619
	Renewable share	n + 1	−0.0006642	0.0000323	0.0007288	0.0003554	0.9276586	0.9677929
			0.6600631	0.6956621	0.7312611	0.0181631	0.0000000	0.9677929
		n + 2	−0.0005429	0.0001038	0.0007504	0.0003299	0.7533335	0.9678031
			0.6588825	0.6947981	0.7307137	0.0183246	0.0000000	0.9678031
		n + 3	−0.0005158	0.0001046	0.0007251	0.0003166	0.7412127	0.9678042
			0.6585848	0.6946307	0.7306767	0.0183911	0.0000000	0.9678042

Source: Own elaboration.

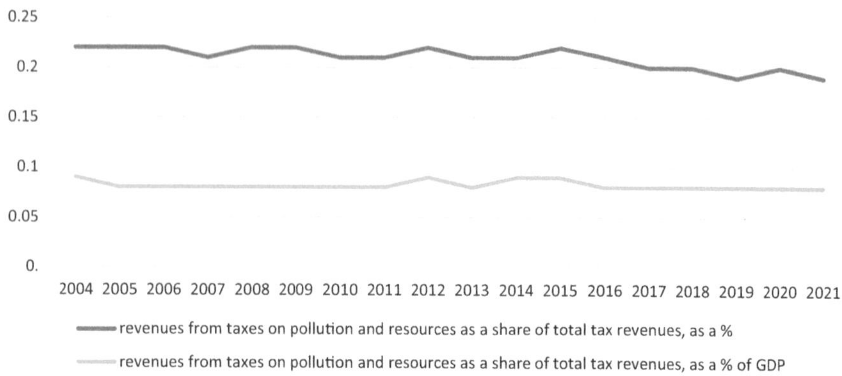

Figure 2.7 Taxes on pollution as a share of total taxes and as a % of GDP in 2004–2021

Source: Own elaboration based on Eurostat data.

Data presented in Figure 2.7 shows a decline in revenues from taxes on pollution and resources as a share of total tax revenues from 2004 to 2021 in EU-27 countries.

The exceptional spikes in 2012, 2014 and 2020 as visible in the figure do not change the overall downward trend in the tax revenue category discussed here. The above figures also show the tax on pollution and natural resources as a share of total tax revenues, measured as a percentage of GDP. In this case, a relatively stable ratio of 0.08% can be observed, except in four years (2004, 2012, 2014, 2015) in the period under review, where the ratio stood at 0.09%.

In 2004, the highest value of revenues from tax on pollution and natural resources as a share of total tax revenues was recorded in the Netherlands (1.33%), Estonia (0.76%) and Denmark (0.67%), with the lowest (zero) in Greece, Cyprus and Luxembourg. Over the years under review, the share of revenues earned from tax on pollution and natural resources changed in respective EU countries and in 2021 the highest share was recorded in Hungary (0.61%), Malta (0.67%) and the Netherlands (1.09%), and the lowest in Germany (0.89%), Ireland (0.01%) and Romania (0.02%).

The downward trend in the share of revenues from tax on pollution and natural resources as presented in Figure 2.8 is confirmed by the falling amount of revenues from those taxes as a share of total tax revenues in respective EU countries in 2004–2021. The sharpest drops were recorded in Romania (by 0.48 p.p.), Bulgaria (0.44 p.p.) and Estonia (0.36 p.p.). In nine EU Member States, this value rose between 2004 and 2021, with increases ranging from 0.03 p.p. to 0.61 p.p. Countries were increases were recorded are Greece, Spain, Luxembourg, Portugal, Croatia, Cyprus, Latvia, Hungary and Malta.

Due to the specificity of tax on pollution and natural resources, the analyses have demonstrated that out of all tax categories, they had the greatest impact on CO_2 reduction in EU countries (see Table 2.5). Raising taxes on pollution and natural resources by one unit causes a reduction of CO_2 emissions by 1.3 unit in the

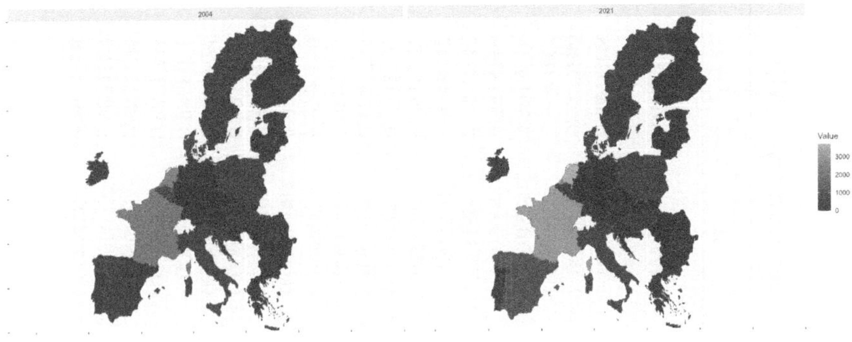

Figure 2.8 Revenues from tax on pollution and natural resources in million euro in EU Member States in 2004 and 2021

Source: Own elaboration based on Eurostat data

years n + 1, n + 2, n + 3 in wealthy countries and by 0.4 in countries with a lower GDP per capita.

When it comes to GHG emissions, taxes on pollution and natural resources also seem to be an effective tool for implementing the climate policy as their increase causes those emissions to go down. This time it is in poorer countries that the impact is stronger, as it stands at ca. 0.1 unit compared to 0.05 in countries with a higher GDP per capita. As was the case of NOx reduction, analyses have demonstrated positive impact of this category of environmental taxes by ca. 0.3 unit in wealthier countries and 0.5 unit in countries with below-average GDP per capita.

2.2 European and national public expenditure – the scale and effectiveness of its impact on the achievement of European environmental goals and on the economic processes

In a fiscal policy intended to support sustainable development, it is necessary to pursue multilateral medium- and long-term actions. Comprehensive actions, however, pose major challenges to effective management and to striking a balance between the fiscal tools in place. It is also the case of environmental protection initiatives as on the one hand, there is a need to generate additional public revenues to finance the related measures, and on the other hand, it is necessary to verify public expenditure in terms of its purposefulness, efficiency and scale. All this overlaps with the ongoing discussion of the maximum acceptable level of financeable public sector deficit and debt that could be additionally contracted as a result of environmental measures (Postuła, 2015b). Considering the substantial complexity of those relationships, sustainable fiscal measures must be coupled with a deep change in public finance to ensure those measures do not have a negative impact on the economic growth rate and on the scale of the public goods provided, which are important for the economic growth. This is especially true considering the ongoing discussion among practitioners and theoreticians alike on how effectively the environmental tasks are delivered by the market and by the government, respectively.

Table 2.5 Impact of taxes on pollution and natural resources in million euro on basic environmental monitoring indicators under climate policy

Group shift	*Dependent variable*		*LB*	*Estimate*	*UB*	*std. er.*	*p*	*R2*
Countries above-average GDP per capita	CO	n + 1	−1.3265716	−1.0089777	−0.6913838	0.1620407	0.0000000	0.9460344
			−40.7525014	−31.9731765	−23.1938516	4.4793297	0.0000000	0.9460344
		n + 2	−1.3532478	−1.0476240	−0.7420003	0.1559333	0.0000000	0.9475078
			−39.4206038	−30.6933872	−21.9661705	4.4527434	0.0000000	0.9475078
		n + 3	−1.2939496	−1.0174934	−0.7410373	0.1410516	0.0000000	0.9490166
			−38.1756326	−29.5205151	−20.8653976	4.4159574	0.0000000	0.9490166
	Greenhouse gases	n + 1	−0.0485006	−0.0250887	−0.0016768	0.0119451	0.0370325	0.9918219
			−3.6645385	−3.0173582	−2.3701779	0.3302001	0.0000000	0.9918219
		n + 2	−0.0514691	−0.0287269	−0.0059848	0.0116034	0.0141806	0.9918942
			−3.6067072	−2.9572941	−2.3078811	0.3313393	0.0000000	0.9918942
		n + 3	−0.0484966	−0.0276568	−0.0068170	0.0106327	0.0100319	0.9919207
			−3.5805026	−2.9280629	−2.2756232	0.3328835	0.0000000	0.9919207
	NOx	n + 1	−0.3253866	−0.2443090	−0.1632315	0.0413669	0.0000000	0.9687237
			−14.6008029	−12.3595564	−10.1183099	1.1435141	0.0000000	0.9687237
		n + 2	−0.3509543	−0.2742573	−0.1975603	0.0391318	0.0000000	0.9706019
			−14.0225876	−11.8324726	−9.6423575	1.1174262	0.0000000	0.9706019
		n + 3	−0.3397630	−0.2708306	−0.2018983	0.0351702	0.0000000	0.9718120
			−13.6299235	−11.4718314	−9.3137393	1.1010876	0.0000000	0.9718120
	Renewable share	n + 1	−0.0055783	−0.0036683	−0.0017583	0.0009745	0.0002307	0.9868621
			0.7790101	0.8329439	0.8868777	0.0275177	0.0000000	0.9868621
		n + 2	−0.0060360	−0.0041528	−0.0022695	0.0009609	0.0000264	0.9871795
			0.7859408	0.8395295	0.8931182	0.0273417	0.0000000	0.9871795
		n + 3	−0.0062902	−0.0044693	−0.0026484	0.0009290	0.0000033	0.9874789
			0.7928519	0.8461845	0.8995172	0.0272110	0.0000000	0.9874789

Countries below-average GDP per capita	CO	n + 1	−0.4714828	−0.2883764	−0.1052701	0.0934233	0.0021998	0.9723269
			−20.4980467	−17.4518510	−14.4056554	1.5542100	0.0000000	0.9723269
		n + 2	−0.4046487	−0.2175248	−0.0304010	0.0954731	0.0233601	0.9719590
			−20.8985365	−17.8289537	−14.7593709	1.5661425	0.0000000	0.9719590
		n + 3	−0.4595366	−0.2665126	−0.0734886	0.0984834	0.0071703	0.9721411
			−20.6435794	−17.5729478	−14.5023161	1.5666776	0.0000000	0.9721411
	Greenhouse gases	n + 1	−0.1011651	−0.0796027	−0.0580403	0.0110014	0.0000000	0.9855592
			−1.8393452	−1.4806293	−1.1219134	0.1830217	0.0000000	0.9855592
		n − 2	−0.0956006	−0.0733999	−0.0511992	0.0113271	0.0000000	0.9851469
			−1.8791621	−1.5149812	−1.1508002	0.1858100	0.0000000	0.9851469
		n − 3	−0.0980210	−0.0750081	−0.0519952	0.0117415	0.0000000	0.9850984
			−1.8726222	−1.5065323	−1.1404423	0.1867840	0.0000000	0.9850984
	NOx	n + 1	−0.5158197	−0.4290030	−0.3421863	0.0442950	0.0000000	0.9509115
			−8.9112932	−7.4669925	−6.0226917	0.7369017	0.0000000	0.9509115
		n + 2	−0.4886831	−0.3984718	−0.3082605	0.0460270	0.0000000	0.9485743
			−9.1168214	−7.6369934	−6.1571655	0.7550281	0.0000000	0.9485743
		n + 3	−0.4948153	−0.4008574	−0.3068995	0.0479386	0.0000000	0.9479128
			−9.1189503	−7.6242650	−6.1295797	0.7626086	0.0000000	0.9479128
	Renewable share	n + 1	−0.0028376	−0.0008119	0.0012137	0.0010335	0.4327563	0.9678611
			0.6633961	0.7003857	0.7373753	0.0188726	0.0000000	0.9678611
		n + 2	−0.0028891	−0.0008433	0.0012026	0.0010438	0.4198336	0.9678650
			0.6635321	0.7005375	0.7375428	0.0188806	0.0000000	0.9678650
		n + 3	−0.0026813	−0.0005771	0.0015270	0.0010736	0.5912786	0.9678244
			0.6619426	0.6990672	0.7361918	0.0189415	0.0000000	0.9678244

Source: Own elaboration.

There are various reasons why the market may fail to achieve the expected effectiveness in this area: imperfect competition, distortions resulting from the existence of public goods, mismatch resulting from externalities, market incompleteness, asymmetry of information, unemployment, inflation and disequilibrium. Market failure is considered a sufficient justification for the government to interfere with the market mechanism, also the one related to the protection of natural goods. However, just like the market, government, too, is not always effective and efficient when it comes to environmental measures. The main reasons in that case include information limitations, limited control over a market dominated by private entities, limited control over bureaucracy as well as political limitations. Opponents of government intervention in the environmental protection or, viewed in a different perspective, proponents of deregulation believe that these sources of government failure are a sufficient argument to call on it to abstain from interfering with the economy and not to try and fix the defects in the market mechanism. Nevertheless, as demonstrated above, the efficiency of market mechanisms also leaves much to be desired; hence, the discussions in this monograph highlight the important role of government for sustainable economic growth, and try to indicate areas and tools with the most effective impacts of the government and market, respectively. This chapter focuses on instruments used by government and that is why it would make sense to start from answering the following question: is the scale of government intervention in the economy of significance to the scale of pollution or are these totally independent variables? Frederik and Lundström (2001) attempted to partly answer that question by examining the impact of political and economic freedom on the CO_2 emissions using a data set from 1975 to 1995 containing 75 countries. They put forward a hypothesis that the government's fiscal impact on pollution level differs depending on the original level of that intervention. In particular, they demonstrated that greater economic freedom and lesser government interference decreases CO_2 emissions, and when government is big, emissions rise. According to Bernauer and Koubi (2006), an increase in such expenses as a share of GDP involves greater air pollution and such a relationship is not affected by the quality of governance. They also successfully confirmed the controversial hypothesis that higher public revenues lead both to higher government impact on economy and to better air quality. Meanwhile, Lopez and Palacios (2010) analysed the impact of spending and tax policy on environmental parameters in Europe using disaggregated data for 21 European countries from 1995 to 2006. The results obtained revealed that public expenditure has a negative impact on the air pollution level, even in a situation where the structure of public expenditure is strictly controlled. A scientific literature review leads to the conclusion that most studies dealt with the impact those in power achieved through public expenditure on the economic growth rather than directly addressing the impact of environmental taxes on this macroeconomic parameter – i.e. an increased relationship, finding a negative impact of the former on the latter. There are quite a number of studies indicating that public expenditure may negatively affect economic growth by crowding out public sector, due to government inefficiency, tax system and incentive system distortions as well as free-market interventions (Barro, 1991; Bajo-Rubio & Ramon, 2000; Afonso &

Furceri, 2008b). Moreover, the share of public expenditure intended to increase private sector productivity is usually lower in countries with big government (Folster & Henrekson, 2001). In addition, the related papers by Bergh and Karlsson (2010) and Afonso and Jalles (2011) demonstrate that the size of government is negatively correlated to the economic growth and commitment of public funds, and that countries with a significant government involvement in the economic processes taking place may leverage improved institutional quality and globalisation to mitigate this negative impact. On the other hand, government expenditure may also have a positive impact on economic performance due to the positive externalities by harmonising conflicts between private and social interests, ensuring socially optimal direction for growth and compensating for market failures (Ghali, 1998). Based on the studies mentioned above, it is hard to draw a clear-cut conclusion on the impact of the government intervention in the economy on the scale of pollution.

The role of public expenditure on environmental protection and measures to reduce pollution has evolved in several stages in line with social and economic development. In the first historical stage when developing countries became independent, emphasis was placed on the economic growth fundamentals and on building the institutional framework for the proper implementation of public service tasks. In that period, the industrial sector was seen as the driving force without which no progress could be achieved, according to economic strategists. That was in the 1980s when governments focused primarily on creating favourable conditions for economic development, including industrial one, without giving much attention to environmental issues. One could even go as far as to say that environmental protection stood in opposition to those economic goals (Gillroy &Shapiro, 1986). Government's spending policy back then focused on developing this branch of economy, putting the protection of natural resources on the back burner. However, over the years, it became evident that the generated national income per capita, as important as it may be, is an insufficient measure for social and economic assessment, and increasingly more attention was given to the significance of human factor and environmental protection as the necessary elements of responsible policy-making. Lack of active environmental measures and the depletion of natural resources quickly came to be a global problem (Barrett & Scott, 1990). To address it, as broadly discussed in Chapter 1, regulations were introduced to foster environmental protection and prevent environmental degradation (Hahn & Stavins, 1992). Environmental protection gradually gained significance, as obviously reflected by the increase in public expenditure on that purpose both at national and international levels (Dunlap & Scarce, 1991b). It is of significance to mention here the Kuznets curve which shows that the environmental quality improves as income rises once the economy reaches a certain income threshold. However, in a country with a low institutional quality, the income curve may never reach the turning point, i.e. the impact of economic growth on limiting pollution worldwide is described by the Kuznets curve (Moshiri & Daneshmand, 2019). On the other hand, some public expenditure items directly promote clean and healthy environment. Such spending categories include subsidised public services related to the basic requirements of waste water and sewage disposal (OECD, 2024), or expenditure on water desalination, expenditure on building RES, etc. Public spending on healthcare is intended to protect the health of citizens and employees, who represent the core part of each country's true wealth. This kind of public spending (financing public goods) has a positive impact on environmental quality. Secondly, public expenditure on education speeds up the transition from capital intensive to labour-intensive branches of industry (Dissou & Karnizova, 2016). Thirdly, increasing public expenditure on R&D and innovation may involve creating and developing new 'clean' technologies such as pro-environment technologies and clean energy, thus improving the efficiency with which inputs are used in the production process and, ultimately, reducing the pollution to performance ratio (Sanberg et al., 2019). This so-called technique effect achieved by adopting clean technology can be even exceeded by the composition effect (education of human capital) (Hua et al., 2018). Lopez et al. (2011) provide theoretical bases for establishing the impact of public expenditure on pollution, which will be further discussed later further in the Monograph. In particular, they emphasise the importance of and help empirically assess the environmental impact of budgetary expenditure. Some of the studies also confirm that reallocating the public expenditure structure towards social and public goods decreases pollution. This outcome is attributed to the combination effect of four factors resulting from such a reallocation, namely the scale (greater environmental pressure resulting from a higher economic growth), composition (a greater share of human-capital intensive activities instead of the more environmentally harmful branches requiring high capital in the form of natural resources), technology (due to higher labour efficiency) and income (higher income increasing the demand for improved environmental quality). Moreover, they believe that increasing the total government involvement in the economy without its reorientation will have no positive impact on the environmental quality. In the 1990s, the problem was still a low economic efficiency of environmental protection expenditure and the devaluation of social benefits (Pearce, 1998). In our day and age, attention to environmental protection has become a norm. Companies are influenced by the government, investors and consumers to adopt proactive environmental management. As demonstrated by research results, such activity ultimately fosters companies' increased productivity and competitiveness (Berry & Rondinelli, 1998). In developed countries, the economic impact on emissions increase is significantly different. Diversified income generates a gap between each country's capability and willingness to pay for environmental protection (Magnani, 2000; Rokicki, 2016). A methodology for counting environmental expenditures has also been developed, making it possible to compare such expenditures across countries and companies. Such accounts do not include external (environmental and social) costs (Jasch, 2003; Soukopová & Struk, 2011). The analysis of environmental expenditure is of strategic importance and enables the evaluation of existing environmental policies. A low level of environmental spending does not always mean that a country is not effectively protecting its environment. Expenditure is often associated with the reduction of adverse effects on nature, the reduction of pollutant emissions or the application of more effective solutions in the form of protective measures (Broniewicz & Poskrobko, 2004; Georgescu & Cabeca, 2010; Rokicki, 2017).

Many scientific publications argue that governments are able to increase public spending on environmental protection in order to simultaneously manage the economy and improve the environment. Even if the arguments given by researchers for increasing government spending on environmental protection to simultaneously support public investment, resulting in reduced unemployment and a better economic situation and reduced pollution, are not always borne out by empirical data, the public perception that this is a phenomenon of interconnected rather than mutually exclusive vessels is equally important. Historical experience shows that societies respond to the onset of recession by significantly reducing their concern for the environment. With regard to the 'Great Recession' of 2008, Kenny (2020) notes that: 'Evidence suggests that the crisis may have affected individuals' environmental protection preferences with a notable decline in environmental concern' (see also European Commission (2014). Kahn and Kotchen (2010) illustrated the impact of rising unemployment on individuals' concern for the environment in the United States. Concern is estimated based on the number of internet search terms. Summarising the results based on an analysis of voter preferences in the United States, the authors concluded: 'During a recession, households are likely to focus on day-to-day wellbeing rather than more abstract, long term, and uncertain threats such as global warming'. Inglehart (2008) distinguishes between materialist (e.g. consumption of private goods and services) and post-materialist (e.g. environmental improvement) objectives, arguing that recessions have an adverse impact on post-materialist values. Climate policy studies also highlight the overarching concern that citizens express for private goods and services when income levels are very low. This observation is important in explaining the shape of the Environmental Kuznets Curve (EKC). At very low-income levels, citizens are willing to accept increasing levels of pollution in order to enjoy economic growth. The EKC indicates that at low-income levels, pollution increases as income levels rise. Obviously, when income reaches a certain higher level, the situation changes. Once higher income levels are reached, individuals continually demand pollution reductions when incomes continue to rise. It is as if private good benefits were considered necessary at low income levels. At higher income levels, the public good benefits of environmental spending become more important. In a recession, risk-averse voters behave as if their overriding concern was to avoid losing income. They place much more importance on the government's ability to manage the economy, which is consistent with this explanation. The evidence is that higher income earners reduce their preference for environmental protection to a greater extent than lower income earners because they stand more to lose if they are put out of work. Reaching quite an opposite conclusion, Kenny (2020) cites Cooper's (2014) empirical results to argue that there is a greater decline in environmental attitudes among those with lower incomes than among those with higher incomes – those experiencing a greater decline in their resources and living standards as a result of unemployment place much less importance on environmental issues.

Another important determinant of environmental quality, which can also impact the effect of government spending, is the quality of governance. In non-democratic regimes, small elites are disproportionately affected by stricter environmental policies because they rely on polluting industrial activities to increase their personal wealth and therefore have incentives to oppose the enactment of environmental regulations (Bernauer & Koubi 2009, 2013; Lake & Baum 2001; Niskanen, 1997; Farzin & Bond, 2006). Consequently, corruption may affect political stability and environmental quality may further deteriorate through reduced stringency of environmental regulations (Fredriksson & Svensson, 2003; Fredriksson et al., 2003; Welsch & Ebert, 2004; Cole, 2007; Halkos & Tzeremes, 2013). On the other hand, in democracies, the median voter faces a relatively lower burden of environmental policy, and therefore more stringent environmental policies are more likely to be implemented in such systems. Better quality of political institutions is expected to strengthen the magnitude of the effect of government anti-pollution spending. Higher levels of government spending help to establish and enforce environmental regulations, which in turn can lead to the development of institutions that improve environmental quality (Fullerton & Kim, 2008). Galinato and Islam (2017) provide evidence that once the government's share of spending on public goods is increased, the effectiveness of environmental regulation in reducing consumption-based pollution is significantly enhanced in democratic regimes. The level and structure of public spending can impact pollution for at least several reasons. Economists continue to predict countercyclical aggregate public spending (Alesina et al., 2008), even though there is growing evidence that aggregate public spending is often procyclical (Gavin & Hausmann, 1996; Kaminsky et al., 2005; Talvi & Végh, 2005; Woo, 2009). Bowen and Stern (2010) provide a general critique of this approach by pointing out that increased spending (including environmental spending) may not always be appropriate in the face of a recession, e.g. if the recession has been caused by adverse supply effects (rather than an autonomous reduction in private sector demand). There are also difficulties in determining the exact timing of increases in public spending (to achieve both objectives) and how to cooperate with other countries. Public spending is pro-cyclical, increasing as national income increases and decreasing as national income declines. There are circumstances in which pro-cyclical spending can maximise community welfare (Lane, 2003), but these are very specific and extremely unlikely (Halland & Bleaney, 2011). Instead, there is a growing consensus that, in practice, governments redistribute spending pro-cyclically as they pragmatically respond to systematic changes in the political pressures experienced during the economic cycle. Lane and Tornell (1996) and Tornell and Lane (1999) speak of 'glutton effects' if political pressures to increase public spending are more intense in good economic times than during economic downturns. Lopez et al. (2020) identify four mechanisms through which the level and structure of government spending can affect the overall level of pollution, namely scale, composition, technique and income effects. The first is generated by economic growth, which in some (most) cases can lead to greater pressure on the environment and the build-up of specific problems, in response to which the government has to implement dedicated solutions, and this entails an increase in specific public spending. The second effect measures the change in environmental degradation due to changes in the mix of goods produced and can be positive or negative depending on the pattern of specialisation induced by trade, leading to the general conclusion that human activity caused by the accumulation of human capital, rather than physical capital, is far more damaging to the environment. The effect of technique, which is based on measuring the pollution that occurs and, as a result of realising its scale, switching to more environmentally sustainable production techniques, is specific and can be better observed in richer countries, which are generally more willing and able to protect their resources mainly in two ways: by setting a higher level of environmental standards and by investing much more in sustainable technologies. A fourth effect accompanies an increase in income, allowing people to care more about themselves and the environment and putting more pressure on the government to increase its spending (Zhang et al., 2017). These effects are directly related to the way the state responds to different phenomena, which is best assessed by looking at specific public spending, in this case related to environmental protection.

In view of the scholarly discussions presented in this subsection on the impact of environmental expenditure on economic growth and, consequently, on environmental quality, the Authors have decided to carry out their own research in this area. As in Section 2.1, the analyses are based on a database from Eurostat covering all EU Member States for the period 2001–2021 and use homogeneous econometric models to maintain comparability of the results obtained. As the literature has repeatedly raised the issue of the impact of public spending on economic growth depending on the wealth of a country, in line with the approach presented in previous chapters, the research sample is divided into two subgroups, i.e. countries with GDP per capita higher than the EU average and those with this parameter at a lower level. The results obtained can be considered quite interesting (see Table 2.6) and, in a certain way, aligned with the scientific discourse on the subject.

The relationships studied showed that public spending on environmental protection can have a positive impact on the level of total consumption in the European Union countries, depending on Member States' wealth level. Admittedly, the magnitude of this effect varies, i.e. in countries with above-average GDP per capita in the following years n + 1, n + 2, n + 3, there is an increase in consumption of around 12.5 units when public spending on environmental protection increases by 1 unit – so it can be seen that public support can be a stimulus in this case. In contrast, in countries with a lower GDP per capita, the relationship looks slightly different, i.e. in period n + 1, n + 2 environmental public expenditure positively translates into consumption increase by about 8.1 and 1.3 units, respectively, while, in year n + 3, the relationship is reversed, i.e. when environmental public expenditure increases by a unit, a decrease in consumption by 9.4 units is observed, bearing in mind that this year an increase in the consumption rate is recorded, i.e. at this point, the expenditure causes the growth of this macroeconomic parameter to slow down.

In turn, studies have shown that environmental expenditures do not create an inflationary impulse; on the contrary, as they increase, the CPI decreases, albeit to a minimal extent, in the period n + 1, n + 2 and n + 3 alike. This phenomenon is observed regardless of the wealth of a given EU Member State.

Table 2.6 Impact of environmental expenditure on selected macroeconomic indicators in EU Member States

Group shift	*Independent variable*		*LB*	*Estimate*	*UB*	*std. er.*	*p*	*R2*
Countries above-average GDP per capita	consumption	n + 1	12.6531246	13.9928098	15.3324950	0.6835254	0.0000000	0.9993478
			1624.5209709	2740.6606557	3856.8003404	569.4694870	0.0000070	0.9993478
		n + 2	12.3237844	14.1287729	15.9337614	0.9209294	0.0000000	0.9992170
			1657.7724370	3098.0825059	4538.3925748	734.8655793	0.0000741	0.9992170
		n + 3	12.5429655	14.6208331	16.6987007	1.0601560	0.0000000	0.9992856
			1636.6444599	3280.6258479	4924.6072359	838.7814271	0.0002399	0.9992856
	CPI	n + 1	−0.0001282	−0.0000368	0.0000547	0.0000467	0.4328032	0.2141074
			−0.1048117	−0.0286331	0.0475456	0.0388674	0.4634954	0.2141074
		n + 2	−0.0001118	−0.0000066	0.0000986	0.0000537	0.9027561	0.2370780
			−0.1679983	−0.0840519	−0.0001056	0.0428306	0.0537464	0.2370780
		n + 3	−0.0000405	0.0000684	0.0001774	0.0000556	0.2233081	0.2162697
			−0.1722403	−0.0860173	0.0002058	0.0439922	0.0552911	0.2162697
	investments	n + 1	4.7671478	6.7137941	8.6604403	0.9932051	0.0000000	0.9915695
			1882.5135468	3504.3341735	5126.1548001	827.4747084	0.0000613	0.9915695
		n + 2	4.4034064	6.8444757	9.2855451	1.2454664	0.0000006	0.9912309
			2284.4420505	4232.3197077	6180.1973648	993.8333931	0.0000638	0.9912309
		n + 3	4.5830595	7.3696345	10.1562094	1.4217481	0.0000028	0.9921418
			2901.5589835	5106.2602939	7310.9616043	#########	0.0000283	0.9921418
Countries below-average GDP per capita	consumption	n + 1	8.0604839	11.5795074	15.0985310	1.7954531	0.0000000	0.9981531
			1820.7365679	2762.2465376	3703.7565072	480.3710563	0.0000001	0.9981531
		n + 2	1.2848035	6.2344288	11.1840541	2.5253654	0.0152729	0.9977273
			2473.1443553	3708.8306746	4944.5169939	630.4637886	0.0000001	0.9977273
		n + 3	−9.3917032	−2.3724357	4.6468318	3.5813247	0.5095428	0.9976076
			3197.5935432	4732.3237287	6267.0539143	783.0399934	0.0000000	0.9976076

CPI	n + 1	−0.0002978	0.0000940	0.0004857	0.0001999	0.6392058	0.2588333
		−0.2242593	−0.1194425	−0.0146258	0.0534789	0.0274371	0.2588333
	n + 2	−0.0004611	0.0000139	0.0004888	0.0002423	0.9544943	0.2704022
		−0.2306216	−0.1120556	0.0065103	0.0604939	0.0669559	0.2704022
	n + 3	−0.0007190	−0.0001457	0.0004275	0.0002925	0.6196737	0.3376849
		−0.2153377	−0.0900014	0.0353349	0.0639483	0.1630853	0.3376849
investments	n + 1	4.4449261	6.4598803	8.4748345	1.0280567	0.0000000	0.9933031
		−262.7720672	276.3261896	815.4244464	275.0551852	0.3171705	0.9933031
	n + 2	1.5686464	4.4070686	7.2454907	1.4482012	0.0029983	0.9915663
		258.9155699	967.5347556	1676.1539413	361.5470444	0.0087181	0.9915663
	n + 3	−3.9507612	−0.1023485	3.7460642	1.9635120	0.9585557	0.9917366
		1011.5764029	1853.0139415	2694.4514802	429.3127554	0.0000441	0.9917366

Source: Own elaboration.

On the other hand, very interesting relationships have been shown for the level of investment, particularly in the context of the literature review presented earlier. In wealthier countries, an increase by one unit of public expenditure on environmental protection is a clear impulse for an increase in total investment as a share of GDP by about 4.8–4.5 units in each year, i.e. n + 1, n + 2, n + 3. In countries with lower disposable income, on the other hand, a positive, but already much smaller, effect is seen in year n + 1 by 4.5 and n + 2 by 1.6 units. A big surprise is the negative effect of environmental expenditure on investment in year n + 3 in this group of countries, as it leads to a decrease in this parameter by about 4 units, which could mean that state interference at this point somehow cannibalises private investment in environmental protection as well.

Summarising the results of the Authors' own research, they indicate a positive effect of environmental expenditure on basic macroeconomic indicators, and its positive effect on economic processes should not be questioned in the context of ongoing discussions about the state's participation in the economy.

Publications on the environmental impact of public spending discuss selected aspects of environmental protection. What is often analysed and linked to its environmental impact is public social spending (e.g. (Halaskova, 2018; Leitner & Stehrer, 2016; Szarowska, 2011). Particularly interesting was the work of Halaskova (2018), who grouped countries by their public social spending taking account of environmental aspects. Others have also analysed convergence in the case of public social spending (De Simone et al., 2010). A much smaller number of publications refer exclusively to public environmental expenditure (Russu, 2017), with a breakdown by subcategory (Ercolano & Romano, 2018). Russu (2017) analysed public expenditure on environmental protection incurred in Romania compared to other European Union countries in 1990, 1995, 2000, 2005, 2010 and 2012. Ercolano and Romano (2018) investigated the existence of convergence in public expenditure on environmental protection in terms of its total amount and for the six environmental aspects highlighted in COFOG, expressed as a percentage of GDP. Data for 21 EU Member States from 2002 to 2010 were used for the analysis. Based on the results, a conclusion was drawn about the lack of convergence in total public expenditure on environmental protection (Pawełek, 2020). In contrast, the results obtained for six aspects of environmental protection were mixed. For 'Biodiversity and landscape protection' and 'R&D Environmental protection' expenditure, convergence was confirmed; for 'Wastewater management' and 'Environmental protection, n.e.c.', divergence was confirmed; and for 'Waste management' and 'Pollution reduction', the results of the analysis were not clear enough to confirm convergence or divergence.

The Classification of the Functions of Government (COFOG) divides public expenditure into ten main categories (known as 'COFOG first level' groups): general public services; defence; public order and safety; economic affairs; environmental protection; housing and community amenities; health; recreation, culture and religion; education; social protection. Within each function, these are further subdivided into 'groups' (COFOG second level). As a first step, it is worth analysing whether the growing public interest in environmental aspects is translating into

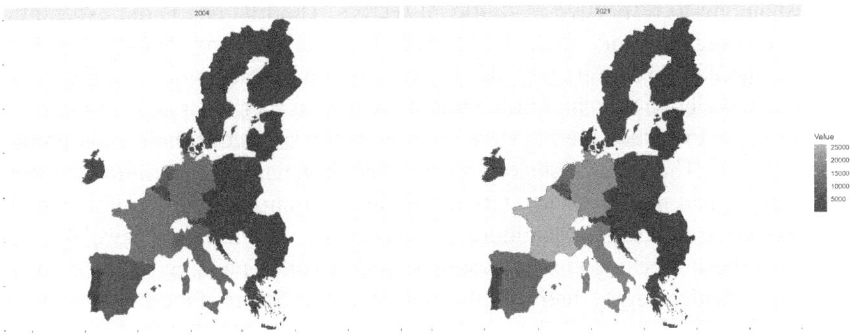

Figure 2.9 Public expenditure on environmental protection in million euro in EU Member States in 2004 and 2021

Source: Own elaboration based on Eurostat data.

an increase in the government's financial commitment in EU countries through public expenditure for this purpose. Observing the data in Figure 2.9 showcasing the scale of public expenditure on environmental protection in individual EU countries from 2004 to 2021, it can be seen that its scale is nominally increasing in a significant way in a great majority of Member States.

An analysis of environmental expenditure in the government sector between 2004 and 2021 shows that France has the highest expenditure in this category (expenditure of EUR 366,615 million), Germany ranks second (EUR 294,060 million) and Italy third, with expenditure of EUR 251,986 million. The smallest expenditure in this category was incurred by Cyprus. Poland ranked ninth among the 30 countries surveyed (in 2021). A general public support for those in power is insufficient to meet the challenges of environmental sustainability. At the same time, there is an urgent need for awareness- and capacity-building in promoting environmental action at the local level. Indeed, it is local governments that do most of the work on environmental protection. An analysis of environmental expenditure in EU Member States in the local government sector between 2004 and 2021 shows France as the leader of this spending category (expenditure of EUR 321,282 million), followed by Italy (EUR 229,357 million) and Germany, with expenditure of EUR 169,342 million. The smallest expenditure in this category was incurred by Malta. Poland ranked eighth out of the 30 countries surveyed (in 2021).

Of course, additional indicators can also be used in the analysis of environmental expenditure, such as those used by Pawełek (2020), i.e. the indicator of the degree of environmental protection in the EU, which is the national expenditure on environmental protection (NEEP). It is calculated as the sum of the running costs of environmental protection activities and investments in environmental protection, taking into account net transfers to the rest of the world. NEEP measures the resources used by a country's resident units (households, corporations and government) to protect the environment over a given period. In the monograph, this indicator is not used because NEEP in total economy is divided into three parts corresponding to respective institutional sectors. The first one is the expenditure of the corporate sector, which includes both specialised environmental producers and ancillary producers who do not sell environmental services on the market but undertake environmental protection activities on their own and for their own use, in order to reduce the negative environmental impact of their main production activities. The second category relates to environmental expenditure of general government and non-profit institutions serving households, and the last category involves environmental expenditure by households. The authors (Pawełek et al.) approach these subcategories separately in each chapter, pointing out their advantages and disadvantages. Interestingly, in the Member States of the 27-strong European Union (EU-27), NEEP is a small percentage of their GDP. More specifically, NEEP in the whole or total economy (households, corporations and government) averaged around 2.2% of the EU Member States' GDP between 2006 and 2021. Of course, there are some noticeable differences between EU countries. In Belgium and Austria, for example, it exceeded 3% of GDP. On the other extreme are Luxembourg (NEEP below 1% of GDP) and Greece (below 1.5% of GDP), well below the EU-27 average.

The high importance of public spending on environmental protection is also confirmed by the fact that, in recent years, several governments in EU Member States and beyond have developed their own Green Budget Tagging (GBT) methodology as an alternative way of accounting for expenditure that contributes to achieving environmental objectives. This has led to the acknowledgement that governments' support for environmental protection requires a specific public financial management process to identify, measure and monitor expenditure linked to policy areas that fall outside existing expenditure classifications. GBT has been in existence for twelve years now and is not a widely used methodology, rather it is still relatively rare among world governments. However, it is considered a key starting point for greening public financial management (Gonguet et al., 2021) and public investment management (IMF, 2021). One good example of such an environmental budget would be the French GBT prepared with the draft budget law for 2021 (September 2020). It was based on the OECD-led Paris Collaborative on Green Budgeting (which France joined in 2017) to integrate 'green' tools into the budget process. The French green budget has four characteristics that, according to experts, make it the most comprehensive in the world so far, as it (1) includes an assessment of the 'green' impact of all state budget expenditure; (2) incorporates tax preferences; (3) reflects not only climate change concerns but also other environmental issues such as biodiversity and the fight against pollution, based on the European Union's sustainable finance taxonomy; and (4) evaluates not only environmentally beneficial expenditures but also those with negative impacts. In practice, the GBT relies on extensive interactions between the relevant ministries and the central budgetary authority as part of the budget preparation process. It analyses at a detailed level the expenditures within the French performance budgeting framework to determine their contribution to environmental objectives. Actual 'green' expenditure is tracked through budget execution reports but not through a specific tag in the financial management information system. The second edition of the French 'Green Budget', produced as part of the draft budget law for 2022, highlights that out of a total of EUR 586.6 billion allocated to the state budget and to tax expenditure, the expenditure of EUR 42.0 billion (1.6% of GDP in 2022), or EUR 53.4 billion including tax expenditure (2.0% of GDP) has an environmental impact. Of this amount, EUR 38.2 billion is assessed as having a positive environmental impact, EUR 4.5 billion as having a mixed impact (positive for one or more elements of the European Union's sustainable finance taxonomy but negative for one or more other elements) and EUR 10.8 billion as having a negative impact (mainly tax expenditure reducing energy costs for specific purposes). For the first time, the French law on the implementation of the 2021 budget includes data on actual 'green' spending. The methodology used for France's green budget is much broader than COFOG's definition of environmental spending, which highlights general government sector's environmental spending of 1.0% of GDP in 2020 alone. This is undoubtedly an example worth following when it comes to presentation of public environmental expenditure, but, as already pointed out, so far few countries can boast having developed such a methodology.

Coming back to the analysis of public environmental expenditure, from the perspective of its share of GDP and of the pool of overall public expenditure (see Table 2.7), one can no longer be so optimistic. In 2021, in eight EU Member States only did public spending on environmental protection account for at least 1% of GDP, the highest Figure 2.9 being 1.5% of GDP in Croatia. In the remaining 19 EU countries, public spending in 2021 ranged from 0.2% of GDP in Finland to 0.9% of GDP in Luxembourg. Meanwhile, in terms of environmental expenditure as a share of total public expenditure, it accounted for at least 3% in three countries only, while in the vast majority, it ranged between 1.4% and 2% of total expenditure.

Obviously, the level of expenditure alone does not indicate the effectiveness of this redistribution instrument on environmental indicators, so in the next step, it was decided to conduct research in this direction. Using data from Eurostat, it was decided to examine the impact of public environmental spending on the key environmental indicators identified in European Commission documents as those that measure the achievement of climate policy objectives, i.e. CO_2, NOx, GHG emissions and the share of energy derived from RES. Obviously, as in the case of environmental taxes, a consideration was given to the distinction between richer countries and those with lower GDP per capita as well as to the time lag effect due to the climate policy specificity, i.e. public funds spent in a given year will not reduce greenhouse gas emissions in the same reporting period, this effect only occurring with a delay (the analyses assume a time lag of one, two and three years).

As a first step, total public environmental expenditure expressed in million euro was analysed and an attempt was made to demonstrate its effectiveness in the implementation of climate policy. The results obtained (see Table 2.8) are quite conclusive and indicate a significant impact of spending policies on the achievement of environmental objectives.

In the group of EU Member States with above-average GDP per capita, public environmental spending has a positive effect on most of the parameters examined. expenditure by a unit results, in successive periods, in a reduction in CO_2 emissions

Table 2.7 Public expenditure on the environment in 2004 and 2021 as a ratio to GDP, as a % of public expenditure and in million euro in EU Member States

Country	*Percentage of gross domestic product (GDP)*		*Percentage of total*		*Million euro*	
	2004	*2021*	*2004*	*2021*	*2004*	*2021*
Austria	0.5	0.4	0.9	0.8	1216.7	1751.4
Belgium	0.9	1.3	1.8	2.4	2594.0	6755.3
Bulgaria	0.8	0.8	2.1	1.9	166.1	559.3
Croatia	0.6	1.5	1.2	3.1	193.2	868.3
Cyprus	0.3	0.4	0.7	0.9	37.3	89.8
Czechia	1.0	0.9	2.4	2.0	979.2	2219.6
Denmark	0.6	0.4	1.1	0.7	1140.9	1243.6
Estonia	0.7	0.6	2.0	1.3	68.2	174.4
Finland	0.3	0.2	0.6	0.4	452.0	579.0
France	0.8	1.0	1.6	1.8	14270.0	26013.0
Germany	0.6	0.6	1.2	1.1	12954.0	20740.0
Greece	0.5	1.2	1.1	2.1	971.0	2187.0
Hungary	0.6	0.7	1.3	1.5	516.3	1098.1
Ireland	0.9	0.3	2.7	1.4	1380.3	1483.4
Italy	0.8	1.0	1.6	1.7	10945.0	16968.0
Latvia	0.5	0.6	1.4	1.3	56.8	188.2
Lituania	0.4	0.5	1.2	1.4	76.5	300.4
Luxembourg	0.7	0.9	1.7	2.2	207.1	667.5
Malta	1.3	1.3	3.2	3.0	65.7	194.7
Netherlands	1.6	1.4	3.7	3.0	8551.0	11938.0
Poland	0.6	0.6	1.3	1.3	1152.9	3224.3
Portugal	0.6	0.8	1.2	1.7	856.6	1720.6
Romania	0.1	0.7	0.4	1.7	77.8	1678.8
Slovakia	1.0	0.9	2.7	2.0	359.2	929.4
Slovenia	0.9	0.7	1.9	1.3	251.7	344.6
Spain	0.9	1.0	2.3	2.0	7809.0	12194.0
Sweden	0.4	0.5	0.8	1.1	1379.4	2935.5

Source: Own elaboration based on Eurostat data.

of 0.95 units in n + 1, 0.82 units in n + 2 and 0.64 units in n + 3, respectively. There is also a positive impact on NOx and GHG reductions, which can be reduced by 0.25, 0.22, 0.17 units and 0.06, 0.046, 0.038 units in years n + 1, n + 2 and n + 3, respectively, due to increased environmental spending by governments. The impact for these indicators is not as large as it is for CO_2, but any positive impulse is important to achieve the aggregate effects. In contrast, no impact of public spending on investment in RES was identified; clearly private spending is more effective in this case, but this will be described in greater detail in the following chapters.

The second group of EU countries analysed, the one with below-average GDP per capita, also showed a positive impact of environmental expenditures on emissions-related indicators. Their level of impact is somewhat lower (e.g. CO_2 reduction is 0.36 in n + 1, 0.45 in n + 2, 0.50 in n + 3, respectively) than in the first group of countries, but there is undoubtedly a case for governments to use the spending instrument in the implementation of climate policies. Compared to

Table 2.8 Impact of public environmental expenditure (in million euro) on selected environmental indicators

Group shift	*Dependent variable*		*LB*	*estimate*	*UB*	*std. er.*	*p*	*R2*
Country above-average GDP per capita	CO_2	n + 1	−0.9429	−0.7111	−0.4792	0.1183	0.0000	0.9423
			−44.6262	−34.5575	−24.4888	5.1372	0.0000	0.9423
		n + 2	−0.8244	−0.5496	−0.2747	0.1402	0.0001	0.9409
			−49.2663	−38.1198	−26.9733	5.6871	0.0000	0.9409
		n + 3	−0.6412	−0.3235	−0.0058	0.1621	0.0481	0.9397
			−55.2649	−42.9788	−30.6928	6.2685	0.0000	0.9397
	Greenhouse gases	n + 1	−0.0536	−0.0383	−0.0230	0.0078	0.0000	0.9930
			−3.3978	−2.7347	−2.0715	0.3383	0.0000	0.9930
		n + 2	−0.0464	−0.0317	−0.0169	0.0075	0.0000	0.9952
			−3.2391	−2.6399	−2.0406	0.3057	0.0000	0.9952
		n + 3	−0.0381	−0.0231	−0.0080	0.0077	0.0033	0.9961
	NOx	n + 1	−0.2504	−0.1965	−0.1425	0.0275	0.0000	0.9723
			−14.5091	−12.1661	−9.8231	1.1954	0.0000	0.9723
		n + 2	−0.2171	−0.1562	−0.0953	0.0311	0.0000	0.9741
			−15.1044	−12.6345	−10.1646	1.2602	0.0000	0.9741
		n + 3	−0.1678	−0.0992	−0.0306	0.0350	0.0053	0.9749
			−16.1069	−13.4551	−10.8033	1.3530	0.0000	0.9749
	Renewable share	n + 1	−0.0011	0.0005	0.0020	0.0008	0.5377	0.9865
			0.7258	0.7897	0.8535	0.0326	0.0000	0.9865
		n + 2	−0.0010	0.0006	0.0023	0.0008	0.4352	0.9869
			0.6898	0.7571	0.8244	0.0343	0.0000	0.9869
		n + 3	−0.0006	0.0011	0.0027	0.0008	0.2015	0.9879
			0.6860	0.7561	0.8261	0.0357	0.0000	0.9879

(*Continued*)

Table 2.8 (Continued)

Group shift	*Dependent variable*		*LB*	*estimate*	*UB*	*std. er.*	*p*	*R2*
Country below-average GDP per capita	CO_2	n + 1	−0.3579	−0.1748	0.0083	0.0934	0.0626	0.9714
			−23.2860	−19.6235	−15.9610	1.8687	0.0000	0.9714
		n + 2	−0.4479	−0.2667	−0.0855	0.0925	0.0043	0.9739
			−23.0624	−19.2901	−15.5179	1.9246	0.0000	0.9739
		n + 3	−0.4954	−0.3037	−0.1121	0.0978	0.0022	0.9751
			−23.7096	−19.7290	−15.7484	2.0310	0.0000	0.9751
	Greenhouse gases	n + 1	−0.0555	−0.0334	−0.0113	0.0113	0.0034	0.9842
			−2.2244	−1.7820	−1.3395	0.2258	0.0000	0.9842
		n + 2	−0.0550	−0.0338	−0.0125	0.0109	0.0021	0.9864
			−2.1550	−1.7123	−1.2696	0.2259	0.0000	0.9864
		n + 3	−0.0686	−0.0466	−0.0246	0.0112	0.0000	0.9875
			−2.2104	−1.7528	−1.2953	0.2335	0.0000	0.9875
	NOx	n + 1	−0.2625	−0.1647	−0.0670	0.0499	0.0011	0.9361
			−11.3088	−9.3534	−7.3980	0.9977	0.0000	0.9361
		n + 2	−0.2775	−0.1806	−0.0836	0.0495	0.0003	0.9421
			−11.5157	−9.4978	−7.4798	1.0296	0.0000	0.9421
		n + 3	−0.2912	−0.1888	−0.0864	0.0523	0.0004	0.9456
			−12.1436	−10.0166	−7.8897	1.0852	0.0000	0.9456
	Renewable share	n + 1	−0.0016	0.0002	0.0021	0.0010	0.8012	0.9716
			0.6277	0.6695	0.7112	0.0213	0.0000	0.9716
		n + 2	−0.0017	0.0003	0.0023	0.0010	0.7851	0.9731
			0.6150	0.6587	0.7024	0.0223	0.0000	0.9731
		n + 3	−0.0012	0.0008	0.0028	0.0010	0.4297	0.9751
			0.6260	0.6718	0.7175	0.0233	0.0000	0.9751

Source: Own elaboration.

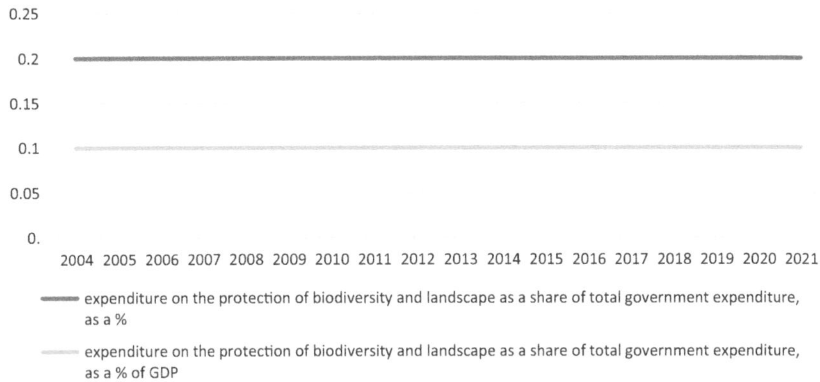

Figure 2.10 Public expenditure on the protection of biodiversity and landscape as a share of GDP and as a % of total expenditure in EU countries in 2004–2021

Source: Own elaboration based on Eurostat data

the wealthier countries, there is another rather interesting difference, i.e. in this case, better environmental effects appear two to three years after the expenditure is made.

As public expenditure on environmental protection (as indicated above) is divided into several subcategories, it is worth verifying whether the situation is similar within the categories identified, or whether some priorities can be observed in a given EU country's climate policy due to significantly higher expenditure on a specific climate-related area. The main categories identified by the European Commission and presented in aggregate by Eurostat are as follows:

- protection of biodiversity and landscape,
- R&D environmental protection,
- waste management,
- pollution abatement,
- wastewater management.

The first subcategory identified involves issues related to the protection of biodiversity and landscape, where different groups of actors are involved in making decisions on biodiversity and landscape conservation, especially in relation to protected areas, a very important political factor for any country. In recent years, there has been a noticeable shift towards an increasing awareness of the needs of local communities in the design and implementation of conservation strategies, leading to a better community-oriented approach to the protection of both biodiversity and landscape. Unfortunately, this is not reflected in the figures indicating a rather constant level of public spending as a share of GDP and as a share of total expenditure (see Figure 2.10), which implies a nominal increase but no growing interest of Member States in these issues at least on the expenditure side.

In addition, an analysis of expenditure on the protection of biodiversity and landscape between 2004 and 2021, conducted based on respective EU countries' data, showed that Italy had the highest expenditure on this heading (expenditure of EUR 34,628 million), followed by France (EUR 24,900 million), Germany (EUR 20,995 million) and Spain with expenditure of EUR 19,976 million. The lowest expenditure in this section was incurred by Cyprus and Romania. Poland ranked 13th out of 30 countries surveyed (in 2021).

Expenditure on the protection of biodiversity and landscape is one of the subcategories that is clearly a very effective tool in the implementation of climate policy in wealthy countries but unfortunately fails completely in those with lower GDP per capita (see Table 2.9). This is a rather surprising result as it might seem that this area of government action is important in maintaining the long-term well-being of natural resources and should be supported directly by public spending.

In fact, analyses reveal that an increase in spending on the protection of biodiversity and landscape by one unit in the first group of countries results in a reduction in CO_2 emissions in each of the three years following expenditure by an average of 2.2 units, a reduction in NOx by 0.55 units and in greenhouse gases by 0.14 units. In contrast, in the group of countries with a below-average GDP per capita, an increase in spending unfortunately results in an increase in emissions in subsequent years of CO_2 by an average of 0.5, units, NOx by 0.5 units and greenhouse gases by 0.1 units. This means that for these countries, governments should use other tools available through fiscal policy in protecting biodiversity and landscapes.

As with other categories of environmental spending, there is no positive impact of these measures on the growth of renewable energy.

It should be noted that the results obtained may have some limitations in this case as the data according to COFOG only include expenditures whose declared primary objective is the protection of biodiversity and landscape, meaning that indirect expenditures that may have a significant impact on the protection of biodiversity automatically are not taken into account. For example, Perry and Karousakis (2020) point out that compared to spending on the protection of biodiversity and landscape, governments in developed countries spend five to six times more on activities that have the opposite effect (e.g. support for fossil fuels or government support for agricultural and fishing activities). Admittedly, recent databases (e.g. CBD-FRF or BIOFIN BER) attempt to account for these indirect effects; however, due to the short periods for which data is available, a comprehensive (dynamic) panel data analysis in this direction cannot be yet conducted as part of this study. Secondly, the protection of biodiversity can also be influenced by policy instruments other than financial flows, such as biodiversity-related taxes, fees and charges as well as subsidies aimed at the protection of biodiversity and tradable permit schemes, which are included in the OECD's Policy Instruments for the Environment (PINE) database (Perry & Karousakis, 2020). Finally, the role of supranational organisations in the protection of biodiversity heritage is also growing in importance, which is, for example, reflected in the formulated objectives of the EU Biodiversity Strategy 2030. Thus, it is worth taking all these aspects into account when making a final assessment of the impact of this category of environmental expenditures and talking about recommendations for the future. This will be described in more detail in Section 2.3.

Table 2.9 Impact of public expenditure on the protection of biodiversity and landscape in million euro on basic environmental indicators

Group shift	*Dependent variable*		*LB*	*estimate*	*UB*	*std. er.*	*p*	*R2*
Country above-average GDP per capita	CO_2	n + 1	−2.3594	−2.0857	−1.8119	0.1397	0.0000	0.9714
			−13.4643	−4.9907	3.4828	4.3233	0.2502	0.9714
		n + 2	−2.2211	−1.8949	−1.5688	0.1664	0.0000	0.9661
			−21.0214	−11.1038	−1.1862	5.0601	0.0299	0.9661
		n + 3	−2.1270	−1.7373	−1.3475	0.1989	0.0000	0.9611
			−29.1512	−17.6450	−6.1387	5.8707	0.0032	0.9611
	Greenhouse gases	n + 1	−0.1493	−0.1316	−0.1139	0.0090	0.0000	0.9967
			−1.3296	−0.7824	−0.2353	0.2792	0.0057	0.9967
		n + 2	−0.1266	−0.1103	−0.0940	0.0083	0.0000	0.9976
			−1.5604	−1.0639	−0.5673	0.2533	0.0000	0.9976
		n + 3	−0.1127	−0.0956	−0.0785	0.0087	0.0000	0.9978
			−1.8736	−1.3687	−0.8637	0.2576	0.0000	0.9978
	NOx	n + 1	−0.6101	−0.5555	−0.5009	0.0278	0.0000	0.9899
			−6.0749	−4.3851	−2.6953	0.8622	0.0000	0.9899
		n + 2	−0.5605	−0.4982	−0.4359	0.0318	0.0000	0.9890
			−7.5573	−5.6641	−3.7709	0.9659	0.0000	0.9890
		n + 3	−0.5229	−0.4479	−0.3729	0.0383	0.0000	0.9871
			−9.2796	−7.0656	−4.8516	1.1296	0.0000	0.9871
	Renewable share	n + 1	−0.0034	−0.0011	0.0013	0.0012	0.3884	0.9865
			0.7386	0.8132	0.8877	0.0380	0.0000	0.9865
		n + 2	−0.0037	−0.0010	0.0016	0.0014	0.4558	0.9869
			0.7003	0.7786	0.8568	0.0399	0.0000	0.9869
		n + 3	−0.0042	−0.0011	0.0020	0.0016	0.4954	0.9877
			0.6971	0.7783	0.8594	0.0414	0.0000	0.9877

(*Continued*)

Table 2.9 (Continued)

Group shift	*Dependent variable*		*LB*	*estimate*	*UB*	*std. er.*	*p*	*R2*
Country below-average GDP per capita	CO_2	n + 1	0.3798	0.5786	0.7774	0.1014	0.0000	0.9747
			−22.2081	−18.7218	−15.2355	1.7788	0.0000	0.9747
		n + 2	0.5379	0.7238	0.9097	0.0948	0.0000	0.9788
			−21.0674	−17.5568	−14.0463	1.7911	0.0000	0.9788
		n + 3	0.6235	0.8012	0.9788	0.0906	0.0000	0.9814
			−20.5812	−16.9588	−13.3364	1.8482	0.0000	0.9814
	Greenhouse gases	n + 1	0.1050	0.1253	0.1456	0.0104	0.0000	0.9900
			−1.9226	−1.5664	−1.2103	0.1817	0.0000	0.9900
		n + 2	0.1155	0.1327	0.1499	0.0088	0.0000	0.9931
			−1.6582	−1.3329	−1.0075	0.1660	0.0000	0.9931
		n + 3	0.0985	0.1169	0.1354	0.0094	0.0000	0.9924
			−1.7065	−1.3298	−0.9532	0.1922	0.0000	0.9924
	NOx	n + 1	0.4593	0.5502	0.6410	0.0464	0.0000	0.9586
			−10.0532	−8.4598	−6.8664	0.8130	0.0000	0.9586
		n + 2	0.5414	0.6194	0.6974	0.0398	0.0000	0.9712
			−9.2089	−7.7363	−6.2638	0.7513	0.0000	0.9712
		n + 3	0.5336	0.6092	0.6848	0.0386	0.0000	0.9743
			−9.1419	−7.6002	−6.0584	0.7866	0.0000	0.9743
	Renewable share	n + 1	−0.0037	−0.0018	0.0002	0.0010	0.0817	0.9728
			0.6115	0.6544	0.6972	0.0219	0.0000	0.9728
		n + 2	−0.0043	−0.0023	−0.0004	0.0010	0.0215	0.9745
			0.5888	0.6338	0.6788	0.0230	0.0000	0.9745
		n + 3	−0.0050	−0.0028	−0.0007	0.0011	0.0111	0.9765
			0.5972	0.6442	0.6912	0.0240	0.0000	0.9765

Source: Own elaboration.

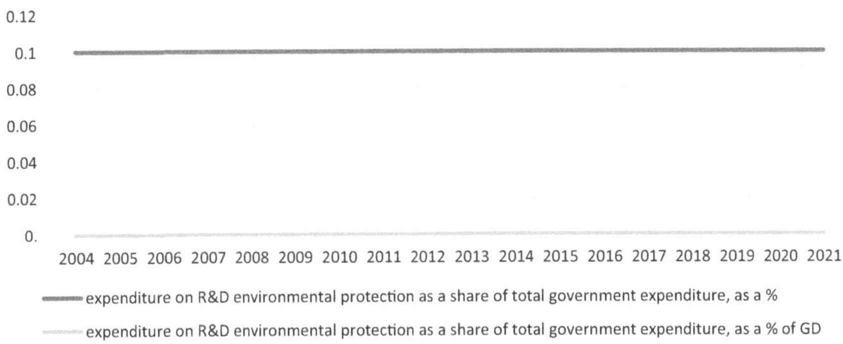

Figure 2.11 Public expenditure on R&D environmental protection as a ratio to GDP and as a % of total expenditure in EU countries in 2004–2021

Source: Own compilation.

It is often argued that policies aimed at protecting the environment can harm economic growth. Moreover, measures introduced unilaterally by a country can reduce the competitiveness of domestic companies. These arguments are generally based on the assumption that environmental objectives should be achieved through the introduction of emission charges (e.g. a carbon tax). However, three points must be made: firstly, a tax is not the only and most effective policy instrument that can be used to reduce emissions; secondly, even when deciding to implement a tax policy, it is particularly important to assess the feedback effects caused by tax revenue recycling; thirdly and most importantly, the role of technological progress cannot be underestimated. Therefore, public spending on R&D should be used as part of climate technology policy. However, the reality is that public support for energy R&D is of little use if the market for new, energy-efficient and carbon-free (or low-carbon) products does not exist or is very limited in size. Furthermore, a direct limited impact on the implementation efforts of companies to bring new energy technology to the market is reported (e.g. Sagar & Holdren, 2002, Sagar & van der Zwaan, 2006), which is somehow confirmed by the studies conducted.

At the same time, the very low level of environmental R&D expenditure (see Figure 2.11) is also surprising. It represents only 0.1% of total public expenditure in the EU as a whole, and the ratio to GDP is so low that Eurostat reports it as 0.0, so having the second curve run along the x-axis in Figure 2.11 is no mistake.

A further analysis of expenditure on R&D environmental protection over the period 2004–2021 shows that Italy has the highest expenditure in this department (expenditure of EUR 20,574 million), followed by Germany (EUR 16,529 million) and France ranking third, with expenditure of EUR 8,916 million. The smallest expenditure on this section was incurred by Malta. Poland ranked ninth out of the 30 countries surveyed (in 2021).

The next step sought to examine the effectiveness of this type of environmental expenditure on selected parameters describing the climate policy pursued (see Table 2.10).

Table 2.10 Impact of public expenditure on R&D environmental protection in million euro on basic environmental indicators

Group shift	*Dependent variable*		*LB*	*estimate*	*UB*	*std. er.*	*p*	*R2*
Country above-average GDP per capita	CO_2	n + 1	−2.3101	−1.9395	−1.5689	0.1891	0.0000	0.9581
			−33.8844	−24.9347	−15.9851	4.5662	0.0000	0.9581
		n + 2	−2.3293	−1.9385	−1.5476	0.1994	0.0000	0.9610
			−34.5246	−24.9962	−15.4679	4.8615	0.0000	0.9610
		n + 3	−2.4930	−2.0805	−1.6680	0.2105	0.0000	0.9648
			−35.1201	−25.0946	−15.0691	5.1151	0.0000	0.9648
	Greenhouse gases	n + 1	−0.1778	−0.1611	−0.1444	0.0085	0.0000	0.9976
			−2.0642	−1.6605	−1.2569	0.2059	0.0000	0.9976
		n + 2	−0.1523	−0.1371	−0.1218	0.0078	0.0000	0.9983
			−2.0019	−1.6306	−1.2593	0.1894	0.0000	0.9983
		n + 3	−0.1400	−0.1247	−0.1094	0.0078	0.0000	0.9986
			−2.0491	−1.6767	−1.3043	0.1900	0.0000	0.9986
	NOx	n + 1	−0.6286	−0.5523	−0.4759	0.0390	0.0000	0.9842
			−11.1912	−9.3470	−7.5029	0.9409	0.0000	0.9842
		n + 2	−0.5822	−0.5019	−0.4216	0.0409	0.0000	0.9853
			−11.3501	−9.3936	−7.4372	0.9982	0.0000	0.9853
		n + 3	−0.5688	−0.4827	−0.3966	0.0439	0.0000	0.9863
			−11.6149	−9.5219	−7.4289	1.0679	0.0000	0.9863
	Renewable share	n + 1	−0.0060	−0.0035	−0.0009	0.0013	0.0087	0.9871
			0.7650	0.8308	0.8967	0.0336	0.0000	0.9871
		n + 2	−0.0066	−0.0038	−0.0011	0.0014	0.0069	0.9876
			0.7331	0.8035	0.8739	0.0359	0.0000	0.9876
		n + 3	−0.0074	−0.0045	−0.0016	0.0015	0.0031	0.9886
			0.7396	0.8140	0.8884	0.0380	0.0000	0.9886

Country below-average GDP per capita	CO_2	n + 1	0.5859	1.1013	1.6167	0.2630	0.0000	0.9731
			−24.4798	−20.8907	−17.3016	1.8312	0.0000	0.9731
		n + 2	1.3776	1.8551	2.3326	0.2436	0.0000	0.9788
			−23.5911	−20.1123	−16.6334	1.7750	0.0000	0.9788
		n + 3	1.6887	2.1513	2.6140	0.2361	0.0000	0.9819
			−22.5722	−19.0173	−15.4624	1.8138	0.0000	0.9819
	Greenhouse gases	n + 1	0.1518	0.2112	0.2706	0.0303	0.0000	0.9865
			−2.4307	−2.0172	−1.6037	0.2110	0.0000	0.9865
		n + 2	0.2468	0.2962	0.3457	0.0252	0.0000	0.9914
			−2.1643	−1.8041	−1.4439	0.1838	0.0000	0.9914
		n + 3	0.2940	0.3381	0.3822	0.0225	0.0000	0.9937
			−1.9580	−1.6191	−1.2801	0.1729	0.0000	0.9937
	NOx	n + 1	0.2566	0.5390	0.8213	0.1440	0.0002	0.9367
			−12.2854	−10.3194	−8.3534	1.0031	0.0000	0.9367
		n + 2	0.6643	0.9292	1.1940	0.1351	0.0000	0.9496
			−11.9490	−10.0195	−8.0900	0.9845	0.0000	0.9496
		n + 3	0.9819	1.2268	1.4718	0.1250	0.0000	0.9612
			−11.3889	−9.5071	−7.6252	0.9601	0.0000	0.9612
	Renewable share	n + 1	−0.0073	−0.0020	0.0032	0.0027	0.4514	0.9726
			0.6179	0.6606	0.7034	0.0218	0.0000	0.9726
		n + 2	−0.0104	−0.0052	−0.0001	0.0026	0.0482	0.9746
			0.5958	0.6408	0.6858	0.0230	0.0000	0.9746
		n + 3	−0.0121	−0.0071	−0.0020	0.0026	0.0066	0.9770
			0.5976	0.6450	0.6924	0.0242	0.0000	0.9770

Source: Own compilation.

R&D environmental protection is one of the activities that offers greater hope of protecting natural resources with as little detriment to economic productivity as possible. Other studies in public spending have also found greater effectiveness of R&D spending in countries with higher income and GDP per capita. This research found a similar relationship, i.e. in more affluent countries R&D spending causes:

- a CO_2 emissions reduction by ca. 2.4 units;
- a NOx emissions reduction by ca. 0.61 unit;
- a GHG emissions reduction by ca. 0.16 unit

in each of the three years following the expenditure in that regard.

In countries with below-average GDP per capita, the situation is quite different and less advantageous, i.e.:

- a CO_2 emissions increase by ca. 0.6 unit in n + 1, 1.4 unit in n + 2, 1.7 unit in n + 3;
- a NOx emissions increase by ca. 0.26 unit in n + 1, 0.66 unit in n + 3, 0.98 unit in n + 3;
- a GHG emissions increase by ca. 0.15 unit in n + 1, 0.25 unit in n + 3, 0.29 unit in n + 3.

When spending public funds on this purpose, it is important to bear in mind that for countries with lower GDP, they will not deliver in the short term – it is definitely a long-term investment in environmental protection.

A widespread uptake of energy innovation can be beneficial for at least three main reasons. Firstly, it can directly mean a reduction in emissions. This is the case as long as adaptation also means use, and not only by installing but also by using energy-saving technologies, which, at the same time, do not cause significant ‘rebound effects’. Secondly, apart from episodes of highly path-dependent sunk investment in certain technologies, which may act as a barrier to entry for alternative solutions of (more cost-effective) innovation, this generally acts backwards on energy innovation incentives, increasing returns from R&D (Popp et al., 2009, Fischer, 2008, Fischer & Newell, 2008). Thirdly, the potential acceleration of learning-by-doing processes that bring additional implementation benefits from the installed technologies (e.g. see the case of sulphur dioxide control technologies for electricity plants analysed by Taylor et al. 2006) or from new installations (e.g. see the case of coal-fired steam power plants between 1960 and 1980 in the United States, discussed by Joskow & Rose, 1985). In conclusion, to realise the potential of targeted R&D, other spending policies are needed as an upstream instrument: complementary measures for new energy technologies (‘demand pull’ policies, see IPCC, 2007) are needed to stimulate the market and to reduce the transaction costs of the ‘interface’ that hinders their implementation (Taylor, 2008). Finally, international markets and international knowledge flows are an increasingly important source of energy innovation (OECD, 2008). In this respect, R&D can act not only as a generator of new knowledge but, in principle, can also enhance the absorptive capacity and increase the speed of deployment of new technologies.

Another subcategory of expenditure is public expenditure related to waste management. Nature does not produce rubbish – all debris, faeces and even river dust and silt are subject to a cyclical transformation called the circulation of matter. Only man produces waste, which nature cannot process or takes an extremely long time to process.

Rubbish surrounds us everywhere. It is thrown out of cars and trains and accumulates along roads. Waste, including used furniture, electronic equipment, tyres or rubble, is deliberately taken to forests, roadsides and thrown into ponds and lakes. In towns and cities, pavements are covered with used chewing gum, candy wrappers, bottles, papers and cigarette butts. Litter mars the beauty of the environment, is a source of environmental contamination and some of it, such as plastic bags and chewing gum, pose a deadly threat to animals.

In affluent countries, the production of rubbish is higher than in poor countries, where things are used for a long time, repaired when necessary or taken apart to reuse their components. A feature of developed societies is over-consumption: buying disposable items, unnecessary goods and quickly replacing the items one owns with others – newer and more fashionable – even though the old ones still perform their primary function well. Another reason for the large amount of rubbish is the diversity of packaging types, and further reasons are the ineffective waste segregation, treatment and management. EU Member States have been spending for decades around 7% of all public expenditure on this area, while when it comes to its share of GDP, a certain decline was visible but has now returned to pre-2016 levels (see Figure 2.12).

An additional analysis of expenditure on waste management between 2004 and 2021 shows that France has the highest expenditure on this heading (expenditure of EUR 156,929 million), followed by Italy (EUR 131,636 million) and Spain ranking third, with expenditure of EUR 86,668 million. The smallest expenditure in this department was made by Slovenia while Poland, cited in all categories by the Authors, ranked 11th out of the 30 countries surveyed (in 2021).

Waste management is a very important part of environmental initiatives and, in addition to the regulatory action, investment of public funds in the related activities is significant here. Public funds spent on this purpose contribute to the reduction of CO_2, NOx and GHG emissions in all EU countries (see Table 2.11). Increasing public spending on waste management by one unit contributes, over the following three years, to an annual reduction in CO_2 emissions of approximately 0.7 units in richer countries and 0.25 units in countries with lower disposable income per capita. Research has confirmed that in countries with higher per capita income, there is a greater awareness of the importance of environmental issues and, due to the high level of satisfaction of other societal needs, better effects can be achieved in this regard.

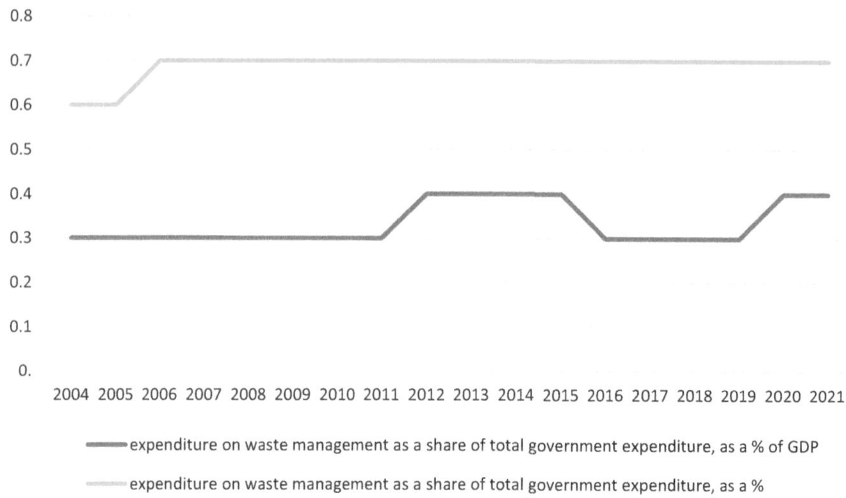

Figure 2.12 Public expenditure on waste expenditure as a ratio to GDP and as a % of total expenditure in EU countries in 2004–2021

Source: Own compilation.

Looking at the impact of this spending subcategory on further selected environmental parameters, the results are quite similar in countries with a higher GDP per capita where there is a reduction in NOx of about 0.16 unit followed by a reduction of 0.14 unit in the second group of countries, i.e. in this case, the effects are small and at a similar level regardless of the wealth of the region. In terms of greenhouse gases, on the other hand, an increase by one unit in public spending on waste management results in their emissions falling by about 0.03 unit across all EU Member States, i.e. a very negligible environmental effect, but the direction of the impact is right. As for renewable energy, no positive impact was found for this expenditure.

Another category of public environmental expenditure relates to pollution abatement. Industrial pollution in Europe is declining due to a combination of regulation, production development and environmentally friendly initiatives. However, industry continues to pollute the environment and the drive to eliminate emissions in this sector is still an ambitious challenge.

These pollutants can be categorised according to where they are found – in the air, water or soil – or considered in terms of different types of pollution, such as chemicals, noise or light. Another way to look at pollution is to analyse its sources. Some of these, such as cars, agriculture and buildings, are quite diffuse but others can be better assessed as individual emission points. Point sources mainly include large installations such as factories and power plants.

Air pollution is often linked to the burning of fossil fuels. This applies to power plants, of course, but also to many other industrial activities that may involve their own electricity or heat production, such as iron, steel or cement production. Some activities generate dust, which contributes to the concentration of

Table 2.11 Impact of public waste management expenditure in million euro on basic environmental indicators

Group shift	*Dependent variable*		*LB*	*estimate*	*UB*	*std. er.*	*p*	*R2*
Country above-average GDP per capita	CO_2	n + 1	−0.6367	−0.5949	−0.5530	0.0214	0.0000	0.9885
			−15.8228	−10.9504	−6.0781	2.4859	0.0000	0.9885
		n + 2	−0.6654	−0.6073	−0.5492	0.0296	0.0000	0.9837
			−18.9690	−12.5888	−6.2086	3.2553	0.0002	0.9837
		n + 3	−0.7112	−0.6311	−0.5511	0.0409	0.0000	0.9783
			−23.5925	−15.4490	−7.3055	4.1549	0.0003	0.9783
	Greenhouse gases	n + 1	−0.0290	−0.0236	−0.0181	0.0028	0.0000	0.9945
			−2.5697	−1.9330	−1.2963	0.3249	0.0000	0.9945
		n + 2	−0.0268	−0.0216	−0.0164	0.0027	0.0000	0.9963
			−2.4385	−1.8677	−1.2969	0.2912	0.0000	0.9963
		n + 3	−0.0266	−0.0212	−0.0158	0.0028	0.0000	0.9971
			−2.4530	−1.9009	−1.3489	0.2817	0.0000	0.9971
	NOx	n + 1	−0.1527	−0.1418	−0.1309	0.0055	0.0000	0.9931
			−8.1599	−6.8958	−5.6316	0.6450	0.0000	0.9931
		n + 2	−0.1548	−0.1427	−0.1306	0.0062	0.0000	0.9937
			−8.2713	−6.9425	−5.6136	0.6780	0.0000	0.9937
		n + 3	−0.1622	−0.1469	−0.1316	0.0078	0.0000	0.9929
			−8.8150	−7.2595	−5.7039	0.7936	0.0000	0.9929
	Renewable share	n + 1	−0.0017	−0.0011	−0.0004	0.0003	0.0012	0.9875
			0.7829	0.8509	0.9189	0.0347	0.0000	0.9875
		n + 2	−0.0022	−0.0014	−0.0007	0.0004	0.0003	0.9882
			0.7570	0.8289	0.9008	0.0367	0.0000	0.9882
		n + 3	−0.0031	−0.0021	−0.0011	0.0005	0.0001	0.9894
			0.7714	0.8473	0.9232	0.0387	0.0000	0.9894

(*Continued*)

Table 2.11 (Continued)

Group shift	*Dependent variable*		*LB*	*estimate*	*UB*	*std. er.*	*p*	*R2*
Country below-average GDP per capita	CO_2	n + 1	−0.2525	−0.2325	−0.2125	0.0102	0.0000	0.9908
			−11.4072	−9.2335	−7.0597	1.1091	0.0000	0.9908
		n + 2	−0.2588	−0.2375	−0.2161	0.0109	0.0000	0.9913
			−11.8126	−9.5202	−7.2278	1.1696	0.0000	0.9913
		n + 3	−0.2741	−0.2491	−0.2241	0.0127	0.0000	0.9908
			−12.7360	−10.1752	−7.6143	1.3066	0.0000	0.9908
	Greenhouse gases	n + 1	−0.0311	−0.0287	−0.0263	0.0012	0.0000	0.9950
			−0.8123	−0.5524	−0.2926	0.1326	0.0000	0.9950
		n + 2	−0.0282	−0.0252	−0.0222	0.0015	0.0000	0.9936
			−1.0030	−0.6833	−0.3636	0.1631	0.0000	0.9936
		n + 3	−0.0277	−0.0240	−0.0203	0.0019	0.0000	0.9924
			−1.2230	−0.8439	−0.4648	0.1934	0.0000	0.9924
	NOx	n + 1	−0.1394	−0.1293	−0.1192	0.0052	0.0000	0.9816
			−5.1002	−4.0031	−2.9059	0.5598	0.0000	0.9816
		n + 2	−0.1369	−0.1247	−0.1126	0.0062	0.0000	0.9782
			−5.8760	−4.5706	−3.2653	0.6660	0.0000	0.9782
		n + 3	−0.1402	−0.1252	−0.1103	0.0076	0.0000	0.9749
			−6.8208	−5.2883	−3.7557	0.7819	0.0000	0.9749
	Renewable share	n + 1	0.0000	0.0004	0.0008	0.0002	0.0348	0.9721
			0.6127	0.6568	0.7009	0.0225	0.0000	0.9721
		n + 2	−0.0001	0.0004	0.0009	0.0002	0.0881	0.9735
			0.5998	0.6460	0.6922	0.0236	0.0000	0.9735
		n + 3	−0.0001	0.0006	0.0013	0.0004	0.0715	0.9754
			0.6032	0.6527	0.7021	0.0252	0.0000	0.9754

Source: Own compilation.

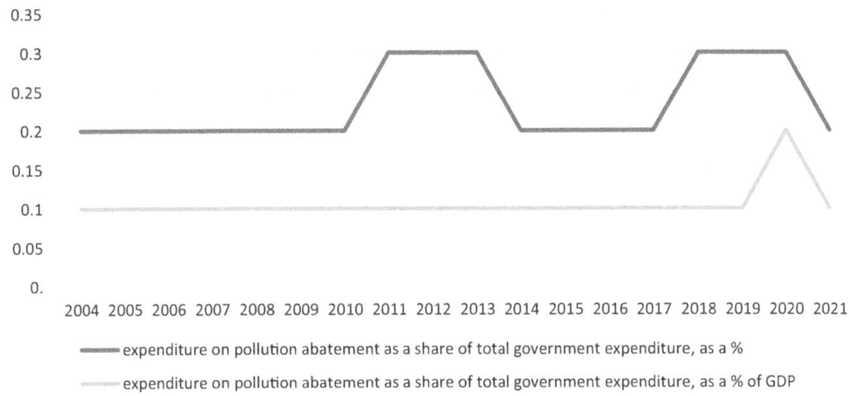

Figure 2.13 Public expenditure on pollution abatement as a ratio to GDP and as a % of total expenditure in EU countries from 2004 to 2021

Source: Own compilation.

particulate matter in the air, while the use of solvents, for example in metalworking or chemical production, can lead to emissions of harmful organic compounds (Figure 2.13).

An analysis of expenditure on pollution abatement between 2004 and 2021 shows that Germany has the highest expenditure in this department (expenditure of EUR 59,027 million), followed by Belgium (EUR 34,939.6 million) and Germany ranking third, with expenditure of EUR 26,173 million. The smallest expenditure on this section was incurred by Cyprus. Poland ranked ninth out of 30 countries surveyed (in 2021).

When it comes to expenditures mainly aimed at pollution abatement, their effectiveness is quite different depending on the wealth level of the relevant country in which they are undertaken (see Table 2.12). In EU countries with above-average GDP per capita, an increase in expenditure in this category will result in a reduction in CO_2 emissions of 2.31 units in the year n + 1, 2.33 units in n + 2 and 2.5 units in n + 3, respectively. A similarly positive effect is seen for the other environmental quality indicators, i.e. the impact on CO_2, NOx and greenhouse gas emissions. In these cases, the magnitude of the impact is definitely lower, but a positive effect can nevertheless be recorded. As in the previous cases, the share of RES energy does not rise in case of increased spending on pollution abatement; on the contrary, a slight inverse relationship was found.

In contrast, selected environmental indicators in countries with a below-average GDP per capita suggest inefficiency in the allocation of public funds to pollution abatement expenditure. An econometric model, whose descriptive statistics indicate a good level of fit when it comes to examining this type of relationship, showed that a one-unit increase in spending in this group of countries would result in a corresponding CO_2 emissions increase of 0.59 units in n + 1, 1.38 units in n + 2 and 1.69 units in n + 3 with a simultaneous reduction in CO_2 emissions observed in these countries. There was also no positive effect on the other environmental

Table 2.12 Impact of public pollution abatement expenditure in million euro on basic environmental indicators

Group dependent shift variable			*LB*	*Estimate*	*UB*	*std. er.*	*p*	*R2*
Countries above-average GDP per capita	CO_2	n + 1	−2.3101	−1.9395	−1.5689	0.1891	0.0000	0.9581
			−33.8844	−24.9347	−15.9851	4.5662	0.0000	0.9581
		n + 2	−2.3293	−1.9385	−1.5476	0.1994	0.0000	0.9610
			−34.5246	−24.9962	−15.4679	4.8615	0.0000	0.9610
		n + 3	−2.4930	−2.0805	−1.6680	0.2105	0.0000	0.9648
			−35.1201	−25.0946	−15.0691	5.1151	0.0000	0.9648
	Greenhouse gases	n + 1	−0.1778	−0.1611	−0.1444	0.0085	0.0000	0.9976
			−2.0642	−1.6605	−1.2569	0.2059	0.0000	0.9976
		n + 2	−0.1523	−0.1371	−0.1218	0.0078	0.0000	0.9983
			−2.0019	−1.6306	−1.2593	0.1894	0.0000	0.9983
		n + 3	−0.1400	−0.1247	−0.1094	0.0078	0.0000	0.9986
			−2.0491	−1.6767	−1.3043	0.1900	0.0000	0.9986
	NOx	n + 1	−0.6286	−0.5523	−0.4759	0.0390	0.0000	0.9842
			−11.1912	−9.3470	−7.5029	0.9409	0.0000	0.9842
		n + 2	−0.5822	−0.5019	−0.4216	0.0409	0.0000	0.9853
			−11.3501	−9.3936	−7.4372	0.9982	0.0000	0.9853
		n + 3	−0.5688	−0.4827	−0.3966	0.0439	0.0000	0.9863
			−11.6149	−9.5219	−7.4289	1.0679	0.0000	0.9863
	Renewable share	n + 1	−0.0060	−0.0035	−0.0009	0.0013	0.0087	0.9871
			0.7650	0.8308	0.8967	0.0336	0.0000	0.9871
		n + 2	−0.0066	−0.0038	−0.0011	0.0014	0.0069	0.9876
			0.7331	0.8035	0.8739	0.0359	0.0000	0.9876
		n + 3	−0.0074	−0.0045	−0.0016	0.0015	0.0031	0.9886
			0.7396	0.8140	0.8884	0.0380	0.0000	0.9886

Countries below-average GDP per capita	CO_2	n + 1	0.5859	1.1013	1.6167	0.2630	0.0000	0.9731
			−24.4798	−20.8907	−17.3016	1.8312	0.0000	0.9731
		n + 2	1.3776	1.8551	2.3326	0.2436	0.0000	0.9788
			−23.5911	−20.1123	−16.6334	1.7750	0.0000	0.9788
		n + 3	1.6887	2.1513	2.6140	0.2361	0.0000	0.9819
			−22.5722	−19.0173	−15.4624	1.8138	0.0000	0.9819
	Greenhouse gases	n + 1	0.1518	0.2112	0.2706	0.0303	0.0000	0.9865
			−2.4307	−2.0172	−1.6037	0.2110	0.0000	0.9865
		n + 2	0.2468	0.2962	0.3457	0.0252	0.0000	0.9914
			−2.1643	−1.8041	−1.4439	0.1838	0.0000	0.9914
		n + 3	0.2940	0.3381	0.3822	0.0225	0.0000	0.9937
			−1.9580	−1.6191	−1.2801	0.1729	0.0000	0.9937
	NOx	n + 1	0.2566	0.5390	0.8213	0.1440	0.0002	0.9367
			−12.2854	−10.3194	−8.3534	1.0031	0.0000	0.9367
		n + 2	0.6643	0.9292	1.1940	0.1351	0.0000	0.9496
			−11.9490	−10.0195	−8.0900	0.9845	0.0000	0.9496
		n + 3	0.9819	1.2268	1.4718	0.1250	0.0000	0.9612
			−11.3889	−9.5071	−7.6252	0.9601	0.0000	0.9612
	Renewable share	n + 1	−0.0073	−0.0020	0.0032	0.0027	0.4514	0.9726
			0.6179	0.6606	0.7034	0.0218	0.0000	0.9726
		n + 2	−0.0104	−0.0052	−0.0001	0.0026	0.0482	0.9746
			0.5958	0.6408	0.6858	0.0230	0.0000	0.9746
		n + 3	−0.0121	−0.0071	−0.0020	0.0026	0.0066	0.9770
			0.5976	0.6450	0.6924	0.0242	0.0000	0.9770

Source: Own compilation.

indicators in these countries, and in the context of such results, one could question whether this is the best way to implement climate policy for these European countries or maybe other more effective tools should be chosen instead, as will be discussed in more detail in Section 2.3.

Fan et al. investigated the relationship between government spending and CO_2 emissions in 30 provinces in China between 2007 and 2015. Their empirical results showed that regional inequalities in emission levels were not only due to economic differences related to the development of the regions, disparities in population density and energy structure, but 3 of 21 were also due to differences in the level of government spending. Zhou and Zhang analysed the impact of fiscal revenue and expenditure decentralisation on the effectiveness of fiscal policy in controlling environmental pollution in Chinese provinces. They confirmed that fiscal expenditure decentralisation negatively affected the effectiveness of fiscal policy in the area of environmental pollution control. The opposite was true for fiscal revenue decentralisation, where the impact was insignificant. Guo et al. conducted a study on the impact of fiscal decentralisation on environmental pollution. The spatial scope of their analysis was also that of Chinese provinces. The results indicate a greater impact of fiscal revenue decentralisation on environmental pollution than that of fiscal expenditure decentralisation. Research in this area has also been conducted at the level of Chinese cities. Cheng et al. investigated the reasons for differences in CO_2 emissions between cities with different socio-economic conditions from the perspective of local fiscal expenditure. When it comes to other countries, it is worth mentioning Galinato and Galinato's research on South American and Asian countries. The empirical analysis shows that an increase in total government spending significantly stimulated the clearing of forest land for agricultural production, which in turn increased CO_2 emissions. However, this relationship was not long-lasting. In the European context, noteworthy are the results of the empirical analysis by López and Palacios, who concluded that fiscal policy and energy taxes are effective in reducing the concentration of certain pollutants through various mechanisms. In another study, the authors noted a similar phenomenon whereby an increased government spending on public goods leads to lower spending on private goods, reducing pollution level.

Access to clean water, safe and readily available for drinking, domestic use, hygiene and food production, is an essential requirement for health, well-being and development of society as a whole. However, this basic need is not being met for a large proportion of the world's population. It is therefore not surprising that access to clean water has been recognised by the United Nations as a Sustainable Development Goal (SDG) and that EU Member States allocate 0.3% of their total public expenditure to wastewater management (see Figure 2.14).

An analysis of expenditure on wastewater management between 2004 and 2021 shows that France has the highest expenditure in this department (expenditure of EUR 68,272 million), followed by Germany (EUR 61,577 million) and the Netherlands ranking third, with an expenditure of EUR 46,743 million. The smallest expenditure on this section was incurred by Iceland. Poland ranked seventh out of the 30 countries surveyed (in 2021).

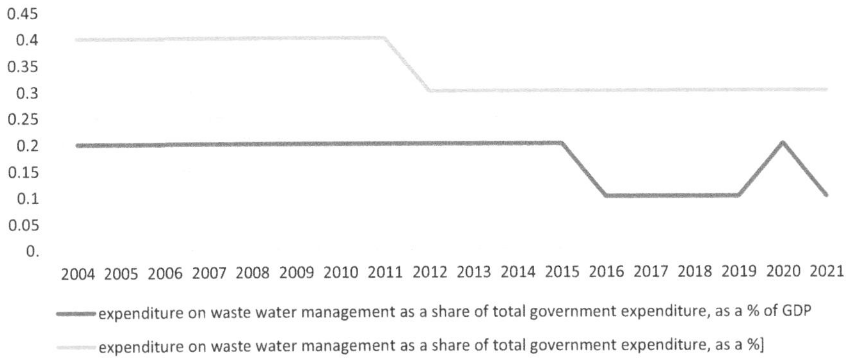

Figure 2.14 Public expenditure on wastewater management as a ratio to GDP and as a % of total expenditure in EU countries from 2004 to 2021

Source: Own compilation based on Eurostat data.

The analyses carried out showed a relatively high effectiveness of wastewater management expenditures on CO_2 emissions, although in this case, as in the previous one, better effects are achieved in wealthier countries (see Table 2.13). Indeed, increasing wastewater management expenditure by a unit in these countries can result in CO_2 reduction of around 0.95 units, while in countries with lower GDP per capita the reduction amounts to only (or as much as – depending on how one looks at it) 0.36 units in the period following expenditure. Subsequent periods also show positive effects of this spending category as, according to statistical models, reductions are achieved in both higher GDP (in n + 2 by 0.82, in n + 3 by 0.64) and less wealthy countries (in n + 2 by 0.45, in n + 3 by 0.5).

A positive effect of wastewater management expenditures can also be noted for NOx emissions as their increase by one unit in all years analysed can result in a decrease of about 0.25 units in the emissions of these pollutants regardless of the wealth of a given EU Member State.

When it comes to the other two environmental variables, the impact of wastewater management expenditure is minimal and in the case of RES share, it's even negative. It is therefore impossible to see any effectiveness of this expenditure on the European objectives measured by these indicators.

Member States' estimated budgetary waste rates are high, both in terms of final results and outputs. Assuming that if resources were allocated at EU level, activities would be carried out on the basis of efficient production function estimated on the basis of a country's actual production, Member States could treat the same amount of waste water and connect the same percentage of their population to a wastewater collection system using 69% and 82% less resources, respectively. In other words, EU Member States could connect the same proportion of their population to the network of wastewater treatment plants and save almost EUR 16 billion per year. In terms of economies of scale and spillover effects, the results are mixed. Authors found evidence that moving wastewater management spending to the EU level would increase the efficiency of the intermediate product manufacturing system

Table 2.13 Impact of public expenditure on wastewater management in million euro on key environmental indicators

Group	*Dependent Variable*	*Shift*	*LB*	*estimate*	*UB*	*std. er.*	*p*	*R2*
Country above-average GDP per capita	CO_2	n + 1	−0.9429	−0.7111	−0.4792	0.1183	0.0000	0.9423
			−44.6262	−34.5575	−24.4888	5.1372	0.0000	0.9423
		n + 2	−0.8244	−0.5496	−0.2747	0.1402	0.0001	0.9409
			−49.2663	−38.1198	−26.9733	5.6871	0.0000	0.9409
		n + 3	−0.6412	−0.3235	−0.0058	0.1621	0.0481	0.9397
			−55.2649	−42.9788	−30.6928	6.2685	0.0000	0.9397
	Greenhouse gases	n + 1	−0.0536	−0.0383	−0.0230	0.0078	0.0000	0.9930
			−3.3978	−2.7347	−2.0715	0.3383	0.0000	0.9930
		n + 2	−0.0464	−0.0317	−0.0169	0.0075	0.0000	0.9952
			−3.2391	−2.6399	−2.0406	0.3057	0.0000	0.9952
		n + 3	−0.0381	−0.0231	−0.0080	0.0077	0.0033	0.9961
	NOx	n + 1	−0.2504	−0.1965	−0.1425	0.0275	0.0000	0.9723
			−14.5091	−12.1661	−9.8231	1.1954	0.0000	0.9723
		n + 2	−0.2171	−0.1562	−0.0953	0.0311	0.0000	0.9741
			−15.1044	−12.6345	−10.1646	1.2602	0.0000	0.9741
		n + 3	−0.1678	−0.0992	−0.0306	0.0350	0.0053	0.9749
			−16.1069	−13.4551	−10.8033	1.3530	0.0000	0.9749
	Renewable share	n + 1	−0.0011	0.0005	0.0020	0.0008	0.5377	0.9865
			0.7258	0.7897	0.8535	0.0326	0.0000	0.9865
		n + 2	−0.0010	0.0006	0.0023	0.0008	0.4352	0.9869
			0.6898	0.7571	0.8244	0.0343	0.0000	0.9869
		n + 3	−0.0006	0.0011	0.0027	0.0008	0.2015	0.9879
			0.6860	0.7561	0.8261	0.0357	0.0000	0.9879

Country below-average GDP per capita	CO_2	n − 1	−0.3579	−0.1748	0.0083	0.0934	0.0626	0.9714
			−23.2860	−19.6235	−15.9610	1.8687	0.0000	0.9714
		n − 2	−0.4479	−0.2667	−0.0855	0.0925	0.0043	0.9739
			−23.0624	−19.2901	−15.5179	1.9246	0.0000	0.9739
		n + 3	−0.4954	−0.3037	−0.1121	0.0978	0.0022	0.9751
			−23.7096	−19.7290	−15.7484	2.0310	0.0000	0.9751
	Greenhouse gases	n + 1	−0.0555	−0.0334	−0.0113	0.0113	0.0034	0.9842
			−2.2244	−1.7820	−1.3395	0.2258	0.0000	0.9842
		n + 2	−0.0550	−0.0338	−0.0125	0.0109	0.0021	0.9864
			−2.1550	−1.7123	−1.2696	0.2259	0.0000	0.9864
		n + 3	−0.0686	−0.0466	−0.0246	0.0112	0.0000	0.9875
			−2.2104	−1.7528	−1.2953	0.2335	0.0000	0.9875
	NOx	n + 1	−0.2625	−0.1647	−0.0670	0.0499	0.0011	0.9361
			−11.3088	−9.3534	−7.3980	0.9977	0.0000	0.9361
		n + 2	−0.2775	−0.1806	−0.0836	0.0495	0.0003	0.9421
			−11.5157	−9.4978	−7.4798	1.0296	0.0000	0.9421
		n + 3	−0.2912	−0.1888	−0.0864	0.0523	0.0004	0.9456
			−12.1436	−10.0166	−7.8897	1.0852	0.0000	0.9456
	Renewable share	n + 1	−0.0016	0.0002	0.0021	0.0010	0.8012	0.9716
			0.6277	0.6695	0.7112	0.0213	0.0000	0.9716
		n + 2	−0.0017	0.0003	0.0023	0.0010	0.7851	0.9731
			0.6150	0.6587	0.7024	0.0223	0.0000	0.9731
		n + 3	−0.0012	0.0008	0.0028	0.0010	0.4297	0.9751
			0.6260	0.6718	0.7175	0.0233	0.0000	0.9751

Source: Own compilation.

as most Member States operate amid demand for increasing returns to scale (four Member States operate on constant returns to scale). Moving wastewater management spending to EU level would enable the EU to exploit economies of scale that result in a 5.1% increase in efficiency (in terms of connecting the population to wastewater treatment plants). When considering the Authors' intermediate production model, a significant spread is observed as well. However, the Court of Auditors did not find evidence of increased economies of scale for joint EU wastewater management activities given the final results. Indeed, the results suggest that wastewater treatment efficiency will decrease. There is also no convincing evidence of spillover effects: although the estimated effects seem to suggest their presence, they are in fact not precisely estimated (the relevant coefficients are statistically insignificant). There is no evidence in favour of moving wastewater management expenditure to EU level and, given the final results, this is not entirely surprising. The appropriate level of governance for broadly defined water resources (i.e. regulating water quantity and quality) has been debated within and outside the EU (for example in Canada) (Hill et al., 2008). While there are arguments in favour of joint action by Member States (for example, because waste water can impact downstream), rationales have also been raised in favour of Member State competence (e.g. national legislation is more reflective of local conditions) (Akhmouch et al., 2018).

2.3 Recommendations for future action using fiscal policy instruments to achieve climate goals

Reports by organisations professionally involved in the scientific monitoring of climate change show that since the 1980s, Europe's climate has been warming twice as fast as the global average – in 2022, Europe's temperature was around 2.3°C above the pre-industrial average (i.e. between 1850 and 1900). Such a phenomenon undoubtedly has social and economic consequences, but it also indicates the scale of challenges the European Union will have to overcome more quickly and effectively as a consequence of such a quick pace. This action should have far-reaching effects on the socio-economic situation and ecosystems of the region. It can therefore be assumed that satisfactory results cannot be achieved in the short term as the laws of nature are stronger and characterised by a high degree of inertia, meaning that a change of direction requires a long-term impact. Nevertheless, the first effects of intensive international and national efforts in the area of climate policy can also be observed. It is worth noting at the outset that, due to the fact that the transformation to a green economy is a long-term process, it must be effectively initiated by government's medium- and long-term economic policy. It is clear that in the long run, the best results will be achieved by those who start the transition as early as possible. However, it is often the 'here and now' that is the priority for governments and businesses, rather than looking at the long-term changes taking place, so an important role for the government should be to build bridges between the 'here and now' and the future. Recognising the consensus around climate issues, an effective regulatory system is a system that incentivises change.

It is important to remember what has already been emphasised many times in this publication – if the change towards protection of natural resources does not start today, we will become less competitive in the long term. Therefore, in the interests of the long-term competitiveness of the economy, both individual Member States and the European Community as a whole should stimulate current measures that need to be adopted urgently. The outcomes of regulatory and support measures taken to date are now becoming tangible, their real-world impact being demonstrable even to sceptics, e.g. in 2022, for the first time in the European Union, renewable energy generated more electricity than polluting fossil gases, with wind and solar power accounting for 22.3%, ahead of fossil gas, which accounted for 20%. Thus, for the first time in the EU, more electricity was generated from wind and sun than from fossil gas. According to Prof Petteri Taalas – Secretary General of the WMO, increasing the use of renewable and low-carbon energy sources is key to reducing dependence on fossil fuels. As recent years have seen major developments in this and many other policy areas, it remains an open question what kind of governance but also fiscal tools should be used to implement climate policy so that the process does not backfire. Russia's full-scale invasion of Ukraine on 24 February 2022 dramatically changed the situation for Europeans when it comes to high imports of fossil fuels (37.5% in 2021), a significant proportion of which came from Russia. As a consequence, there was a risk that EU action to move away from Russian energy would become more important than action on climate policy. On the other hand, however, the challenges faced by the world as a result of this armed conflict may accelerate action on green energy, as it has become essential to:

- rapidly reduce energy dependence on Russia, which would enable Member States to impose an embargo on imports of Russian oil and possibly gas;
- build new partnerships with third countries to protect European energy security in the long term;
- implement the Fit for 55 package to make the European Green Deal a reality.

The above-mentioned factors have caused energy prices in Europe to soar, entailing previously unforeseen and unplanned support for energy infrastructure investment, social support for vulnerable households and businesses, and the emergence of additional political and diplomatic capital related to energy. Some Member States believe that a shift towards clean and renewable energy sources would not reduce energy prices fast enough. This is why Austria, Germany, Greece, the Netherlands, Poland and the Czech Republic have recently postponed the planned decommissioning of their coal-fired power plants. Member States are again focusing on the infrastructure dedicated to fuels that were seen as transitional before Russia's war with Ukraine. Germany is exploring the possibility of building liquefied natural gas (LNG) import terminals to replace Russian pipelines; France and Spain have resumed talks on the construction of the Midi-Catalonia pipeline; Bulgaria and Greece have also recommitted to pipeline plans. France now plans to build fourteen new nuclear power plants by 2050; EU governments are racing to deepen their relationships with gas suppliers other than Russia, from Algeria to Qatar. The paradigm shift that occurred on 24 February could be seen as the geopolitical pressure the EU needed to accelerate its move away from fossil fuels. From this perspective, the EU now has the opportunity to focus on the medium-term climate challenge and accept as inevitable what might otherwise seem a daunting political cost. The course of the EU's energy transition will depend heavily on national policies in its Member States as well as on the leadership of national governments to navigate through a painful dual energy transition – away from dependence on both Russia and fossil fuels. Actions in this area have shown how Member States and political groups approach different solutions to the EU's energy dilemma, meaning that it will be difficult to strike a balance between them. As outlined more fully in Chapter 1, on 22 June this year, MEPs voting in favour of a compromise agreement in relation to the SDGs merely put on hold the disagreements that had arisen between them on this topic. As a result, most Member States have unfortunately scaled back their climate ambitions in 2022, although everyone is aware that there is no turning back from them.

In this context, it becomes all the more important to look for ways to support governments in the implementation of climate policy using the most effective, simple and fast solutions. Before going on to identifying specific instruments of government action, it is worth mentioning the importance of policy coherence, which requires that when a country decides to act within the framework of the green economy, it should do so consistently. Let us take an example from a recent publication by the European Court of Auditors (ECA, 2023), which looked at the consistency of the application of one of the instruments for achieving climate goals, namely energy taxation. Its effectiveness can be significantly undermined if, at the same time, the same country applies fossil fuel subsidies. The Court found that Member States' fossil fuel subsidies total more than €55 billion per year. They have remained relatively stable over the past decade, despite calls for them to be phased out. And, most worryingly, some Member States tax energy on the one hand and, on the other, spend more on fossil fuel subsidies than on environmental subsidies.

In spite of the general progress in the implementation of environmental policies, there are a number of concerns as to how this area is managed in the EU, for example, further to unpredictable external phenomena such as wars, increasingly strong national interests resulting from changes in the political scene, and income polarisation across European countries. Undoubtedly, one should applaud that since the end of the 1990s, the European Union has developed a number of climate-related policies and objectives, often using any tools possible to get the Member Countries on-board, especially that these were often quite innovative on the global scale. Actions taken over the past decade include an increasingly broad range of instruments (e.g. market-based, informational and voluntary, as well as regulatory) compared to what was traditionally the norm in earlier EU environmental policy. In most (if not all) Member States, current national climate policies were either developed directly in the country but inspired by the European Commission or indirectly prepared by its officials.

The main objective of the Authors in this part of the monograph was to verify the long-term effectiveness of fiscal instruments used by EU Member States to reduce environmental pollution and to examine the extent to which they also affect selected macroeconomic indicators. The results of the analyses presented in the previous subsections indicate that the implementation of environmental protection tasks at national level depends on a number of factors and, in many cases, fails to achieve the intended objectives. This is due, inter alia, to the different priority assigned to the various segments of these activities. With regard to NH_3 emissions, studies have shown that public expenditure is a relatively ineffective tool for reducing them, and when it comes to attempts to increase the share of RES in the energy mix, such expenditure has no impact at all. The main source of NH_3 emissions is agriculture and so far public policies have failed to achieve the expected level of ammonia reduction. Nitrogen management is a key element in reducing nitrogen losses. It is based on the premise that reducing surplus nitrogen (surplus N) and increasing nitrogen use efficiency (NUE) contribute to reducing NH_3 emissions. Nitrogen management also aims to identify and prevent any exchange of pollutants between different N compounds and environmental elements. Creating a nitrogen input/output balance in a given economic entity is a prerequisite for integral optimisation of the N management. In this case, the analyses indicate that an increasing government involvement in public spending does not lead to more efficient results, which may come as a big surprise. A possible reason for this is that public spending is allocated in response to the increasing pollution and is undertaken on an ad hoc basis rather than on a preventive and long-term basis. This may be due to the choice of ineffective forms of support that do not yield the desired effects, or perhaps their effects take longer than five years to be visible. Global man-made CO_2 emissions have been steadily decreasing in EU countries, but the process is not evenly spread across Member States. The largest sources of emissions of this pollutant are the combustion of fossil fuels in power stations, road and air transport and processes associated with the manufacture of industrial products. The general public support for actions to reduce pollution at EU level may make it easier to implement public spending in this area. At the same time, further research may be needed at national level to examine in detail which tools are most effective in terms of their environmental impact. Sustainable development means 'better development' and 'better finance' in all its aspects: environmental, economic and social. The challenge facing the modern world is to allocate available resources even more efficiently, so that the classically understood development of the present generations does not mean the existential decline of future generations.

Of course, the positive effects of the current activities of the European Union and its Member States are worth mentioning as monitoring data show that the EU's GHG emissions fell by 23% between 1990 and 2014 and that the EU reached its lowest level ever – despite the fact that the European economy had grown by 46% over the same period (EEA, 2015). Projections show that the EU is heading for a 24% reduction in future years. To what extent these reductions are due to effective EU policies and to what extent they were driven by unexpected factors such as economic restructuring and recession is a matter for debate. Similarly, a question should be asked whether the right policy mix, taking account of the interactions between instruments at EU and national level (both in climate policy and, more broadly, in energy policy) can be an effective driver of emissions reduction. It is important to recognise how EU energy policy-makers pursue several important agendas at the same time, including energy security, market liberalisation and climate protection as well as the enforcement of internal market rules while maintaining the EU's growth aspirations. Research carried out for the monograph showed that public spending can be an effective tool for authorities to reduce these emissions, along with investment in biological projects that absorb CO_2 from the environment. However, the effectiveness of tax instruments to reduce CO_2 emissions was found to be lower than that of spending instruments. It should also be stated that the results of the study showed that, in general, in the area of environmental protection, fiscal instruments only produce results after a few years, so decisions should be taken across political divides, with relevant actions continued after a change of government as only then can the expected results be achieved. In addition, the level of government involvement should be adapted to the wealth of respective societies as in poorer countries the government should take on a greater burden in terms of environmental action, compensating for the less active citizens in this area. In general, the low effectiveness of environmental tax revenues in countries with lower GDP per capita can be partly explained by the fact that their level generally decreases while emissions of some key pollutants (e.g. CO_2 or NH_3) increase, suggesting that taxes are not imposed consistently enough. In addition, pollution taxes account for only a small proportion of total environmental tax revenues, and their distribution varies considerably between Member States. For example, pollution taxes on farmers (which applies to NH_3 emissions, for example) were generally very low, with the exception of a few Member States.

Data indicating inadequate efficiency of national expenditures suggests the need for action at international and intercontinental levels to protect the environment. This is in line with the position of the EU, which has emphasised the international nature of environmental pollution ever since the adoption of the first Environmental Action Programme in 1973. To those who are sceptical of such proposals and only recognise the national dimension of such actions, it is worth giving examples from recent years that suggest very strongly that such a direction does not yield results in the long term (Postuła & Radecka-Moroz, 2021). A particularly clear example of transnational and global environmental problems is air pollution. Despite noticeable improvements in air quality globally, efforts by national authorities do not sufficiently protect citizens' health, and the problem of air pollution is particularly acute for urban dwellers. Poor air quality is a phenomenon that ignores administrative boundaries as locally generated emissions of air pollutants can contribute significantly to their concentration in another area, so transnational action is required to combat this threat effectively. One should also emphasise the international dimension of environmental policies in ensuring competitive balance. Only the adoption of uniform rules and objectives at a global level avoids distortions of competition resulting from advantages gained by economies not covered by environmental targets and charges. The best example in this regard would be the issue of reducing atmospheric emissions. In the absence of a harmonised approach, serious inequalities in the competitiveness of economies would arise, including higher energy prices or production costs. Therefore, only a common approach to the problem, both at EU and global level, will allow individual economies not to build their competitive advantage on higher (unregulated by relevant standards, etc.) emissions compared to other countries. Similarly, in the case of manufacturing, relevant entities subject to norms, standards and emission reduction targets are obliged to bear the costs of implementing state-of-the-art solutions and technologies to meet the requirements. Competition of such entities with companies not subject to these restrictions and requirements would not ensure equal treatment and would result in a loss of market due to higher operating costs. Studies have confirmed that 'punishing' polluters through the tax system has relatively little impact on reducing this harmful activity in the future in countries with a below-average GDP per capita, while it is an effective tool for climate policy in wealthier countries. This points to one of the most important dilemmas in the area of environmental protection at the supranational level – the significant differences in the level of development of individual countries. The proposed global solutions can be introduced in developed countries without significantly compromising their further economic development and can even sometimes stimulate it, for example through the development of new sectors or branches of the economy. On the other hand, in countries with a low level of development and developing countries, the introduction of environmental policies such as the taxation discussed above may significantly reduce the economic growth rate. In view of the above, there is a particular need to design appropriately differentiated global policies that are tailored to economies with different levels of development while ensuring that objectives are met.

Research has shown that when making decisions affecting the scale and structure of environmental spending and taxes, fiscal authorities need to consider two main aspects. Firstly, the specific effect of the time dimension and, secondly, the type of fiscal instruments, otherwise the effectiveness of these measures may be significantly reduced. Within the policy mix, possible fiscal instruments include tax credits for companies investing in environmentally friendly solutions, additional taxation of polluting companies or non-refundable subsidies to support spending on environmentally friendly investment projects, public spending on environmental measures, interest subsidies for entities implementing environmentally friendly investments or other measures. The research carried out has shown that it is necessary to create the right policy mix of pro-environmental measures, adapting the appropriate tools to the type of environmental challenge as decisions in this area should always take into account the costs and benefits translated into living standards as measured by GDP per capita. There is the phenomenon of a time lag between fiscal decisions and their implications for the improvement of public expenditure indicators measuring the scale of pollution. There is also the rather curious phenomenon of taxes having no impact on decisions taken to reduce greenhouse gas emissions and the scale of environmental pollution in the medium term. The second finding demonstrates the limited effectiveness of the polluter-pays principle, suggesting that this tool is not effective or applied rigorously enough so the use of this type of instrument would only make sense if applied consistently. The results indicating a positive long-term impact of public spending speak in favour of increasing public spending on environmental protection, preferably at a supranational level and in a coordinated manner. For many years, the academic literature has attempted to answer the question of whether the solutions proposed and then implemented are adequately consistent with each other and implemented in a coordinated manner as failing that it is difficult to achieve effectiveness regardless of the amount of expenditure incurred or taxes imposed (Strambo et al., 2015; Tosun, 2019) In addition, it is also widely agreed among economists – and a diverse group of other policy analysts – that, at least in the long term, in many industrialised countries, economy-wide carbon pricing will be an essential component of any policy meant to achieve significant reductions in CO_2 emissions (Metcalf, 2009; Kaplow, 2010; Borenstein & Bushnell, 2018). The ubiquitous nature of energy generation and use, and the diversity of CO_2 sources in the modern economy mean that the application of conventional technology and uniform standards would be unfeasible or in any case prohibitively expensive (Newell & Stavins, 2003). The cost advantage of carbon pricing arises from the flexibility of the policy and from the incentive it creates for all sources of emissions to be controlled at the same marginal cost of emission reductions, thereby achieving aggregate cost efficiency. Moreover, in the long run, pricing approaches can further reduce the cost of emission reductions by inducing carbon-friendly technological change (Newell et al., 1999). There is less consensus among economists on the choice of specific carbon pricing policy instruments, with some favouring carbon taxes (Mankiw, 2006; Nordhaus, 2007) and other cap-and-trade mechanisms (Ellerman et al., 2003; Keohane, 2009). This gives rise to the need to address two questions: how the two main approaches to carbon pricing compare in terms of their respective dimensions, including efficiency, cost-effectiveness and distributive justice, among others, and which of the two approaches is more likely to be adopted in the future in developed countries. Academic economists have written extensively on the first issue, while the second issue has been addressed more by social scientists as well as commentators from the wider policy community, analysing it from an interdisciplinary perspective.

For some 40 years before Coase (1960), the literature had focused on finding a single economic answer to the problem of taxing externalities. In principle, a regulator could ensure that emitters internalise the damage they have caused by charging a tax on each unit of pollution equal to the marginal social loss, with an effective level of pollution control (Pigou, 1920). Such a system makes it profitable for firms to reduce emissions to a level where their marginal abatement costs equal the common tax rate. Thus, the marginal abatement costs will be equalised for all sources, meeting the necessary cost-effectiveness condition. Theoretically, this will happen in both the short and long term, by providing incentives for the diffusion (Jaffe & Stavins, 1995) and innovation (Newell et al., 1999) of low-cost abatement technologies. The work of Coase (1960) made it possible to think about solving the pollution problem by clarifying poorly defined property rights. If resources, such as clean air and water, could be recognised as a form of property whose corresponding rights could be traded on the market, private actors could allocate the use of this property in a cost-effective manner. More than 50 years ago, Thomas D. Crocker (1966) and J. H. Dales (1968) proposed a system of tradable permits for pollution discharges that could provide such a market-based solution. In their proposal, the regulator only needs to determine the total amount of emissions allowed (the cap), allocate allowances corresponding to this total and allow individual emission sources to trade allowances until the optimum allocation is reached. This was the basic premise behind the so-called cap-and-trade. Under this approach, the government sets an acceptable overall level of pollution (not necessarily at an efficient level) and distributes it to companies in the form of tradable allowances. Companies that keep their emissions below their allocated level can sell their excess allowances to other companies or use them to offset excess emissions in other areas of their operations. Under these conditions, it is in the interest of the owner of each source to drive reductions to the point where its marginal control costs equal the market-determined price of tradable allowances. Although the two instruments – carbon taxes and cap-and-trade – can be said to derive from two distinct perspectives: that of externalities (Pigou, 1920) and that of property rights (Coase, 1960), respectively, yet the two approaches are similar. A carbon tax would directly impose an additional cost on carbon (most likely in the upstream portion of the supply chain, where fossil fuels, i.e. coal, oil and natural gas enter the economy), due to the need to adjust the amount of carbon consumption and CO_2 emissions. An upstream cap-and-trade system would reduce the amount of CO_2 entering the economy through carbon allowances for fossil fuels, among others, with prices determined indirectly in the allowance market. In some cases, what may at first glance appear to be key differences between the two instruments disappears upon closer examination, while other less obvious differences emerge upon such assessment.

Another issue that can serve as a methodological basis for determining the effectiveness or ineffectiveness of the respective solutions is whether research is based on the right input data on the scale of actions. This is where the first weakness of the EU's solutions emerges, namely the lack of a homogeneous infrastructure for monitoring and evaluating climate policy across the EU, resulting in considerable uncertainty about its effects (Hildén et al., 2014). Critics of the arrangements in place for at least a decade emphasise that European targets defined at the strategic level were set too prudentially. They were based on past changes in the approach to natural resource management but mainly on the rate of restructuring processes taking place naturally in two countries (UK and Germany) which in the 1990s generated up to 50% of the recorded CO_2 savings (Eichhammer et al., 2001). Those savings however did not result directly from EU action but from macro- and microeconomic phenomena (Kerr, 2007). In this context, it is important to realise that most existing studies using data on changes in environmental indicators are subject to this kind of limitation. At the same time, just how it would be possible to 'decouple' the effects of public policies in European and national statistics remains an open question. In the Authors' opinion, this is virtually impossible as there is a conglomerate of activities impacting emissions through changes in the socio-economic environment. These include not only financial solutions but also legal ones and those related to awareness-raising and promotion, etc. In spite of the analytical and research difficulties, it is clear that action must be taken to bring about change in this area, chiefly in terms of aligning short-term policies with long-term goals, particularly in planning documents. For example, looking at the content and subsequent implementation of the National Energy and Climate Plans (NECPs) it can unfortunately be seen, in selected cases, that the main purpose is to communicate goals and policies for 2030 – and to align long-term goals with them, rather than indicating the real effects planned to be achieved at national level. At least a few NECPs are incomplete in this way. Policies were described in very little detail, investment needs were not identified, and their implementation process involved hardly any public participation (Knodt & Schoenefeld, 2021; Serafini, 2021). In addition, a number of Member States were late in submitting their national long-term strategies (LTSs). As of July 2023, five Member States had not yet submitted their own strategies, which is more than 3.5 years late compared to the early 2020 deadline. Several older LTSs, which have not been revised in line with the evolution of key policies, are already outdated and can no longer sufficiently inform current policy-making. This state of affairs exacerbates the existing design flaw of this area of legislation, namely that the deadline for submission of draft NECPs is set earlier than the deadline for the preparation of the LTS. Without proper sequencing, the LTSs will not be able to fulfil their primary purpose, i.e. to inform Member States' short- and medium-term policy decisions. Moreover, the information contained in many national LTS is not sufficiently detailed and precise. At EU level, the Clean Planet for All project (European Commission, 2018) has had a major impact on setting the climate neutrality target, but it is now outdated on several levels and can no longer be an appropriate and adequate basis for further policy-making. Additionally, its update is not anticipated by the European Commission. However, at COP26 in Glasgow, a call for regular updates of the LTSs was adopted – imposing updates of the relevant models and scenarios in the context of changes to the EU's 2040 target proposal. As indicated earlier, certainly Russia's aggression against Ukraine is an important factor in changing the targets, but in the context of the EU's overall climate policy, changing them may have the effect of reducing the policy effectiveness.

Another structural weakness in the EU actions, and consequently, in those by Member States, is how the target and the indicator to measure its achievement are defined for the period after 2030. Indeed, the European Union has set in its climate law an expected level of CO_2 reduction at 55% by 2030 (Article 4(1)), in principle also defining a maximum volume of acceptable emissions. However, this has not been translated into targets for 2050, nor is it explicitly stated in the 2040 target proposal (Article 4(3) EUCL). This is problematic as there are significant policy implications arising from divergent assumptions as to the magnitude of remaining emissions and as to the sectors in which they would still occur (Duwe, 2022; Meyer-Ohlendorf, 2020). The same applies to different assumptions about natural and technical potential and sources of carbon dioxide removal. Acknowledging the complexity of the phenomena and in order to remove possible inconsistencies, the Commission conducted its own LTS survey. It revealed extreme approaches of Member States to achieving the net zero emissions target in 2050, both in the context of abatement solutions to achieve this but also of the so-called eliminators (adsorbents) of pollutants emitted. However, as mentioned above, there is no updating process for the LTS itself, which has become outdated as a result of the need to quickly adapt to new external conditions, among other things. Shocks were evident both during the pandemic and now in the face of Russia's war with Ukraine. These events, obviously unforeseen in the analyses, required corresponding changes in targets (e.g. by 2030) and policies (e.g. the addition of IAS to the EU ETS). Response capacity is stronger if policy and system updates are conducted in cycles, so that they will be more frequent, increasing the timeliness of plans and thus their effectiveness. This is currently lacking in the EU climate policy management, and there is some concern as to whether new information can be effectively taken into account after 2030, maintaining the course towards climate neutrality by 2050. Hopefully so, but for this to happen, a further consistent improvement is needed in the instruments of government action in the area of fiscal policy, efficient planning systems and feedback management systems on the results achieved.

Mitigation of such risks underlies the 'Fit for 55' package, in particular through introduction of a social climate fund (European Commission, 2021), the purpose of which is twofold: (1) 'to finance temporary direct income support for vulnerable households' and (2) 'to support measures and investments that reduce emissions in road transport and the buildings sectors and as a result reduce costs for vulnerable households, micro-enterprises, and transport users' (European Commission, 2021), promising a socially just transition (EEA and Eurofound, 2021). Funding for the Social Climate Fund is envisaged to represent 25% of the expected revenues from the sale of emission allowances under the EU Emissions Trading Scheme, covering buildings and road transport (see Defard et al., 2021). In addition, it is proposed that the majority of ETS revenues should be spent entirely on climate and energy projects as a key policy instrument to finance the energy transition. Such a proposal goes beyond the current policy target, according to which Member States should spend at least half of their ETS auctioning revenues on climate and energy goals. The 'Fit for 55' package makes it less likely that tax-shifting programmes will be implemented in the short term. Other environmental taxes do not generate sufficient revenue, limiting the scope for revenue-neutral tax changes. A study commissioned by the European Commission modelled a tax-shifting programme which increased revenue from pollution and natural resource taxes while reducing labour costs, revealing positive but almost negligible macroeconomic effects in terms of GDP and employment growth. Undoubtedly, the time is ripe for environmental taxes and carbon pricing policies to take centre stage, and it can be expected that their importance and relevance will increase during the transition to a climate-neutral economy. These economic instruments must, however, be designed to support the transition to sustainability by adhering to the principle of 'keeping prices right' in line with the 'polluter pays' principle. The revenue-generating aspect of environmental taxes, including carbon pricing policies, should no longer be at the centre of political discussions. Offsetting, or at least compensating for, the expected revenue shortfalls in the coming decades will require a review of current tax regimes to bring them into line with interim targets as well as accelerating the phasing out of environmentally harmful subsidies. In addition, concepts and proposals for redesigning transport taxes, including distance-based road tolls, can be found (Gago et al., 2019; OECD & ITF, 2019; Blank et al., 2021). One of the challenges of such solutions is to ensure timely implementation of new tax schemes. Running existing and new schemes in parallel can lead to undesirable outcomes. Such outcomes could be expected if, for example, distance-based charges were introduced alongside current road fuel taxation schemes, as this would have a negative impact on owners of fossil-fuelled passenger vehicles, which could exacerbate inequalities and reduce the mobility of the poorer sections of society. Nevertheless, such a tax could be an important element in shifting transport to more sustainable modes such as rail, although before it is introduced, access must be first guaranteed to forms of passenger and goods transport that are alternative to individual means of transport. Finally, this may be a good time to revisit the concept of environmental fiscal/tax reform – shifting the tax burden from labour to pollution and natural resource use – in order to achieve sustainable fiscal reform. Fiscal challenges are expected to continue.

More recent analysis suggests that without the combined effect of the EU ETS, instruments to promote renewable energy and of the environmental tax reforms, CO_2 emissions in 2008 would have been around 5% higher, meaning that a positive impact has already been achieved in the first decade of the 21st century. At the same time, further work to develop an effective implementation pattern of various policies in the context of the multifold transition (EEA, 2020) is of utmost importance. Indeed, fiscal sustainability, understood as the 'solvency' of the public sector, will be crucial in the transition towards sustainable development, meaning that available resources must be allocated prudently to models that bring the greatest added value to the broadly defined (economic, environmental or social) environment.

3 Involvement of the financial sector in green investments

3.1 The role and importance of the financial sector in the process of achieving climate goals

As indicated in Chapter 1, the implementation of a rational climate policy requires involving financial resources on a significant scale from all participants in the economic processes (international organisations, central and local governments, the financial sector, economic actors and households) and using capital of varying nature (i.e. both equity and debt). However, the mobilisation of these funds and their efficient redirection to sustainable development requirements will not be possible, or at least very difficult, without ensuring the right conditions and infrastructure. This means that of major significance to the process discussed here is the financial sector, understood by the Authors as a group of entities offering and providing financial services to other sectors of the economy. This sector is also an element of the financial system, by which the Authors mean the system of financial institutions, financial markets and institutional and technical infrastructure whose interrelations lead to the flow of purchasing power and capital (usually using financial instruments) (cf. Hubbard, 2005; Merton, 2004).

The services provided to real-economy entities by the financial system can be delivered either through market and public mechanisms. This distinction determines the division of the financial system into a market segment and a public segment, while some of those services may be provided by both. The process of financing investment to transform the European economy towards a low-carbon economy, which is the main focus of this discussion, should be carried out by the financial system's market segment and public segment alike. The modern financial system is a dynamic structure, changing under the influence of international finance processes taking place in the economic, legal and technological spheres. Special attention should also be paid to the internationalisation of respective countries' financial systems, the important role of financial conglomerates and the wide scale of money flows between countries. However, despite the above interconnections and dependencies, as well as the activities undertaken, when it comes to the European Union's financial system, it can hardly be said to constitute a single market. It is more reasonable to say that it consists of the financial systems of individual Member States. At the same time, the growing importance of the financial sphere

DOI: 10.4324/9781003434689-4

in recent years, as shown by the crisis of 2008, creates the need for a new understanding of the financial system, particularly in terms of assessing and ensuring its stability and its impact on sustainable development and economic growth. Today's national financial systems are also undergoing a transition towards meeting the needs of sustainable development, in order to support its objectives in the most effective way possible. In this context, both the public and free-market financial systems face a number of challenges that require action leading to broader integration with Sustainable Development Goals (SDGs) (see Zioło, 2020).

When analysing the impact of the financial system and its potential for supporting the process of mobilising capital for green investments, the Authors believe that three aspects should be given special attention

- the level of development of the financial system,
- the shape of the financial system and
- the stability of the financial system.

The first of the above-mentioned factors determining the process of financing green investments is the level of development of the financial system. However, this development is not an end in itself; what is assessed is the ability of a given system to fulfil its assigned tasks of reducing transaction costs, including the costs of financial intermediation. A well-developed financial system, due to a richer range of financial instruments and lower transaction costs, provides broader opportunities to use financial instruments that are better tailored to the purpose of funding than a financial system with a lower level of development (Schoenmaker & Schramade, 2019). A better developed financial system can also foster economic growth (Levine, 1997, 2005; Puscasu, 2022).

The level of development of the financial system, reflecting its ability to perform its functions effectively, can be measured in a variety of ways. A common approach in empirical studies is to use one of the two typical measures of financial depth, i.e. the private credit-to-GDP ratio or market capitalisation-to-GDP ratio. However, these indicators do not take into account the complex and multidimensional nature of financial development. An example of a more sophisticated approach in this regard is the Financial System Development Index ('FD') developed by the International Monetary Fund (IMF) (Sahay et al., 2015; Svirydzenka, 2016). The authors of this approach, in order to overcome the shortcomings of single indicators, constructed a comprehensive index, since it refers to the level of depth, accessibility and efficiency, covering both financial institutions and markets. Thus, the final value of the index results from the level of its sub-indices, i.e. the Financial Institutions Index (FI) and the Financial Markets Index (FM), which reflect the varying degree of development of different segments of respective countries' financial system. The values of the FD index from 2010 to 2021 for selected European countries and groups of countries are presented in Table 3.1.

The metric in question takes values in the range [0;1], where the higher the level of system development, the higher the index value. Countries with the highest level of financial system development have index values of 0.90 (e.g. Switzerland 0.94

Table 3.1 Financial System Development Index 2010–2021 for selected European countries and groups of countries

	2010	*2011*	*2012*	*2013*	*2014*	*2015*	*2016*	*2017*	*2018*	*2019*	*2020*	*2021*
Czech Republic	0.45	0.45	0.46	0.48	0.47	0.48	0.47	0.47	0.47	0.33	0.32	0.32
France	0.80	0.81	0.77	0.75	0.77	0.80	0.80	0.83	0.82	0.81	0.81	0.81
Germany	0.74	0.72	0.74	0.72	0.72	0.74	0.69	0.68	0.70	0.67	0.71	0.70
Greece	0.63	0.63	0.54	0.59	0.62	0.55	0.52	0.53	0.49	0.50	0.49	0.47
Hungary	0.56	0.53	0.47	0.47	0.43	0.43	0.43	0.43	0.43	0.44	0.47	0.46
Italy	0.76	0.74	0.76	0.74	0.76	0.78	0.76	0.79	0.77	0.77	0.79	0.77
Japan	0.82	0.81	0.81	0.84	0.84	0.86	0.86	0.90	0.89	0.91	0.93	0.89
Luxembourg	0.74	0.72	0.72	0.72	0.73	0.72	0.74	0.73	0.73	0.73	0.72	0.71
Norway	0.75	0.74	0.68	0.65	0.67	0.69	0.68	0.66	0.66	0.65	0.66	0.64
Poland	0.45	0.48	0.46	0.46	0.45	0.46	0.45	0.47	0.44	0.43	0.45	0.43
Portugal	0.72	0.67	0.65	0.68	0.74	0.69	0.72	0.71	0.69	0.66	0.65	0.65
Romania	0.29	0.31	0.30	0.30	0.26	0.29	0.28	0.28	0.28	0.26	0.27	0.28
Slovakia	0.28	0.28	0.28	0.29	0.29	0.29	0.29	0.29	0.29	0.29	0.29	0.28
Spain	0.84	0.83	0.83	0.84	0.88	0.88	0.87	0.90	0.85	0.81	0.83	0.80
Sweden	0.81	0.81	0.81	0.81	0.81	0.81	0.79	0.78	0.78	0.79	0.78	0.78
Switzerland	0.97	0.99	0.95	0.95	0.95	0.98	0.97	0.96	0.97	0.93	0.95	0.94
Turkey	0.47	0.46	0.47	0.49	0.50	0.49	0.48	0.50	0.50	0.50	0.51	0.50
United Kingdom	0.91	0.91	0.90	0.86	0.84	0.83	0.82	0.85	0.85	0.85	0.84	0.84
United States	0.91	0.89	0.91	0.91	0.91	0.92	0.91	0.92	0.92	0.92	0.91	0.92
Advanced Markets	0.66	0.65	0.64	0.64	0.64	0.64	0.64	0.64	0.64	0.63	0.63	0.62
Africa	0.14	0.14	0.14	0.15	0.15	0.15	0.15	0.15	0.16	0.15	0.16	0.16
All Countries	0.31	0.31	0.31	0.31	0.32	0.32	0.32	0.32	0.32	0.32	0.33	0.32
Asia and Pacific	0.33	0.33	0.33	0.34	0.34	0.35	0.35	0.36	0.36	0.36	0.37	0.36
Emerging Markets	0.31	0.31	0.31	0.31	0.32	0.32	0.33	0.33	0.33	0.33	0.34	0.33
Europe	0.54	0.53	0.52	0.52	0.51	0.51	0.51	0.52	0.51	0.50	0.50	0.50
Low-Income and Developing Countries	0.13	0.13	0.13	0.13	0.13	0.13	0.14	0.14	0.14	0.14	0.14	0.15
Middle East and Central Asia	0.25	0.24	0.25	0.24	0.26	0.26	0.26	0.26	0.27	0.26	0.27	0.28

Source: Own elaboration based on IMF data.

in 2021; or USA 0.92), while the lowest levels (around 0.15) can be found, for example, in African countries. Europe compares favourably in this respect since the value of 0.50 recorded at the end of 2021 is a level reflecting the range of development similar to that of Advanced Markets (0.62–0.66 in the period under review), while, by way of comparison, for Emerging Markets, the index value stood at 0.31–0.33 and for low-income and developing countries at 0.13–0.15. Admittedly, over the period under review, the aggregate index value for European countries fell from 0.54 to 0.50, but this change does not significantly alter the picture. When analysing the situation in individual European countries, significant variations can be seen, with a lower level of development in Central and Eastern European countries (close to levels characteristic of Emerging Markets) compared to Western European countries (a level reflecting development adequate for Advanced Markets). In both cases, however, it should be noted that the European financial system is, in most cases, well developed and can successfully fulfil its functions, including in terms of enabling the transfer of money for green investments.

With regard to the second aspect that is the shape of the financial system, a bipolar classification of financial systems is widespread in the literature, one of the basic distinguishing criteria being the dominant type of institution. Hence, a distinction is made between bank-oriented systems (financial system model also referred to as continental) and systems based on securities markets (otherwise known as the Anglo-Saxon model) (Heffernan, 2005).

Bank-oriented financial systems (e.g. in Germany) are mainly characterised by the predominant role of banks as intermediaries in the flow of capital between economic players. When it comes to the issue under analysis, this means funds for development are raised predominantly in the form of bank credit. The dominant types of institution in this model are universal banks, combining deposit and credit (commercial) banking with investment banking services within the scope of their activities (Moles & Terry, 1997).

In market-oriented systems (e.g. the United States and the United Kingdom), capital is raised and invested primarily through financial markets. In this model, deposit and loan banking is separated from capital market-related investment banking and a strong tendency towards specialised banks can be noted (separation of deposit and loan banks, and investment banks) (see Allen & Gale, 2000, p. 4).

In addition to the different types of dominant institutions, the aforementioned models are also characterised by other differences, the most important of which include controlling methods and information distribution (Kozłowski, 2007). As research to date has shown, the financial systems of the vast majority of economies are a mixture of securities markets, and banking and non-banking financial intermediaries. It should be pointed out, though, that their weight tends to vary – both across the economy as a whole and across groups of real sector entities – and the clear division between the above two types of systems is blurred. It should be stressed that processes of convergence between financial systems have gained importance with the globalisation processes, stimulated in the pre-crisis period by deregulation and other institutional changes, as well as by dynamic changes in information technology. These convergence processes are stimulated by the search for the most efficient solutions, allowing entities to maximise their revenues.

However, the differences between systems, despite the aforementioned convergence processes, are still significant and each financial system has its own peculiarities, both in terms of structural and legal/institutional solutions in place. As noted earlier, the components of the FD Financial System Development Index reflect the degree of development of its individual segments, i.e. financial institutions (FI Index) and financial markets (FM Index). The values of these metrics for selected European countries for the period 2010–2021 are presented in Table 3.2.

The data presented in Table 3.2 shows the variance both in terms of the level of individual indices for specific countries and in terms of the level of development of financial institutions, represented mainly by the banking sector and financial markets. At the same time, however, the differences in the level of development of the banking sector and financial markets are becoming noticeably blurred. An interesting example in this respect is Germany, often cited as an example of a bank-based financial system. Meanwhile, the data in the table shows that while the indices for both segments were at similar levels in 2010 (0.72 FI Index and 0.73 FM Index), the following years saw a development for financial markets (index value increasing to 0.76 FM Index in 2021) combined with a decrease in the level of the index of development of financial institutions (down to 0.62 in 2021). By way of comparison, for the UK, whose financial system is often indicated as characteristic of marked-based financial systems, in 2010, the FI Index stood at 0.92 and the FM Index at 0.86. In subsequent years, a decrease was recorded for the FI Index to 0.79, with the FM Index value virtually unchanged, at 0.85. The data presented confirms the blurring of differences between the two models of financial systems. At the same time, it should be noted that for smaller and less economically developed countries (e.g. the Czech Republic, Slovakia or Romania), a significantly lower level of development of financial markets is visible (marginal index values compared to the financial institutions index).

The above data indicates that for some countries in the European Union, financial markets can only marginally and narrowly be used as a tool in the green investment financing process. In these countries, the banking sector will be the main channel for obtaining financing, and the special role of the public sector in supporting green financing should be emphasised.

Stability is another important feature of an efficient financial system on which its effective functioning depends. Various definitions of this concept can be found in the literature (Mikita, 2021). Referring to the European Central Bank's definition, a stable financial system is one that can withstand shocks without major disruptions (ECB, 2023a). In other words, it is a state in which the financial system performs its functions continuously and efficiently, even in the event of unexpected and adverse disturbances of significant magnitude (Allen & Wood, 2006). Since financial stability is one of the basic conditions for a sustainable economic growth that ensures a high utilisation of factors of production, achieving it ensures efficient functioning of both the financial system and of the economy as a whole. In addition, it is worth emphasising that with the increasing number of financial institutions conducting their operations internationally, and with the growing capital flows between countries' financial systems, the global financial stability grows in importance. In the European Union, in order to increase stability, work is underway

Table 3.2 Financial Institutions Development Index (FI Index) and Financial Markets Index (FM Index) 2010–2021 for selected European countries

		2010	*2011*	*2012*	*2013*	*2014*	*2015*	*2016*	*2017*	*2018*	*2019*	*2020*	*2021*
Czech Republic	FI Index	0.50	0.50	0.52	0.53	0.53	0.52	0.52	0.53	0.53	0.53	0.51	0.52
	FM Index	0.38	0.38	0.39	0.41	0.40	0.41	0.40	0.40	0.39	0.11	0.11	0.10
France	FI Index	0.90	0.90	0.88	0.88	0.87	0.88	0.88	0.86	0.85	0.85	0.85	0.85
	FM Index	0.68	0.70	0.63	0.59	0.63	0.69	0.70	0.77	0.75	0.75	0.74	0.75
Germany	FI Index	0.72	0.71	0.71	0.71	0.71	0.71	0.64	0.63	0.62	0.62	0.62	0.62
	FM Index	0.73	0.71	0.73	0.70	0.70	0.75	0.71	0.70	0.74	0.70	0.78	0.76
Greece	FI Index	0.64	0.62	0.60	0.62	0.54	0.52	0.52	0.51	0.49	0.48	0.46	0.43
	FM Index	0.60	0.61	0.46	0.53	0.67	0.55	0.50	0.53	0.47	0.49	0.50	0.50
Hungary	FI Index	0.51	0.47	0.46	0.47	0.43	0.44	0.47	0.48	0.48	0.53	0.53	0.53
	FM Index	0.59	0.57	0.46	0.46	0.41	0.40	0.39	0.37	0.36	0.34	0.38	0.38
Italy	FI Index	0.79	0.74	0.75	0.73	0.75	0.76	0.74	0.76	0.75	0.73	0.73	0.72
	FM Index	0.70	0.70	0.74	0.72	0.75	0.76	0.74	0.80	0.76	0.78	0.81	0.78
Luxembourg	FI Index	0.84	0.81	0.81	0.81	0.85	0.83	0.85	0.84	0.87	0.88	0.84	0.82
	FM Index	0.60	0.60	0.60	0.60	0.59	0.57	0.59	0.60	0.56	0.56	0.56	0.56
Norway	FI Index	0.58	0.56	0.57	0.56	0.57	0.58	0.58	0.58	0.55	0.56	0.58	0.55
	FM Index	0.88	0.90	0.76	0.71	0.75	0.77	0.77	0.72	0.74	0.71	0.72	0.70
Poland	FI Index	0.54	0.54	0.57	0.57	0.56	0.55	0.56	0.56	0.55	0.54	0.51	0.48
	FM Index	0.34	0.39	0.33	0.34	0.33	0.34	0.33	0.37	0.32	0.31	0.38	0.36
Portugal	FI Index	0.84	0.80	0.80	0.81	0.82	0.72	0.78	0.75	0.74	0.72	0.70	0.73
	FM Index	0.57	0.52	0.47	0.53	0.63	0.63	0.64	0.64	0.61	0.58	0.58	0.55
Romania	FI Index	0.51	0.51	0.48	0.48	0.47	0.50	0.49	0.49	0.48	0.46	0.46	0.47
	FM Index	0.06	0.10	0.10	0.11	0.05	0.06	0.06	0.07	0.07	0.05	0.07	0.07
Slovakia	FI Index	0.48	0.48	0.50	0.51	0.53	0.53	0.54	0.54	0.53	0.53	0.53	0.52
	FM Index	0.06	0.07	0.04	0.05	0.04	0.04	0.04	0.04	0.03	0.03	0.03	0.02

Spain	FI Index	0.83	0.82	0.81	0.83	0.83	0.83	0.83	0.82	0.81	0.81	0.81	0.78
	FM Index	0.82	0.80	0.81	0.83	0.89	0.89	0.87	0.95	0.85	0.79	0.81	0.80
Sweden	FI Index	0.81	0.81	0.80	0.81	0.80	0.79	0.77	0.76	0.76	0.76	0.75	0.74
	FM Index	0.78	0.77	0.78	0.78	1.0.79	0.79	0.78	0.78	0.78	0.78	0.78	0.78
Switzerland	FI Index	0.96	0.97	0.99	1.00	0.99	0.99	0.99	0.98	0.97	0.94	0.94	0.92
	FM Index	0.94	0.97	0.87	0.86	0.87	0.93	0.92	0.90	0.92	0.87	0.92	0.92
Turkey	FI Index	0.37	0.38	0.39	0.42	0.43	0.43	0.43	0.43	0.43	0.43	0.42	0.42
	FM Index	0.56	0.53	0.53	0.54	0.55	0.53	0.51	0.55	0.55	0.55	0.58	0.56
United Kingdom	FI Index	0.92	0.91	0.91	0.94	0.81	0.81	0.81	0.81	0.81	0.81	0.79	0.79
	FM Index	0.86	0.87	0.85	0.74	0.83	0.82	0.80	0.86	0.85	0.85	0.85	0.85

Source: Own elaboration based on IMF data.

to create a single financial market, i.e. a market with free movement of capital between Member States. As a result of its construction, consumers will have free and unrestricted access to all EU financial institutions and their products, and these institutions will be able to operate in all EU countries under the same rules as those applicable to national entities. In addition, the stability of the EU financial system is being enhanced by building a financial infrastructure at EU level and creating a banking union, as well as by implementing plans to establish a capital union. All measures taken so far increase the financial stability of the EU, although it is difficult to determine whether they are satisfactory (Mikita, 2021).

Taking care of the financial system stability is one of the central bank's tasks, as it is closely linked to this institution's primary task of maintaining price stability. As the financial system plays a key role in the process of transmitting monetary policy impulses to the real economy, its instability may hinder and undermine the effectiveness of the measures taken by the central bank. The financial system stability is also a necessary component of the central bank's effective regulatory and supervisory policy, as well as a necessary condition for the effective functioning of the payment clearing system (see Thompson, 2023). Thus, due to the key importance banks play in the financing of the economy and because they clear payments, maintaining the banking system stability is of great importance in this respect.

It is an international standard for central banks to publish reports assessing the stability of a given financial system, including its resilience to possible shocks. In euro area countries, materials of that type are published by the European Central Bank on a semi-annual basis as Financial Stability Review. They contain key information and data on, inter alia, the current financial situation of the banking sector and of non-bank financial institutions, the ability of the banking sector to absorb shocks, the outlook for the euro area's economic environment or a synthetic assessment of the outlook for financial system stability. Risk factors and mitigation recommendations are also provided.

For example, the ECB's November 2023 report (ECB, 2023a) identifies increased interest rates as a key area of challenge, which, combined with a difficult macro-financial outlook and geopolitical tensions, translates into increased financing costs for all sectors of the economy, including the ability to finance and implement green investments. The associated tightening of financial and credit conditions is also affecting the economic activity and poses additional challenges to respective countries' financial and non-financial sectors alike. Those concerns are also compounded by rising geopolitical tensions in the Middle East. They increase the uncertainty related to the macro-financial outlook, not only due to the possible adverse repercussions on energy commodity supplies in the event of further conflict escalation, but also given their potential to trigger risk aversion in financial markets and undermine confidence in the real economy. In this context, three key themes shape the euro area's financial stability outlook, according to the report's authors (ECB, 2023a):

vulnerability of markets and non-bank institutions to adverse macro-financial and geopolitical surprises and related shifts in market sentiment;

- an increase in debt service costs due to tighter financial and credit conditions, translating into higher debt service costs and weaker resilience of firms, households and sovereigns;
- the risk of deterioration in banks' asset quality due to increasing vulnerabilities in the real economy, which, combined with lower loan volumes and rising funding costs, could undermine their viability prospects.

It is worth emphasising that the central bank is usually only one element of a system that ensures stability of the financial system. The institutions that regulate and supervise financial systems also play an important role in this respect. In the case of the euro area, the European Central Bank is part of the European System of Financial Supervision, which is a cooperation network comprising three European Supervisory Authorities, the European Systemic Risk Board and national supervisory authorities. Its main task is to ensure consistent and effective financial supervision throughout the European Union. The European System of Financial Supervision includes both macro- and micro-prudential supervisions (ECB, 2023b).

At the global level, the IMF plays an important role in the context of ensuring economic stability by analysing risks to the stability, for example that of the European financial system. In the *Global Financial Stability Report* (IMF, 2023), published in October 2023, its authors highlight, among other things, the issue of interest rate rises and the resulting increasing risk of debt default (as does the ECB), as well as the economic challenges facing the Chinese economy and its implications. Past experience suggests that in the face of such external conditions, banks' credit exposures may deteriorate rapidly and demand for loans may fall sharply when the economy enters recession, thus affecting banks' profitability. The report also points to the presence of an extremely weak 'tail' of banks. Stress tests indicate that many banks will suffer capital losses in an adverse stagflationary scenario. This includes several systemically important institutions in Europe, in addition to Chinese and US entities. The report under discussion also addresses the transfer of funds needed to implement investments towards the transition to low-carbon economy. According to the authors, by 2030, climate mitigation investment needs in emerging and developing economies (EMDEs) will rise to around $2 trillion per year (IMF, 2023). In addition to a properly functioning financial system, the private sector, which is vital to financing the required investments in EMDEs, given limited fiscal space and difficult market conditions, will have a key role to play in this context. By 2030, the share of private finance must increase to around 80% of climate mitigation investment needs in EMDE countries.

The authors of the study in question not only identify the challenges facing the international financial system but also make recommendations for action that can prevent disturbances and help improve the situation. A good example would be recommendations on measures in the field of price stability and financial stability, which are essential elements for building sustainable economic growth. Thus, in the IMF's view, central banks should (IMF, 2023):

- remain determined in their fight against inflation until there is tangible evidence that it is moving sustainably towards targets, although the stance of monetary

policy should reflect a country-specific pace of economic recovery and disinflationary processes;
take care of communication, which remains crucial to convey policymakers' resolve;
exercise caution when cutting interest rates;
integrate their measures with other elements of the macroeconomic policy, taking account of risks stemming from volatile capital flows amid uncertainty in global monetary policy and the foreign exchange environment.

The IMF also draws attention to the threat to stability from the financial system due to the presence of capital-weak banks in the global financial system and the consequent risk of the crisis spreading to sound institutions. This implies an urgent need for consistent implementation of international standards. In addition, adequate minimum capital and liquidity requirements for large and small institutions are necessary to mitigate risks to financial stability. The authorities should intervene as early as possible to address vulnerabilities in banks, for example ensure that they have access to central bank facilities, and that their resolution regimes are strengthened and ready for implementation. Institutions where real estate (both residential and commercial) is a significant part of the portfolio are identified as a particularly vulnerable segment.

IMF believes that when it comes to 'green investment', a broad set of structural and financial policies are needed to create an attractive investment environment for private capital to support financing needs. A stronger climate information architecture – data, disclosures and alignment approaches (including taxonomies) – is essential to attract private investors. This is particularly important for EMDEs. At the same time, the European Union should be identified as the part of the world that often sets the direction for economic transition efforts. Policies on finance provided by the financial sector should focus on climate impacts. Transition taxonomies in EMDE countries can help institutions identify GHG mitigation actions, including in the most carbon-intensive sectors. Disclosures and labels for sustainable investment funds should enhance market transparency, market integrity and alignment with climate impact-oriented outcomes (IMF, 2023).

The impact of non-financial factors on the economy and on financial markets, in particular those related to climate change effects, makes it necessary to take transition measures to adjust financial systems to financing sustainable development and achieving its objectives. Indeed, only sustainable financial systems can ensure the achievement of all the SDGs, including in particular the environmental goals, which represent the greatest challenge for both developing and developed countries. For sustainable financial systems to be efficient, a series of actions must be ensured that determine their sustainability, namely actions at the stage of system planning, organisation, operation and control. The quality of financial reporting and controls is a vital aspect in this context, other important areas being decision-making and ESG risk management. As indicated earlier, cooperation between the public and private sectors also plays a significant role, as without it the integration of the market and public financial system towards satisfying the needs of sustainable development financing is not possible. These systems are complementary and interact with each other. Thus it is essential to develop methodologies for evaluating financial systems – not only evaluation criteria, but also evaluation methods. Of significance are the so-called sustainable benchmarks and targets that financial systems aim to achieve. An idea worth considering in this regard is building an integrated measure or index for assessing a sustainable financial system, which, in addition to economic variables, would also take into account environmental factors, providing a comprehensive view of the financial system as a necessary condition for the achievement of economic, social and environmental goals (Ziolo, 2020).

The above analysis points to the broad importance of both external and internal factors in preserving the financial system stability. These factors may pose threats to the liquidity situation of the financial sector and, in particular, of the banking sector, which plays a key role here, translating into the finances of real economy entities, including the process of green investment implementation and financing. At the same time, however, in Europe, one should emphasise the sophistication level of the solutions in place when it comes to the ability to absorb disturbances in the financial sector. A good example would be the case of the Swiss bank Credit Suisse which, in the first half of 2023, found itself in a difficult situation following the turbulence in international financial markets (caused by the difficult liquidity situation of a group of medium-sized US banks). Action by the country's central bank, supervision authority as well as the government led to the takeover of this entity by another Swiss banking group UBS, without the wave spreading to further markets and institutions.

3.2 The need to adapt the financial sector to sustainable development requirements

Respective EU countries' financial systems are influenced by a number of factors and processes. Among the key ones are the following (see Claessens, 2016; Hynes et al., 2020; Ziolo, 2020):

- environmental factors (climate risk, environmental degradation, increase in the share of environmental risk-weighted assets which affects the valuation of legal security interests, a growing risk faced by the banks, in particular credit and liquidity risk);
- technological factors (e.g. development of fintechs, blockchain technology, change in business models, digitisation of services, cyber-attacks);
- social factors (health risk, social exclusion which determines financial risk);
- changing consumption patterns and consumer expectations, sustainable household consumption patterns (accessibility of services, speed of transactions, ability to transact anytime and anywhere, socially responsible consumption).

The importance of environmental aspects stems from regulations adopted at the UN level (Agenda 2030 and the Paris Agreement signed in 2016), committing its member economies to adaptation and mitigation actions, which has led to the need for an increase in the volume of capital allocated in this direction. In the European Union, the increase in the value of capital linked to the concept of sustainable development results, among other things, from the Community's 2019 decision to achieve climate neutrality by 2050. The intermediate target set by the EU is to reduce greenhouse gases by 55% by 2030. These objectives are set out, among others, in the framework of the European Green Deal, a development strategy that describes the EU's transition towards sustainable development. The EU wants to allocate EUR 100 billion between 2021 and 2027 to achieve these goals (European Parliament, 2023). These initiatives also imply the need to adapt individual European countries' financial systems to measures oriented to the low-emission transition.

In the above context, it is worth noting the changes in household consumption that translate into financial systems and expectations regarding the provision of financial services. With increasing public awareness of the consequences of climate change, or more broadly of the effects of environmental degradation, households' requirements for the products and services they purchase, including financial products and services, are changing. A consumer approach based on environmental concern (increasingly also referring to other ESG elements) and conscious purchasing results in a change in demand structure (an increase in demand for products reflecting environmental concerns) or a reduction in consumption. Such household decisions also apply to financial products and services, translating into a model of sustainable household finance. Sustainable household finance refers to decisions made by households to accumulate, spend, invest or incur liabilities, taking into account the environmental and social impacts of the actions taken, while aiming to reduce environmental and social risks. Examples of such decisions include taking out a so-called green mortgage and, in terms of investment, investing only in shares of companies listed on sustainable stock exchange indices. Households' expectations of green products and services stimulate demand for such solutions, which are an impulse for the financial institutions responsible for this demand (Zioło, 2020).

The importance of non-financial factors, mainly the environmental factor, in influencing respective countries' financial systems is highlighted in the study by S. Krogstrup and W. Oman (2019). They point out that climate change requires, on the one hand, taking mitigation measures and, on the other hand, measures to adapt financial markets and systems to these changes, and this raises the need for financial capital and the implementation of appropriate instruments and regulations. Financial markets alone cannot, due to their imperfections, ensure sufficient mitigation – hence, the need for coordinated action at different levels of macroeconomic policy (in particular fiscal, financial and monetary policy). When it comes to fiscal policy tools, options involving carbon pricing (explicit and implicit), spending and investment and public guarantees are usually identified in the literature. For financial policy, major options that can play a key role in financing low-emission transition include reflecting and pricing climate risk better on financial institutions' balance sheets, creating financial stability frameworks and supporting climate-related financial market development and reforms. The aforementioned authors also draw attention to the role of monetary policy tools, such as reflecting climate risk better in the portfolios of large-scale asset purchase programmes or collateral frameworks, which are within central banks' current mandates. In a more controversial approach, proposals include financial regulations explicitly favouring green investments, central bank credit allocation and adapting monetary policy framework.

Financial and monetary policy tools can be divided into:

those focused on climate risk and
policies that promote climate finance.

The former is aimed at correcting respective financial institutions' current lack of or insufficient consideration for climate risk while the latter are oriented towards internalising externalities and co-benefits at the society level. The first set supports climate change mitigation through changing the demand for green and carbon-intensive investments and through applying price differentiation. The latter, on the other hand, may be effective for respective solutions' relative prices and may induce investment (Krogstrup & Oman, 2019).

The importance of ensuring access to adequate levels of finance for the green transition and of the consequent need for change in the financial sector is pointed out in the IPCC report (IPCC, 2023). One of the key points in this context is the recommendation whereby resources for tackling climate change should be significantly increased simultaneously in developed and developing countries in the coming years, as climate risk has a major impact on financial markets. First and foremost, global warming affects the valuation of fossil fuels, which are likely to lose value. In turn, the increasing frequency of natural disasters triggered by climate change may lead to a significant reduction in asset values and an increase in insurance losses (Wu et al., 2023). The magnitude of the impact of climate change on markets and institutions is thus sufficiently complex to significantly affect the security and stability of financial systems over the long term. A significant risk associated with climate change is that, in an environment of intensifying and increasingly frequent weather threats, the resulting losses will not be insured because premiums will prove too high. This practice increases the indirect risk to the financial market (so-called secondary effects), as uninsured losses may result in lowering the company value and a greater risk of borrower insolvency (Zioło, 2020).

The consequences of climate change associated with extreme weather events can also create direct risks for the financial market. This risk manifests itself in creating higher and volatile costs for the insurance sector and involves a potential operational risk related to closure of bank branches in the event of extreme events.

The extent of the impact of climate risk on financial risk is shown in Figure 3.1.

The impact of climate risk on the financial system varies in strength. In the short to medium term, the climate change effects are not expected to pose a significant risk to the stability of financial systems. The insurance sector is able to adapt to the risk in the short to medium term, as insurance premiums can be changed accordingly each year and risk capital can be continuously adjusted. A higher risk for the

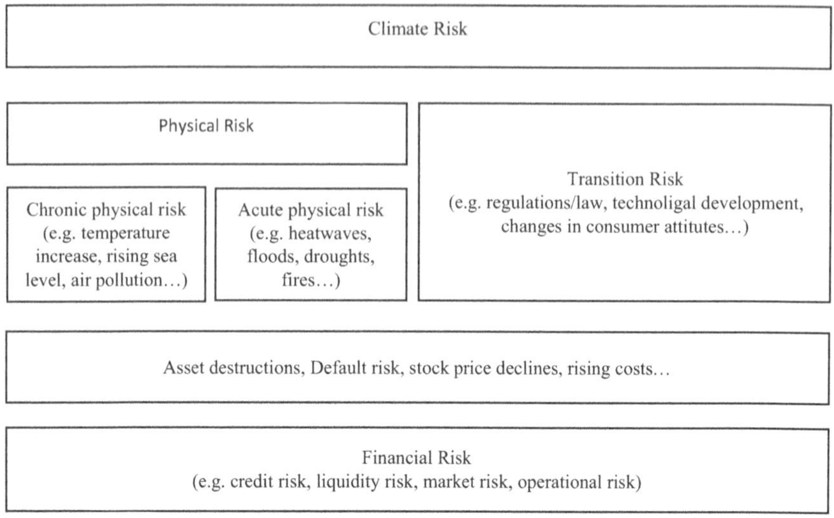

Figure 3.1 Impact of climate risk on financial risk

Source: Own elaboration.

insurance sector is related to the variable probability of extreme events generating very high losses, which are not directly reflected in insurance models because the models are based on historical and statistical data. The same is true for short-term funding provided by banks.

However, in the long term, climate change has negative consequences for financial institutions and financial markets. They lead to a decline in the growth rate of financial assets and investment returns (Krueger, 2020), which increases the volatility of financial markets. The level of systemic financial risk increases indirectly through the banking sector, securities markets and the insurance sector amid high frequency of climate risks. Insurance companies are directly affected as they provide insurance against the loss of physical assets and property (Massa & Zhang, 2011). Climate change affects aggregate economic indicators such as GDP (Nurke et al., 2015) and shows regional differences (Rahul & Anisur, 2023).

As presented in Figure 3.1, climate change causes physical and transition risks, leading to economic losses and deterioration of human quality of life (Grippa & Demekas, 2021). The potential economic costs and financial losses resulting from long-term gradual climate change are considered typical of physical risks. The frequent occurrence of extreme climate events can reduce production efficiency, affect business profitability and increase firms' borrowing costs. The consequence is an increase in loan defaults and a decrease in cash flow. At the same time, asset devaluation is inevitable. Risks will also increase for the banking sector (Wu et al., 2023).

Transition risk refers to policy and regulatory change, technological modernisation and market development in response to the financial risk arising from climate change. This typically occurs during the low-carbon transition process. Rising energy and emissions costs may lead to cost shifts within the green transition, resulting in higher overall production costs. Companies with high energy and emissions consumption may face production cuts, shutdowns or even withdrawal from the market. Climate change policy may affect employment, inflation and GDP, at least in the short to medium term (Marin & Vona, 2019; Ali & Nida, 2018).

The emergence of climate extremes poses a serious threat to the security of human life and social prosperity. It is necessary to focus on potential negative externalities between climate change and financial institutions (Nieto, 2019). Also linked to climate risk is the issue of the impact of CO_2 emissions on the financial market. Transition risk affects this market (secondary effects) through investments by financial market actors in emissions-affected companies. Companies may be affected, for example, by increased prices for CO_2 and other greenhouse gas emissions, regulation of their energy efficiency or a decrease in demand for carbon-intensive products.

Alongside climate risk management, it is also important to ensure that the right conditions are in place to secure adequate levels of capital. In this context, climate change can be neutralised through innovation, which is also one of the key drivers of change for building sustainable financial systems, i.e. systems that are environmentally (as well as socially) oriented. The financing of innovative solutions results in the need to develop financial innovations that allow for this type of financing. Potential areas worth mentioning include (Zioło, 2020):

new forms and types of financial institutions and new organisational solutions – e.g. special funds for counteracting negative environmental changes;
new segments of the financial market along with new infrastructural solutions – e.g. green venture, green energy crowdfunding, green private equity;
new financial products and services along with new distribution and customer service channels – a range of sustainable financial products and services is developing and evolving;
new standards and regulations in relation to sustainable finance and financial systems particularly at the international level, e.g. *United Nations Environment Programme (UNEP) Finance Initiative*.

Both public and free-market segments are faced with the challenge of adapting their financial systems towards green finance.

The public financial system is the mechanism that secures funding for public goods and services provided by the government, local government and social security sectors. It is an area that, in addition to having an impact on the economic situation (e.g. through fiscal policy), is seen as one that supports and stimulates financing for sustainable development. According to the World Bank's *Roadmap for a Sustainable Financial System*, sustainability-oriented government interventions can take the form of (World Bank, 2017): direct support to the financial system, direct financing and risk-sharing, or activities in support of the 'enabling environment' that can facilitate the operation of a sustainable financial system. With regard to intervention in the area of sustainable public financial system, it is important to pay attention to the impact of the system on stakeholder attitudes. Thus, it can be said that a sustainable public financial system is a mechanism in which environmental and social criteria – in addition to economic ones – are included in the decision-making criteria of the process of financing public goods and services.

When analysing the public financial system, it is worth noting that the system plays an important role in financing sustainable development in the sustainable finance model and is typical of developing countries, where the government plays the most important role in providing resources to finance sustainable development objectives. In these countries, the financial sector is currently in the phase of developing and adapting financial products and services to the needs and specificities of sustainable development. The financial market is in the 'greening' phase in terms of environmental financing and adapting financial instruments to finance the above-mentioned projects. In the above context, it is also important to highlight the role of public sector investors in allocating financial resources and creating financial flows to support sustainable development objectives. Sovereign wealth funds and public pension funds are actively investing in green bonds. A good example in this respect is Norway's Norges, which is the world's largest SWF and with $1bn in assets under management, remains a leader in the sustainable investment sphere. At the same time, central banks play a much smaller role as investors compared to funds, due to numerous legal restrictions determined by the need to ensure safety, stability and liquidity. This often stands in the way of investments in green bonds, which do not always meet stringent conditions in terms of credit rating, liquidity, maturity or currency.

Meanwhile, in the case of the market-based financial system, the increasing role of non-financial factors and their impact on the stability and security of the overall structure should be highlighted. The impact of non-financial factors on the financial system is increasingly being taken into account by financial institutions, as evidenced by initiatives such as the so-called climate stress tests.

As the World Bank points out in the aforementioned *Roadmap for a Sustainable Financial System*, a sustainable financial system is a stable system that creates, prices and processes financial assets to ensure prosperity and meet the long-term needs of an inclusive and sustainable economy across all dimensions relevant to meeting those needs, including economic, social and environmental needs; sustainable employment; education; retirement finance; technological innovation; and climate change mitigation and adaptation infrastructure (World Bank, 2019). The authors of the aforementioned study point to three important types of initiatives that ensure change within the financial system towards sustainable finance, among them:

market-based initiatives for the development of collective projects such as the *Sustainable Banking Network* (SBN) or the *Finance* Initiative (UNEP FI), through which private and public financial institutions worked to integrate ESG risks into financial institutions' business models;

national initiatives – originally, actions to develop sustainable finance stemmed from country-level initiatives, which in many cases were linked to national planning processes implemented to apply climate change policies or other long-term strategic pro-development initiatives;

international initiatives – activities implemented by the G20, G7, INZ and the Financial Stability Board (FSB) that addressed various aspects of sustainable and green finance, while increasingly involving the private sector. These efforts have been complemented by multilateral development banks and other international financial institutions that promote sustainable finance, including by adopting sustainable practices in financial activities or introducing sustainable financial products in their product and service mix.

Changes in the market-based financial system towards a sustainable system are evolving and are being implemented on a voluntary basis, among others, by means of financial institutions implementing initiatives, such as (UNEP FI, 2016)

Equator Principles,
Principles for Responsible Investment (PRI),
Principles for Sustainable Insurance (PSI),
UNEP Finance Initiative.

It should be emphasised that the above initiatives are at varying levels of progress depending on the country and continent. In connection with initiatives to ensure sustainability of the market-based financial system, systematic progress is being made towards:

financial institutions disclosing their carbon footprint,
the integration of ESG factors into decision-making (financial, investment) and risk assessment processes,
integrated reporting,
stress testing,
taking account of the so-called 'stranded assets',
moving away from analysing sustainability threats to looking for business opportunities provided by sustainability.

When analysing respective segments of the market financial system, it is important to identify trends in banking, insurance and broadly defined investments that support the emergence of a sustainable market financial system. In the banking sector, a trend can be discerned in which a sustainable approach is becoming one of the main strategies for avoiding credit and reputational risks. These risks manifest themselves particularly in: default, rescheduling of payments, and loss of liability insurance or negative reputation among shareholders or customers. At the same time, the banking system, after the 2008 crisis, is among the sectors experiencing the highest regulatory pressure and, at the same time, a sector in which customers place relatively less trust. These factors mean that liquidity risk in the banking sector is increasing due to capital adequacy regulatory requirements and, in addition, due to the increased competitiveness of parabank institutions, especially fintechs, with which banks find it difficult to compete. At the same time, there are also opportunities for the banking sector, which are linked to the development of initiatives for inclusive growth and the 'greening' of the economy. These initiatives require not only funding but also specialised services, including advisory services, which banks offer (Banking on Climate Change, 2019).

It should be noted that a sustainable market-based financial system is found in developed countries with stable financial markets. In these countries, public awareness of the need to protect the environment, including the awareness of financial sector's customers, is high enough to be an important factor in driving change towards a sustainable financial system. Households and entrepreneurs expect institutions to engage and transform their business models to harmonise with the sustainability concept, and consciously choose sustainable financial products and services. Financial institutions that fail to align their product and service mix with market expectations will cease to be attractive to customers. Developed countries are characterised by a higher degree of integration between the free-market and public financial systems, which work together to align with SDGs.

3.3 Green finance – current state and outlook

The use of financial sector is crucial to achieving sustainable development and its defined goals, in particular to carry out an effective energy transition. The growing role of the financial sector in engaging and directing capital to the implementation of 'green transition' oriented investment projects is confirmed by data from the United Nations Conference on Trade and Development. According to the results presented by this organisation, the value of sustainable financial products globally at the end of 2022 was USD 5.8 trillion, with Europe playing a dominant role in this respect. In product terms, sustainable funds had a major share of this amount, with assets accounting for USD 2.7 trillion (a year-on-year decrease of 7%) (UNCTAD, 2023). The scale of equity exposure by region for this class of instruments over the period 2012–2022 is presented in Figure 3.2.

As evidenced by the data presented in Figure 3.2, Europe is the dominant market for sustainable financial products, of which climate- and environmentally oriented products play an important role. Both in Europe and globally, the year 2022 closed at a lower level than the year before, which was caused by the economic downturn and higher interest rates, among other things.

The above data confirms that capital market participants are increasingly recognising sustainability challenges in their investment strategies in addition to economic indicators. The last decade has seen a surge in the number of financial products dedicated to sustainability across a range of asset types, and an emergence of entities specialising in investing in such instruments. Sustainability funds are mainly oriented to ESG or SDG topics or sectors, such as clean energy, clean technology, sustainable agriculture and food security. ESG funds contribute indirectly to achieving SDGs: on the secondary market where outstanding securities are traded, they increase demand for shares of companies that meet various ESG/sustainability criteria. Sustainability-oriented funds include mutual funds and

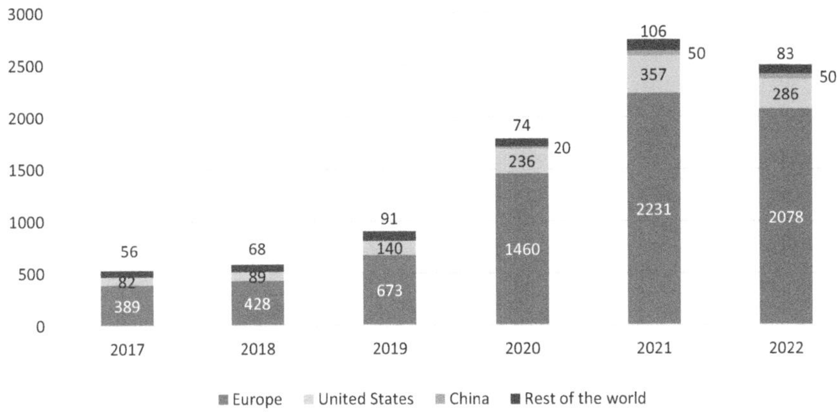

Figure 3.2 Value of sustainable funds globally between 2017 and 2022 (USD billion)

Source: Own elaboration based on UNCTAD, Morningstar data.

exchange-traded funds that apply ESG criteria as part of their securities selection process or seek to have a measurable positive impact alongside financial returns. Currently, UNCTAD estimates that there are more than 7,000 such funds operating globally, managing approximately USD 2.5 trillion in assets, mostly in developed economies (UNCTAD, 2023).

The number of sustainability-themed funds in Europe and the United States, the two largest markets for sustainable investments, has grown rapidly in recent years. At the end of 2022, Europe's sustainable fund market continued to dominate, with more than 5,300 sustainable funds, representing 76% of all sustainable funds globally. The number of sustainable funds is also growing in other parts of the world. With regard to Europe, it is worth highlighting the relatively high market maturity and the relatively advanced regulatory environment for sustainable investments on that continent. The United States has the second largest share of sustainable funds, while Luxembourg is by far the largest single host country with a market share of almost 30% in assets (although tax residence does not necessarily mean the fund is managed from that location). The rapid growth of sustainable funds, particularly in 2020, reflects an accelerated adoption of sustainability criteria in the investment community, particularly in developed countries. Increasingly, institutional investors such as pension and insurance funds are prioritising sustainability in their investment decisions, especially in light of their long-term commitments to beneficiaries and the significant risks associated with climate change and other sustainability crises such as the COVID-19 pandemic. Investors are also increasingly convinced that a shift towards sustainable investments does not necessarily mean an additional cost but rather an opportunity. Over the past two years, major fund providers and asset owners such as BlackRock (US) and the Norwegian government pension fund have taken measures to step up their sustainable investment efforts, for example by announcing the divestment of carbon-related assets from their portfolios.

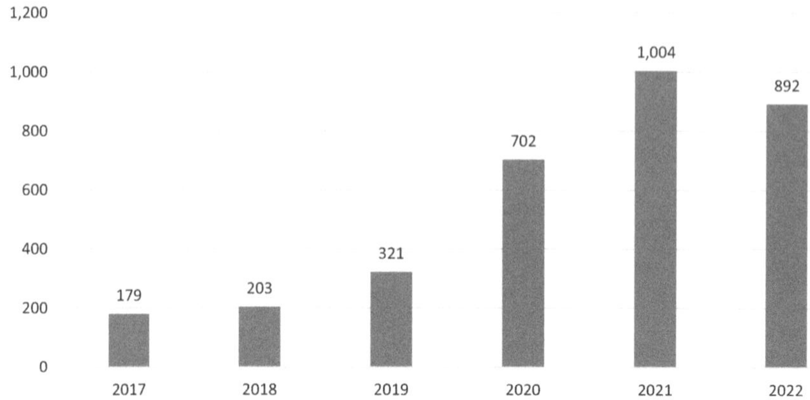

Figure 3.3 The value of sustainable debt instruments globally between 2017 and 2022 (USD billion)

Source: Own elaboration based on UNCTAD, Environmental Finance data.

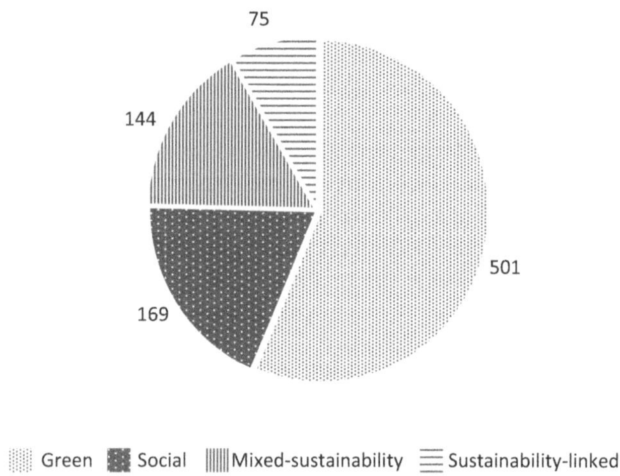

Figure 3.4 Product structure of the sustainable debt instrument market (as of the end of 2022)

Source: Own elaboration based on UNCTAD, Environmental Finance data.

Debt capital market financing has also seen dynamic growth in recent years. Globally, the value of debt securities issued and outstanding by various groups of issuers to finance SDGs amounted to USD 3.3 trillion as of the end of 2022.

Admittedly, as indicated by data shown in Figure 3.3, the scale of new issuance in 2022 was 11% lower than the previous year, amounting to USD 892 billion. In terms of products, the amount of green bonds issued was USD 501 billion (Figure 3.4). However, this result was shaped by several factors resulting from international economic circumstances.

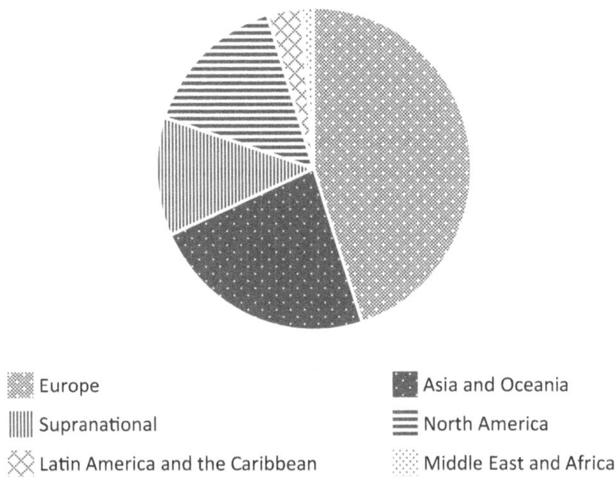

Figure 3.5 Geographical structure of the sustainable debt instrument market (as of the end of 2022)

Source: Own elaboration based on UNCTAD, Environmental Finance data.

When analysing the market for sustainable debt instruments by geography, the clear dominance of Europe is evident, accounting for 45% of the global value of this class of financial instruments at the end of 2022 (Figure 3.5).

It should be noted that debt financing (from bank and capital market alike) can address a specific purpose (green loans, green bonds) or general corporate needs (sustainable linked loans [SLLs], sustainable linked bonds). Entities in sectors for which there are already established sustainability transition pathways can more easily identify green/sustainable financing objectives. On the other hand, entities from industries that are difficult to replace and at the same time difficult to decarbonise (e.g. cement, chemicals) can test new decarbonisation solutions. For them, flexible SLL financing may be a better solution due to the possibility to match overall financing to their respective potential to meet ESG targets expressed by established sustainability performance targets (SPTs) and key performance indicators (KPIs). It is worth emphasising that the effect of SLL instruments on sustainability transition processes depends on the borrower's credibility and achievement of the stated objectives.

The data presented confirms that the capital market, through proprietary instruments and debt instruments granted at market conditions, can be another important 'actor' in the pursuit of sustainable development and investments made as part of it. In the search for optimal solutions combining these characteristics, i.e. investment and tackling the consequences of unsustainable development, debt securities such as 'thematic' bonds are increasingly appearing on the capital market. Bonds are securities created on the primary market, for specific sustainable development objectives in this case. Thematic bonds are instruments where funds raised through issuance are allocated to investment projects with environmental (or social) benefits, thus bridging the financing gap for their implementation. These bonds are often effective investment vehicles that can unlock investment flows by directing institutional and private capital towards sustainable development.

Another, very important, type of bonds intended to achieve SDGs is the 'green bonds', already mentioned here as those gaining importance in recent years. In this class of financial instrument, the capital raised is allocated to new or existing projects with environmental benefits. The purpose of this financing instrument is similar to that of an ordinary bond, the difference being how the funds raised are used. This is because in the case of green bonds, the funds raised are allocated to the implementation of environmentally friendly projects, whereas in the case of ordinary bonds, this restriction does not exist.

In practice, one can also identify a number of other types of bonds that are linked to the achievement of climate goals: climate bonds, sustainability bonds; social bonds, ESG bonds; blue bonds (ocean-related), etc. (Michalski, 2022).

Sustainability bonds are used to finance projects with clear environmental and social benefits. The aim in this case is to achieve positive economic results for a specific target group, while at the same time having a neutral or positive impact on the environment. It is worth noting that in the transition period, transition bonds are emerging to finance activities of entities from less green economic sectors, which often can make the most difference in the fight against climate change by transforming their business model to a more sustainable one (Michalski, 2022).

In order for bonds to be called green, they must meet certain requirements, such as transparency and disclosure, and the funds from their issuance must be allocated to projects that support environmental protection. In order to verify the proper use of funds raised through issuance, specific standards have been developed, the fulfilment of which increases the credibility of issuers and ensures the pro-environmental use of the funds raised in the future.

The most widespread and commonly used standard is the *Green Bond Principles* (GBP) developed by the International Capital Market Association (ICMA). These criteria help both investors and bond issuers to assess the environmental impact of investments financed by these bonds. ICMA's principles and guidelines address issuance rules and reporting to investors. The GBP is a set of guidelines recommending transparency and promoting consistency in the green bond market. Among the most important of these are:

- funds must be used for environmentally friendly purposes only – the GBP includes a corresponding list of acceptable purposes;
- transparent project appraisal and selection processes must be applied – guidelines on how the decision-making process is to take place for the selection of 'green' investments;
- procedures must be in place for managing funds according to their purpose – the obligation of high transparency in the disbursement of funds;
- reporting must be ensured on the project progress and disbursement of funds – obligations to provide information on the achievement of 'green' objectives;
- an independent auditor's opinion must be obtained to verify that the issuer meets the GBP criteria.

The ICMA describes in detail the standards governing the project selection process, managing of funds raised through issuance, and reporting. As an additional control measure, an external audit is used to give credibility to the issuing entity's project activities.

According to the ICMA guidelines, there are several thematic areas of projects that fall under the green project framework. These include (ICMA, 2021):

Renewable energy,
Energy efficiency,
Pollution prevention and control,
Environmentally sustainable management of living natural resources and land use,
Terrestrial and aquatic biodiversity conservation,
Clean transportation,
Sustainable water and wastewater management,
Climate change adaptation,
Circular economy adapted products, production technologies and processes,
Green buildings.

Thus, an issuer of green bonds under the Green Bond Framework should clearly state:

- Environmental sustainability objectives (bond issuance objectives);
- The process used by the issuer to classify projects as 'green';
- The eligibility criteria and the process for identifying potential risks in implementing green projects.

An alternative to the system developed by ICMA is the Climate Bonds Initiative (CBI), whose standards set out sector-specific eligibility criteria for assets and projects. The CBI ensures transparency of the underlying assets, which is extremely important for investors to make informed decisions.

Thus, it can be said that the green bond market bridges the gap between capital providers and investors who finance assets aimed to fulfil green transition goals, providing both investors and issuers with access to finance for projects relevant to fulfilment of climate goals. Thus, green bonds, together with other innovative capital market instruments, support new or existing green projects by enabling the availability of long-term capital (Michalski, 2022).

The information presented above shows a great diversity but also an overlap among the defined types of thematic bonds. It is definitely evident that the most frequently mentioned area they are intended to serve is climate change financing. This is hardly surprising, as it is the activities in this sustainability area that are the most capital-intensive and have the greatest impact on ESG objectives.

This is also confirmed by data from the aforementioned United Nations Conference on Trade and Development presented in the World Investment Report 2022. According to the report, in addition to bonds meant to counter the impact of the COVID-19 pandemic crisis, those for financing sustainable development also played a significant role. It can therefore be concluded that thematic bonds are valuable capital market instruments that have the potential to accelerate and unlock sustainable finance flows. They can attract local and international investors, and thus positively impact the issuer's ability to diversify funding sources, while promoting investments with social and environmental benefits.

Becoming a thematic bond issuer reflects a commitment to sustainability, enhances transparency among the investment community about a company's environmental and social impacts and further strengthens leadership in achieving sustainability goals (Table 3.3).

Green financial instruments are very similar to traditional financial instruments, the main difference being there's a need to identify specific purposes for which the funds raised can be used and what measurable environmental effects this will achieve. A key distinction for green finance is how it can be demonstrated that the investment is delivering the expected environmental benefits, and some products may be subject to penalties if such verification is missing. Green finance may also have more stringent requirements as to decarbonisation efforts and ambitions of the suppliers responsible for project delivery. From the point of view of delivery of public service tasks, this approach is very beneficial as it involves accountability for the efficiency and effectiveness of a given investment, not only public but also private, and environmental impact assessment. Green finance includes non-repayable aid in the form of grants for implementing environmental protection projects as well as financing such projects through equity (acquisition of shares) or debt (green bonds).

Measures involving the use of green bonds were also indicated directly by the European Commission in 2018, with the publication of its action plan on financing sustainable growth, outlining a comprehensive strategy to further strengthen the link between finance and sustainable development. The main objectives defined in this document are as follows:

reorient capital flows towards sustainable investment, in order to achieve sustainable and inclusive growth;

manage financial risks stemming from climate change, environmental degradation and social issues; and

foster transparency and long-term thinking in financial and economic activity

Despite such support from international organisations, however, green bonds are undoubtedly not the first choice of finance for entities implementing green projects – they often prefer to opt for classic financing instruments that do not require them to demonstrate the scale of their energy transition.

The green bond market began just over fifteen years ago with the European Investment Bank's first, EUR 600 million climate bond issue in 2007. Since then, the green bond market has grown significantly, recording notable year-on-year increases. As the amount of capital raised using green bonds has grown, the market has also expanded to include an increasing diversity of issuers from different regions – first Europe, then North America and, more recently, increasingly

Table 3.3 Benefits for Issuers and Investors

	Benefit	*Description*
Issuers	Upgrade sustainability credentials	The process of issuing a thematic bond can be a catalyst to solidify sustainability in the DNA of the organisation as it allows management to align their financial actions to their sustainability goals resulting in a more faithful investor base and more engaged workforce.
	Increase investor demand and diversification	Thematic bond issuers can attract new investors with sustainability mandates.
	Achieve higher levels of oversubscription	Anecdotally, demand for thematic bonds generally outstrips supply. Given the strong demand, some issuers claim to achieve a tighter yield at issuance, especially for bonds denominated in EUR or USD.
	Establish a loyal investor base	Impact investors tend to hold bonds to maturity, which can provide stability for thematic bond issuers.
	Enhance market and brand value	A thematic bond issuance allows management to promote the organisation's sustainability practices which is well received by key stakeholders like investors, employees, regulators and consumers.
	Enhance reputation and visibility	Thematic issuers can brand themselves as forward thinking, innovative, and sustainable, which demonstrates their commitment to addressing climate and social issues.
	Promote intra-company collaboration	The process of issuing a thematic bond makes it possible to strengthen internal communication between the finance and sustainability teams.
Investors	Provide a long-term impact investment option for institutional investors	For asset managers, investment in thematic bonds provides a market return plus a measurable impact at the same time. For pension funds, investment in thematic bonds provides an opportunity to finance green and/or social infrastructure, which matches long-term liabilities while also helping to build a sustainable society for pensioners to retire into.
	Generate investment opportunity in quality assets with transparent reporting	Thematic bonds are inherently more transparent because their allocation and impact are reported annually, providing investors with a greater understanding of the impact of their investment for their own reporting purposes.
	Address environmental and social issues	Thematic bonds direct capital to activities that can generate positive environmental and social impact. They advance adoption of innovative new technologies, finance projects that provide green jobs, and promote economic opportunities, equal access to basic services and climate resiliency across regions.
	Enhance risk management	Issuers provide a solid due diligence for the selection of projects, which provides investors with a clear way to get both economic and environmental returns without significant additional risk.
	Meet sustainability objectives	Investing in thematic bonds can help investors meet their sustainability objectives (i.e., decarbonising their portfolios).

Source. https://cgdevelopmentframework.com/wp-content/uploads/2022/01/Thematic_BONDS_MAY26_FINAL.pdf

Asia-Pacific and, to a slightly lesser extent, Latin America and Africa. Diversification has also been noticed when it comes to type of issuers and currencies in which green bonds are offered. On a market originally driven mainly by multilateral development banks and development finance institutions, green bonds are now issued by public and private institutions, including governments, government agencies as well as private corporations and financial institutions. Such data suggests that the green bond market is well-established, and indeed it is a fact in both developed and emerging countries, supported by a growing awareness of the need for climate action among investors.

Green investments increase GDP while reducing global coal consumption, expanding the market for non-fossil fuels and lowering CO_2 emissions (Wang & Zhi, 2016). Thus, one way to finance environmentally friendly initiatives is through green bonds. Green bonds are a relatively new product, which, as previously mentioned, improves the stability in financial circles; a financial instrument whose proceeds are used to finance low-carbon and environmentally beneficial projects (Flammer, 2020). In order to achieve sustainability goals, various institutions such as municipalities, companies, government agencies and supranational organisations issue green bonds. It has been documented that the issuance of green bonds signals the involvement of various stakeholders, such as managers, shareholders, customers and the public, and helps the issuer gain positive recognition among investors (Tang & Zhang, 2018). Signalling theory states that the issuance of green bonds signals companies as environmentally friendly in society (Wang & Zhi, 2016), and such signals serve as a reliable source of information for investors (Flammer, 2020). Investors have been found to be less sensitive to financial returns and more patient with cash flows when investing in socially responsible companies (Flammer, 2020; Riedl & Smeets, 2017; El-Ghoul & Karoui, 2017). In support of the signalling argument, the resource-based view (RBV) argues that companies issuing green bonds gain social acceptance, enabling them to access cheaper finance, allowing investors to exchange financial returns for social development. In capital markets, there is evidence that firms issuing green bonds experience positive share price reactions and improved trading liquidity (Tang & Zhang, 2018; Nanayakkara & Colombage, 2019). In addition, increased media coverage of green bonds attracts investor interest and improves the visibility of the issuance, enabling existing shareholders to earn dividends. An issuer may be able to solve its financial problems with the efficient use of such instruments due to positive impact of the issuance of green bonds on its financial and environmental performance. In addition, green issuers have a significant impact on the environment (as can be seen from their CO_2 emissions and environmental assessments), supporting the view that green bonds are an effective engagement mechanism for issuing companies, and investors appreciate such a strategy. The impact of green bonds on companies' ownership structure is that investors intensify their interest in companies issuing green bonds, and in the projects in which the company invests capital. Moreover, green bond issuers solicited by institutional investors have higher returns for early users than experienced issuers. In addition, the impact of investor attention on the green bond market means that green bond issuers receive more attention in the short term, which helps investors understand the characteristics of green bonds (Pham & Huynh, 2020).

Regarding the pricing of green bond issuance, the premium for green bonds has been proven in several studies (Karpf & Mandel, 2018; Hyun et al., 2020; Febi et al., 2018; Flammer, 2020; Baker et al., 2018; Ehlers & Packer, 2017). For example, the issuance price of green bonds in the United States is significantly higher than that of regular bonds (Baker et al., 2018). For green bond issuances in different countries, it has been observed (Ehlers & Packer, 2017) that green bonds get a premium at issuance compared to ordinary bonds, while the performance of the two different types of bonds in secondary markets is almost the same. In addition, the favourable share price reactions to green bond issuance announcements in 28 global green bond markets show that green bond issuance helps equity investors. In China's corporate bond market, green bonds are issued at lower yields and sold at a premium in the main market. The premium is much higher than in other global markets and enables the green bond issuer to obtain more advantageous terms. Moreover, a positive stock market reaction is associated with a price premium for green corporate bonds, making them more expensive than traditional bonds. Using data from 12 countries (Zerbib, 2019), it was found that the relative yield of green bonds in the US bond market decreases with lower ratings and is slightly lower than that of conventional bonds. Similarly, US green bond yields are lower than US municipal bonds (Karpf & Mandel, 2018). Green bonds trade at lower spreads than conventional bonds. The green label provides an incentive for issuers to generate cash by issuing green bonds, while allowing investors to diversify their investment returns through a regular premium in the green bond market. It also helps them understand the market risk and return trends resulting from green bonds and discover that green and traditional bonds are valued very closely. Co-movement of green bonds with several other financial instruments showed that other fixed-income securities and green bonds move significantly on average and towards the tail of distributions. Issuing green bonds can improve collateral liquidity, reduce information asymmetry and lower the perceived risk of bond issuers (Huang, 2022). Being one of the signals of companies' fulfilment of their social responsibilities, green bonds can help reduce interest costs (Li et al., 2023). Overall, green bond certification reduces information asymmetry and improves corporate disclosure, resulting in investors being willing to pay a higher price. Several studies have been conducted to understand the reasons for such a green bond premium. For example, one reason for the green bond premium is investors' environmental preferences. Other factors considered are bond ratings and the type of issuer (Zerbib, 2019). Premiums for green bonds are not driven by liquidity risk (Febi et al., 2018). However, the social reputation of issuers can increase the green bond premium (Wang et al., 2022). In summary, in the international market, green bonds generally have a premium at issuance and third-party certification helps to improve the price of green bonds, while it has a lower yield than regular bonds.

Renewable energy financing is present in about half of all green bonds issued. However, the relevance of green bonds remains well below their potential, and issuances are too small to drive the global transition to renewables. Another instrument referred to as a source of equity is the so-called capital entry, which allows an external source of finance to be raised in exchange for a share of equity in a company or municipal corporation. This type of instrument is not referred to as a 'green' instrument but is a typical capital measure aimed to financially strengthen the newly created entities, for example those operating in the field of energy and waste management.

Thematic bonds have shown that they can be used as effective investment instruments to help close this financing gap, directing institutional and private capital to prioritise the sustainable development agenda.

The economy transition towards a sustainable model will also not be possible without the participation of the banking sector. This part of the financial system, like its other elements, is being transformed to adapt to financing sustainable development. However, it should be noted that both the transition mode and the conceptual apparatus accompanying these changes remain heterogeneous. As M. Zioło et al. (2021) points out, the literature lacks consistency in defining the terms 'sustainable', 'green', 'ethical' or 'socially responsible' banking. For example, green banking is often equated with sustainable banking or ethical banking, or even the terms are combined and used to describe sustainable green banking. Meanwhile, the term green banking refers only to the environmental area of sustainability, while sustainable banking is a broader concept and means that not only environmental but also social and governance impacts are taken into account in a bank's operations. The sustainable bank model describes a knowledge-based organisation that participates in changing socio-economic practice in accordance with the principles of sustainable development. In such a model, the principle of profit maximisation must give way to other priorities. This change requires implementing appropriate modifications in various areas of the institution's activity (Zioło et al., 2021).

The importance of the banking sector in the context of financing opportunities for sustainable development-oriented investment projects is primarily due to:

- its size and role in respective countries' financial systems – this applies in particular to those countries where the financial system is based on banks, which are the main providers of debt capital;
- the wide scope of banking regulation – due to its importance for the economy and the proper functioning of the financial system, the banking sector is subject to a wide range of regulations, which improves security, but also makes it easier to direct money flows towards financing projects that fit with the premises of sustainable development.

The aforementioned broad scope of banking regulation means at the same time that the sector is heavily burdened by processes to adapt to the requirements of sustainability finance. This is because of banks' exposure to and need to manage new ESG-related risks arising from changes in the business and regulatory environment. As part of their operations, banking institutions are progressively integrating the assessment of ESG factors into their processes while involving their clients in these tasks. EU taxonomy regulations require the banking sector to increasingly disclose its commitment to financing sustainable activities. The European Commission has made it mandatory in 2022 and 2023 for non-financial reports to show the portfolio structure in terms of compliance with the Taxonomy. This means that banks' reports should present information as to what part of an institution's exposure (to selected clients) finances the activities described in the Taxonomy, and what else is included in the portfolio (appropriately divided into exposures to central banks and derivatives). From 2024 onwards, on the other hand, a second phase of disclosure will be implemented, under which banks will be required to report on the so-called KPIs. In this context, the term refers to various 'green asset ratios' measuring the proportion of a bank's exposure used to finance sustainable operations.

As mentioned above, these obligations raise a number of challenges on the part of financial institutions in obtaining the necessary data from customers. This often means the need to significantly expand the scope of information that is obtained both to analyse a given loan application and at the stage of monitoring the customer's economic and financial situation and transactions. Thus, it can be said that this situation implies a process of building a sustainable relationship with the customer. Credit institutions not only perform a credit analysis but also analyse the potential borrower's exposure to sustainability risks, the scale of its carbon footprint, the energy efficiency of its collateral or the scale of divergence of its loan portfolio from the International Energy Agency's 'net zero' pathway. However, obtaining such a wide range of information from customers also represents an opportunity for banks to capture more customer data, including ESG factors (Schoenmaker & Schramade, 2019).

In turn, a good example of an initiative that brings the sector together around the topic of sustainable finance would be the document prepared by UNEP FI (The United Nations Environment Programme Finance Initiative), 'Principles for Responsible Banking' (PRB), which serves as sort of guidelines whose implementation in the banking practice is supposed to lead to the fulfilment of SDGs (Niedziółka, 2021, p. 181).

The role that banks have to play in addressing the investment gap in order to move towards a more sustainable economy is also creating changes in terms of product offerings. It is worth emphasising that despite the growing range of instruments observed in recent years, their scope is still in a development phase. However, taking the type of financing as a classifying criterion, sustainable bank financing can be divided into sustainability-linked and targeted (e.g. 'green' or 'social').

SLLs have the following characteristics:

general purpose financing,

an open catalogue of risk instruments that can underlie the transaction,

loan pricing linked to the performance in meeting ESG targets adopted by the borrower,

loan margin directly linked to key sustainability indicators (ESG scoring, strategic objectives or other selected indicators), voluntary guidelines in place (SLL Principles) as regards transparency of transactions, reporting to lender, audits of adopted ESG targets, etc.,

the available guidelines are not binding rules – the SLL loan market is unregulated as regards the criteria to be met for SLL loans to be clearly distinguished from other loans (including syndicated loans).

When analysing this type of financing, it is important to note that definitions of sustainability may vary depending on geography, industry and regulations. Borrowers should consider regional and industry guidelines and constraints when selecting KPIs as well as SPTs.

SLL loans are a tool to support the borrower in its sustainable transition and in improving sustainability performance. In principle, any type of borrower can apply for an SLL loan, assuming they are able to provide the strategic elements necessary for the transaction structure to be in line with the guidelines of international associations of financial institutions (ICMA, LMA and similar). SLL loans may disappear within a decade, and having an ESG strategy and sustainability targets in place may become a conditio sine qua non for accessing external capital.

Another group is targeted loans. In this context, green loans as well as social loans should be mentioned as the most popular type. The specificity of green loans is presented in Table 3.4.

The above analysis indicates that SLLs are an interesting source of finance both for those with a clear transition pathway and those at an earlier stage of these efforts.

Globally, SLLs have been gaining significantly in importance in recent years. Figure 3.6 shows the volume of this type of financing over the period 2016–2022.

An analysis of the information and communications provided by banking sector players also indicate that it is becoming increasingly difficult to find an institution that accepts financing for companies in the coal sector, for example. At the same time, there are a growing number of banks described as 'green', which are focusing their attention on environmentally friendly projects and implementing ESG

Table 3.4 Targeted loans

Green loans
• any credit risk instrument (including guarantees and letters of credit) that (re)finances / guarantees fully/in a specific part new/existing projects from an identified pool of targeted projects qualified as green; • identifying the funding objective is a key structural element (including expenditure directly linked to the achievement of the objective, e.g. R&D); • all environmental (green) objectives identified as available for funding should be objectively measurable and transparent; • funding may include social elements, but these must not determine the green nature of the funding; • funding objectives may be directly based on the technical criteria of the EU Taxonomy, those of an extra-regulatory market standard, e.g. CBI, Loan Market Association, ICMA or another widely recognised and recognisable institution.

Source: Own elaboration.

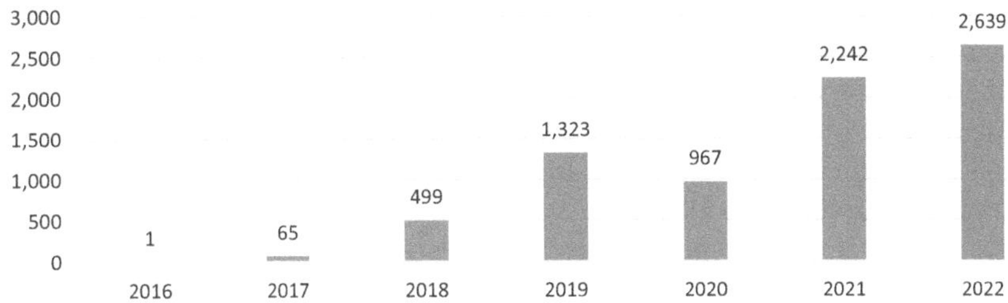

Figure 3.6 Sustainability-linked loans in 2016–2022 (USD billion)

Source: https://greenfinanceportal.env.go.jp/en/loan/sll_issuance_data/sll_market_status.html (doi: 25/11/2023).

risk factors into their lending policies, thereby switching to a sustainable banking strategy.

Hence, business entities that do not meet sustainability requirements (e.g. have not developed an energy transition strategy) have increasingly fewer opportunities to obtain financing. At the same time, institutions that are willing to provide this financing tend to expect a higher remuneration than is the case for ESG-compliant companies. The aforementioned group of companies also has limited leverage – the Net Debt/EBITDA ratio for European companies is in many cases higher than for Polish entities. For such entities, there is a clear risk of abandoned assets – which is both a burden on commercial bank' balance sheets and impedes access to debt financing.

The level of and the potential to incur debt depends, among other things, on the type of operating activity (generation/distribution); fuel mix (RES/fossil fuels/nuclear); age of generating units; planned capital expenditure for the coming years. The deterioration of credit ratings is also an important aspect, with a significant group of banks planning to quantify the impact of ESG factors on a borrower's processes and risk profile in the lending process (Lipski, 2021).

For companies whose operations involve increased sustainability risks, access to bank financing is conditional on strictly addressing the objective of the debt funds. This objective must be sustainable and meet market or regulatory technical and sectoral criteria.

The above-mentioned sources of project financing are not the only tools that can be used in the financial assembly. They are the most popular and play a major role, but also other ways to raise capital can be identified, both as equity and debt capital.

Business angels are an example of this type of solution. These are wealthy investors who provide capital for new business ventures (Scott, 2003). Business angels are interested in funding small- and medium-sized enterprises, which are mostly at an early stage of development and have a high potential to increase their value (Tamowicz, 2007). These are usually entrepreneurs with extensive professional experience, with significant assets of their own, who engage not only their accumulated savings but also their business experience, knowledge and business contacts. This group, as is the case with venture capital (Breuer & Pinkwart, 2018), is characterised by its significant importance for economic development due to its acceptance of greater risk and willingness to finance ventures of an innovative nature (Drover et al., 2017).

Market data for both the United States and Europe indicate that business angels are an important component of the capital market (Bonini et al., 2018). This is because they represent an alternative source of capital for high-risk ventures. This source of capital can also be used for investments linked to sustainable development, especially for projects characterised by an increased rate of return or using various types of modern solutions. This is confirmed by statistics from the European Business Angels Network, an organisation that brings together this group of investors in Europe (EBAN, 2022).

High-risk capital represented by venture capital and private equity funds can be indicated as another potential source of funding. This group is often identified as potential investors at the next stage of business entity development (after business angels). Private equity refers to medium- to long-term equity investments. Usually, transactions of this type are carried out in the non-public market, but there are exceptions such as investments in support of a company's delisting process. The investor and the company agree on a strategy of action for the period defined by the investor, to enable the company to grow in value. The investment period is usually between three and seven years. Considering the early stages of the company's development, the fund usually takes a majority stake in the beginning, while at later stages the involvement is often of a minority nature, however, usually not less than 20% (Sobańska-Helman & Sieradzan, 2013).

Venture capital funds are mostly considered a subset of private equity that deals with investments made in the start-up phase. However, for different countries or continents, there may be differences in the exact definition of these terms (Podedworna-Tarnowska, 2015, p. 9). The main criterion for selecting projects for this group of investors is a market analysis in terms of feasibility of the ideas, entrepreneurs' qualifications and high rate of return combined with acceptable risk. Investment success is determined by the market: high risk indicates that not every investment will be profitable. As with business angels, VCs also recognise the changes taking place in the environment, the increasing role of sustainable growth and the need to address these issues in the investment process. In a global survey on responsible investment conducted by PwC (2021), its authors analysed the views of general partners and limited partners on responsible investment among global private equity firms. In this survey, 209 firms from 35 countries or territories responded. According to its results:

56% of respondents discuss ESG issues at board meetings more than once a year;
66% consider value creation as one of the top three drivers of responsible investment and ESG activities;
72% always check companies being taken over for ESG risks and opportunities at the pre-acquisition stage;
56% have refused to enter into agreements with partners or have rejected investments on ESG grounds.

These results confirm the growing importance of an investment category that can be described as sustainable investing. C. Alfonso-Ercan notes that private equity investors are strategically positioned to drive a shift towards ESG-informed investment standards and to create sustainable investment vehicles that provide greater transparency, better asset management, better risk management and higher returns than conventional investment strategies (Alfonso-Ercan, 2020).

Another example of an alternative source of funding that can be used as a source of capital in the implementation of sustainability-related investment projects is crowdfunding. The essence of this form of financing is that money is provided by distributed, online investors to implement a specific business activity (usually at an early stage of development) (Ordanini et al., 2011). In crowdfunding, several players play an active role: most of all individuals proposing new ideas and projects for potential implementation. The goal of these individuals is to gain market access and attract financial support from community investors (who find the project in question attractive). In a standard transaction, it is this very community that decides to finance the proposed projects and assumes the risk of failure. The participants in a crowdfunding initiative not only contribute their funds but often can also influence the final shape of a given project or product being the subject of a campaign. The above-mentioned groups are linked by the platform/organisation that brings together funding recipients and potential funding providers.

One can provide examples of where funds are raised this way also for sustainability-linked projects. This is not an easy task, but when it comes to projects that involve a lower expenditure and are attractive in marketing terms, crowdfunding can be identified as an interesting alternative. Especially following the implementation of regulations governing this form of financing into European legislation, it has become both more secure and more transparent. And, as research results reveal, although sustainability orientation does not always increase the chances of success or the involvement of professional investors in a project, it often attracts more investors willing to entrust their funds (Vismara, 2019).

The above-mentioned ways to finance investment projects, including those oriented towards sustainable growth, do not exhaust the catalogue of available possibilities. This means that when it comes to projects that are important from the ESG perspective, it is worth analysing the options available on the market, as the growing number of participants (various types of institutions, often mission-driven ones), as well as the increasingly wide range of financial instruments, mean that the method of financing can be tailored to specific needs.

The increasing importance of non-financial (ESG) factors is driving the need for more non-financial reporting on the part of investors and debt capital providers. The contemporary framework for non-financial reporting comprises standards and regulatory requirements, of which Regulation (EU) 2020/852 of the European Parliament and of the Council of 18 June 2020 on the establishment of a framework to facilitate sustainable investment 2020/852 (the 'Taxonomy Regulation') is paramount. It is currently one of the most important sets of regulations for the financial and real sector alike. The Taxonomy Regulation aims to make it easier for investors and entrepreneurs to assess economic activities in terms of sustainable use of the resources required to implement them. The requirements of the EU Taxonomy also provide the regulatory background for a number of pieces of legislation currently being drafted (or revised), such as the Non-financial Reporting Directive (NFRD), the Corporate Sustainability Reporting Directive (CSRD), the Sustainable Finance Disclosures Regulation (SFDR) and the recommendations of the Task Force on Climate-related Financial Disclosures (TFCD).

However, the lack of legally binding regulation of financial products and reliance merely on 'best practice' mean that sustainable finance runs a significant risk of 'greenwashing' (activities that deliberately mislead investors or customers and create a false impression of environmental sustainability). At the same time, the entry into force of the EU sustainability regulations creates new tasks for the financial and real sectors, relating to adjustment processes at operational level and changes in reporting. Meeting regulatory requirements for business transparency involves processing new types of information (e.g. greenhouse gas emissions and energy efficiency, e.g. the use of renewable energy sources to power the company's facilities).

3.4 Development trends and challenges for the financial sector in the context of green finance

As indicated in the preceding discussion, the transition of the EU economy, as expressed, among others, in the European Green Deal, which assumes building a highly competitive, resource-efficient and zero-carbon economy, poses a number of challenges to the financial sector. Planned and anticipated activities, fundamental changes in the functioning of a number of industries and economic sectors, efforts to stimulate technological and product innovations as well as transform public transport and energy production methods, all of this involves the need to organise appropriate funding. The financial system, with its array of available sources of funding and mechanisms to assess risks and costs of this funding, has a special role to play (Stern, 2007; Gerster, 2011). As shown in the previous subsections of this chapter, characterising the current situation and assessing the level of financial sector's willingness to participate in climate finance, the development of both equity and debt-based 'green finance' has been evident in recent years. Some areas can be said to be prepared better and others less so (both geographically and in terms of products), but even for segments considered stable and developed, care should be taken to develop them further and strive for optimal solutions, given the scale of the needs. This means the need to get not only credit or lending institutions involved in the process of change but also investors, individual ones managing their own capital as well as those managing entrusted capital, such as investment or pension funds. In the latter case, this is done through legal tools introducing the requirement to take sustainability criteria into account both at the due diligence stage and in the selection of financial instruments for the portfolio as well as in the investment risk management process.

The financial sector can and should actively participate in the process of raising and mobilising capital and directing it towards financing activities that directly address one or more of the defined SDGs. For example, this could involve financing of projects related to renewable energy generation, improved economic efficiency or more accessible and efficient public transport. That kind of finance can also stimulate a change in strategies of economic actors, especially companies operating in sectors associated with the so-called 'brown economy', where, unlike the green economy, there is a strong link between economic growth, on the one hand, and resource use, environmental degradation and increasing social inequality on the other. The financial system aims to allocate resources to the most efficient projects. Therefore, finance is used in sustainable investments and sustainable companies. It also helps to transform the economy into a low-carbon and circular economy. Thus, this aspect concerns sustainable finance, which bridges the gap between finance (investments and loans) and economic, social and environmental issues. Sustainable finance plays a key role in allocation, as it helps achieve sustainable goals by focusing on strategic sustainable development action (Schoenmaker, 2017).

The importance of the financial sector and, in particular, of the banking sector in terms of its impact on carbon emissions is pointed out in the study by Obiora et al. (2020), who, based on their analysis of a sample of 45 countries (economically developed, emerging and developing alike) for 1990–2017, concluded that financial institutions reducing the level of lending to large GHG emitters from private sector in all economies contribute to lower emissions.

As S. Thompson (2023) points out, the contemporary financial system exhibits three key features that can lead to problems meeting environmental challenges and other sustainability factors. These are:

a short-term orientation in decision-making – the time horizon adopted by financial institutions and investors when making decisions is often too short to see the long-term environmental or social impacts of investment decisions or other actions. This short-term outlook is largely due to the pressure to produce attractive (e.g. quarter-on-quarter) results, which at the same time often discourages long-term investment;

profit and shareholder focus – despite the increasing popularity in recent years of theories about maximising the utility of all stakeholders in a company (cf. Morrison, 2021), a theory initiated in economics in the 1960s by the so-called 'Chicago School', according to which the main purpose and role of a company is to maximise profits for shareholders, is still popular. This idea has had a major impact on the conduct of business and the approach to company regulation. At the same time, such an approach displayed by companies, including financial institutions focused on maximising returns from shareholders' perspective alone, can lead to environmental and social damage. It is worth noting that the consequences of a profit maximisation approach are not always immediately apparent. This is because they are often cumulative, as in the case of water pollution caused by the release of industrial chemicals; or in the case of climate change caused by the burning of fossil fuels;

the tendency not to take 'externalities' into account – externalities are the side effects of economic activity that are not disclosed in cost-effectiveness accounting or quantified. In other words, it is the impact of decisions on stakeholders (such as individuals, communities and the environment) who are not in a position to influence the content of those decisions. Externalities can be both positive and negative, although in the context of climate change and the environment, most externalities are negative. Externalities refer to a situation where financial institutions assess the risks and benefits of lending or investment decisions relying on criteria based on maximising shareholder returns, while not taking account of other factors, including environmental and social costs. This attitude leads to investing in sectors and projects that generate pollution, carbon emissions, habitat destruction and other environmental and social damage because their costs are 'hidden'.

PWC (2020), on the other hand, identifies the following 6 main challenges facing the financial sector as regards sustainability and green investment management:

striking the right balance by adequately anticipating risks that are relevant from a given organisation's perspective – for a bank, this challenge will refer to the ability to properly identify risks and value the risk of funding a given sector/entity, or companies operating in a given geographical area;

integrating ESG into the credit or investment cycle (rather than creating new processes with parallel characteristics) – the credit or investment cycle as a formal decision flow plays a key role in the management of funds or assets, and therefore these processes represent a natural framework for ESG integration in financial institutions. This means that investors/lenders should consider ESG factors throughout the entire credit or investment cycle: from loan origination to termination or renewal. The importance of such an approach is also confirmed by the results of a study conducted by Grygiel and Lipski (2023) on investment funds in Poland;

adapting stakeholder management and sharing ESG knowledge – financial institutions' stakeholders include a wide range of actors (from capital providers to collaborators, employees to customers); at the same time, access to different types of information can create a number of different opportunities for financial institutions, such as the ability to influence risk management when it comes to companies from the investment portfolio;

collecting, managing and using ESG data for risk modelling – data collection is essential for the effective identification and assessment of ESG risks and their integration into overall risk modelling. For example, information on clients' ESG emissions or the location of their production facilities allows investors to assess exposure to physical and transitional risks. Information on the structure of a client's supply chain, including exposure to geographical areas with higher human right risks or poor governance risks, can give investors an idea of their exposure to social and governance risks. However, collecting this information requires adequate resources and may require investors/finance providers to contact individual clients. There being no standards in place, and data being often of poor quality, this is a significant challenge from the financial institutions' perspective, particularly when it comes to extensive investment/credit portfolios. The use of third parties, such as ESG data providers, is helpful, although the information obtained through these channels is not always comparable and is not equally mature for all asset classes. Where possible, investors can use existing customer due diligence procedures such as 'Know Your Customer' (KYC) to collect and process data. This type of approach also reduces the risk of so-called 'reporting fatigue' among clients;

delivering on and communicating ESG commitments – each financial institution may at some point need to indicate how it has addressed ESG risks and whether it has successfully harnessed the available opportunities in this area; an interesting example would be, for example, communication on the tools used to decarbonise the portfolio (for example through participation in the Science Based Targets initiative);

integrating ESG into existing risk practices – by integrating ESG risks (in particular climate risk) at every stage of the risk management framework, financial institutions can prepare for the future. To identify potential risks, investors should consider whether their investments are concentrated in specific industries or regions, for example. Stress tests can be used to assess ESG risks. Last but not least, ESG risk can be mitigated by exclusion policies or adjusted risk premiums.

As can be seen, overcoming the problems outlined above will be one of the key challenges facing the financial sector in order to encourage investors and lenders to take the described broader environmental context into account in their investment and lending decisions. The development of the financial system towards financing sustainable investments requires a multi-dimensional transition, including the implementation of a number of legal and regulatory solutions. Some of the needed changes have already been initiated under the following sustainability-related acts/solutions (AIMA, 2020):

Taxonomy Regulation, through which sustainable activities are classified according to a standardised system;

Benchmarks Regulation, enabling green products to be classified according to sustainable standards;

Markets in Financial Instruments Directive and Insurance Distribution Directive, addressing the classification of financial advice according to sustainability principles,

UCITS Directive and Alternative Investment Fund Management Directive – legislative acts that integrate sustainability risks and factors into asset management,

Non-financial disclosure for companies – focus on ESG data reporting and accounting,

Green bonds – increasing comparability and transparency based on common standards

EU Ecolabel – sustainable products (including financial products) are labelled with the common EU Ecolabel,

Corporate governance – sustainable corporate governance supports and prevents short-term capital market pressures,
Capital Requirements Regulation (CRR)/Solvency II – integration of sustainability into prudential requirements,
Credit ratings – incorporation of sustainability into the credit rating and market research process.

With regard to legal and regulatory issues, it can be said that an entire architecture for the development of sustainable finance has been built in the European Union. This includes the European Green Deal, which is a multi-vector strategy for climate neutrality by 2050, and the taxonomy of 'green' finance, which classifies activities that meet sustainability criteria. There is also a whole network of organisations looking after the transparency of the sustainable investment market and countering greenwashing (green PR and marketing, i.e. pretending to comply with sustainability goals, fake eco-policy).

An important area for development in this respect is planning and designing systems to assess a given business activity's level of sustainability, where such assessment is as standardised and objective as possible, thus helping redirect funding towards genuinely sustainable projects. This requires, on the one hand, creating an appropriate formal legal environment for non-financial reporting in this area, and mechanisms for verifying and assessing the information provided, as well as, on the other hand, developing market and industry standards. It can lead to creating unique, individualised methods for assessing the sustainability of projects and operations, which in the medium and long terms can serve as a mechanism for building competitive advantage both in terms of due diligence and investment risk management.

The effects of applying a combination of diverse ESG criteria in the process of investment portfolio creation and management are multifold. On the one hand, they can be analysed in terms of successful implementation of the leading objective for which, in principle, all investment portfolios are created, namely the pursuit of the expected return on investment, while reducing investment risk through portfolio diversification. In this context, it is crucial to ask about the impact of additional selection and risk management criteria, such as ESG criteria, on investment returns and volatility. On the other hand, the inclusion of sustainability-linked criteria may raise expectations as to achieving additional, non-financial objectives, as part of investments. From this perspective, it becomes interesting to analyse both the formula for defining these objectives and how they relate to the guiding objective of the entire ESG transition in the EU economy that is trying to build resilience, particularly to climate change. This naturally raises further questions about the possibility to parameterise the investment process, but also the investment itself, in such a way as to make it more resilient – both to the typically long-term negative effects of the ESG risks materialising, and to the risk of financial or economic crises occurring globally and locally.

The growing importance of climate risk and its impact on the financial sector, particularly the banking sector, also determines the need for developments in analysing and measuring the impact of such risks on financing providers. In case physical risks materialise, or the implementation of international agreements on the economic transition brings about negative effects, this can adversely affect the financial standing of economic entities whose activities are harmful to the environment. A negative demand shock affecting carbon-intensive assets (loans, debt and equity securities) cannot be ruled out either, causing a sharp fall in their value on financial markets. Another important issue when it comes to transition risk is the uncertainty regarding the scale and timing of the expected CO_2 reduction, which, at the same time, in countries with a high dependence on fossil energy, will lead to a price increase and, sometimes, to importing cheaper electricity (Giuzio et al., 2019). Thus, this phenomenon will contribute to inflation and economic changes.

As mentioned earlier, the financial system's stability is determined by the banking sector's stability. At the same time, the latter depends on the financial standing of banks in the sector, or rather on the economic and financial situation of the weakest links in this banking system. The key determinants of a bank's financial strength, in addition to its profitability and asset quality, are capital adequacy and liquidity. Given the above, the perception of green assets remains a particularly important issue from the capital adequacy and liquidity perspective. If banks perceive the risks associated with such financial instruments as high and their liquidity as low, these will become unattractive in terms of the parameters determining quantitative supervisory standards. Hence, the initiatives for regulatory change towards being able to capture them in a more favourable way from the perspective of how they impact bank performance (Niedziółka, 2021).

The growing need for implementing appropriate regulations and solutions is addressed in a way by European Banking Authority actions aimed at (Ziemba, 2023), among others:

reorienting capital flows towards sustainable investments to achieve sustainable growth conducive to social inclusion;
managing financial risks arising from climate change, resource depletion, environmental degradation and social issues;
promoting transparency and long-term perspective in financial and business activities.

EBA has transformed these objectives into real actions, ready to be implemented in the financial sector, including (Ziemba, 2023) through sustainable operations that are classified by a common EU system; green financial products marked with EU standards and labels; support for investment in sustainable projects, and development of sustainability models.

The plan to make the financial industry more sustainable requires the banking sector participants to disclose whether their funds are exposed to ESG risks, and to report on how they invest in sustainability. These issues are addressed by the SFDR, which is at the heart of the European Commission's 2018 Sustainable Finance Roadmap (SFDR, 2019). With the SFDR, consumers have greater transparency on the sustainability of financial products. The aim of the SFDR is to channel private investment towards sustainable investments while preventing 'greenwashing'.

Specific SFDR obligations for financial institutions depend on a given legal entity's role. This is important because different disclosure obligations apply to financial market participants (who provide SFDR products) and to financial advisers (who advise on SFDR products). The first group has to disclose on their website their policy on incorporating sustainability risks both into their investment decision-making, and into investment or insurance advice provided to clients. Financial market participants should disclose (whenever large entities and large holdings are involved), or (in other cases) warn against or explain the main negative sustainability impacts of investment decisions and provide information on due diligence. On the other hand, financial advisers should explain the negative sustainability impacts of investments. In summary, this regulation aims to set out rules on obligations as regards sustainability information. Specifically, the three main pillars of these new rules are limiting the potential for greenwashing, ensuring regulatory neutrality (developing a disclosure toolkit) and defining regulated financial service sectors (Deloitte, 2021).

In order to be able to determine the impact of climate risk on the health of the banking system, it is therefore not superfluous to introduce mandatory stress tests, primarily for systemically important institutions. These tests should cover scenarios involving a significant increase in charges payable by polluters (Huang et al., 2019). These measures are justified insofar as some financial institutions have significant exposure to corporate clients operating in carbon-intensive sectors. The need to integrate climate risk into the financial stability monitoring system and to identify areas where climate change can impact financial stability can also be identified as an important demand in this regard (NGFS, 2019). As P. Niedziółka (2021) points out, Key Risk Indicators (KRIs), which use mathematical formulas and models to estimate the potential for a specific type of natural resource degradation, are useful as a tool in this regard. KRIs can act as early warning indicators of an increasing risk exposure. They differ from KPIs in that the latter measure how well something is being done, whereas KRIs serve to quantify the potential for future negative impacts (Niedziółka, 2021). An increase in the level of total risk, determined by climate risk evaluation, will probably increase the price of financing. This makes it necessary to provide incentives to finance climate and environmental projects (especially with banks showing a tendency for deleveraging and avoiding exposures with unsatisfactory risk-to-return ratio, such as exposures related to energy generation).

In the context of challenges facing the financial sector, it is also important to emphasise the fact that efforts to slow down global warming and environmental and climate action must be long-term and coordinated in order to have the expected effect. It is also important to share experiences and applied practices and implement internationally those developments that have been identified as optimal. An example of such an initiative is the Network of Central Banks and Supervisors for Greening the Financial System, NGFS, which, as at the end of 2022, had 134 members and 21 observers (NGFS, 2023). In addition to central banks, this community includes national and international supervisory institutions and international development banks. The primary objective of this initiative is to develop awareness of the need to manage environmental and climate risks. It is noteworthy that NGFS members particularly emphasise the need to strengthen the role of the financial system in achieving the goals set out in the Paris Agreement. Indeed, the financial system can significantly accelerate but also slow down the achievement of emission reduction targets.

While central banks and financial regulatory authorities play an important role in promoting green and sustainable finance at a global level, this role, as noted by Thompson (2023), could be greater. In banking, Basel III requires banks to assess the impact of specific environmental risks but does not explicitly address broader risks to financial stability associated with systemic environmental risks. The Network for Greening the Financial System helps coordinate the work of central banks and regulators to address climate and environmental risks and foster the development of green and sustainable finance (Thompson, 2023).

A wide range of alliances, initiatives and groups have been established to align financial sector activities with the goals of the Paris Agreement, the UN SDGs and broadly defined sustainability goals. Many of these are partnerships between intergovernmental agencies, such as the UNEP, and financial sector institutions and associations. A key partnership in this area is the UNEP Finance Initiative (UNEP FI), which developed the PRI, PRB and PSI, among others (Thompson, 2023).

The development of financial instruments segment creates the need to work out mechanisms related to reporting not only by financial institutions but also by economic entities. With the increasing importance of ESG factors, reporting of non-financial data, in addition to strictly financial data, is becoming a vital element of decisions made by a number of economic actors (Dagiliene & Nedzinskiene, 2018; Stolowy & Paugam, 2018). Thus, investors, analysts, banks, debt financing providers and asset managers should expect and require additional information from economic actors on environmental, social and corporate governance factors.

It is worth noting that companies' level of reporting has been on the rise for both European entities and in other parts of the world. For example, according to the 2023 Sustainability Reporting in Focus report by the Governance & Accountability Institute (G&A Institute, 2023), in 2022, 98% of the 500 largest and most liquid US companies reported on their ESG activities, compared to less than 20% in 2011. Further growth in this area is particularly important, both in terms of improving the quality of information provided and broadening the range of actors to also include those with smaller business operations. Companies are demonstrating their commitment to sustainability, for example through ISO certification (Weston & Nandi, 2023) and inclusion of non-financial factors in data on their ownership structure. Thus, further development of the tools in place is needed in investment processes to ensure environmental and social factors are also taken into account when making investments, in addition to the traditional fundamental financial analysis (Kim & Li, 2021).

ESG factors also influence the cost of capital when contracting a debt, or issuing bonds or equity instruments, and are important when capital market instruments are outstanding. Compliance with ESG standards has a positive impact on a company's reputation and, in the case of highly capitalised companies, makes it possible to obtain an ESG rating from one of the leading institutions (for example, Reuters/Refinitiv provides rating for around 9,000 companies). A high rating increases investor interest in the stock and thus its price. It does not directly affect the company's capital but increases its recognisability and prestige, which can translate positively into its operating performance. In addition, the margin is reduced if a bond issuance is planned in the future. It is worth mentioning that a high ESG rating has a significant impact on the share price, especially when the company is included in an ETF that holds companies with a high ESG rating. As a result, the share price of high ESG-rated companies is less dependent on specific risk than it used to be, while becoming more impacted by the risk of other ETF companies. This is a favourable phenomenon that, in most cases, supports the share price.

The role of the financial sector in financing green investments is also that of educating key stakeholders (in particular customers and ultimate beneficiaries). There is ample scope for financial institutions to actively communicate the need to implement sustainability-oriented changes, thus supporting the processes underway, as well as pointing out the risks associated with failure to take adaptation measures (which risks may include, inter alia, reduced liquidity, reduced or no access to finance and increased financing costs). Financial market institutions can act as ambassadors of sorts for the ESG transition, pointing out the benefits it entails and actively promoting investment opportunities meeting the sustainability principles. In addition, they can create or support the creation of investment or insurance solutions, both those that actively promote ESG-compliant investment and those that enable clients to meet their own sustainability goals, such as seeking to reduce their carbon footprint.

Summarising the challenges and prospects of the financial sector in light of climate challenges, further initiatives should focus on the following areas of action:

public incentives – e.g. in the form of special investment funds, or advice for projects that support sustainable development;

standardisation – efforts to increase transparency in the financial market, especially in terms of comparability of the available information, making it easier for investors to select genuinely sustainable issuers or assets. A good example of a particularly useful tool is the Taxonomy, which serves to verify respective types of business activity but not a whole company or a specific issuer;

disclosures – these are designed to improve the quality and availability of non-financial information in the financial market, which will have a positive impact on its transparency and efficiency. From the point of view of capital-seeking companies, the direct benefit of disclosures containing high-quality ESG data will be to make them more attractive to those offering financing. Another significant macroeconomic effect of disclosures may be to increase the financial system stability by improving risk management within financial institutions and among companies;

corporate governance and strategic management – corporate governance proposals are expected to reduce the aforementioned problem of the so-called capital market myopia. As with disclosures, improvements in this area can result in increased financial stability at a macroeconomic level;

financial regulation – aimed at influencing the allocation of private capital by creating incentives to encourage investment in more sustainable assets.

To ensure the existing opportunities are adequately harnessed, and risks minimised, a commitment is required from all market participants, including the government, with a particular role to play for the financial system as a whole. Thus, the following should be identified as possible courses of action:

stable institutional and regulatory environment – the need for a stable regulatory environment applies to many markets that are key to the success of the transition to sustainable finance: energy, gas, utilities (including waste) and transport;

systemic education of the market – it is necessary to carry out educational activities and organise information campaigns aimed at business leaders, entrepreneurs and representatives of central and local government administration;

competitive financing – the development of the capital market should continue to be supported by mobilising long-term savings but also a thorough analysis should be conducted of the potential benefits of developing alternative trading platforms based on blockchain, as well as fintech and insurtech;

technological and expert support – updating business strategy and adapting to new risks will not be possible without access to relevant data, as well as the ability to analyse it. That is why the capacity for micro-level data collection and analysis must be strengthened as it is of essential significance to improving the process of planning and implementing private investments as well as the quality of evidence-based policies.

4 Assessing the efficiency of public and private sector financing of environmental measures

4.1 Level of achievement of climate objectives in light of the available financial sources and solutions

As the discussion so far has shown, the last decades have seen an increase in public awareness on a number of ethical levels, especially on the issues of sustainability, climate change or equality in the broadest sense. Recent years have also been characterised by a growing environmental awareness and demand for the promotion of renewable energy sources. This is confirmed by alarming reports from various institutions and organisations indicating that climate change is an urgent issue requiring decisive action (cf. UNCC, 2023). At a summit in New York on 25–27 September 2015, the leaders of UN member states made a number of ambitious commitments when they signed the document 'Transforming our world: the 2030 Agenda for Sustainable Development'. The resolution they signed outlines 17 goals (Sustainable Development Goals, SDGs) and 169 targets to be achieved by 2030. The act encourages collective action to reduce poverty in all its forms, ensure access to education, food and clean water as well as actively promote equal opportunities, support human rights, peace and stability in the world, protect the environment, mitigate climate change and ensure access to sustainable energy sources. It is noteworthy that in addition to the goals themselves, more specific tasks were identified to enable the achievement of overall objectives. They are all divided into five thematic groups directly related to each objective. These areas coincide with sustainable development foundations relating to three dimensions: economic, social and environmental. In addition, the implementation of the individual goals is monitored on an ongoing basis by specially designed indicators, verified at national level by governmental institutions (United Nations, 2015).

As the sustainable development targets are ambitious, their implementation requires significant financial resources and the cooperation of many communities, from public and private sectors alike. At the same time, there is a need globally to ensure policy coherence for sustainable development, and to carry out educational and promotional activities. This role has been largely assumed by the United Nations.

According to the United Nations Framework Convention on Climate Change (UNFCCC), which sets out the principles for international cooperation to reduce

DOI: 10.4324/9781003434689-5

emissions of greenhouse gases (GHG) responsible for global warming, climate finance has been defined as funding source at the local, national or supranational level – from public, private and alternative funding sources – to support mitigation and adaptation measures to counter climate change. It is about the investments that governments, corporations and households need to make to shift the global economy to the low-carbon pathway to reduce GHG emissions and build countries' resilience to climate change (cf. Hong et al., 2020).

Of the aforementioned 17 SDGs, several are directly or indirectly related to green and low-carbon energy development and the environment. These are: SDG7 (affordable and clean energy) and SDG13 (climate action), which relate directly to the aforementioned aspects. There are also SDG3 (good health and well-being), SDG14 (life under water) and SDG15 (life on land), which can be identified as indirectly linked.

As indicated above, environmental and climate issues are directly addressed by

SDG7 – oriented towards ensuring access to clean and affordable energy for all, which is key to the development of agriculture, business, communications, education, healthcare and transport (UN Energy, 2024) and

SDG13 – related to urgent action to combat climate change and its impacts (UN Climate Change, 2024).

As revealed by the results of a study by Carvalho and Santos (2024) based on an analysis of 363 articles, the energy sector plays a key role in achieving the aforementioned two SDGs. Critical issues in this regard include governance, policy frameworks and technological innovation. At the same time, this research also highlights the need for interdisciplinary collaboration and a holistic approach to the complex challenges of sustainable energy development.

As far as SDG7 is concerned, its importance stems from the role energy plays in today's world. Overcoming challenges and seizing opportunities is directly linked to having access to it. Electricity and heat energy are essential for doing work, ensuring security, combating climate change and producing food. At the same time, however, energy consumption is a major contributor to climate change, accounting for ca. 60% of total global GHG emissions. While it is evident that action is being taken to achieve sustainable energy goals, it is not enough. In the last decade, progress has been made in the use of electricity from renewable sources like water, solar and wind power and the ratio of energy consumed per unit of gross domestic product (GDP) is also falling. However, the problem is far from being solved.

As indicated by the UN, between 2015 and 2021, the percentage of the global population with access to electricity increased from 87% to 91%. Ensuring universal access to affordable electricity by 2030 means investing in clean energy sources such as solar, wind and thermal energy (UN Energy, 2024).

Expanding infrastructure and upgrading technology to provide clean energy in all developing countries is a key objective that can both stimulate economic growth and help the environment. At the same time, in terms of financing, adequate support is necessary in the form of appropriate financial mechanisms (Manko &

Table 4.1 SDG 7 targets (included in the 2030 Agenda for Sustainable Development)

7.1	By 2030, ensure universal access to affordable, reliable and modern energy services.
7.2	By 2030, increase substantially the share of renewable energy in the global energy mix.
7.3	By 2030, double the global rate of improvement in energy efficiency.
7.A	By 2030, enhance international cooperation to facilitate access to clean energy research and technology, including renewable energy, energy efficiency and advanced and cleaner fossil-fuel technology, and promote investment in energy infrastructure and clean energy technology.
7.B	By 2030, expand infrastructure and upgrade technology for supplying modern and sustainable energy services for all in developing countries, in particular least developed countries, small island developing states and land-locked developing countries, in accordance with their respective programmes of support.

Source: Own elaboration based on https://www.un.org/sustainabledevelopment/energy.

Watkins, 2022). The main tasks of this objective included in the 2030 Agenda for Sustainable Development are presented in Table 4.1.

As can be read in a special report on the SDGs prepared by the UN (UN, 2023, p. 26):

> the world continues to advance towards sustainable energy targets – but not fast enough. At the current pace, about 660 million people will still lack access to electricity and close to 2 billion people will still rely on polluting fuels and technologies for cooking by 2030;
>
> renewable sources power nearly 30% of energy consumption in the electricity sector, but challenges remain in heating and transport sectors. Developing countries experience 9.6% annual growth in renewable energy installation, but despite enormous needs, international financial flows for clean energy continue to decline;
>
> to ensure access to energy for all by 2030, we must accelerate electrification, increase investments in renewable energy, improve energy efficiency and develop enabling policies and regulatory frameworks.

Monitoring SDG 7 in the EU context requires looking at changes in energy consumption, energy supply and energy access. As Eurostat points out in its report on the level of implementation of the SDGs in the European Union covering the period 2016–2021, the European community has made little progress towards this SDG during the period mentioned. In the area of energy consumption, the EU needs to accelerate in light of the more ambitious energy reduction targets agreed for 2030. In the area of EU energy supply, on the other hand, improvements towards the newly agreed 2030 target of 42.5% renewable energy (although this rate has slowed down in recent years) are evident. It is worth noting that the EU has achieved its 2020 renewable energy target of 20% and has slightly reduced its dependence on imports. At the same time, access to conventional energy has improved over the past few years (Eurostat, 2023). It should be noted that the figures quoted refer to the period before the outbreak of the war in Ukraine, which had a significant impact on the energy market situation.

An in-depth analysis of the implementation of SDG7 between 2015 and 2020 for respective EU countries was carried out by Dmytrów et al. (2022), who found that Norway, Denmark, Estonia, Croatia, Latvia, Sweden and the UK were the best performing countries, while Belgium, Bulgaria, Cyprus, Lithuania and Finland were the worst.

The guiding element of the EU action in the context of SDG7 is the European Green Deal (EGD), which envisages the decarbonisation of European energy systems to achieve climate neutrality by 2050. Furthermore, in order to achieve the new EU climate target in 2030, the Commission has proposed a set of interlinked measures in the areas of energy, transport, taxation and climate policy, also known as 'Fit for 55'. The European Instrument for Recovery and Resilience, too, supports reforms and investments in sustainable mobility, energy efficiency and renewable energy. When discussing the topic under consideration, mention should also be made of the new EU strategic plan to reduce the community's dependence on imports (in particular from Russia) of energy and energy resources, the REPowerEE. In March 2022, the communication on security of supply and stable energy prices outlined immediate measures to prepare for the next two winters, including mandatory gas storage. Importantly, the EU has since agreed on emergency rules for gas supply that set out voluntary and mandatory reductions in energy consumption and introduced an emergency regulation that includes joint gas purchasing, a market correction mechanism for gas trade, market interventions in the electricity sector and the promotion of solidarity between Member States.

In terms of energy consumption, it is worth highlighting that the directive was revised to improve energy efficiency by at least 32.5% by 2030 compared to the reference year 2007. In July 2021, the Commission proposed a revision that would implement energy efficiency as a priority in all sectors, furthermore increasing the ambition of the 2030 target and making it binding for the whole EU. Negotiations between the EU co-legislators concluded in March 2023 with an agreement to reduce total energy consumption by at least 11.7% in 2030, compared to 2020 energy consumption projections by 2030 (Eurostat, 2023, p. 135).

In terms of energy supply, the 2018 Renewable Energy Directive set a binding target for the share of renewables in total energy consumption to reach at least 32% by 2030. The Commission proposed a revision of the directive in July 2021, including an increase to 40% and strengthening measures for transport, heating and cooling, and a more circular energy system. In May 2022, the REPowerEU plan proposed a further increase in the target to 45% by 2030. Negotiations between the EU co-legislators concluded in March 2023 with an agreement to increase the share of renewable energy in total EU energy consumption to 42.5% by 2030, with an additional 2.5% indicative top up to reach 45% (Eurostat, 2023, p. 135).

Regarding access to sustainable energy, the European Pillar of Social Rights lists the area in question among the essential services to which everyone should have access. In April 2022, The Commission set up a Coordination Group on energy poverty and vulnerable consumers to help Member States in the fight against energy poverty. The SAFE (Supporting Affordable Energy) measures proposed in October 2022 under the Cohesion Policy aim to allow Member States to use unspent funds under 2014–2020 to provide direct support to vulnerable families and small- and medium-sized enterprises (SMEs) to help them face increased energy costs. The EU Energy Poverty Advisory Hub is an initiative that provides a central platform offering expertise on energy poverty to local authorities and other stakeholders (Eurostat, 2023, p. 135).

It is noticeable that in an era of rapid climate change and uncertain geopolitical situation caused by the war in Ukraine, the problem of energy access is a serious issue (Dmytrów et al., 2022). It is becoming important to use renewable energy sources and to ensure as much energy independence as possible. All the more so as European countries' power systems are interconnected, so it is in everyone's common interest to have access to cheap, clean and sustainable energy.

As far as SDG 13 is concerned, the climate changes currently taking place are being felt in every country on all continents. They are disrupting the development of national economies and threatening human lives and entire societies. For economic actors, this often means having to remodel the way they do business. Table 4.2 presents the change in average global temperatures from 1953 to 2022. As this data shows, every corner of the world has seen an increase in temperature over time.

Combating climate change is costly already, and further increases in expenditure are to be expected in the future. Societies in various countries are experiencing severe impacts of climate change, including those related to changing weather conditions, rising sea levels and extreme weather events. At the same time, as can be seen, man-made GHG emissions continue to rise, resulting in further climate change. This implies the need for action on an appropriate scale, otherwise the average temperature of the globe will rise to more than 3°C this century, with some regions of the world experiencing even higher temperatures. The poorest countries and vulnerable groups will suffer the most. Admittedly, effective and inexpensive solutions are becoming more widely available that can help countries transition to a resilient economy based on cleaner technologies. Change is accelerating as, for

Table 4.2 Average air temperatures worldwide in 1953–2022

Region	*1953–1962*	*1963–1972*	*1973–1982*	*1983–1992*	*1993–2002*	*2003–2012*	*2013–2022*
Europe	7.4°C	7.1°C	7.2°C	7.5°C	8.0°C	8.3°C	8.8°C
Asia	15.8°C	15.5°C	15.6°C	15.7°C	16.2°C	16.5°C	16.9°C
North America	9.8°C	9.0°C	8.9°C	9.6°C	9.9°C	10.2°C	11.0°C
Central America	27.0°C	27.0°C	27.2°C	27.2°C	27.8°C	27.5°C	27.6°C
Africa	20.0°C	19.9°C	19.8°C	20.2°C	20.2°C	20.7°C	20.8°C
Australia	19.4°C	19.6°C	19.6°C	19.9°C	19.8°C	20.0°C	20.6°C
Worldwide	12.4°C	11.9°C	12.1°C	12.4°C	12.9°C	13.1°C	13.7°C

Source: Own elaboration based on https://www.worlddata.info/global-warming.php.

Table 4.3 SDG 13 targets (included in the 2030 Agenda for Sustainable Development)

13.1	Strengthen resilience and adaptive capacity to climate-related hazards and natural disasters in all countries.
13.2	Integrate climate change measures into national policies, strategies and planning.
13.3	Improve education, awareness-raising and human and institutional capacity on climate change mitigation, adaptation, impact reduction and early warning.
13.A	Implement the commitment undertaken by developed-country parties to the United Nations Framework Convention on Climate Change to a goal of mobilizing jointly $100 billion annually by 2020 from all sources to address the needs of developing countries in the context of meaningful mitigation actions and transparency on implementation and fully operationalize the Green Climate Fund through its capitalization as soon as possible.
13.B	Promote mechanisms for raising capacity for effective climate change-related planning and management in least developed countries and small island developing States, including focusing on women, youth and local and marginalized communities.

Source: Own elaboration based on https://www.un.org/sustainabledevelopment/climate-change.

example, more and more people embrace renewable energy and other measures that reduce GHG emissions and strengthen adaptation efforts, but more action is needed. Since GHG emissions in any place on the earth affect people all over the world, tackling climate change should be seen as a global challenge. Therefore, this issue requires coordinated cooperation and internationally developed solutions as this is the only way to help developing countries make the transition to a low-carbon economy (UN Climate Change, 2024). The main tasks of this goal included in the 2030 Agenda for Sustainable Development are included in Table 4.3.

The above-mentioned UN special report on SDGs (UN, 2023, p. 38) presents the following conclusions with respect to SDG13

with a climate cataclysm looming, the pace and scale of current climate action plans are wholly insufficient to effectively tackle climate change. Increasingly frequent and intense extreme weather events are already impacting every region on Earth. Rising temperatures will escalate these hazards further, posing grave risks;

the Intergovernmental Panel on Climate Change (IPCC) emphasises that deep, rapid and sustained reductions in greenhouse gas (GHG) emissions are essential in all sectors, beginning now and continuing throughout this decade. To limit global warming to 1.5°C above preindustrial levels, emissions must already be decreasing and need to be cut by almost half by 2030, just seven years away;

urgent and transformative action is crucial, going beyond mere plans and promises. It requires raising ambition, covering entire economies and moving towards climate-resilient development, while outlining a clear path to achieve net-zero emissions. Time is running out, and immediate measures are necessary to avoid catastrophic consequences and secure a sustainable future for generations to come.

SDG 13 aims to achieve a climate-neutral world by mid-century and limit the global warming to well below 2°C – with a target of 1.5°C – compared to pre-industrial times. Its goal is to strengthen countries' climate resilience and adaptive capacity, with a particular focus on supporting the least developed countries.

Climate change increases global temperatures, alters rainfall patterns, raises global average sea levels, triggers extreme weather events, damages biodiversity and increases ocean acidity. Its effects affect social, environmental and economic factors and may cause some regions to face food and water shortages. For the European Union, the monitoring of SDG13 focuses on climate change mitigation, climate impacts and initiatives to support climate action. As the above-presented rising surface temperature trend continues, the European Union faces environmental, social and economic losses. In the case of net GHG emissions, an increase was recorded for 2021 (after a decrease at the peak of the COVID-19 pandemic in 2020). Although a decline has been evident over recent years, the ambitious target of a 55% reduction in net GHG emissions by 2030 is still a long way off. As mentioned earlier, these additional costs are already foreseen in the Fit for 55 package with the revision of the EU Emissions Trading System (ETS), and the Emissions Sharing Regulation, which sets binding annual targets for Member States. The 2030 target includes net removals of GHG emissions from land use, land use change and forestry, which continue to decline and thus contribute less to progress towards the net GHG target. The share of renewables has been increasing in the EU in recent years, but more progress will be needed to reach the new, more ambitious 2030 target. On a positive note, there has also been an increase in the number of local and regional governments that have joined the Covenant of Mayors on Climate and Energy on implementing adaptation measures. Significant progress has also been made in terms of financial support, and climate-related spending for developing countries is also increasing (Eurostat, 2023, p. 235). At the same time, however, it is important to note that not all parts of the world are taking such advanced action and on such a scale. The investments that are being made as well as the economic and social transition are generating costs that various communities or professional groups are having serious trouble accepting, which manifests itself, among other things, in various forms of protest.

In terms of climate change mitigation, the EU signed the Paris Agreement in 2015. European climate law sets a target of reducing net GHG emissions by at least 55% between 1990 and 2030 and achieving climate neutrality by 2050, a key objective of the EGD. In 2021, the European Commission proposed a package of new and revised energy legislation – the so-called Fit for 55. This package comprises a set of interconnected measures and includes strengthened and extended carbon emission prices, targets, standards and support measures. It also sets a target for natural carbon sinks of 310 million tonnes CO_2 equivalent. Some of these measures have already been adopted, while for others provisional agreements or discussions are still ongoing. The Just Transition Mechanism supports regions with the highest carbon intensity or with the largest number of people working in fossil fuels. The Social Climate Fund will support vulnerable households, micro-enterprises and transport users to cope with impacts in road transport and buildings (Eurostat,

2023, p. 237). At the same time, the EU's adaptation strategy calls for smarter, faster and more systematic adaptation so that by 2050 the European community becomes a climate-resilient society, fully adapted to the inevitable impacts of climate change. Climate law mandates continued progress in increasing adaptive capacity, strengthening resilience and reducing vulnerability.

Regarding climate finance, it is important to highlight that support for climate action comes from the EU budget, Recovery and Resilience Facility and climate-related funds, including modernisation funds. An important aspect in this context is the sustainable business taxonomy, requiring sustainability-related disclosures to investors for financial products and establishing new climate-friendly labels for investment portfolios. This implementation is oriented towards shifting private and public resources towards sustainable activities. The REPowerEU plan aims to deliver EUR 210 billion in additional investment in energy efficiency, energy infrastructure and renewable energy. The new Green Deal plan includes significant support for solar panels, wind turbines, heat pumps, hydrogen, energy storage, electric vehicles and critical raw material extraction, processing and recycling. In order to support developing countries, the EU and its Member States are contributing to delivering on the developed countries' pledge under the Paris Agreement to provide USD 100 billion per year in climate finance by 2025 (Eurostat, 2023, p. 237).

It is worth pointing out that, despite the large sums of money allocated to climate finance, the scale of the needs as well as its accessibility and the way it is allocated, often arouse strong emotions (Economist, 2023).

As mentioned earlier, in addition to the SDGs, which are directly related to environmental and climate protection, it is possible to identify those that address these issues indirectly, namely: SDG3 (good health and well-being), SDG14 (life under water) and SDG15 (life on land).

SDG3 is oriented towards ensuring healthy lives and promoting well-being for all at all ages. It is worth noting that much progress has been made in this area in recent years. As the UN points out, 146 out of 200 countries or areas have already achieved or are on track to achieve the SDG target for under-5 mortality. Effective HIV treatment has reduced global AIDS-related deaths by 52% since 2010, and at least one neglected tropical disease has been eliminated in 47 countries (UN Health, 2024). However, inequalities in access to healthcare persist and the COVID-19 pandemic and other ongoing crises have hindered progress towards the goal, e.g. childhood immunisation has seen the largest decline in three decades and deaths from TB and malaria have increased from pre-pandemic levels. It is worth noting that the SDGs represent a bold commitment to end the epidemics of AIDS, TB, malaria and other infectious diseases by 2030. In addition, the goal is to achieve universal health insurance and ensure access to safe and affordable medicines and vaccines for all. Therefore, in order to overcome these failures and address long-standing health care shortcomings, increased investment in health systems is needed to support countries to recover and build resilience to future health threats. For EU countries, the main focus is on healthy lives, determinants of health, causes of death and access to healthcare. Over the period 2016–2021, the

EU has made progress on most health-related indicators, although the impact of the COVID-19 pandemic is now clearly visible in some areas (Eurostat, 2023).

SDG14 is about the conservation and sustainable use of oceans, seas and marine resources. Healthy oceans and seas are essential for human existence and life on the Earth. It should be noted that the oceans cover three-quarters of the Earth's surface, contain 97% of the Earth's water and account for 99% of the planet's living space by volume. They provide key natural resources, including food, medicines, biofuels and other products. In addition, they help decompose and dispose of waste and pollution, and their coastal ecosystems act as buffers to reduce storm damage. It is worth noting that they also act as the largest carbon sink on the planet (UN Oceans, 2024).

It is worrying that marine pollution is reaching extreme levels, with forecasts predicting further increase. Plastic is the most damaging type of ocean pollution. Increasing levels of waste in oceans around the world also have a serious environmental and economic impact. It is estimated that between 5 and 12 million metric tonnes of plastic enter the oceans each year, costing an estimated USD 12 billion a year – including clean-up costs and financial losses to fisheries and other industries. About 89% of the plastic litter found on the ocean floor are single-use items such as plastic bags.

In the context of environmental protection, the ocean's role stems from the fact that it absorbs around 23% of annual CO_2 emissions generated by human activities and helps mitigate climate change. The ocean has also absorbed more than 90% of the excess heat in the climate system. Ocean heat is reaching record levels, causing widespread marine heat waves, threatening rich ecosystems and killing coral reefs around the world (UN Oceans, 2024).

Today, the average pH of the ocean is 8.1, about 30% more acidic than in pre-industrial times. Ocean acidification threatens the survival of marine life, disrupts the food web and undermines the vital services provided by the ocean and our own food security. Therefore, careful management of this vital global resource is a key component of a sustainable future. This includes increasing funding for ocean science, stepping up conservation efforts and urgently turning the tide on climate change to protect the planet's largest ecosystem. Current conservation efforts are not yet meeting the urgent need to protect this vast but fragile resource.

As far as the EU is concerned, SDG14 monitoring mainly covers trends in the areas of ocean health, marine conservation and sustainable fishing. Moderate progress towards the goal in the period 2016–2021 should be noted in this regard. On the positive side, marine protected areas have increased and fish stocks in EU marine waters (especially in the North-East Atlantic) seem to be recovering due to reduced fishing pressure. However, unsustainable trends are evident in the areas of ocean acidification (due to carbon emissions from human activities) and eutrophication (Eurostat, 2023).

SDG15 addresses the conservation of life on land. More specifically, it focuses on protecting, restoring and promoting the sustainable use of terrestrial ecosystems, sustainably managing forests, combating desertification, halting and reversing land degradation and stopping the biodiversity loss.

As the UN points out, the Earth's ecosystems are critical to sustaining human life, contribute to more than half of global GDP and encompass a variety of cultural, spiritual and economic values. The main concerns to be identified here are the threat of a triple crisis of climate change, pollution and biodiversity loss. Between 2015 and 2019, at least 100 million hectares of healthy and productive land were degraded every year, affecting the lives of 1.3 billion people. Furthermore, agricultural expansion is the direct cause of almost 90% of deforestation. This is directly linked to our food systems, with oil palm harvests accounting for 7% of global deforestation between 2000 and 2018. This means that global and regional efforts to maintain forest ecosystems as well as their social, economic and environmental functions are essential, particularly for developing and tropical countries. It is worth noting that forests cover almost 31% of the world's surface and are home to more than 80% of all terrestrial animal, plant and insect species. However, biodiversity is declining faster than at any other time in human history. Globally, one-fifth of the Earth's surface is degraded, an area almost the size of India and the Russian Federation combined. Land degradation is driving species extinction and exacerbating climate change, and the biodiversity and ecosystem services that underpin it can also be the basis of climate change adaptation and disaster risk reduction strategies as they can provide benefits that enhance human resilience (UN Biodiversity, 2024).

As far as the EU is concerned, SDG15 monitoring focuses on trends in ecosystem condition, land degradation and biodiversity. On average, the EU has moved slightly away from the SDG15 targets over the course of 2016–2021. While the EU's terrestrial protected areas and forest area have grown, recent trends in pollutant concentrations in EU rivers have been mixed. Species biodiversity indicators show a long-term and steady decline in common birds in the EU (Eurostat, 2023).

To conclude this part of the monograph, it is important, in the Authors' view, to highlight the commitment, legislative, organisational and also in terms of capital in the EU, which often stands out above other world regions in the fight for climate and environmental protection.

In spite of the challenges and recent crises, the EU is fully engaged and committed to making progress towards all the SDGs and will continue to monitor them.

At the same time, however, the scale of the challenge remains large, confirming the need to secure significant financial resources. This creates the need also to educate and promote, within the society as well as among entrepreneurs, investors or financial institutions, the knowledge and objectives of sustainable development. In addition, in many cases, the study of the implementation of individual goals is limited by the lack of access to relevant data (an example is the inability to include information on access to electricity in many analyses) or long delays in accessing them.

As can be seen, external events, such as the COVID-19 pandemic and the war in Ukraine, to which the next subsection of the monograph is dedicated, also have an impact on the achievement of the goals outlined in the Paris Agreement.

4.2 Impact of external factors (COVID-19 and the war in Ukraine) on the financing of environmental objectives

The instability of the macroeconomic environment due to various events, whether regional or global in nature, causes risk factors to materialise, affecting the level of respective actors' capacity and potential commitment to meet the environmental and climate challenges. They also affect the scale of funding allocated to environmental objectives. Examples include the problems experienced by economic actors in such situations when it comes to the availability of raw materials and production inputs from the East, fuel supply shocks (price increases), constraints related to the labour availability as well as limited access to funds from capital markets and the banking sector.

There is a prevailing view among business stakeholders that sustainability with the accompanying CSR and environmental, social and governance (ESG) is an approach that can be implemented and applied on a large scale mostly in good economic times, while in times of recession and greater risks, it becomes less urgent and relevant (cf. Giannarakis & Teotokas, 2011). A financial crisis is usually experienced by companies in the form of liquidity constraints. At the same time, it can be pointed out that expenditure reductions are often linked to new growth strategies in times of recession, which aim to increase economic efficiency and productivity. Amid recession, taking care of, for example, environmental aspects is seen purely as an expense as it is difficult to find its tangible benefits in the form of incoming cash flows.

Understanding of the organisation, its constraints and its processes, gained through the implementing CSR or ESG strategies, makes it possible to limit the negative recession impact of the organisation – both in the financial and social sphere (Miedziak, 2023). The measurements associated with preparing sustainable reporting help determine an organisation's ability to function under different conditions as well as test its capacity to achieve goals that may be consistently overshadowed by other priorities (Stainer, 2006).

In times of recession or economic crisis, the potential for adaptation is greatly limited, resulting in a reduction of non-compulsory inputs to the necessary minimum, most often that required by law, e.g. the need to use purification filters in factories. The 'new deal' efforts within an organisation are often determined by factors arising from its environment, e.g. globalisation (Tanimoto, 2004), which influences domestic actors to become socially responsible by following the example of newcomers.

Sustainable development has long-term effects (e.g. more efficient development), through which different groups of actors (including economic actors) can achieve the desired benefits and overcome obstacles and crises caused by various events (Ziemba, 2023).

An event that put in jeopardy the achievement of environmental goals was the COVID-19 pandemic, which confronted much of the world with a new crisis in late 2019 and early 2020. This situation meant a significant hurdle to implementing sustainable development policies due to the need for countries and actors to focus on tackling this threat (also using financial resources). It is not an exaggeration to say that the unexpected COVID-19 pandemic of 2020–2023 posed the greatest threat to human health in decades. It caused almost 7 million deaths and changed the world in many dimensions. On 5 May 2023, the World Health Organisation recognised the end of the pandemic by declaring that COVID-19 is no longer a global health threat (UN NEWS, 2023).

Free movement of people and goods around the world is an important part of the global economy and globalisation. Unfortunately, this also enables viruses and bacteria to spread. In the case of COVID-19, the route of transmission was primarily through air links as well as large concentrations of people, especially in cities. In the spring of 2020, in order to combat COVID-19, most countries around the world imposed full lockdowns, which had a particular impact on both social and economic life.

D'Anselmi (2020) points out that the coronavirus pandemic represented a critical test for the whole social corporate responsibility concept. He also notes how crucial it is to involve public actors in defending this approach. In order to maintain the concept of sustainability and climate protection as a viable way to influence the environment, governmental support and the creation of a common global protection and support system is necessary. Carroll (2021) points out that the global pandemic put SCR approaches to the test, and the emerging evidence supports the view that many companies were trying to reset their thinking to cope with the crisis and meet public expectations. An approach where owners' risk is the main value is highlighted, among others, by Chang (2011), who points out that it leads to a sort of passive consent for companies to focus their activities on maximising owners' benefits at the expense of their environment (including natural environment and workers). It is then assumed that the benefits generated for the owners will return to society in the form of investment (whether in the company or in the community). Meanwhile, empirical studies indicate that the share of profits returned to society by owners is relatively low (30–60%, depending on the study). Most of the profits generated are consumed or stored as savings, which do not generate benefits for other stakeholders. A kind of acquiescence to the drip economy phenomenon is largely due to stakeholders' belief in the good intentions of the owners – without which it would have no rationale to exist.

What distinguished the COVID-19 pandemic crisis from previous crises (e.g. the economic crisis in 2008) was its causes. COVID-19 had physical causes, whereas the previous one had been due to, for example, a loss of confidence. Many organisations were forced to fight for survival, so the topic of sustainability was put on hold in the face of the pandemic as all attention focused on countering this extreme threat (IFLR, 2021). Some countries and companies argue that events such as a pandemic are not the right time for sustainability due to excessive costs, which can be seen as justified when viewing this time as a struggle for survival (Lofts, 2020). However, from a broader perspective, sustainable investments create opportunities for business growth and generate positive impacts for society, companies and the environment. Therefore, looking at the long term, the transition to a low-carbon economy is an optimal and beneficial direction. The European Commission has committed to the EGD (estimated at over EUR 1 trillion), despite the emerging claims that the cost of this investment is too high in the face of a pandemic. Central banks and governments have undertaken to support the financial system to help it survive COVID-19. In this case, this is a short-term support rather than a long-term policy, but it may be important in dealing with the immediate impact of the pandemic and driving sustainable development policies (UNDP, 2020).

COVID-19 highlighted several important ESG risks and opportunities that financial institutions and other economic actors should consider. One example is that the economic crisis increased the likelihood of the 'disorderly transition' scenario, and therefore regulators and the financial industry should focus on less optimistic climate scenarios (Klein, 2020). A number of COVID-19 crisis consequences manifested themselves immediately (e.g. business closures, bankruptcies, rising unemployment, falling interest rates), but some of the effects appeared with a delay, revealing themselves gradually (e.g. permanent changes in supply chains, working from home and reducing the need for office space and thus reducing the use of means of transport), and could also threaten the balance sheets of both economic actors and financial institutions. The pandemic and the lessons learnt from it are important for sustainable development as awareness of the links between the economy, society and government helps to decarbonise the economy and make important changes. Financial institutions and their key role in financing the transition, given their influence and capacity for financing, underwriting and investment in the long term, make it possible to follow through on set goals. Countries are committed to the low-carbon transition, and sustainable financing is key in this context. At the same time, COVID-19 has contributed, among other things, to highlighting the complexity of climate and transition risks in the financial sector (Lofts, 2020).

Cherednichenko et al. (2022) found that COVID-19 exacerbated the primary impacts of climate change, threatening food and water security. Widespread starvation due to the effects of COVID-19 is capable of causing more deaths than the virus. Improving water availability and food production is therefore crucial to eradicating hunger and poverty. This means that there is a need to strengthen adaptation and mitigation capacities. International cooperation is urgently needed to support the adaptation of climate-smart agriculture to reduce GHG emissions and thereby mitigate climate impacts, resulting in higher productivity, food security, poverty reduction and sustainable development.

The risk of gradual changes brought by COVID-19 becoming a new pandemic and post-pandemic normalcy is also pointed out by Miedziak (2023), while emphasising the need to address these challenges, and the significant role that properly standardised reporting has to play in this case. At the same time, he points to the importance of supranational standards such as the Global Reporting Initiative (GRI), which can play a significant normative role in guiding immediate and short-term best practices for COVID-19 reporting (Zharfpeykan & Ng, 2021; Pavlović & Denčić-Mihajlov, 2022).

The increasing importance of ESG factors in the activities of companies and financial institutions during the pandemic is confirmed by the research presented in a joint report by ING and EY (2021). One sign of this change is the increasing number of companies worldwide that have undertaken to report data on their emissions. These trends are also confirmed by the results of a survey conducted by KPMG (KPMG International, 2022), according to which 79% of the N100 companies (the 100 largest companies in each country surveyed) and 96% of the 250 largest global companies issued sustainability reports in 2022. This compares to 41% of the N100 and 64% of the G250 15 years earlier, in 2008.

Among the effects of the COVID-19 pandemic and the resulting global economic recession was a significant drop in ongoing investment in renewable energy, energy efficiency and other green projects. At the same time, global markets saw a dramatic decline in fossil fuel prices. Low fossil fuel prices negatively impact the development of renewable energy projects, making solar, wind and other renewable energy sources less competitive (Lu et al., 2022). This reduces investor interest in clean fuels, which could jeopardise the Paris Agreement on climate change and several SDGs. Economic recovery plans for 2021–2022 have increased global energy demand, causing a surge in the price of oil and other fossil fuels. However, the increase in fossil fuel prices was not able to immediately stimulate new investment in renewable energy and energy efficiency projects. The main reason for this low level of investment and the private investors' reluctance about the green sector is the existence of various risk factors and economic uncertainty, making investors seek safer assets.

However, positive signals can also be found, as Pawłowski and Rydzewski (2023) point out: despite tight restrictions, the highest-ever annual number of global renewable energy installations, including onshore wind and photovoltaic plants, was completed in 2020. At the same time, they stress that, regardless of the pandemic, public support for renewable energy remains strong in different regions of the world. In their view, while COVID-19 caused serious health risks and severely impacted the global economy, its consequences for climate change and energy markets were not as devastating. In the context of climate change, the impact of the COVID-19 pandemic appears to have been neutral. The reduction in air pollution levels during the 2020 lockdown was impressive but temporary. Many negative practices, such as deforestation, have not been stopped. On the other hand, despite the pandemic, the global engagement in climate change policy and commitments to decarbonise the global economy remained unwavering. It is also worth highlighting the introduction (in 2021, the second year of the pandemic) of a new and ambitious strategy to reduce an important GHG that is methane. In the context of renewable energy development, COVID-19 has not had a significant negative impact in the long term on the rapid development of solar and wind power, in terms of either the number of new installations or their capacity. Nor has it impeded the progress of new hydropower installations (less significant but still important). The above is even more interesting in light of the fact that most other industries have been hit hard by the pandemic. Moreover, the renewable energy sector growth also seems to be stable in the post-pandemic COVID-19 era, at least in the coming years.

It was not only the real economy that faced crisis amid the COVID-19 pandemic; so did the financial system itself. In other words, it was forced to tackle problems including life-or-death challenges. In just a few weeks, the financial system was subjected to changes of a magnitude similar to major world events since the World War Two (McDaniels, 2020). As pointed out by the authors of a study prepared by the consulting firm McKinsey (2020), the financial system faced great future uncertainty. Thus, understanding the similarities, differences and broader relationships between pandemics and climate risk is a critical first step towards drawing practical implications that will influence further action. As Shipalana and Chigwenya (2021) point out, efforts to overcome COVID-19 should not only be comprehensive but also involve a wide range of stakeholders. In developing countries in particular, there are many competing priorities, such as budget constraints coupled with the urgent need to revitalise the health sector and respond to the socio-economic impacts of COVID-19. Nevertheless, their governments should promote green development, which is multidimensional in nature and therefore also improves social, economic and even political aspects of human life. The need for green development is particularly urgent in economically less developed countries, whose citizens are more vulnerable to the long-term effects of climate change. Thus, the following aspects should be pointed out:

- the need for institutional reforms to develop a green financial market (with a particular role for developing country governments);
- the need to increase the level of cooperation at international level;
- the need for a globally coordinated green development effort.

Jiang et al. (2023), based on the experience of the Chinese economy, conducted a study on how the COVID-19 pandemic causes spillover effects between green finance, carbon market and renewable and non-renewable energy. The authors assessed the dynamic and directional linkages between risk factors, indicating the importance of linkages between these areas and their impact on investor attitudes. Taghizadeh-Hesary et al. (2021) highlighted, based on the experience of South Asian countries, that, due to the COVID-19 pandemic and the global recession, the scale of investment in green projects worldwide has been reduced. They propose that the post-COVID-19 world should adopt a green financial system by introducing new financial instruments, among other things. While appreciating the growing popularity of green bonds, the authors pointed to their weaker sides, namely the increased level of risk and low returns associated with this instrument. They also highlighted the dominant role of the banking sector, proposing in their conclusions the introduction of tax incentives and support for greater diversification of issuers with greater public sector participation and risk reduction policy.

The need for proactive measures in combating the challenges caused by the pandemic is pointed out by Ngo et al. (2022), who analyse in their study the impact of economic growth on environment, health of the general public and national economies in light of the extended threat of the COVID-19 pandemic. Their results indicated that loans provided on favourable terms by banks or financial institutions for environmentally friendly projects make it easier for companies to overcome the environmental issues and adverse effects resulting from the COVID-19 pandemic. This, in turn, contributes to improving a country's GDP. Similarly, the investment in acquiring green resources or technologies and the adoption of green technologies helps create and promote sustainable economic development. Their findings also showed that the issuance of green securities encourages investment in green economic projects, which minimises the chances of COVID-19 proliferation and ensures healthy human resources, thus sustaining economic growth. This study also confirmed that improvements in the capital market help control the situation in the country and sustain economic growth in times of COVID-19. In addition, increased government spending on resources used in the education sector can potentially act as a powerful tool to cope with the COVID-19 pandemic and sustain education sector's contribution to economic growth. The findings presented in this study also showed that incorporating environmental issues and requirements into financial policy-making, in addition to fostering environmental protection, also enables economic sectors to overcome COVID-19, maintain labour productivity and ultimately increase the country's economic growth. Furthermore, the results of this study indicate that business organisations should pay special attention to capital accumulation in their policy-making efforts to cope with the sudden economic crisis while maintaining the pace of economic growth.

In contrast, a more pessimistic approach is presented by Stuart et al. (2022), pointing out that the imperative for economic growth not only drives climate change and has created the conditions for the development and spread of phenomena such as the COVID-19 pandemic but also creates favourable conditions for climate inaction and ineffective responses to the pandemic. Focusing on the United States, the authors identified reasons for collective inaction on COVID-19, which in their view are similar in content to known delays in climate action: (1) denialism, (2) individualism and (3) techno-optimism. While emphasising that adequately addressing climate change and future pandemics requires overcoming these narratives and moving towards social conditions that are resilient, healthy and sustainable – in particular conditions where social and environmental well-being takes precedence over economic growth for maximised profits. As they note, the imperative for growth is often an indisputable policy goal as steadily increasing production and consumption levels are necessary to accumulate capital and sustain GDP growth. However, because growth makes it difficult to deal effectively with both climate change and global pandemics, these priorities must be confronted. Examining the negative ecological and social costs of growth requires rethinking the structural conditions of capitalist societies. Thus, the COVID-19 pandemic presents an opportunity to move towards a more sustainable society and a 'green recovery' that can reduce emissions while increasing prosperity without relying on economic growth, and a greater resilience to shocks. Stuart et al. (2022) refer, among others, to a Dutch manifesto signed by 170 scientists, which prioritised five policies to achieve goals relating to environmental and climate protection, among other things.

Summarising this discussion, it can be said that the impact of the COVID-19 pandemic on the implementation of green investments caused temporary concerns about the sustainability of the environmental and climate measures. However, as time went by, economic and political actors start to see this event as an opportunity to drive further change. Of course, further initiatives are needed from those in power, but the direction in which things are going is encouraging.

The war in Ukraine is another event having a major impact on the achievement of environmental goals and on the capacity to finance them. Against the backdrop of a tense economic situation and strained social security systems due to the

COVID-19 pandemic, the Russian invasion of Ukraine led to the largest forced displacement of people in Europe since the 1940s, while also confronting countries, households and businesses with unprecedented increases in energy and food prices.

In addition, the outbreak of war came at a rather peculiar time, i.e. when supply chains remained disrupted due to the COVID-19 pandemic and many companies had accumulated record levels of debt, often as a result of loans granted on favourable terms. As EBRD (2023) points out in its investment report, wars have a profound impact on people's livelihoods and economic activity. During a typical war, public debt increases by 47 percentage points of GDP and the government takes a more active role in the economy. Even if per capita income manages to recover after a few years of reconstruction, there can still be lasting scars affecting labour and capital resources. As mentioned, many companies have recently experienced major disruptions in their supply chains. For the most part, these entities have adapted to these disruptions, primarily by increasing their raw material stocks and sourcing more goods from more suppliers (mainly from abroad). At the same time, after a decade of rising debt and the shocks caused by the COVID-19 crisis, corporate debt levels often remain at record highs. Various types of 'green' cheap financing for vulnerable businesses are also a serious risk as some of the so-called zombie companies (those operating only because of the various forms of support they receive) create negative spillover effects for healthy businesses. As can be seen, therefore, the conflict in Ukraine has added another factor to the multiple existing challenges, namely an armed conflict on the EU border.

In the Authors' opinion, the Russian-Ukrainian conflict and its impact on the achievement of environmental objectives should be considered from several perspectives. Firstly, this event has created the need for EU countries to reorient towards military expenditure and, although social risk factors play a predominant role in this context, environmental risks are also important in this case. Secondly, the war has highlighted the drawbacks of EU countries' strong dependence on raw materials supplied by Russia (in particular gas and oil). Thirdly, the humanitarian aspect is also important.

As far as the arms industry is concerned, both governments and financial institutions displayed, in recent years, a negative approach to it, or in fact an eagerness to consider the industry as socially and environmentally harmful. However, the outbreak of the war taking place on the EU border has forced a revision of this approach. An expression of this change of attitude can be seen, for example, in the adjustment made by the Swedish bank SEB, which, although it had adopted, just before the war, a sustainability policy that excluded shares in defence companies from its funds, turned back from this path after 24 February 2022 and, from 1 April 2022, some funds can again be invested in the defence sector (Hollinger, 2022). It should be noted that this bank, one of the largest in the Nordic region, has not been the only one to avoid financing arms companies. For years, investors and financial institutions have been withdrawing from the defence sector for fear of controversy over the arms trade and out of concern for reputational risk. Increasing pressure on banks and fund managers to comply with environmental, social and corporate governance guidelines has resulted in a significant reduction in investment in the sector. This trend is particularly noticeable in Europe. Thales, a French arms company, has seen its shareholdings held by European investors (outside France) halve since 2016. Admittedly, arms companies have warned that an ESG-based label could limit their access to capital, particularly for the small- and medium-sized companies that make up the supply chain, pointing to banks in Germany, Belgium, the Netherlands, Sweden and Finland that have already cut ties with companies generating just 5–10% of defence revenues.

However, the contradiction inherent in declaring the arms sector unsustainable, while at the same time the EU calls for greater strategic autonomy over its own military capabilities, is apparent. It would instead be appropriate to suggest an approach whereby a negative label should be reserved for those who violate international conventions on the production, use and deployment of arms.

On the negative side, it took a war to realise the importance of the European defence industry. Certainly, as an important element of the bloc's ability to ensure the safety and security of its citizens, it should qualify for some recognition in the societal element of the ESG, especially that without a strong and resilient defence industry, it will be difficult if not impossible for Europe to achieve its strategic goals of autonomy.

It should also be stressed that not all arms companies are created equal. Those that do not comply with international treaties on arms development and sales, or that have not developed appropriate anti-corruption programmes, should rightly be excluded. There are also legitimate concerns about where permitted exports ultimately go. There may be a need to tighten the conditions attached to arms sales, for example, by strengthening monitoring of the end use of equipment.

So, as can be seen, the issue of development, support and financing of the defence industry is very much about social aspects. However, this does not mean that it has no impact on environmental risks. The defence industry is known for its significant consumption of natural resources, energy and water in the production of weapons and military equipment. Furthermore, the production of weapons often involves the emission of toxic chemicals and GHGs. The extraction of raw materials, such as metals or fuels, can also contribute to environmental degradation and pollution (Arak, 2023). A number of examples can be provided demonstrating a positive impact of ESG investments and green financing in conflict zones. Examples include the sustainable development programme in Afghanistan, clean water access projects in Syria, renewable energy implementation in the Democratic Republic of Congo, biodiversity conservation in Myanmar, disaster risk reduction in Ethiopia and sustainable infrastructure development in Iraq. At the same time, however, it is hard to conclude that armed conflict and sustainable development go hand in hand. On the one hand, under the pressure of increasing geopolitical tensions and in particular the war in Ukraine, Europe is undertaking to strengthen its defence capabilities and sovereignty. On the other hand, however, it tends to weaken its companies in this sector by not spontaneously including them in sustainable financing. Certainly, the extent and impact of this exclusion should not be underestimated for it is already having significant consequences for European defence companies (Arak, 2023).

According to the EIB's Annual Investment Report 2022/2023 (EIB, 2023), the volume of green investment in the EU has increased after the pandemic-induced decline, but more is still needed if Europe is to meet its targets. Investments of EUR 1 trillion per year are needed to reduce GHG emissions by 55% by 2030, a level that is EUR 365 billion per year higher than between 2010 and 2020. In addition, the Russian aggression against Ukraine has further increased the scale of challenges facing Europe. As a result of the outbreak of war, the EU decided to accelerate the energy transition and increase the share of renewables in the economy. Thus, European countries increased the budget for the development and use of environmentally friendly energy in order to become independent of gas and oil from Russia, while believing that environmentally friendly energy could become the primary source of energy in the future. With the outbreak of the war in Ukraine, European countries have become more aware of the need to break free from their dependence on energy imports from Russia (Saktiawan et al., 2022). The sanctions applied also affected energy prices and availability in other sectors of the economy. It should be noted that the value of European energy imports from Russia prior to the outbreak of war averaged EUR 100 billion per year, contributing significantly to this exporter's GDP. The most significant energy commodity imported in Europe was natural gas, followed by oil. Especially in the case of natural gas, European countries, confronted with the new situation, were forced to look for suppliers in other countries than Russia. Hence, a need arose to overcome this dependency by, among other things, maximising and optimising the use of renewable energy as an alternative.

Although the use of alternative energy in Europe is increasing year on year and has reached 22.09% in 2020 alone, this amount is not enough to cover the energy demand that Russia has supplied so far. As mentioned, the war and embargo on Russia have forced European countries to increase their renewable energy target from 40% to 45% in 2030. The increase in this target has also resulted in a required increase in the budget as the implementation of this plan requires at least EUR 210–300 billion. The war, directly or indirectly, caused an increase in renewable energy budgets in EU countries. This is in order to reach the target by 2030. They believe that environmentally friendly renewable energy will be the primary source of energy in the future. The aim is to free European countries from energy dependence on Russia, which makes embargoes less than optimal.

An important factor in this situation is the increase in funding for businesses affected by the war in Ukraine and support for the green transition. For the 12 months following the outbreak of the war, the European Commission approved EUR 733 billion in state aid for these entities (Johnston & Espinoza, 2023). Only grants approved during the COVID-19 pandemic were higher than that. It is worth noting that Germany accounts for almost half of the total EU state aid funding approved under the emergency crisis programme (Temporary Crisis Framework) introduced in 2022 to protect economies from the war in Ukraine and support green investment. A total of EUR 90 billion of approved funding was allocated in 2022. Admittedly, those grants are lower than the record aid allocated in the amount of almost EUR 900 billion, out of more than EUR 3 trillion of approved spending for

COVID-19 in 2021. However, EU diplomats in smaller countries have criticised the tendency to continually relax emergency state aid rules, which they say favours larger economies that can afford to offer such support to their companies.

It should be noted that Margrethe Vestager, the EU Competition Commissioner, first relaxed state aid rules in 2020 to help sectors such as airlines and hotels affected by lockdowns during the pandemic. Another Temporary Crisis Framework was adopted in March 2022 to allow Member States to help companies affected by the war in Ukraine and compensate those affected by higher energy costs. Since then, Vestager has expanded and extended the policy until the end of 2025 to support investment in the green transition, approving 270 national measures under the programme to date. France is the second largest user of the programme, accounting for 23% of approved projects, followed by Italy with 8%. Other EU legislation supporting the production of semiconductors, munitions and critical raw materials will also facilitate more direct investment from Member States in their industries (Johnston & Espinoza, 2023).

The growing expenditure also comes at a time when the EU is seeking to become more independent from other economies, including China. E. Letta, president of the Jacques Delors Institute, a Paris-based think-tank on European affairs, emphasises the importance of the single market in the EU's process of building 'strategic autonomy'. This implies the need for further conceptual development of projects such as the capital markets union, in order to give companies better access to finance across the bloc.

The importance of green investment in light of challenges caused by the war in Ukraine is broadly captured in a report by the European Think Tanks Group (ETTG, 2022), analysing the implications of the war in Ukraine for the EU and developing countries in four areas: energy security, industrial supply chains, food security and environmental protection. In the latter section, the report also addresses the deteriorating environmental situation in Ukraine. In addition, it explores three approaches to mitigating these impacts: policy coherence, social protection and international cooperation.

ETTG argues that the EGD may be the best EU policy tool to address the repercussions of Russia's invasion of Ukraine and avoid exacerbating climate change-related disruptions. The implementation of the EGD should be accelerated by all 27 EU Member States. At the same time, this should not come at the expense of sustainable development priorities and equitable transitions in other parts of the world, especially in developing countries. On the contrary, the international component of the EGD calls for global, coordinated and coherent action to achieve sustainable development, climate change mitigation and adaptation and a transition to clean energy.

To simultaneously address energy security and the climate crisis, the energy transition needs to be accelerated worldwide. At the national level, the EU can speed up renewable energy production, phase out fossil fuels (including liquefied natural gas (LNG)) and improve energy efficiency in all sectors and industries. The EU should avoid measures that block pathways to green transition. In parallel, the EU has the capacity to build strong international partnerships to help other interested countries in their own energy transition and support them to become key trading partners for renewables. However, it is important to note that energy transition is a significant expense and not all countries are ready for this type of action.

As mentioned earlier, global supply chains, particularly industrial ones, have been disrupted by the war and the related sanctions. Ukraine, Russia and Belarus were, until recently, responsible for the supply of many of the world's key raw materials such as neon, nickel, aluminium and palladium as well as key commodities such as iron and its derivatives and fertilisers. Soaring energy prices and inaccessible transport routes have further exacerbated previous disruptions. As companies relocate their production and look for new suppliers, the EU should aim to encourage low-carbon options, boost innovation and material efficiency and support developing countries to build their own green industries (ETTG, 2022).

Demonstrating leadership (often expressed by a pioneering approach to different initiatives) and upholding multilateralism will, in the think-tank's view, ensure that the EU does not act in isolation but takes account of the needs of countries equally affected by Russia's invasion of Ukraine. War on the EU's doorstep is as much a security threat as an opportunity to bring about a lasting change towards a more resilient world. As such, the EU can and should take a strong stance in the face of Russia's geopolitical belligerence, while championing sustainable development and a just transition, both domestically and globally.

War-disrupted supply chains have also had a negative impact on food security. In particular, developing countries relying on food imports face serious challenges due to record high prices. The EU has already implemented measures to support short-term food security, both domestically and internationally. To mitigate future crises, it should develop long-term sustainability measures and support the development of resilient food systems in developing countries (ETTG, 2022).

Another important point is that the war in Ukraine poses a serious threat to global environmental governance, particularly with regard to environmental protection and biodiversity. The war is likely to contribute to deforestation and ecosystem degradation in the supply chain, partly due to increasing food insecurity. The EU can support efficient and smart agriculture to minimise or avoid land conversion for food or energy production, both domestically and in developing countries. In addition, the EU can play an active role in supporting Ukraine in its increasingly precarious environmental situation as well as supporting neighbouring countries such as Poland, Slovakia, Romania and Hungary, which may suffer from cross-border pollution.

The war in Ukraine has also revealed the urgent need for effective coordination and coherence between respective EU policy frameworks. To implement the EGD, internal and external trade-offs should be minimised between key areas such as food and environment, energy and industrial supply chains as well as between energy and industrial supply chains, and between short- and long-term impacts. At the same time, synergies should be increased. At present, however, the content and implementation of the EGD is still based on a sectoral and siloed approach, which runs counter to the EU's policy coherence ambitions. More than ever, achieving the EGD goals requires an integrated approach to facilitate effective alignment with long-term global programmes such as the 2030 Agenda for Sustainable Development and the Paris Agreement.

In terms of international cooperation, the EU still needs to define the goals it wants to achieve in the external dimension of the EGD strategy. These will need to be translated into concrete actions in close dialogue with the EU's partner countries. In addition, international cooperation must be aligned to support long-term strategies for the implementation of the 2030 Agenda for Sustainable Development and the Paris Agreement. This requires a space for political ownership and learning through continuous monitoring and evaluation of relevant international cooperation activities and partnerships. The EU also plays an important role in building trust between partner countries and demonstrating international leadership in the face of Russia's geopolitics (ETTG, 2022). In conclusion, it can be said that the wide range of activities indicated by the above-mentioned think-tank is mainly based on the implementation of the EGD concept, which, however, is facing increasing public resistance, including from farmers (Euronews, 2024).

Despite the concerns mentioned above, the green transition is considered the best response to the energy price crisis caused by the Russian invasion of Ukraine, as revealed by the survey of more than 28,000 people in 30 countries conducted by the European Investment Bank (Knight, 2022) in collaboration with consultancy and research firm BVA Group in August 2022. It should be noted that the majority of Europeans believe that the war in Ukraine provides an incentive to save energy and reduce dependence on fossil fuels, with 66% saying that the consequences of the invasion on oil and gas prices should spur action to accelerate the green transition. British and Chinese respondents share this view, although Americans are divided. Also a large number of EU respondents (84%) said that unless energy and commodity consumption is drastically reduced in the near future, humankind will face a global catastrophe. 63% of people in the EU want energy prices to be linked to consumption, with individuals or companies consuming the most energy paying higher prices.

The significant impact of the war in the neighbourhood and the resulting energy crisis on social behaviour (in terms of energy saving) is also pointed out by an interesting study by Liobikiene et al. (2023) in relation to Lithuanian society. The energy crisis caused by the war in Ukraine and uncontrollable climate change revealed the importance of energy-saving behaviour in this country. The authors conducted a survey in Lithuania in 2022 with 1,000 respondents. The results showed that war in Ukraine was the most worrying issue for them, the level of concern about climate change ranking slightly lower. Interestingly, the COVID-19 pandemic was the least important concern at the time. Furthermore, respondents stated that the COVID-19 pandemic contributed less to changes in environmental concern and energy-saving measures than the war in Ukraine. At the same time, the results of a generalised linear model showed that only the war in Ukraine positively and significantly influenced energy-saving behaviour. Concern about the COVID-19 pandemic negatively influenced energy-saving behaviour, while the climate change factor influenced it indirectly, as an interaction of attitudes towards energy consumption. The study thus revealed a major method of encouraging energy-efficient behaviour in the context of the main current crises.

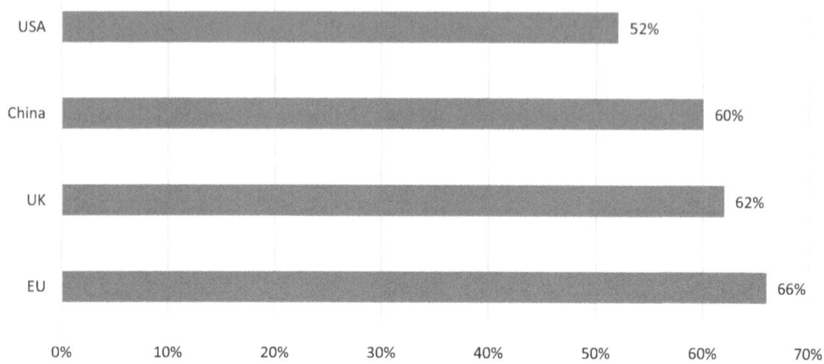

Figure 4.1 Percentage of people saying the war in Ukraine should accelerate the green transition

Source: EIB, BVA.

The war in Ukraine is an important issue for many of those surveyed by the EIB as Russia's invasion triggered a global energy crisis, increasing inflation and damaging economies across Europe and beyond. Record heat waves and droughts in many countries have contributed to a greater awareness of the impact of climate change and the urgent need for action. In addition, rising living costs and general financial issues topped the list of concerns in a survey among those living in the EU, UK and US. In China, the COVID-19 pandemic remained the biggest concern (Knight, 2022).

It should be noted that the vast majority of EU and Chinese citizens surveyed say they feel the effects of climate change in their daily lives (80% and 91% respectively). A significant proportion of these societies also suggest that the war in Ukraine should accelerate the green transition (Figure 4.1).

Importantly, 87% of respondents in the European Union and 85% in the UK believe their government is acting too slowly to prevent climate change. A minority of UK, EU and US respondents believe their government will succeed in reducing carbon emissions by 2030. In addition, nearly half of EU and UK citizens surveyed (47% and 45%) want the government to prioritise the development of renewable energy sources. 64% of EU citizens want polluting activities such as air travel and SUVs to be taxed more to take into account their environmental costs.

Other important conclusions to be drawn from this survey involve fiscal aspects as 40% of respondents in the EU believe that their government should reduce energy-related taxes in the short term (compared to 29%, 24% and 23% who hold this view in the UK, China and the US). Other measures, such as capping or regulating gas, oil and coal prices, are more favoured by the British, Chinese and Americans.

With the faltering pace of economic growth in a number of EU member economies in 2023, an analysis of macroeconomic data shows that the European economy is under pressure. Growth is slowing and challenges to competitiveness are on the rise, while EU companies are tackling the demands of the green transition. As the results show, coordinated support from national governments and EU institutions proved crucial in the aftermath of the COVID-19 pandemic, while helping Europe strengthen its resilience to future shocks and spurring the investment needed to transform and modernise the economy. Consequently, progress has been made on digitalisation, energy efficiency, decarbonisation and strengthening supply chains. However, the pace of change needs to accelerate, even as investments become more difficult to maintain. To remain competitive, the European Union and its members must improve productivity, encourage innovation, address skills gaps, develop new technologies and support young, dynamic companies (EIB, 2024).

In conclusion, as the above discussion shows, both the COVID-19 pandemic and the war in Ukraine have had an impact on the green transition. However, despite concerns about the sustainability of this trend and the numerous challenges, the direction taken has not been abandoned. In fact, one could say it has accelerated. As the last few years have shown, despite the aforementioned challenges, new regulatory and economic initiatives are being implemented. New legislative proposals and the general trend towards decarbonisation have not been halted by the crisis caused by the COVID-19 pandemic or by the war in Ukraine. Examples in this regard include legislation on Taxonomy (Regulation 2020/85), the Corporate Sustainability Reporting Directive and the proposal for a Directive on substantiation and communication of explicit environmental claims (Green Claims Directive), among others.

4.3 Recommendations for further action to achieve climate goals

As indicated by the results of PWC's (2023a) survey, climate change risk is among the top five most frequently cited risks identified by business and risk leaders (at executive level), in the areas of technology, operations and finance and risk and audit.

The discussion so far illustrates how demanding and costly a task it is to strive for environmental protection and for climate change to stop. However, when analysing the events taking place in the environment, it is difficult to question the need for decisive action. Observing the natural environment, it is easy to see the widespread and often intense changes in the atmosphere, oceans, cryosphere and biosphere. Human-induced climate change is already causing many extreme weather events and increasingly unpredictable weather and climate conditions around the world. This situation is causing a number of negative impacts and associated losses for nature and people. At the same time, it is important to emphasise that it is often the most affected communities that have contributed the least in the past to the current climate change.

The aforementioned climate change as well as the growing awareness and public pressure are the main catalysts for new climate regulations. Societies in respective countries recognise and often demand greater responsibility from those acting as employers, suppliers, business partners or beneficiaries of the invested funds. Thus, one can conclude that the pressure for change is triggered by (ING & EY, 2021):

a more informed public which pushes regulators;
regulators who understand that their constituents expect change;
customers who support the change leaders with their everyday consumer decisions;
financial institutions which demand a different way of doing business from companies, and at the same time have to comply with new regulations themselves;
employees who prefer to work for companies that do not overconsume natural resources.

However, despite the implementation of new regulations and the measures adopted, the global as well as the European economy is not able to balance economic growth and resource consumption. Without drastic changes in consumption and production practices, the demand for non-renewable resources may double between 2015 and 2050. In addition to problems such as insufficient resources, the issue of increased migration may also arise. More than 20 million people a year are forced to leave their homes due to extreme weather events such as floods, torrential rains, fires and extreme heat. Climate change is also likely to trigger major conflicts, leading to forced displacement of entire populations (ING & EY, 2021). Thus, the climate crisis phenomenon points to the weaknesses of the existing solutions, which raises the need, on the one hand, to reinforce positive measures and, at the same time, to seek new solutions at different levels of implementation and often ones that are fundamental in nature. This situation also creates a special role for science and the application of its latest developments. An interesting perspective in this context was provided by J. Ravetz (2006) in his and S. Funtowicz concept of postnormal science, which argues that the positivist, linear approach to science is part of the problem that is the contemporary environmental crisis. They also demonstrate that the ineffectiveness of the 'puzzle-solving' suggestions proposed so far is due, among other things, to the failure to take account of the complexity of the problem. Post-normal science accepts the existence of inherent contradictions and inconsistencies. A good example of such seemingly irresolvable conflicts might be the constant drive to develop and get rich while the limited planetary resources necessary to realise this ambition are being depleted (Rockström et al., 2009). There is no single scientific method for resolving this antagonism, which is why the role of science in this perspective is defined as an initiator of a mutual learning process rather than as an objective provider of final solutions.

Regarding the involvement of science in environmental protection and climate efforts, a good example is the Science Based Targets initiative aimed at a voluntary reduction of GHG emissions based precisely on a scientific approach. This initiative is the result of a partnership between the World Resources Institute (WRI), the World Wide Fund for Nature (WWF), Carbon Disclosure Project (CDP) and the United Nations Global Compact, which supports its member organisations in preventing the negative effects of climate change by determining the necessary level of carbon emission reductions (Michalski, 2022). This initiative is gaining momentum, as the number of companies and financial institutions that set GHG emission reduction targets and have them validated under the aforementioned initiative doubled in 2023 (from 2079 in 2022) to 4,204 companies. This significant demand for corporate decarbonisation standards and target validation services has prompted SBTi to undertake a far-reaching operation to rapidly develop a wider range of trusted, credible emission reduction standards and increase the capacity to validate corporate targets, while pursuing the highest level of service excellence for companies and financial institutions. SBTi has also established a subsidiary company that, once fully operational, will provide target validation services with all profits being donated to the charity. The organisation plans to review the Corporate Net-Zero Standard in the coming years as well as work to develop sector standards for six high-impact sectors: oil and gas, power companies, automotive companies, chemicals, insurance and clothing. In addition, SBTi is to pilot a hybrid model for developing sector standards, working with external organisations and pooling expertise (SBTi, 2024). This model could lead to further diffusion of this initiative. Thus, **what the Authors recommend is the widest possible use of science and its accomplishments (along the lines of SBTi) for environmental and climate protection activities, both in real and financial economy**.

Environmental action is also an example of a collective impact area. It is a typical area where spending at one level only (household, business, country or EU) will not be effective (such thinking being confirmed by the results of the Paris Consensus reached in this regard). Therefore, only coordinated action at the global level, whether by individual companies, countries, regional organisations or communities such as the EU, will help achieve the desired results. If the way resources flow, particularly financial ones, and the rules to account for them are not changed, some of these funds will be merely a window dressing and some of them (which is often why global tasks are criticised) will be spent more on administrative issues than on concrete actions to solve a given environmental problem. **When these resources of different origin are centralised and managed in a well-defined, coordinated way, the implementation efficiency of the tasks financed by these resources will be much higher**. Public resources, both domestic and international, are a very important source of funding for various types of sustainable investment as public sector investors have a longer investment horizon compared to private investors and play a key role particularly in the case of countries with a lower level of development of their economy and financial system.

It is worth emphasising an increasingly strong common phenomenon over the last few years, i.e. the fact that national and international authorities consider sustainable development measures a priority and identify with its stated objectives. As a result, **providing funding for such actions seems natural to them, while the financial return from these investments is less important in the decision-making process. This approach is definitely expected to continue**, especially that investors from the public sector often finance sustainable development measures in several formulas, i.e. through non-refundable aid or debt instruments. At the same time, the effects of such multi-level actions are visible. Various initiatives at international level (e.g. the UNFCCC, the Kyoto Protocol or the Paris Agreement) support measures reflecting respective governments' ambitions at national level. The Paris Agreement, with almost universal participation, has led to the development of policies and the setting of targets at national and sub-national levels, particularly with regard to mitigation as well as increased transparency of action and support for climate change. A number of regulatory and economic instruments have already been successfully implemented. In many countries, policies have increased energy efficiency, reduced deforestation rates and accelerated technology deployment, thus helping avoid and in some cases reduce or eliminate emissions. Abundant evidence suggests that mitigation policies have led to 24 Gt CO_2 equivalent per year of avoided global emissions. At least 18 countries have sustained production-based CO_2 and GHG and consumption-based CO_2 absolute emission reductions for longer than ten years. At the same time, however, these reductions have only partially offset the global emissions increase (IPCC, 2023) and each increment of global warming exacerbates a number of coexisting risks. Deep, rapid and sustained reductions in GHG emissions would lead to a noticeable slowdown in global warming within about two decades as well as noticeable changes in atmospheric composition within a few years.

It is important to stress that climate and non-climate risks will increasingly interact, creating complex and cascading threats that are more difficult to manage. Some future changes are inevitable and/or irreversible, but they can be mitigated by deep, rapid and sustained reductions in global GHG emissions. The likelihood of sudden and/or irreversible environmental changes increases with higher levels of global warming. Similarly, the likelihood of unlikely effects associated with potentially very large adverse impacts increases with higher levels of global warming. Climate change also poses a threat to human wellbeing and planetary health. As the IPCC (2023) points out in its report, there is a rapidly closing window of opportunity to secure a sustainable and liveable future for all.

Over the past three decades, the European Union has positioned itself as a guardian of relatively steady improvements in environmental and public health protection. This has been achieved, among other things, through the implementation of common standards and the integration of numerous nature and public health protection instruments into national law. However, measurable emission reductions are still lagging behind. Financial barrier is the main factor causing the gap between the ambitious scale of the targets set and the actual implementation of policies at both EU and Member State level (Institut Rousseau, 2024).

Deep, rapid and sustained mitigation and accelerated implementation of adaptation actions in this decade would reduce projected loss and damage to people and ecosystems and bring a range of co-benefits, especially in terms of air quality and health. Ambitious adaptation and mitigation targets and climate-resilient development could become reality through prioritising climate equity, climate justice, social justice, inclusiveness and equitable transition. Adaptation outcomes are improved through increased support for the most climate-vulnerable regions and people. Furthermore, integrating climate change adaptation into social protection programmes increases resilience. A range of options are available to reduce intensive emissions, including through behavioural and lifestyle changes, with co-benefits for societal well-being (IPCC, 2023).

Effective climate action is possible through political commitment, well-aligned multi-level governance, appropriate institutional frameworks, laws, policies and strategies and increased access to finance and technology. **Measures such as clearly articulated goals, coordination across multiple policy areas and inclusive governance processes will facilitate effective climate action**. Regulatory and economic instruments can support deep emission reductions and climate resilience if widely applied. The development of climate resilient technologies benefits from diverse knowledge. Thus, finance, technology and international cooperation are key enablers to accelerate climate action. If climate targets are to be met, both adaptation and mitigation funding would need to increase multifold. Currently allocated capital is often sufficient to close the global investment gap, but there are barriers to redirecting capital towards climate action. Streamlining systems is key to accelerating the widespread adoption of technologies and practices. Enhancing international cooperation is possible through multiple channels including at the level of financial sectors. A number of examples can be identified of financial sector activities which should be supported and developed, e.g. banks supporting the fight against climate change (Michalski, 2022), but even a broader integration and unification of that approach seems justified. As indicated in Chapter 3, Banks, the main representatives of the financial sector when it comes to fulfilling economic actors' needs, must be at the forefront of changing financial flows in order to encourage benefits to nature rather than loss of nature. Thus, they have a key role to play in achieving the objectives underlying 'sustainable banking'. This is partly due to their activities in high-impact sectors as well as their high levels of funding in emerging markets, and their ability to direct financial flows towards nature-positive activities. As PWC (2023) points out, more than half of the global economic value, i.e. around USD 58 trillion, is moderately or highly dependent on nature. By the same token, this leads central banks and financial regulators in many countries around the world to recognise that nature degradation, and actions to protect and restore nature can have significant macroeconomic, macroprudential and macroeconomic impacts (NGFS, 2023). **Thus, attention to the quality of loan portfolios and the appropriate steering of cash flows should be considered as another recommendation for meeting the ambitious environmental goals set by the European Union.**

According to a study by the Institut Rousseau, featuring over 150 experts, researchers and volunteers from more than 20 organisations across Europe, including economists, engineers and public policy experts, the benefits of climate transition will only be unlocked if public spending across Europe doubles to EUR 510 billion per year. In addition, EUR 40 trillion worth of investment is needed to put Europe on the path to climate neutrality, while letting Europe stay in the global race for competitiveness, in line with the EU's strategic autonomy agenda (Institut Rousseau, 2024). Currently, Europe's territorial emissions are mainly due to energy production (26%), transport of goods and people (23%) and industry (22%). Agriculture and buildings contribute more or less equally (around 13% each). Despite meeting the 2020 target, Europe does not currently meet the 2050 target and the Fit-for-55 target for 2030. **Therefore, in the Authors' view, more sectoral targeting would be needed to strengthen emission reductions.** This is confirmed by the think-tank's opinion, which, in an optimum transition scenario, points to the possibility of achieving a stringent 85% reduction in annual emissions in the EU compared to 2021, resulting in a reduction of 519 million tonnes of CO_2 in 2050. However, a number of so-called levers need to be activated to achieve these targets. A total of 37 decarbonisation levers are identified in the report, with particular potential for significant emissions reductions in key levers related to energy (power generation), transport (cars, trucks) and building renovation. Implementing all of these levers, regardless of scale, is essential to achieving carbon neutrality.

In addition to the above aspects, among the authors' key conclusions are the following (Institut Rousseau, 2024)

Europe needs to invest EUR 40 trillion by 2050 to decarbonise the EU economy, equivalent to around 10% of the current EU GDP. An additional investment of EUR 10 trillion is needed by 2050, which is on average about 2.3% of current GDP per year. This is about half of what the EU spent on fossil fuel imports in 2022. Public spending needs to double from EUR 250 billion to EUR 510 billion per year to stimulate private investment, and finance unprofitable decarbonisation solutions. With public deficit and debt ratios limited by the Stability Pact, countries find themselves restricted in their efforts so transition investments should be excluded from these budgetary rules. This additional public investment of EUR 260 billion per year represents around 1.6% of current EU GDP. This is less than EU spending on post-Covid-19 reconstruction (EUR 338 billion per year) or fossil fuel subsidies in the EU-27 (EUR 359 billion per year);

The renovation of buildings and the promotion of modal shift from cars and airplanes should be priority targets for additional public support, although public involvement is required in all sectors;

The additional investment required as a percentage of GDP may vary by 2.5 from country to country depending on the current carbon intensity of their economies and the current level of investment. These investments will be higher if delayed. These amounts are estimates of the lowest investment required as net carbon neutrality is only part of the environmental transition and does not fully address the challenges of biodiversity or natural resource scarcity.

The above investment plan is not only necessary but also beneficial (Institut Rousseau). It will create local jobs and increase the purchasing power of most Europeans in the short term. If self-sufficiency and local production options are chosen, they will also strengthen the EU's energy security as well as economic sovereignty, competitiveness and trade balance. What's more, these public investments will pay dividends by reducing the need for future public spending, such as unemployment insurance, climate spending and climate change adaptation costs.

While actions of all actors will be very important in achieving climate goals, the Authors believe that of greatest significance will be the actions of

companies that take up the challenge of transforming their business model and obtaining financing for this purpose. This type of approach is a challenge but at the same time also a business opportunity. Friede et al. (2015) point out that around 90% of more than 2,000 studies identified show a non-negative relationship between ESG and corporate financial performance, with the vast majority highlighting a positive relationship in the short as well as the long term. This data indicates that commitment to ESG practices translates into real financial success for the company. It is common for companies to implement environmental best practices related to modern technology use and to encouraging pro-environmental behaviour among employees, in order to enhance the company's capacity to reduce environmental costs and burdens on customers as well as generating advantages at the level of financial operations (Tarmuji et al., 2016).

In addition, integrating ESG aspects, particularly environmental ones, into a company's management system requires their strategic prioritisation. It should be noted that it is not enough to develop an ESG strategy; it also needs to be integrated into the company's business strategy. Unfortunately, Baumgartner and Korhonen (2010) observe a lack of strategic orientation in pro-environmental and pro-social activities. In many companies, ESG practices are implemented because of regulatory requirements, stakeholder pressure or as a result of bottom-up initiatives within the company. A strategic orientation, on the other hand, seems necessary if a company wants to realise the long-term benefits of ESG engagement.

However, the long-term benefits are not only about reputational changes and improved competitive position but, above all, about satisfactory financial performance (Taliento et al., 2019). Leaders will bear the greatest costs, while the falling price of new technologies over time will make it easier to follow their example. To make changes using fully mature technology, with lower implementation costs and less risk of failure, may prove more efficient on the cost side. However, it is the leaders who receive a kind of 'risk premium' from customers in the form of greater trust, and the acceptance of higher unit margins and limited turnover (PWC, 2023). In addition, leaders will have access to preferential funding sources. Furthermore, implementing change earlier, ahead of competitors, brings yet another benefit: a change in organisational culture. Thus, business owners should accept the current costs of change in favour of the long-term and multidimensional benefits they will reap in the future, especially that, in the long term, failure to act will lead to the cost of inaction. Companies ignoring social and environmental responsibility may face penalties from regulators and rejection by consumers seeking brands that meet sustainability standards.

Members of an organisation (e.g. employees) prefer rapid implementation of changes that are perceived as positive. As a result, the sense of identification with the organisation increases, change is adopted more quickly at all levels, and the whole operation, from the strategy level all the way to the lowest process level, runs consistently. The transition to low- or zero-carbon is costly, but companies that do not make it will find it difficult to raise capital and grow. They may also struggle to sell their products or services as consumers are already measuring their carbon footprint and expect the same from suppliers. Financing institutions are increasingly refusing to finance non-environmental projects such as coal-fired power units, for example. Transition supports the development of innovative products and business models, while reducing the competitiveness of companies that do not keep up with changes. At its core, it is about investing in new technologies that are zero-emission and increasingly economically competitive, such as renewable energy sources. By the same token, this means that business operators should analyse their level of resilience to environmental and climate change events on an ongoing basis.

A study carried out on a sample of companies listed on the Warsaw Stock Exchange in 2023 (Lipski, 2024) to assess the maturity of ESG management in listed companies and their resilience to crises indicates that smaller companies have both lower resilience to crises and a lower level of maturity. It is clear that companies with higher capitalisation exhibit greater management maturity in every aspect and higher levels of crisis resilience. As demonstrated by the World Economic Forum, companies that have created sustainable supply chains can see an increase in revenue of up to 20% compared to companies that have not implemented similar solutions. They can also reduce costs associated with supply chain operations by 16%. This applies to entire chains, including suppliers and sub-suppliers, often supporting them on the road to sustainability. Global corporations, operating in multinational supply chains, are already choosing partners that not only have transparent sustainability policies but require the same from their sub-suppliers (ING & EY, 2021).

Analysis to date indicates that ESG activity and reporting loosen capital constraints and can contribute to greater financial flexibility for economic entities. Non-financial aspects are seen as impulses influencing the decisions of both equity (e.g. private equity funds) and debt capital providers. As revealed by the results of a qualitative study of representative Polish companies (Lipski et al., 2023), environmental investments have a direct impact on efficiency as they can, among other things, reduce operating costs, though it should be noted that the specific nature of the enterprise is also important. For service companies, investments in human resources are an important channel of value creation by influencing the quality of services provided or staff retention. Respondents in this study were unanimous about the impact of ESG investment and indicated it stimulates and enhances enterprise development. At the same time, when it comes to corporate finance activities, respondents often indicated that ESG was a key element of the overall capital raising strategy for companies using external sources. In their view, taking ESG factors into account can contribute to lowering the cost of external financing, for example, through lower margin. Most importantly, however, the experts surveyed pointed to the relevance of non-financial aspects in making a financing decision. The possibility of obtaining cheaper financing compared to classical sources is particularly manifested in the targeted financing of ESG projects. The results obtained indicate that the scope of analysis in the decision-making process, in the context of a company's investment and financing activities alike, should definitely include the extended dimension of ESG factors. The broader range of aspects that need to be taken into account, in essence, does not undermine the capital raising theories formulated to date (such as Modilliani and Miller's theory, substitution theory or the pecking order theory. **It does, however, suggest the need to factor in not only the interests of the owners but also those of other stakeholders.**

Sustainable transition in the context of ESG aspects related to the environmental protection and degradation prevention is becoming an inevitable direction of socio-economic development. It encompasses and relates to the activities of financial institutions, manufacturing and commercial enterprises and local government units, whose operations are interdependent. In pursuit of the overarching goal of sustainable development, it is intended to serve as an effective means of achieving resilience to climate change. A particular area in this regard is the real estate sector, which is crucial from the perspective of how the economy, society and financial markets function. At the same time, it is also among the sectors with the greatest environmental impact, accounting for a crucial percentage of GHG emissions. Taking ESG criteria into account in asset allocation decision-making in the real estate market has become a leading need for investors. This is due to formal requirements and market expectations alike. **By the same token, environmental protection is nowadays one of the leading challenges of real estate portfolio management, and a deeper market monitoring of the solutions applied is a desirable state of affairs.**

Given the urgent need for significant climate finance, all parties involved need to adopt a new ambitious target in 2025 that aims to rectify previous shortcomings. At the same time, the majority of climate finance, as noted earlier, remains allocated to debt and loans to developing countries, which, given the repayable nature of these instruments, may raise concerns about the ability to effectively implement mitigation and adaptation projects. Furthermore, the lack of consensus as to the definition and measurement of climate finance presents challenges in accurately assessing and tracking progress.

Nevertheless, this phenomenon can be mitigated by so-called green aid, which stimulates technological transition towards more environmentally conscious and sustainable technologies. This result is in line with the conclusions presented in recent literature examining this topic. Furthermore, aid distribution is driven by factors representing recipients' needs as well as donors' concerns. Climate finance should be effectively delivered and aligned with national development strategies and needs. And yet, some factors are surprisingly irrelevant when it comes to aid allocation, for example, donor countries do not necessarily reward bilateral trade ties. In contrast, their commitments are sensitive to foreign direct investment inflows. Against this backdrop, it becomes clear that scaling up private climate finance in developing economies often requires a complex strategy with enhancements covering many aspects, including support from multilateral development banks, the IMF and the public sector. This reflects not only the enormity of the financing requirements but also the diversity of investments needed to achieve important climate change mitigation and adaptation goals. Innovative financing instruments can help overcome some of the challenges facing the private sector in emerging markets and developing economies, such as credit and political risks and lack of economies of scale. In larger emerging markets with functioning bond markets, investment funds are a good example of how to attract institutional investors. Such funds should grow in number and be scaled up to encourage issuers in emerging markets to generate a sufficient supply of green assets to finance green projects (Grygiel & Lipski, 2023). By relying on public markets, these funds can attract large amounts of private finance with relatively little use of multilateral institutions or public sector resources. New types of performance-based debt instruments – particularly sustainability-linked bonds – can help reduce environmental burdens. **For these instruments to achieve a significant climate impact, sustainability targets should be linked to emission reduction targets in line with the Paris Agreement.** The set of potential actions focused on strengthening sustainable bond issuance by the private sector, local governments and government agencies is broad. Indeed, these could include providing technical assistance, capacity building, creating a favourable regulatory framework for sustainable financing and promoting transparency and standardisation of sustainable bonds.

At the same time, expanding the portfolio of green financial instruments only is not sufficient to achieve the necessary scale of private climate finance in developing economies. Indeed, there may be additional opportunities to find the necessary finance by leveraging the allocative function of the financial and capital market, and by exploiting opportunities for financial hedging of environmental and climate risks. The existing theoretical concepts of climate risk mitigation emerge as encouraging opportunities. Extending the application of these in less developed countries can strengthen and expand domestic financial markets. These concepts demonstrate the potential to mitigate climate risk and contribute to favourable financial outcomes.

At the same time, it should be noted that, in light of the observed needs, the concept of transition finance has been gaining popularity in recent years. This approach complements the existing green finance efforts of governments, donors and multilateral development banks, while at the same time ensuring the flow of private finance to more sustainable activities. As noted by the OECD (2023), transition finance focuses on raising and providing funds to decarbonise carbon-intensive economic activities and industries that currently do not have a fully viable zero- or near-zero-emission alternative. Thus, more and more jurisdictions are beginning to put forward elements of a policy framework for transition finance, such as transition taxonomies and requirements for business transition plans. Given this emphasis, a key issue in transition finance is how to ensure that eligible investments are aligned with the Paris Agreement temperature target. The debate largely focuses on investments involving fossil fuels in energy-intensive industries, and loans to companies with fossil fuel assets. These investments carry a high risk of 'carbon dependency'. To prevent carbon dependency to the extent possible, and to ensure the environmental integrity of transition financing, relevant investments must be carefully selected and implemented with appropriate safeguards.

The existing approaches and policy frameworks for transition finance emphasise the need to avoid carbon dependency but largely fail to provide clear guidance or criteria on how to do so. In the absence of consensus on how to avoid carbon dependency, funding may be directed to projects that do not have sufficient safeguards to ensure compliance with the temperature target of the Paris Agreement. Similarly, corporations seeking transition finance may fear accusations of greenwashing. The concept of carbon dependency is a recurring theme in discussions on climate change mitigation policy and financing. The existing financial and investment frameworks and tools reflect, to varying degrees, the growing importance of carbon dependency risk. However, as the window of opportunity to stay within the Paris temperature target closes, the risk and questions about how best to mitigate it will need to take centre stage.

In summary, public awareness of sustainability, climate change and climate equity issues have increased in recent decades. The SDGs and climate-related tasks are key to achieving global sustainability. Cooperation between the public and private sectors is essential, and investment in renewable energy sources is an important part of the fight against climate change. It is worth emphasising that climate action requires policy coherence, education and promotion. At the same time, global spending on clean energy is still insufficient, and more action is needed to achieve sustainable energy development goals. Promoting climate action is a global challenge, and coordinated international cooperation is key to tackling climate change. Valuable initiatives such as the EGD are supporting economic and social transition towards a sustainable future. However, further action is needed to achieve ambitious climate and environmental goals.

Conclusion

In recent years, as demonstrated by the analyses and data presented in the monograph, there has been an increasing emphasis on the importance of green finance and environmental sustainability in decision-making at the macro- and microeconomic levels, leading to increased attention and focus on both academic research and practical applications on these issues. The world is currently experiencing an unprecedented environmental crisis, with issues such as resource depletion, biodiversity loss and climate change becoming more pressing and affecting the pace of socio-economic development. Increasingly, the physical hazards caused by natural disasters and climate change are impacting on societies and economic actors leading to the destruction of capital stocks, loss of life and disruption of economic activity. Discussions among policy-makers and theoreticians alike indicate a growing concern that climate change problems may hit financial markets and it is necessary to test financial institutions for climate resilience as well (Adams & Abhayawansa, 2022). Climate change is undoubtedly, as mentioned many times in the monograph, a pressing problem requiring immediate attention and action not just by individuals or single countries. Instead, as research indicates, collective, global efforts across environmental, social and economic dimensions are needed, especially that environmental pollution is likely to worsen, leading to irreversible damage to the planet and its inhabitants. The Authors concluded that social preferences have a significant impact on economic decisions and a simple method should be proposed to ensure institutional investors are able to satisfy the social expectations of their clients. Investors' willingness to invest in sustainable projects, as well as transparency and standardisation of sustainability reporting, influences the effectiveness of Green Finance in achieving the Sustainable Development Goals (SDGs). Transparency, standardisation and social equity are essential to creating a sustainable and equitable future.

In addition, the outbreak of the Russian-Ukrainian conflict in 2022 has significantly increased uncertainty about energy supplies in Europe. The instability of oil and gas markets made the EU, Asia and other regions aware of the urgent need to find alternative energy sources. This reprehensible event leading to a military conflict in Europe imposed an immediate change in economic policy by accelerating the processes of renewable energy development, and the resources available at the European Union level were directed towards financing energy independence

DOI: 10.4324/9781003434689-6

efforts, e.g. by authorising EU co-funding of the construction of nuclear power plants, also increasing the overall pool of financial resources for this purpose, as described in more detail in Chapter 1. Following Russia's military aggression in Ukraine, European countries became more aware of their dependence on energy imports from Russia. Although sanctions in other sectors of the economy have been applied, it is still not optimal to take energy from there. Europe's energy imports from Russia used to amount to an average of EUR 100 billion a year, having a significant impact on the gross domestic product generated. The most important (by value) energy resource imported to Europe is natural gas, followed by oil. European countries are looking for suppliers in countries other than Russia, especially when it comes to natural gas, as it is much cheaper than other fuels. Therefore, a solution is needed to overcome this dependency, the aim of which is to maximise and optimise the use of renewable energy as an alternative. On the other hand, the use of alternative energy sources in Europe is steadily increasing year on year. In 2020 alone, the use of alternative energy reached 22.09%. However, this amount is not sufficient to cover energy needs after ceasing the cooperation with Russia. The war and the embargo on Russia have forced European countries to increase their ambitions expressed in their renewable energy targets from 40% to 45% in 2030. Due to the higher target, a budget increase is also required. The implementation of this plan requires at least EUR 210–300 billion. The idea is for European countries to be able to break free of their energy dependence on Russia, but for this to happen it will take time and large-scale funding from both public and private sources. The Russian military invasion of Ukraine has also shown that such an unexpected event, aside from being a human tragedy and despicable event, has significant economic implications disrupting the energy supply cycle and clearly demonstrating how dependent we are on traditional natural resources. In an empirical analysis, Nerlinger and Utz (2022), similarly to Boubaker et al., 2022; Boungou and Yatié, 2022; Deng et al., 2022; Huang and Lu, 2022; Tosun and Eshraghi, 2022, see Russia's invasion of Ukraine as an unforeseen, abrupt change in the market environment affecting the economic environment not only across Europe but also globally. An example of an unexpected change in the market environment was the significant change in commodity prices, for example, the price of coal immediately after 24 February 2022 increased by almost 150%. The onset of the Russia-Ukraine armed conflict indicated the need to step up efforts and redirect financial resources towards national energy independence plans (Tollefson, 2022).

In those circumstances, climate action and action for a sustainable future for all has been a priority for some time now, as the discussion presented in this book has confirmed. To combat the negative effects of climate change but also to take action to become less dependent on Russian natural resources in the European Union, all available green finance solutions are being used in the economic sphere, e.g. through technological innovations, etc.

The factors considered by the Authors throughout the monograph have shown that addressing and confronting climate change require access to significant financial resources and investments, which can then be used to reduce emissions. The literature reviews presented in the monograph but also practical regulations and solutions used by financial institutions indicate that green finance issues are crucial to promoting sustainable development and combating environmental problems. Green finance is a relatively new way of integrating environmental issues not only into the financial sector but also into decisions made by governments at the level of fiscal policy-making.

Green finance is a financial tool aimed at achieving economic, social and environmental sustainability (Scholtens, 2006). According to experts (Hartzmark & Sussman, 2019; Heine, 2019), green finance focuses primarily on reducing carbon emissions by financing green projects and participating in the carbon market. On the one hand, green finance focuses on financing or providing regulatory support for environmental investments and, by issuing green bonds, reduces the financing and operating costs of environmental projects. This helps improve the effectiveness of environmental initiatives and promotes the development of green technologies while reducing greenhouse gas emissions. Green finance, as confirmed by the monograph's research, is essential to achieve sustainable growth by financing sustainable environmental, economic and social projects in line with international standards (Xie & Chen, 2020). Green finance is also an innovative financial tool that bridges the gap between the environment and sustainable development (Labatt & White, 2002). In the context of marketing principles and mechanisms, the concept of green finance is based on the idea that the government should place resources on the market while respecting environmental resources (Li et al., 2022) but also, through its fiscal policy, support actions that reduce pollution caused by other market players. In concluding our opinion, it is worth using the concept created by Cowan (1999), who believes that effective financing of pro-environmental actions should be based on three perspectives, which also emerged directly from our analyses. Firstly, when allocating capital resources to environmental investments, financial institutions have a clear methodology for evaluating them, which is referenced by regulations. Assumptions made in this regard are audited by independent bodies, which make the concept available for government oversight to avoid greenwashing. Secondly, the concept is innovative in solving environmental problems. Last but not least, the concept aims to improve the environment and reduce pollution while providing renewable energy services.

Research findings reported in the literature, but also in reports from major international institutions, emphasise the importance of large investments in sustainable and low-carbon projects and point to the need for a robust regulatory framework to facilitate the availability of green finance and its integration with carbon-neutral solutions in practical terms. The studies analysed highlight the positive impact of climate finance on economic growth in the vast majority of EU Member States in the medium to long term and the positive impact on the decarbonisation index. Our own analyses, but also those presented in the literature, have shown that it is possible to improve climate finance strategies by analysing the benefits of carbon-neutral practices such as the Green Climate Fund. Some developing countries have established regional and national channels and funds for various purposes, funded by international resources and/or national budget allocations as well as the domestic private sector. The Indonesia Climate Change Trust Fund was among the first entities of that kind to be established. The Amazon Fund, operated by Banco Nacional de Desenvolvimento Econômico e Social (BNDES, Brazil's National Development Bank), is the world's largest national climate fund, with combined commitments from Norway and Germany.

Moreover, important issues include integrating environmental, social and governance criteria into investment decisions, but also successfully coping with implementation challenges and improving data collection in green finance activities. Supporting activities related to green finance, sustainable economic development and environmental risk mitigation requires cooperation, involvement of the stakeholders of the market processes taking place but also political measures. As regards the aspects of finance and supported development, researchers have investigated the impact of green finance on sustainability through interrelations, indicators and techniques to assess the green finance expansion in Europe and globally. Zeng et al. (2014) attempted to design an evaluation system for the expansion of green economics. The results indicate that green investment significantly influences the overall economic development. On the other hand, there are some bottlenecks at the regional level that need to be addressed.

In the Authors' opinion, the analyses showed that concerted action and infrastructure are needed to address the need for climate change finance. This is necessary to mobilise sufficient monetary resources for climate change action and gaining energy independence from Russia resources. The architecture of international climate change finance is extremely complex, as are the mechanisms for monitoring the sources of money and disbursements, and the systems for controlling them to track results in order to achieve beneficial outcomes for recipients. Discussions presented in the monograph have shown that institutions such as development banks, which finance climate change projects with the support of the authorities in power, often use a decision-making process that differs from what commercial financial institutions usually have in place, making it possible to find financial resources for projects involving a greater market risk. Of course, it is important to recognise such activities and agree with the substantial role played by development banks in the sub-segment of green finance by increasing the efficiency of the measures taken. An excellent example of this is provided in Chapter three, which shows how eagerly the financial market gets involved in financing the construction of renewable energy sources (wind farms), whereas hardly any information can be found on its involvement in the construction of pumped storage power stations, which, if we look at the example of Switzerland, are built only with the involvement of public development resources.

In addition, also the analyses prepared for this monograph showed that intensive efforts still need to be made to increase participation and transparency in the multilateral governance of climate finance bodies. For example, it is important to define the role of non-governmental actors as observers and establish committees inside relevant funds with various powers to participate in decision-making. Although many countries have established multilateral climate funds, most funding for climate change initiatives is bilateral and mainly managed by development organisations operating within a given European country. In order to increase the efficiency of green finance activities, the Authors believe that more concrete and consistent steps should be taken in defining a reporting format, and ensuring an independent entity's verification of how Member States classify and publicly report on climate finance. Unfortunately, this limitation was significantly felt by the Authors when carrying out the statistical research presented in Chapter 2 as they were unable to obtain certain information either from Eurostat or when contacting respective Member States' national statistical institutions.

The content of the monograph confirms a great potential for green financing to support sustainable economic development, but to ensure its efficient use, concrete multifaceted measures are needed, for example, specific financial incentives (tax breaks, public subsidies and regulations to reduce the need for financial institutions to build up reserves, interest rate subsidies) while at the same time consistently monitoring environmental issues, as environmental policy is undoubtedly based on market power. In this context, it is important to note that as economic and financial globalisation, market integration and economic interrelations between countries (regions) are progressing, their financial markets are becoming increasingly close to each other. An increasing scale of interaction can be seen between financial markets not only in terms of asset prices but also in terms of asset volatility. This implies volatility in the financial market. What happens on the market of one country (region) can rub off on the financial market of another country (region), which implies 'volatility' ('spillover effect'), given that the development of green finance is to become a major trend for future development.

The research carried out has shown that a wide range of climate finance instruments are available to facilitate the initiation of national climate change programmes to address the country's climate finance needs related to both mitigation and adaptation. However, it is necessary to tailor climate finance to the individual needs of each country, taking into account its specific economic conditions and climate requirements. The financial tools used for climate finance are mainly based on established mechanisms often used in traditional finance. Debt and equity are two frequently used capital mechanisms in climate change financing. These instruments are primarily used to bridge the financing gap in long-term finance, project finance, equity finance and fees related to capital intensive and unpredictable implementation costs.

Green finance has emerged as a new financial tool to promote sustainable development, but its precise impact has not yet been conclusively proven, neither was it possible to do so in the discussions presented in this book. Research, for example, by Wang et al. (2022), suggests that policy-makers promote the greening of finance and its contribution to sustainability through governmental guidelines, improved classification and evaluation of green finance and better disclosure. The Authors as well as other researchers, e.g. Shih et al. (2023), Feng et al. (2023) and IMF (2024), opined the following:

- Green finance efforts should focus, in the near term, on creating opportunities for far better understanding, measurement, extraction and incorporation of climate risk data into business decisions, and developing robust models to assess the impact of climate on the macroeconomic risk as well as on the risk for financial institutions (this is in line with global efforts towards consistent and comparable risk measurement and assessments by standard-setting bodies such as the Basel Committee, the International Association of Insurance Supervisors, the Network for Greening the Financial Sector). To increase the resilience of economies and the financial sector to climate change risk, it is important to develop tools to better measure and understand climate risks: effective climate risk management starts with accurate measurement and understanding of such risks.

- In the context of Russia's aggression against Ukraine, which has a significant impact on energy policy but also other sectors such as agriculture, reviewing and updating climate strategies at EU and Member state level, and creating green financial ecosystems (which involves establishing a framework for sustainable financing and a taxonomy of responsible investments, improving access to reliable information on climate-related investments and green products as well as building capacity to overcome the constraints on climate action implementation).
- Policy action should continue to prioritise the implementation of standardised methods for quantifying and reporting climate risks. This entails the development of a comprehensive framework that takes into account both physical risks (for example, extreme weather events, rising sea level) and transitional risks (for example, policy changes and changes in consumer preferences). By adopting consistent methodologies and indicators, financial institutions (as well as their regulators and supervisors) can better assess and compare their exposure to climate risk, facilitating informed decision-making. Transparency plays a key role in promoting market efficiency and supporting prudent risk management. This disclosure should go beyond mere compliance and the pursuit of comprehensive and consistent reporting to enable stakeholders to make an informed assessment of an institution's exposure to climate risk.
- Creating a standardised reporting framework, for example as proposed by initiatives such as the Task Force on Climate-related Financial Disclosures and the International Sustainability Standards Board.
- Using new financial technologies, which are developing very rapidly, their applications becoming increasingly widespread in the fight against climate change. Through the use of green technologies and approaches, the environmental impacts of economic activities, such as carbon footprint and greenhouse gas emissions, can be accurately measured and tracked to promote environmental efforts and actions that contribute to a net-zero carbon future. The real-world case studies presented in this monograph help point to the tangible benefits of adopting green technologies in achieving sustainability goals and mitigating the effects of climate change. The future of finance lies in promoting sustainable practices, with green fintech, among others, playing a key role in enabling this transition. As such, it is critical for financial institutions to adopt sustainable financial practices and integrate green fintech solutions into their operations to support them in their transition to a more sustainable and equitable future. In

doing so, financial institutions must operate on a sound ethical basis and comply with relevant laws, regulations and standards. Indeed, to ensure this, aspects of sustainable finance management and green fintech, taking into account environmental and social responsibilities, are required. By putting ethics and compliance first, financial institutions can build trust among their stakeholders such as customers, investors and the wider community. Trust can foster collaboration between stakeholders and lead to more effective action on environmental efforts as they work together to mitigate climate change. This book explores the emerging areas of green finance, regenerative finance and green fintech. Green fintech, on the other hand, has the potential to transform the financial sector by improving the efficiency and transparency of investments, while enabling new forms of impact measurement and reporting. With the upward trend towards greener finance, these technologies and approaches can help address this urgent environmental and social challenge, thus creating a more positive future for all.

- Promoting initiatives that can redirect financial flows towards sustainable projects and investments. Green finance has the potential to drive this transition to a low-carbon economy. Regenerative finance, on the other hand, goes beyond sustainability by seeking to restore natural capital and support better ecosystem health.

References

Acevedo, M. S., Mrkaic, M., Novta, N., Pugacheva, E., & Topalova, P. B. (2018). The effects of weather shocks on economic activity: What are the channels of impact? *IMF Working Paper No. 18/144*. Available at SSRN: https://ssrn.com/abstract=3221232.

Adams, C. A., & Abhayawansa, S. (2022). Connecting the COVID-19 pandemic, environmental, social and governance (ESG) investing and calls for 'harmonisation' of sustainability reporting. *Critical Perspectives on Accounting, Elsevier, 82*(C). https://www.ncbi.nlm.nih.gov/pmc/articles/PMC8882606/pdf/main.pdf

Adebayo, T. S., Altuntaş, M., Goyibnazarov, S., Bonah, E., Hossam, M. Z., & Kamel, S. (2022). Dynamic effect of disintegrated energy consumption and economic complexity on environmental degradation in top economic complexity economies. *Energy Reports, 8*, 12832–12842. https://doi.org/10.1016/j.egyr.2022.09.161.

Afonso, A., & Furceri, D. (2008a). EMU enlargement, stabilization costs and insurance mechanisms. *Journal of International Money and Finance, 27*(2), 169–187. https://EconPapers.repec.org/RePEc:eee:jimfin:v:27:y:2008:i:2:p:169-187.

Afonso, A., & Furceri, D. (2008b). Government size, composition, volatility and economic growth, No 2008/04. Working Papers Department of Economics, ISEG - Lisbon School of Economics and Management, Department of Economics, Universidade de Lisbon.

Afonso, A., & Jalles, J. T. (2011). Growth and productivity: The role of Government Debt. Working Papers Department of Economics 2011/13, ISEG - Lisbon School of Economics and Management, Department of Economics, Universidade de Lisboa.

Afonso, A., & Jalles, J. T. (2012). Growth and productivity: The role of government debt (June 23, 2012). *International Review of Economics & Finance*, Forthcoming. Available at SSRN: https://ssrn.com/abstract=2089739.

Aghion, P., Boneva, L., Breckenfelder, J., Laeven, L., Popov, A., Olovsson, C., & Rancoita, E. (2022). Financial markets and green innovation. ECB Discussion Paper, forthcoming.

Aghion, P., & Roulet, A. M. (August 2014). Growth and the smart state. *Annual Review of Economics, 6*, 913–926. Available at SSRN: https://www.annualreviews.org/content/journals/10.1146/annurev-economics-080213-040759

Agovino, M., Casaccia, M., Ciommi, M., Ferrara, M., & Marchesano, K. (2019). Agriculture, climate change and sustainability: The case of EU-28. *Ecological Indicators, 105*, 525–543. https://doi.org/10.1016/j.ecolind.2018.04.064.

AIMA (2020). The alternative investment management association, guide to the EU sustainable disclosure regulation, 8. https://maples.com/-/media/files/pdfs/articles-and-chapters/maples-group--aima-guide-to-the-eu-sustainable-finance-disclosure-regulation--regulatory-technical-s.pdf.

Akhmouch, A., Clavreul, D., & Glas, P. (2018). Introducing the OECD principles on water governance. *Water International*, *43*(1), 5–12.

Akyapi, B., Bellon, M., & Massetti, E. (2022). Estimating macro-fiscal effects of climate shocks from billions of geospatial weather observations. *IMF Working Papers*.

Alesina, A., Campante, F., & Tabellini, G. (2008). Why is fiscal policy often procyclical? *Journal of the European Economic Association*, *6*(5), 1006–1036. https://econpapers.repec.org/article/tprjeurec/v_3a6_3ay_3a2008_3ai_3a5_3ap_3a1006-1036.htm.

Alfonso-Ercan, C. (2020). Private Equity and ESG Investing. In: Esty, D. C., Cort, T. (Eds.), *Values at work*. Cham: Palgrave Macmillan. https://doi.org/10.1007/978-3-030-55613-6_9.

Allen, F., & Gale, D. (2000). *Comparing financial systems*. Cambridge, MA: The MIT Press.

Allen, R. I., & Tandberg, E. (2021). How to Manage Public Investment during a Postcrisis Recovery. IMF How to Notes, 2021(007), A001. Retrieved May 25, 2024. https://doi.org/10.5089/9781513584416.061.A001.

Allen, W. A., & Wood, G. (2006). Defining and achieving financial stability. *Journal of Financial Stability*, *2*, 159–160. https://doi. org/10.1016/j.jfs.2005.10.001.

Ali, R., McFarlane, D., Varma, S., Dawes, W., Emelyanova, I., & Hodgson, G. (2012). Potential climate change impacts on the water balance of regional unconfined aquifer systems in south-western Australia. *Hydrology and Earth System Sciences*, *16*(12), 4581–4601. https://doi.org/10.5194/hess-16-4581-2012, 2012.

Ali, R. S., & Nida, S. (2018). Testing environmental Kuznets curve hypothesis in G7 countries: The role of renewable energy consumption and trade. *Environmental Science and Pollution Research*, *25*, 26965–26977. https://doi.org/10.1007/s11356-018-2673-z.

Ambhore, S., & Ofori, E. K. (2023). Exploring psychological well-being in business and economics arena: A bibliometric analysis. *Health Science Reports*, January 6, *6*(1), e1044. https://doi.org/10.1002/hsr2.1044. PMID: 36620512; PMCID: PMC9817197.

Arak, P. (2023). Czy inwestowanie w broń może być etyczne? In Zielone Finance w Polsce, L. Kotecki (Eds.), *UN global compact network Poland* (pp. 72–75). Warsaw. UN global compact network Poland.

Arora, N. K. (2019). Impact of climate change on agriculture production and its sustainable solutions. *Environmental Sustainability*, *2*, 95–96. https://doi.org/10.1007/s42398-019-00078-w.

Aydin, C., & Esen, O. (2018). Reducing CO_2 emissions in the EU member states: Do environmental taxes work? *Journal of Environmental Planning and Management*, *61*(13), 2396–2420. https://doi.org/10.1080/09640568.2017.1395731.

Azzari, G., Grassini, P., Edreira, J. I. R., Conley, S., Mourtzinis, S., & Lobell, D. B. (2019). Satellite mapping of tillage practices in the North Central US region from 2005 to 2016. *Remote Sensing of Environment*, *221*, 417–429, ISSN 0034-4257, https://doi.org/10.1016/j.rse.2018.11.010.

Bailey, I., & Compston, H. (2012). *Feeling the heat. The politics of climate policy in rapidly industrializing countries*. Hampshire: Palgrave Macmillan.

Bajo-Rubio, O., & Ramon, M.-D. (2000). Exchange rate pass-through in the new member states of the European Union: Some explanatory factors. *Research Papers of Wrocław University of Economics*, *14*(201), 88–94.

Baker, M., Bergstresser, D., Serafeim, G., & Wurgler J. (2018). Financing the response to climate change: The pricing and ownership of US green bonds. NBER Working Paper Series, Working Paper 25194. http://www.nber.org/papers/w25194.

Bamidele, R., Ozturk, I., Gyamfi, B., & Bekun, V. F. (2022). Tourism-induced pollution emission amidst energy mix: Evidence from Nigeria. *Environmental Science and Pollution Research*, *29*, 19752–19761. https://doi.org/10.1007/s11356-021-17233-8.

Banking on Climate Change (2019). Fossil fuel finance report card 2019. https://www.ran.org/wp-content/uploads/2019/03/Banking_on_Climate_Change_2019_vFINAL1.pdf.

Bansal, R., Kiku, D., & Ochoa, M. (2016). What do capital markets tell us about climate change? *Working Paper*, Duke University.

Bargiel, D. (2017). A new method for crop classification combining time series of radar images and crop phenology information. *Remote Sensing of Environment, 198*, 369–383. https://doi.org/10.1016/j.rse.2017.06.022.

Barnett, J. (2003). *Redesigning Cities*. Chicago: APA Planners Press.

Barreca, A., & Schaller, J. (2020). The impact of high ambient temperatures on delivery timing and gestational lengths. *Nature Climate Change, 10*(1), 77–82. https://doi.org/10.10.1038/s41558-019-0632-4.

Barrett, T. W., & Scott, T. B. (1990). Suicide bereavement and recovery patterns compared with nonsuicide bereavement patterns. *Suicide and Life-Threatening Behavior, 20*, 1–15. https://doi.org/10.1111/j.1943-278X.1990.tb00650.x

Barro, R. J. (1991). Economic growth in a cross section of countries. *The Quarterly Journal of Economics, 106*(2), 407–443. Handle: RePEc:oup:qjecon:v:106:y:1991:i:2:p:407-443.

Basnet, D. M. (2022). Investigating the validity of the Wong and law emotional intelligence scale in a Nepali student sample (November 19, 2022). *Emotional Intelligence*.

Baumgartner, R. J., & Korhonen, J. (2010). Strategic thinking for sustainable development. *Sustainable Development, 18*(2), 71–75.

Bekkhus, N. B. (2007). Energy and climate change in the European Union. *Studia Diplomatica, 60*(2), 157–211. http://www.jstor.org/stable/44839184

Bennett, B., Salawitch, R., Canty, T. Hope, A., & Tribett, W. (2017). *Paris climate agreement: Beacon of hope*. https://doi.org/10.1007/978-3-319-46939-3.

Berg, F., Fabisik, K., & Sautner, Z. (2021). *Is history repeating itself? The (un)predictable past of ESG ratings*. Mimeo. Finance Working Paper N° 708/2020 August 2021, https://www.ecgi.global/sites/default/files/working_papers/documents/bergfabisiksautnerfinal_3.pdf.

Bergh, A., & Karlsson, M. (2010). Government size and growth: Accounting for economic freedom and globalization. *Public Choice, 142*, 195–213. https://doi.org/10.1007/s11127-009-9484-1.

Bernauer, T., Böhmelt, T., & Koubi, V. (2013). Is there a democracy–civil society paradox in global environmental governance? *Global Environmental Politics, 13*(1), 88–107.

Bernauer, T., & Koubi, V. (2006). States as providers of public goods: How does government size affect environmental quality? Available at https://ssrn.com/abstract=900487

Bernauer, T., & Koubi, V. (2009). Globalization, democracy and the environment. *National Centre of Competence in Research (NCCR)-Challenges to Democracy in the 21st Century, 32*. https://citeseerx.ist.psu.edu/document?repid=rep1&type=pdf&doi=b029e88284f660e0ff2723566dfbbcc67d89fd29.

Bernauer, T., Böhmelt, T., & Koubi, V. (2013). Is There a Democracy–Civil Society Paradox in Global Environmental Governance? *Global Environmental Politics*, MIT Press, *13*(1), 88–107.

Bernstein, A., Gustafson, M. T., & Lewis, R. (2019). Disaster on the horizon: The price effect of sea level rise. *Journal of Financial Economics, 134*(2), 253–272. https://doi.org/10.1016/j.jfineco.2019.03.013.

Berry, M. A., & Rondinelli, D. A. (1998). Proactive corporate environmental management: A new industrial revolution. *The Academy of Management Executive (1993–2005), 12*(2), 38–50. http://www.jstor.org/stable/416545.

Blank, L., Baxter, S., Buckley Woods, H., & Goyder, E. (2021). Interventions to reduce the public health burden of gambling-related harms: A mapping review. *Lancet Public Health*, *6*(1), e50–e63. https://doi.org/10.1016/S2468-2667(20)30230-9.

Bonini, S., Capizzi, V., Valletta, M., & Zocchi, P. (2018). Angel network affiliation and business angels' investment practices. *Journal of Corporate Finance*, 50 pp. 592–608.

Borenstein, S., & Bushnell, J. B. (2018). *Are residential electricity prices too high or too low? Or both?* Cambridge: National Bureau of Economic Research.

Bosco, G., & Simeoni, L. (2018). Environmental impact of intensive farming in sloping areas MATEC Web of Conferences, Trento. *EDP Sciences*, Article 01001. https://doi.org/10.1051/matecconf/201817401001

Bosello, Francesco and Eboli, Fabio and Pierfederici, Roberta, Assessing the Economic Impacts of Climate Change (February 10, 2012). FEEM (Fondazione Eni Enrico Mattei), Review of Environment, Energy and Economics (Re3), February 2012, Available at SSRN: https://ssrn.com/abstract=2030223

Boston, J., Martin, J., Pallot, J., & Walsh, P. eds. 1991. *Reshaping the State: New Zealand's Bureaucratic Revolution*. Auckland: Oxford University Press.

Boubaker, S., John, W., Goodell, Dharen Kumar Pandey, & Vineeta Kumari (2022). Heterogeneous impacts of wars on global equity markets: Evidence from the invasion of Ukraine. *Finance Research Letters*, *48*, 102934. https://doi.org/10.1016/j.frl.2022.102934.

Boungou, W., & Yatié, A. (2022). The impact of the Ukraine–Russia war on world stock market returns. *Economics Letters*, *Elsevier*, *215*(C).

Bowen, A., & Stern, N. (2010). Environmental policy and the economic downturn. *Oxford Review of Economic Policy*, *26*(2), 137–163.

Braun, S., Enculescu, M., Setty, S. T., Cortés-López, M., de Almeida, B. P., Sutandy, F. R., Schulz, L., Busch, A., Seiler, M., Ebersberger, S., Barbosa-Morais, N. L., Legewie, S., König, J., & Zarnack, K. (2018). Decoding a cancer-relevant splicing decision in the RON proto-oncogene using high-throughput mutagenesis. *Nature Communications*, *9*(1), 3315. https://doi.org/10.1038/s41467-018-05748-7. PMID: 30120239; PMCID: PMC6098099.

Brännlund, R., & Nordström, J. (2004). Carbon tax simulations using a household demand model. *European Economic Review*, *48*(1), 211–233.

Breckenfelder, J., Mackowiak, B., Marques, D., Olovsson, C., Popov, A., Porcellacchia, D., & Schepens, G. (2023). The climate and the economy, ECB. Working Paper Series.

Bressers, J. T. A., & Lulofs, K. R. D. (2004). Industrial water pollution in the Netherlands: A free-based approach. In W. Harrington, R. D. Morgenstern, & T. Sterner (Eds.), *Choosing environmental Policy: Comparing instruments and outcomes in the United States and Europe* (pp. 91–116). Resources for the Future Press.

Breuer, W., & Pinkwart, A. (2018). Venture capital and private equity finance as key determinants of economic development, *Journal of Business Economics*, *88*, 319–324.

Brocca, L., Tarpanelli, A., Filippucci, P., Dorigo, W., Zaussinger, F., Gruber, A., & Fernández-Prieto, D. (2018). How much water is used for irrigation? A new approach exploiting coarse resolution satellite soil moisture products. *International Journal of Applied Earth Observation and Geoinformation*, *73*, 752–766, ISSN 1569-8432, https://doi.org/10.1016/j.jag.2018.08.023.

Broniewicz, E., & Poskrobko, B. (2004). *Nakłady na ochronę środowiska. Metodyka i wyniki badań*. Wydawnictwo Ekonomia i Środowisko, Białystok.

Bruvoll, A., & Larsen, B. M. (2004). Greenhouse gas emissions in Norway: Do carbon taxes work? *Energy Policy*, *32*(4), 493–505. https://EconPapers.repec.org/RePEc:eee:enepol:v:32:y:2004:i:4:p:493-505.

Buchner, B., Naran, B., de Aragão Fernandes, P., Padmanabhi, R., Rosane, P., Solomon, M., Stout, S., Wakaba, G., Zhu, Y., Meattle, C., Guzmán, S., & Strinati, C. (December 14, 2021). Global Landscape of Climate Finance 2021 - CPI (climatepolicyinitiative.org).

Burke, M., Hsiang, S., & Miguel, E. (2015). Global non-linear effect of temperature on economic production. *Nature*, *527*, 235–239. https://doi.org/10.1038/nature15725.

Burke, M., & Tanutama, V. (2019). Climatic constraints on aggregate economic output. *NBER Working Paper* No. w25779. Available at SSRN: https://ssrn.com/abstract=3390983.

Callaway, J. M. (2003). Adaptation benefits and costs–measurement and policy issues. *Environment Directorate, Environment Policy Committee, OECD, Paris, France, ENV/EPOC/GSP*, *10*(2002), 44.

Calliari, E., Staccione, A., & Mysiak, J. (2019). An assessment framework for climate-proof nature-based solutions. *Science of the Total Environment*, March 15, *656*, 691–700. https://doi.org/10.1016/j.scitotenv.2018.11.341. Epub November 24, 2018. PMID: 30529972.

Campos-Taberner, M., García-Haro, F. J., Martínez, B., Izquierdo-Verdiguier, E., Atzberger, C., Camps-Valls, G., & Gilabert, M. A. (2020). Understanding deep learning in land use classification based on Sentinel-2 time series. *Scientific Reports*, *10*, 17188. https://doi.org/10.1038/s41598-020-74215-5.

Caney, S. (2012). Just emissions. *Philosophy & Public Affairs*, *40*(4), 255–300. http://www.jstor.org/stable/23323980.

Carroll, A. (2021). Corporate social responsibility (CSR) and the COVID-19 pandemic: Organizational and managerial implications. *Journal of Strategy and Management*, *14*(3), 315–330. https://doi.org/10.1108/JSMA-07-2021 0145.

Carvalho, L., & Santos, M. R. C. (2024). The role of the energy sector in contributing to sustainability development goals: A text mining analysis of literature. *Energies*, *17*. https://doi.org/10.3390/ en17010208. https://www.preprints.org/manuscript/202311.1241/v1.

Cevik, S., & Jalles, J. (2020). This changes everything: Climate shocks and sovereign bonds, No 2020/0132. Working Papers REM, ISEG - Lisbon School of Economics and Management, REM, Universidade de Lisboa. https://EconPapers.repec.org/RePEc:ise:remwps:wp01322020.

Cevik, S., & Jalles, J. T. (2021). An apocalypse foretold: Climate shocks and sovereign defaults. *Open Economies Review*, *33*, 89–108.

Cevik, S., & Jalles, J. T. (2022). This changes everything: Climate shocks and sovereign bonds. Energy Economics, Elsevier, *107*(C).

Cevik, S., & Jalles, J. T. (2023). For whom the bell tolls: Climate change and income inequality, *Energy Policy*, *174*. https://doi.org/10.1016/j.enpol.2023.113475.

Chang, H. (2011). 23 *Things they don't tell you about capitalism*. New York: Bloomsbury Press; London: Allen Lane.

Cherednichenko, O., Dovgotko, N., Rybasova, Y., Vorontsova, G., & Momotova, O. (2022). Implementation of the UN sustainable development goals in the agri-food system of Russia: regional and sectoral features. *International Journal of Sustainable Development & World Ecology*, *29*, 483–498. https://doi.org/10.1080/13504509.2022.2040635.

Claessens, S. (2016). Regulation and structural change in financial systems. ECB Forum on Central Banking. https://www.ecb.europa.eu/pub/conferences/ecbforum/shared/pdf/2016/claessens_paper.pdf.

Cline, W. R. (1992). *The economics of global warming*. Washington, DC: Institute for International Economics.

Coase, R. H. (1960). The problem of social cost. *The Journal of Law and Economics*, *3*, 1–44.

Colacito, R., Hoffmann, B., & Phan, T. (2019). Temperature and growth: A panel analysis of the United States. *Journal of Money, Credit and Banking*, *51*(2–3), 313–368. https://doi.org/10.1111/jmcb.12574.

Cooper, R., Burton, E., & Cooper, C. (Eds.). (2014). *Wellbeing: A complete reference guide, wellbeing and the environment* (Vol. 2). Chichester: John Wiley & Sons.

Cooper, D. & Pankaj, P. & Sherry, T. (2014). It depends: Environmental context and the effects of faultlines on top management team performance. *Organization Science*, *25*, 633–652. https://doi.org/10.1287/orsc.2013.0855.

Council of State (2008). Long term climate and energy strategy. Government Report to Parliament 6 November 2008. Summary in English. http://www.tem.fi/files/20587/Climate_Change_and_Energy_Strategy_2008_summary.pdf, The whole strategy available in Finnish. http://www.tem.fi/files/20585/Selontekoehdotus_311008.pdf.

Cowan, M. M. (1999). Plant products as antimicrobial agents. *Clinical Microbiology Reviews*, *12*, 564–582.

Crawford, I., Keen, M., & Smith, S. (2008). Preference structures and optimal commodity taxation. Institute for Fiscal Studies, *Working Paper.*

Cremer, H., & Gahvari, F. (2002). Imperfect observability of emissions and second-best emission and output taxes. *Journal of Public Economics*, *85*(3), 385–407. https://www.sciencedirect.com/science/article/abs/pii/S0047272701001207.

Crocetti, D., Monro, S., Vecchietti, V., & Yeadon-Lee, T. (2021). Towards an agency-based model of intersex, variations of sex characteristics (VSC) and DSD/dsd health. *Culture, Health & Sexuality*, *23*(4), 500–515. https://doi.org/10.1080/13691058.2020.1825815.

Crocker, T. D. (1966). The structuring of atmospheric pollution control systems. In H. Wolozin (Ed.), *The economics of air pollution* (pp. 61–86). New York: W. W. Norton & Co.

Cruz, J.-L., & Rossi-Hansberg, E. (2021). The economic geography of global warming. *Working Paper 28466*, National Bureau of Economic Research. http://www.nber.org/papers/w28466.

Cuaresma, J. C. (2010). Natural disasters and human capital accumulation. *The World Bank Economic Review*, *24*(2), 280–302. http://www.jstor.org/stable/40891368.

Dagiliene, L., & Nadzinkiene, R. (2018). An institutional theory perspective on non-financial reporting: The developing Baltic context. *Journal of Financial Reporting and Accounting*, *16*(4), 490–521. https://doi.org/10.1108/JFRA-06-2016-0054

Dales, J. H. (1983). Distortions and dissipations. *Canadian Public Policy/Analyse de Politiques*, *9*(2), 257–263.

Dall'erba, S., & Fang, F. (2017). Meta-analysis of the impact of European Union structural funds on regional growth. *Regional Studies*, *51*, 1–12. https://doi.org/10.1080/00343404.2015.1100285.

D'Anselmi, P. (2020). CSR and Covid-19 what CSR has to say about coronavirus. *Academy of Strategic Management Journal*, *20*(4), 168–189. https://doi.org/10.13140/RG.2.2.20728.26883.

Dantas de Paula, M., Forrest, M., Langan, L., Bendix, J., Homeier, J., Velescu, A., Wilcke, W., & Hickler, T. (2021). Nutrient cycling drives plant community trait assembly and ecosystem functioning in a tropical mountain biodiversity hotspot. *New Phytologist*, *232*, 551–566. https://doi.org/10.1111/nph.17600.

Davis, S. J., Caldeira, K., & Matthews, H. D. (2010). Future CO2 emissions and climate change from existing energy infrastructure. *Science*, September 10, *329*(5997), 1330–1333. https://doi.org/10.1126/science.1188566. PMID: 20829483.

Defard, T., Setkov, A., Loesch, A., & Audigier, R. (2021, January). Padim: A patch distribution modeling framework for anomaly detection and localization. In *International*

Conference on Pattern Recognition (pp. 475–489). Cham: Springer International Publishing.

de Graaf, I. E. M., Gleeson, T., van Beek, L. P. H., Sutanudjaja, E. H., & Bierkens, M. F. (2019). Environmental flow limits to global groundwater pumping. *Nature*, *574*, 90–94. https://doi.org/10.1038/s41586-019-1594-4.Dell, M., Jones, B. F., & Olken, B. A. (2009). Temperature and income: Reconciling new cross-sectional and panel estimates. *American Economic Review*, *99*(2), 198–204. https://doi.org/10.1257/aer.99.2.198.

Dell, M., Jones, B. F., & Olken, B. A. (2012). Temperature shocks and economic growth: Evidence from the last half century. *American Economic Journal: Macroeconomics*, *4*(3), 66–95. https://doi.org/10.1257/mac.4.3.66.

Dellink, R., Lanzi, E. & Chateau, J. The Sectoral and Regional Economic Consequences of Climate Change to 2060. Environ Resource Econ 72, 309–363 (2019). https://doi.org/10.1007/s10640-017-0197-5

Deloitte (2021). The EU is getting closer to disclosure rules on sustainable finance. https://www.deloitte.com/content/dam/Deloitte/lu/Documents/sustainable-dev/lu-regnewsalert-eu-disclosure-rules-sustainable-finance_14032019.pdf.

Deng, A., & Hernández, C. (2022). Algorithmic pricing in horizontal merger review: An initial assessment (October 21, 2021). *Antitrust*, Spring 2022, *36*(2), 36–41. Available at SSRN: https://ssrn.com/abstract=3971920 or https://doi.org/10.2139/ssrn.3971920.

Desmet, K., Nagy, D., Rossi-Hansberg, E., 2015. The Geography of Development: Evaluating Migration Restrictions and Coastal Flooding, Princeton University.

Deschênes, O., Greenstone, M., & Guryan, J. (2009). Climate change and birth weight. *American Economic Review*, *99*(2), 211–217.

Deyle, R. E., & Bretschneider, S. (1995). Spillovers of state policy innovations: New York's hazardous waste regulatory initiatives. *Journal of Policy Analysis and Management*, *14*, 79–106.

De Simone, E., Gaeta, G. L., & Ercolano, S. (2010). Exploring convergence in some OECD public social expenditure trends. *MPRA Paper*, 22496, 2–24.

Dissou, Y., Didic, S., & Yakautsava, T. (2016). Government spending on education, human capital accumulation, and growth. *Economic Modelling*, *58*, 9–21.

Di Cosmo, V., & Hyland, M. (2013). Carbon tax scenarios and their effects on the Irish energy sector. *Energy Policy*, *59*, 404–414. ISSN 0301-4215. https://doi.org/10.1016/j.enpol.2013.03.055.

Dissou, Y., & Karnizova, L. (2016). Emissions cap or emissions tax? A multi-sector business cycle analysis. *Journal of Environmental Economics and Management*, *79*, 169–188. https://doi.org/10.1016/j.jeem.2016.05.002

D. J. Maddison. The amenity value of the climate: the household production function approach. Resource and Energy Economics, 25(2):155–175, 2003. 19

Dmytrów, K., Bieszk-Stolorz, B., & Landmesser-Rusek, J. (2022). Journal sustainable energy in European countries: Analysis of sustainable development goal 7 using the dynamic time warping method. *Energies*, *15*. https:// doi.org/10.3390/en15207756.

Downing, T. E., Eyre, N., Greener, R., & Blackwell, D. (1996). *Projected costs of climate change for two reference scenarios and fossil fuel cycles*. Oxford: Environmental Change Unit.

Downing, T. E., Ringius, L., Hulme, M., & Waughray, D. (1997). Adapting to climate change in Africa. *Mitigation and Adaptation Strategies for Global Change*, *2*, 19–44. https://doi.org/10.1007/BF02437055.

Drover, W., Busenitz, L., Matusik, S., Townsend, D., Anglin, A., & Dushnitsky, G. (2017). A review and road map of entrepreneurial equity financing research: Venture capital,

corporate venture capital, angel investment, crowdfunding, and accelerators, *Journal of Management, 43*(6) 111–124.
Dunlap, R. E., & Scarce, R. (1991a). Poll trends: Environmental problems and protection. *The Public Opinion Quarterly, 55*(4), 651–672. http://www.jstor.org/stable/2749413
Dunlap, R. E., & Scarce, R. (1991b). Risk scare. Environmental problems and protection. *Public Opinion Quarterly, 55*, 651–672.
Duwe, M. (2022). *Making EU climate governance fit for net zero.* https://www.ecologic.eu/de/18516.
EBRD, 2023, Sustainability Report 2023. https://www.ebrd.com/sustainability-report-2023.html#.
EC (2018). A Clean Planet for all: A European strategic long-term vision for a prosperous, modern, competitive and climate neutral economy - Transport aspects – Policy debate, Brussels.
EC (2021). Social Climate Fund. Social Climate Fund | EUR-Lex (europa.eu).
EC (2023). Commission legislative proposals on sustainable finance. Commission legislative proposals on sustainable finance. European Commission (europa.eu).
ECA (2021). Climate Change & Audi. journal20_02_en.pdf (europa.eu).
ECA (2023). Special report 18/2023: EU climate and energy targets – 2020 targets achieved, but little indication that actions to reach the 2030 targets will be sufficient, Luksemburg | European Court of Auditors (europa.eu).
ECB (2023a). Financial stability review. https://www.ecb.europa.eu/pub/financial-stability/fsr/html/ecb.fsr202311~bfe9d7c565.pl.html#toc2.
ECB (2023b). https://www.ecb.europa.eu/ecb/tasks/stability/html/index.en.html.
EEA (2020). EEA Programming Document 2020–2022.
EEA and Eurofound, 2021 Anticipating and managing the impact of change Anticipating and managing the impact of change | European Foundation for the Improvement of Living and Working Conditions (europa.eu).
Economist (2023). Will climate finance make or brake COP28? https://impact.economist.com/sustainability/circular-economies/will-climate-finance-make-or-break-cop28.
EIB (2023). EIB investment report 2022–2023: Resilience and renewal in Europe. https://www.eib.org/en/publications/20220211-investment-report-2022.
EIB (2024). Investment report 2023/2024. Transforming for competitiveness. European Investment Bank. https://www.eib.org/attachments/lucalli/20230323_economic_investment_report_2023_2024_en.pdf.
Eichhammer, W., Boede, U., Gagelmann, F., Jochem, E., Kling, N., Schleich, J., Schlomann, B., Chesshire, J., & Ziesing, H. J. (2001). Greenhouse gas reductions in Germany and the UK—coincidence or policy induced? An analysis for international climate policy. Germany.
Ehlers, T., & Packer, F. (2017). Green bond finance and certification. *BIS Quarterly Review*, 89–104. https://www.bis.org/publ/qtrpdf/r_qt1709h.pdf.
El-Ghoul, S., & Karoui, A. (2017). Does corporate social responsibility affect mutual fund performance and flows? *Journal of Banking and Finance*, *77*, 53–63. https://doi.org/10.1016/j.jbankfin.2016.10.009.
Ellerman, A. D., Joskow, P. L., & Harrison Jr, D. (2003). Emissions trading in the US. *Pew Centre on Global Climate Change*. Pew Center on Global Climate Change Report, May. http://www.pewclimate.org/global-warming-in-depth/all_reports/emissions_trading/emisstrad_contents.cfm.

Ercolano, S., & Romano, R. (2018). Spending for the environment: General government expenditure trends in Europe. *Social Indicators Research, 138*, 1145–1169. https://doi.org/10.1007/s11205-017-1695-0

Estrada, Á., & Santabárbara, D. (2021). Recycling carbon tax revenues in Spain. Environmental and economic assessment of selected green reforms. *Working Papers* 2119, Banco de España.

ETTG (2022). European think tanks group, The European Green deal and the war in Ukraine addressing crises in the short and long term. The-European-Green-Deal-and-the-war-in-Ukraine.pdf (ettg.eu).

Euronews (2024). Farmers from 12 EU countries continue to protest agricultural policies, 23 February 2024. https://www.euronews.com/my-europe/2024/02/23/farmers-from-12-eu-countries-continue-to-protest-agricultural-policies.

European Commission (2014). Directorate-General for Communication, Directorate-General for Environment, Attitudes of European citizens towards the environment – Report, Publications Office. https://data.europa.eu/doi/10.2779/25662.

European Business Angels Network (2022). EBAN Statistics Compedium. European Early-Stage Market Statistics. https://www.eban.org/wp-content/uploads/2022/10/Statistics-Compendium-2021-FINAL-3.pdf.

European Central Bank (2023). Towards an orderly energy transition. Press release, 29 September.

European Commission (1977). The perception of poverty in Europe. Report on a public opinion survey carried out in the member countries of the European Community as part of the programme of pilot projects to combat poverty. V/171/77-E EU, European Commission - Working Document.

European Commission (1995). European Environment Agency, Eurostat, Wieringa, K., *Environment in the European Union 1995 – Summary: Report for the review of the fifth environmental action programme*, Publications Office.

European Commission (2017a). Special Eurobarometer 468: Attitudes of European citizens towards the environment. *European Economic Review*, *45*(8), 1501–1520.

European Commission (2017b). The European Green Deal sets out how to make Europe the first climate neutral continent by 2050, boosting the economy, improving people's health and quality of life, caring for nature, and leaving no one behind. European Commission - Press release.

European Commission (2019). *Term sheet on the budgetary instrument for convergence and competitiveness*. https://www.consilium.europa.eu/en/press/press-releases/2019/06/14/term-sheet-on-the-budgetary-instrument-for-convergence-and-competitiveness/ [accessed: 20.07.2019].

European Court of Auditors (2019). Annual report: 2019 EU accounts: Clean, but too many spending errors. European Court of Auditors (europa.eu).

European Environment Agency (1998). *Europe's environment – The second assessment: Data pocketbook*. Publications Office, 1998.

European Parliament (2023). *Cutting EU greenhouse gas emissions: National targets for 2030*. https://www.europarl.europa.eu/news/en/headlines/society/20180208STO97442/cutting-eu-greenhouse-gas-emissions-national-targets-for-2030.

Eurostat (2023). Sustainable development in the European Union Monitoring report on progress towards the SDGs in an EU context 2023 edition, Sustainable development in the European Union - Publications Office of the EU (europa.eu).

Fankhauser, S. (1995). Protection versus retreat: The economic costs of sea level rise. *Environment and Planning A*, *27*, 299–319.

Fankhauser, S., & Tol, R. (1996). Climate change costs: Recent advancements in the economic assessment. *Energy Policy*, *24*(7), 665–673.

Fankhauser, S., Smith, J., & Tol, R. (1999). Weathering climate change: Some simple rules to guide adaptation decisions. *Ecological Economics*, *30*(1), 67–78. https://doi.org/10.1016/S0921-8009(98)00117-7.

Fankhauser, S., Tol, R., & Pearce, D. (1997). The Aggregation of climate change damages: A welfare theoretic approach. *Environmental & Resource Economics*, *10*(3), 249–266.

Farzin, Y. H., & Bond, C. A. (2006). Democracy and environmental quality. *Journal of Development Economics*, *81*(1), 213–235.

Febi, W., Schäfer, D., Stephan, A., & Sun, C. (2018). The impact of liquidity risk on the yield spread of green bonds. *Finance Research Letters*, *27*, 53–59. https://doi.org/10.1016/j.frl.2018.02.025.

Feng, Jing-Chun, Sun, L., & Yan, J. (2023). Carbon sequestration via shellfish farming: A potential negative emissions technology. *Renewable and Sustainable Energy Reviews*, *171*, 113018. https://doi.org/10.1016/j.rser.2022.113018.

Fernando, J. (2020). Climate finance: Meaning, contributors, example. investopedia.com.

Filipović, S., & Golušin, M. (2015). Environmental taxation policy in the EU – new methodology approach. *Journal of Cleaner Production*, *88*, 308–317. https://doi.org/10.1016/j.jclepro.2014.03.002.

Fischer, C. (2008). Feedback on household electricity consumption: A tool for saving energy? *Energy Efficiency*, *1*, 79–104. https://doi.org/10.1007/s12053-008-9009-7.

Fischer, C., & Newell, R. G. (2008). Environmental and technology policies for climate mitigation. *Journal of Environmental Economics and Management*, *55*(2), 142–162.

Flammer, C. (2020). Green bonds: Effectiveness and implications for public policy. *Environmental and Energy Policy and the Economy*, *1*, 95–128. https://doi.org/10.1086/706794.

Folster, S., & Henrekson, M. (2001). Growth effects of government expenditure and taxation in rich countries. *European Economic Review*, *45*(8), 1501–1520. https://www.sciencedirect.com/science/article/abs/pii/S0014292100000830.

Foster, T., Mieno, T., & Brozovic, N. (2020). Satellite-based monitoring of irrigation water use: Assessing measurement errors and their implications for agricultural water management policy. *Water Resources Research*. https://doi.org/10.5281/zenodo.4079027.

Frederik, C., & Lundström, S. (2001). Political and economic freedom and the environment: The case of CO2 emissions. *Working Paper in Economics no. 29*. University of Gothenburg, Gothenburg.

Fredriksson, P. G., List, J. A., & Millimet, D. L. (2003). Bureaucratic corruption, environmental policy and inbound US FDI: Theory and evidence. *Journal of Public Economics*, *87*(7–8), 1407–1430.

Fredriksson, P. G., & Svensson, J. (2003). Political instability, corruption and policy formation: The case of environmental policy. *Journal of Public Economics*, *87*(7–8), 1383–1405.

Freire-González, J. (2018). Environmental taxation and the double dividend hypothesis in CGE modelling literature: A critical review. *Journal of Policy Modeling*, *40*(1), 194–223.

Friede, G., Busch, T., & Bassen, A. (2015). ESG and financial performance: Aggregated evidence from more than 2000 empirical studies. *Journal of Sustainable Finance & Investment*, *5*(14), 210–233. https://doi.org/10.1080/20430795.2015.1118917.

Fullerton, D., & Kim, S. R. (2008). Environmental investment and policy with distortionary taxes, and endogenous growth. *Journal of Environmental Economics and Management*, *56*(2), 141–154.

Fullerton, D., & West, S. (2002). Can Taxes on cars and on gasoline mimic an unavailable tax on emissions? *Journal of Environmental Economics and Management*, *43*(1), 135–157. https://www.sciencedirect.com/science/article/abs/pii/S0095069600911690.

Gago, J., Filgueiras, A., Pedrotti, M. L., Caetano, M., & Frias, J.(2019). Standardised protocol for monitoring microplastics in seawater. Deliverable 4.1. JPI-Oceans BASEMAN Project, 33pp. https://doi.org/10.25607/OBP-605.

Galinato, G. I., & Islam, A. (2017). The challenge of addressing consumption pollutants with fiscal policy. *Environment and Development Economics*, *22*(5), 624–647.

Gallup, J. L., Sachs, J. D., & Mellinger, A. D. (1999). Geography and economic development. *International Regional Science Review*, *22*(2), 179–232. https://doi.org/10.1177/016001799761012334

Gans, J. S. (2012). Innovation and climate change policy. *American Economic Journal: Economic Policy*, *4*(4), 125–145.

Gavin, M., & Hausmann, R. (1996). The roots of banking crises: The macroeconomic context (January 1996). IDB Working Paper No. 262, Available at SSRN: https://ssrn.com/abstract=1815948 or https://doi.org/10.2139/ssrn.1815948.

Gassebner, M., Keck, A., & Teh, R. (2010). Shaken, not stirred: The impact of disasters on international trade. *Review of International Economics*, *18*, 351–368. https://doi.org/10.1111/j.1467-9396.2010.00868.x.

Georgescu, M. A., & Cabeca, J. C. (2010). Environmental protection expenditure and revenues in the EU, EFTA and candidate countries 2001–2006. In *Eurostat. Statistics in Focus*, 31/2010.

Geraldini, S., Bruschi, A., Bellotti, G., & Taramelli, A. (2021). User needs analysis for the definition of operational coastal services. *Water*, *13*, 92. https://doi.org/10.3390/w13010092.

Gerlagh, R., & Lise, W. (2005). Carbon taxes: A drop in the ocean, or a drop that erodes the stone? The effect of carbon taxes on technological change. *Ecological Economics*, *54*(2–3), 241–260.

Gerlagh, R., & van der Zwaan (2006). Climate sensitivity uncertainty and the necessity to transform global energy supply. *Energy*, *31*(2006), 2571–2587.

Gerster R. (2011). Sustainable finance: Achievements, challenges, outlook. http://www.gersterconsulting.ch/docs/Sustainable_finance_final_11.02.10.pdf.

Ghali, K. (1998b). Public investment and private capital formation in a vector error-correction model of growth. *Applied Economics*, *30*(6), 837–844. https://EconPapers.repec.org/RePEc:taf:applec:v:30:y:1998:i:6:p:837-844.

G&A Institute (2023). Governance & accountability institute, Inc., sustainability reporting in focus. https://www.ga-institute.com/research/ga-research-directory/sustainability-reporting-trends/2023-sustainability-reporting-in-focus.html.

Giannarakis, G., & Theotokas, I. (2011). The effect of financial crisis in corporate social responsibility performance. *International Journal of Marketing Studies*, *3*, 2–10. https://doi.org/10.5539/ijms.v3n1p2.

Gielen, A. C., & Zwiers, E. (2018). Biology and the gender gap in educational performance: The role of prenatal testosterone in test scores. IZA Discussion Papers 11936, Institute of Labor Economics (IZA).

Giglio, S., Bryan, K., & Johannes, S. (2021). Climate finance (November 1, 2021). *Annual Review of Financial Economics*, *13*, 15–36. Available at https://ssrn.com/abstract=3957028 or https://doi.org/10.1146/annurev-financial-102620-103311.

Giglio, S., Maggiori, M. Krishna Rao, Stroebel, J., & Weber, A. (August 2021). Climate change and long-run discount rates: Evidence from real estate, *The Review of Financial Studies*, *34*(8), 3527–3571. https://doi.org/10.1093/rfs/hhab032.

Gilroy, J. M., & Shapiro, R. Y. (1986). The polls: Environmental protection. *Public Opinion Quarterly*, *50*, 270–279.

Ginglinger, E., & Moreau, Q. (2019). Climate risk and capital structure. Université Paris Dauphine Research Paper 3327185.

Giuzio, M., Krusec, D., Levels, A., Melo, A. S., Mikkonen, K., & Radulova, P. (2019). Climate change and financial stability. Financial Stability Report 2019. https://www.ecb.europa.eu/pub/financial-stability/fsr/special/html/ecb.fsrart201905_1~47cf778cc1.en.html.

Global Compact (2004). Who cares wins: Connecting financial markets to a changing world. https://www.unepfi.org/fileadmin/events/2004/stocks/who_cares_wins_global_compact_2004.pdf.

Gomarasca, M., Banfi, G., & Lombardi, G. (2020). Myokines: The endocrine coupling of skeletal muscle and bone. *Advances in Clinical Chemistry*, *94*, 155–218. https://doi.org/10.1016/bs.acc.2019.07.010. Epub 2019 August 8. PMID: 31952571.

Gonguet, F., Wendling, C., Aydin, O., & Battersby, B. (2021). Climate-sensitive management of public finances—"Green PFM". IMF Staff Climate Notes 2021/002. https://www.imf.org/en/Publications/staff-climate-notes/Issues/2021/08/10/Climate-Sensitive-Management-of-Public-Finances-Green-PFM-460635.

González-Sánchez, M. B., & Martín-Ortega, J. J. (2020). Greenhouse gas emissions growth in Europe: A comparative analysis of determinants. *Sustainability*, *12*, 1012.

Griffith-Jones, S., Marodon, R., & Ocampo, J. A. (2020a). Mobilizing $400 billion: Using the visible hand of development banks. Center for Global Development, April 10. https://www.cgdev.org/blog/mobilizing-400-billion-using-visible-hand-development-banks.

Griffith-Jones, S., Attridge, S., & Gouett, M. (2020b). Securing climate finance through national development banks. Overseas Development Institute, London. G7 Leaders' Declaration, 8 June 2015. https://sustainabledevelopment.un.org/ content/documents/7320LEADERS%20STATEMENT_FINAL_CLEAN.pdf.

Grippa, P., & Demekas, M. D. G. (2021). Financial Regulation, climate change, and the transition to a low-carbon economy: A survey of the issues. *IMF Working Papers*. International Monetary Fund: Washington, DC, USA.

Grygiel-Tomaszewska, A., & Lipski, M. (2023). ESG w zarządzaniu aktywami funduszy inwestycyjnych w Polsce – wyniki badan. In B. Ocicka & K. Gemra (Eds.), *Zrównoważona transformacja. Stan i uwarunkowania w kontekście ESG* (pp. 115–132). Warsaw: Oficyna Wydawnicza SGH.

Gyamfi, B. A., Bein, M. A., Udemba, E. N., & Bekun, F. V. (2022). Renewable energy, economic globalization and foreign direct investment linkage for sustainable development in the E7 economies: Revisiting the pollution haven hypothesis. *International Social Science Journal*, *72*(243), 91–110. https://doi.org/10.1111/issj.12301

Hahn, R., & Stavins, R. (1992). Economic incentives for environmental protection: Integrating theory and practice. *American Economic Review*, *82*(2), 464–468.

Haites, E. (2018). Carbon taxes and greenhouse gas emissions trading systems: what have we learned? *Climate Policy*, *18*(8), 955–966. https://doi.org/10.1080/14693062.2018.1492897.

Halaskova, R. (2018). Structure of general government expenditure on social protection in the EU member states. *Montenegrin Journal of Economics*, *14*, 007–021. https://doi.org/10.14254/1800-5845/2018.14-4.1.

Halkos, G. E., & Tzeremes, N. G. (2013). A conditional directional distance function approach for measuring regional environmental efficiency: Evidence from UK regions. *European Journal of Operational Research*, *227*(1), 182–189.

Halland, H., & Bleaney, M. (2011). *Explaining the procyclicality of fiscal policy in developing countries* (No. 11/09). CREDIT Research Paper.

Hammar, H., Lofgren, A., & Sterner, T. (2004). Political economy obstacles to fuel taxation. *The Energy Journal, International Association for Energy Economics*, *0*(3), 1–18.

Hannam, P. M., Vítor, V. V., Levin, S. A., & Pacheco, J. M. (2015). Incomplete cooperation and co-benefits: Deepening climate cooperation with a proliferation of small agreements. *Climatic Change*, *144*, 65–79. https://doi.org/10.1007/s10584-015-1511-2.

Hao, Y. & Peng, Y. (2017). On the convergence in China's provincial per capita energy consumption: New evidence from a spatial econometric analysis. *Energy Economics*, *68*, 31–43. ISSN 0140-9883. https://doi.org/10.1016/j.eneco.2017.09.008.

Hartzmark, S. M., & Sussman, A. B. (2019). Do investors value sustainability? A natural experiment examining ranking and fund flows, 1–49. (March 25, 2019). European Corporate Governance Institute (ECGI) - Finance Working Paper No. 565/2018, Available at SSRN: https://ssrn.com/abstract=3016092 or https://doi.org/10.2139/ssrn.3016092.

Hashmi, R., & Alam, K. (2019). Dynamic relationship among environmental regulation, innovation, CO2 emissions, population, and economic growth in OECD countries: A panel investigation. *Journal of Cleaner Production*, *231*, 1100–1109.

Haug, L. S., Salihovic, S., Jogsten, I. E., Thomsen, C., van Bavel, B., Lindström, G., & Becher, G. (2010). Levels in food and beverages and daily intake of perfluorinated compounds in Norway. *Chemosphere*, *80*, 1137–1143.

He, J-J., Zheng, Y-H., Qiu, L., Che, Y-L. & Wang, Z-Q. (2019). Two new species and a new combination of Allacta (Blattodea, Ectobiidae, Pseudophyllodromiinae) from China, with notes on their behavior in nature. *Zookeys*, *836*, 1–14. https://doi.org/10.3897/zookeys.836.31673

Heal, G. M., & Kunreuther, H. C. (2012). Managing catastrophic risk. *NBER Working Paper* No. w18136. Available at SSRN: https://ssrn.com/abstract=2085124.

Heine, D., Semmler, W. Mazzucato, M. Braga, J. P. Gevorkyan, A., Hayde, E. K., Radpour, S. (2019). Financing low-carbon transitions through carbon pricing and green bonds. World Bank Policy Research Working Paper 8991. https://ssrn.com/abstract=3440367.

Heffernan, S. (2005). *Modern banking*. Chichester: John Wiley & Sons.

Hengge, M., Panizza, U., & Varghese, R. (2023). Carbon policy surprises and stock returns: Signals from financial markets. *IMF Working Papers WP/23/13*. https://www.imf.org/en/Publications/WP/Issues/2023/01/27/Carbon-Policy-Surprises-and-Stock-Returns-Signals-from-Financial-Markets-528644.

Hildén, M., Jordan, A., & Rayner, T. (2014). Climate policy innovation: Developing an evaluation perspective. *Environmental Politics*, *23*(5), 884–905.

Hill, P. R., Conway, K., Lintern, D. G., Meulé, S., Picard, K., & Barrie, J. V. (2008). Sedimentary processes and sediment dispersal in the southern Strait of Georgia, BC, Canada. *Marine Environmental Research*, *66*, S39–S48.

Hill, W. D., Davies, N. M., Ritchie, S. J., Skene, N. G., Bryois, J., Bell, S., Di Angelantonio, E., Roberts, D. J., Xueyi, S., Davies, G., & Liewald, D. C. (2019). Genome-wide analysis identifies molecular systems and 149 genetic loci associated with income. *Nature Communications*, *10*, 5741. https://doi.org/10.1038/s41467-019-13585-5.

Hischemöller, M., & Hoppe, R. (2001). Coping with intractable controversies: The case for problem structuring in policy design and analysis. In M. Hischemöller, R. Hoppe, W. N. Dunn, & J. R. Ravetz (Eds.), *Knowledge, power, and participation in environmental policy analysis*. New Brunswick, NJ: Transaction Publishers, pp. 391–416.

Hively, W. D., Lamb, B. T., Daughtry, C. S., Shermeyer, J., McCarty, G. W., & Quemada, M. (2018). Mapping crop residue and tillage intensity using WorldView-3 satellite shortwave infrared residue indices. *Remote Sensing*, *10*(10), 1657. https://doi.org/10.3390/rs10101657.

Hollinger, P. (2022). Ukraine war prompts investor rethink of ESG and the defence sector. *Financial Times*, 9 March 2022. https://www.ft.com/content/c4dafe6a-2c95-4352-ab88-c4e3cdb60bba.

Hope, L. and Wright, D. (2007), Beyond unusual? Examining the role of attention in the weapon focus effect. Appl. Cognit. Psychol., 21: 951–961. https://doi.org/10.1002/acp.1307

Hong, H., Karolyi, G. A., & Scheinkman, J. A. (2020). Climate finance. *The Review of Financial Studies*, *33*(3), 1011–1023.

Horowitz A. Attention to attention in domestic dog (Canis familiaris) dyadic play. Anim Cogn. 2009 Jan;12(1):107–18. doi: 10.1007/s10071-008-0175-y. Epub 2008 Aug 5. PMID: 18679727.

Horowitz, C. A. (2016). Paris agreement. *International Legal Materials*, *55*(4), 740–755. http://www.jstor.org/stable/10.5305/intelegamate.55.4.0740.

Howard, P. H., & Sterner, T. (2017). Few and not so far between: A meta-analysis of climate damage estimates. *Environmental and Resource Economics*, *68*(1), 197–225. https://doi.org/10.1007/s10640-017-0166-z.

Howard, P. H., & Sylvan, D. (2020). Wisdom of the experts: Using survey responses to address positive and normative uncertainties in climate-economic models. *Climatic Change*, *162*(2), 213–232.

Hua, Y., Xie, R., & Su, Y. (2018). Fiscal spending and air pollution in Chinese cities: Identifying composition and technique effects. *China Economic Review*, *47*, 156–169.

Huang, B., Punzi, M. T., & Wu, Y. (2019). Do banks price environmental risk? Evidence from a quasi natural experiment in the People' Republic of China. *ADBI Working Paper Series 2019*, No. 974. https://www.adb.org/sites/default/files/publication/511356/adbi-wp974.pdf.

Huang, L., & Fangzhou, L., & Sixuan, L. (2022). The cost of Russian sanctions on the global equity markets (March 18, 2022). Available at SSRN: https://ssrn.com/abstract=4060927 or https://doi.org/10.2139/ssrn.4060927.

Hubbard, R. G. (2005). *Money, the financial system and the economy*. Boston, MA: Addison-Wesley.

Huitema, D., Mostert, E., Egas, W., Moellenkamp, S., Pahl-Wostl, C., & Yalcin, R. (2009). Adaptive water governance: Assessing the institutional prescriptions of adaptive (co-) management from a governance perspective and defining a research agenda. *Ecology and Society*, *14*(1), 26.

Huitema, D., Jordan, A., Massey, E., Rayner, T., Asselt, H., Haug, C., Hildingsson, R., Monni, S., & Stripple, J. (2011). The evaluation of climate policy: Theory and emerging practice in Europe. *Policy Sciences*, *44*(2), 179.

Hynes, W., Love, P., & Stuart, A. (Eds.). (2020). *The financial system, new approaches to economic challenges*. Paris: OECD Publishing. https://doi.org/10.1787/d45f979e-en.

Hyun, S., Park, D., & Tian, S. (2020). The price of going green: The role of greenness in green bond markets. *Accounting Finance*, *60*, 73–95. https://doi.org/10.1111/acfi.12515.

ICMA (2021b). Green project mapping. https://www.icmagroup.org/sassets/documents/Sustainable-finance/2021-updates/Green-Project-Mapping-June-2021-100621.pdf.

IFLR (2021). Sustainable finance will emerge stronger from Covid-19 rebalancing. https://www.iflr.com/article/b1mq8sprtjdz01/sustainable-finance-will-emergestronger-from-covid-19-rebalancing.

IMF (2020a). An apocalypse foretold: Climate shocks and sovereign defaults, prepared by Serhan Cevik and João Tovar Jalles. *IMF Working Papers*. wpiea2020231-print-pdf.pdf.

IMF (2020b). IMF annual report 2020. A year like no other. Washington.

IMF (2023). Global financial stability report. Financial and climate policies for a high-interest-rate era. Washington. https://www.imf.org/en/Publications/GFSR/Issues/2023/10/10/global-financial-stability-report-october-2023.

IMF (2024). Preparing financial sectors for a green future. Managing risks and securing sustainable finance, DP/2024/002, Middle East and Central Asia Department. https://www.imf.org/en/Publications/Departmental-Papers-Policy-Papers/Issues/2024/02/12/Preparing-Financial-Sectors-for-a-Green-Future-Managing-Risks-and-Securing-Sustainable-540602.

Institut Rousseau (2024). Road to net zero, bringing the green investment gap. https://drive.google.com/file/d/1cDQmQB0iezwthxiaoM83VxbllhrNz-0O/view.

ING and EY (2021), Biznes dla klimatu. Raport o zmianie priorytetów, https://www.ey.com/pl_pl/climate-change-sustainability-services/raport-ey-ing-biznes-dla-klimatu

Inglehart, R., Foa, R., Peterson, C. & Welzel, C. (2008). Development, Freedom and Rising Happiness: A Global Perspective 1981-2006. *Perspectives on Psychological Science*, *3*(4), 264–285.

IPCC (2007). Summary for policymakers in: Climate change 2007: The physical science basis. Contribution of Working Group I to the Fourth Assessment Report of the Intergovernmental Panel on Climate Change. Cambridge University Press.

IPCC (2013). *Working Group I contribution to the IPCC fifth assessment report. Climate change 2013: The physical science basis*. Geneva, Switzerland.

IPCC (2014). Summary for policymakers in: Climate change 2014: Impacts, adaptation, and vulnerability. Part A: Global and sectoral aspects. Contribution of Working Group II to the Fifth Assessment Report of the Intergovernmental Panel on Climate Change ed CB Field et al. Cambridge: Cambridge University Press; Cambridge, United Kingdom and New York, NY, USA, pp. 1–32.

IPCC (2023). Climate change 2023. Synthesis Report. https://www.ipcc.ch/report/ar6/syr/downloads/report/IPCC_AR6_SYR_FullVolume.pdf.

Jaffe, A. B., & Stavins, R. N. (1995). Dynamic incentives of environmental regulations: The effects of alternative policy instruments on technology diffusion. *Journal of Environmental Economics and Management*, *29*(3), S43–S63.

Jasch, C. (2003). The use of Environmental Management Accounting (EMA) for identifying environmental costs. *Journal of Cleaner Production*, *11*(6), 667–676.

Jiang W, Dong L, Liu X. (2023). How does COVID-19 affect the spillover effects of green finance, carbon markets, and renewable/non-renewable energy markets? Evidence from China. *Energy*, *281*:N.PAG. doi:10.1016/j.energy.2023.128351.

Johnston, I., & Espinoza, J. (2023). Ukraine was and green transition keep EU state aid near record level. www. Ft.com, 2 August 2023. Ukraine war and green transition keep EU state aid near record level (ft.com).

Jones, R. (2019). Climate change and indigenous health promotion. *Global Health Promotion*, *26*(3_suppl), 73–81. https://doi.org/10.1177/1757975919829713.

Jongeneel, R., Erjavec, E., & García Azcárate, T. Silvis (2019). Assessment of the common agricultural policy after 2020 EU Bioeconomy Economics and H. Policies, vol. I (pp. 207–228). Cham: Palgrave Macmillan. https://doi.org/10.1007/978-3-030-28634-7_14.

Joskow, P. & Rose, N. (1985). The effects of technological change, experience, and environmental regulation on the construction cost of coal-burning generating units. *RAND Journal of Economics*, *16*(1), 1–17.

Kahn, M. E., & Kotchen, M. J. (2010). *Environmental concern and the business cycle: The chilling effect of recession* (No. w16241). National Bureau of Economic Research.

Kahn, M. E., Mohaddes, K., Ryan, N. C., Ng, M., Pesaran, H., Raissi, M., & Yang, J-Ch (2021). Long-term macroeconomic effects of climate change: A cross-country analysis. *Energy Economics*, *104*. https://doi.org/10.1016/j.eneco.2021.105624.

Kalkuhl, Matthias, and Leonie Wenz. 2020. "The Impact of Climate Conditions on Economic Production. Evidence from a Global Panel of Regions." Journal of Environmental Economics and Management 103: 102360.

Kaminsky, G., Reinhart, C., & Vegh, C. (2005). When it rains, it pours: Pro-cyclical capital flows and macroeconomic policies. Working paper series (National Bureau of Economic Research). https://doi.org/10.1086/ma.19.3585327.

Känzig, D. R. (2021). The macroeconomic effects of oil supply news: Evidence from OPEC announcements. *American Economic Review*, *111*(4), 1092–1125. https://doi.org/10.1257/aer.20190964.

Kaplow, L. (2010). Concavity of utility, concavity of welfare, and redistribution of income. *International Tax and Public Finance*, *17*, 25–42.

Karakosta, Ch., Flamos, A., Doukas, H., & Vaturi, A. (2010). Sustainable energy technology transfers through the CDM? Application of participatory approaches for decision making facilitation. *International Journal of Environmental Policy and Decision Making*, *1*, 1–16. https://doi.org/10.1504/IJEPDM.2010.033908.

Karl, T. R., & Trenberth, K. E. (2003). Modern global climate change. *Science*, *302*(5651), 1719–1723. https://doi.org/10.1126/science.1090228. PMID: 14657489.

Karpf, A., & Mandel, A. (2018). The changing value of the 'green' label on the US municipal bond market. *Nature Climate Change*, *8*, 161–165, https://doi.org/10.1038/s41558-017-0062-0.

Karvosenoja, N. (2008). Emission scenario model for regional air pollution. Monographs of the Boreal Environment Research 32. Finnish Environment Institute. http://www.ymparisto.fi/ download.asp?contentid=92446&lan=en.

Kastrinos, N., & Weber, K. M. (2020). Sustainable development goals in the research and innovation policy of the European Union. *Technological Forecasting and Social Change*, *157*, 120056. Elsevier.

Kelly, P. M., & Adger, W. N. (2000). Theory and practice in assessing vulnerability to climate change and facilitating adaptation. *Climatic Change*, *47*, 325–352 https://doi.org/10.1023/A:1005627828199.

Kenny, J. (2020). Economic conditions and support for the prioritisation of environmental protection during the Great Recession. *Environmental Politics*, *29*(6), 937–958.

Keohane, R. O. (2009). The old IPE and the new. *Review of International Political Economy*, *16*(1), 34–46.

Kerr, J. (2007). Watershed management: Lessons from common property theory. *International Journal of the Commons*, *1*, 89–109.

Keynes, J. M. (1926). *The end of Laissez-Faire*. London: Hogarth Press.

Kim, S., & Li, Z. (2021). Understanding the impact of ESG practices in corporate finance. *Sustainability*, *13*(7). https://doi.org/10.3390/su13073746.

Klein, A. (2020). When it comes to sustainable finance in the COVID era, let the private sector lead the way. https://blogs.worldbank.org/climatechange/when-it-comes-sustainable-finance-covid-era-let-private-sector-lead-way.

Klein, R., Nicholls, R., & Thomalla, F. (2004). Resilience to natural hazards: How useful is this concept? *Environmental Hazards*, *5*, 35–45. https://doi.org/10.1016/j.hazards.2004.02.001.

Klimakomissionen (2010). Green energy – the road to a Danish energy system without fossil fuels. Summary of the work, results and recommendati. 2010, Danish Commission on Climate Change Policy, https://ens.dk/sites/ens.dk/files/Globalcooperation/green_energy_eng_publication.pdf

Kluza, K., Ziolo, M., & Postuła, M. (2024). Climate policy development and implementation from the Sustainable Development Goals perspective. Evidence from the European Union countries. *Energy Strategy Reviews*, *52*, 2024. https://doi.org/10.1016/j.esr.2024.101321.

Knodt, M., & Schoenefeld, J. (2021). How 'harder soft governance' might help deliver the EU's new 55 per cent emissions reduction target. LSE European Politics and Policy (EUROPP) blog.

Knight, C. (2022). Crisis to spur green transition, 16 November 2022. www.eib.org. https://www.eib.org/en/stories/ukraine-war-energy-climate#.

Kompas, T., Pham, V. H., & Che, T. N. (2018). The effects of climate change on GDP by country and the global economic gains from complying with the Paris Climate Accord. Earth's Future, 6, 1153–1173. https://doi.org/10.1029/2018EF000922

Kosonen, K. (2012). Regressivity in environmental taxation: Myth or reality? In J. Milne & M. S. Andersen (Eds.), *Handbook of research on environmental taxation*. Cheltenham: Edward Elgar. https://doi.org/10.4337/9781781952146.00018.

Kozłowski, T. (2007). Problem struktury systemu finansowego w kontekście relacji pomiędzy przedsiębiorstwami niefinansowymi i sektorem finansowym, Bank i Kredyt, No. 1, p. 71.

KPMG International (2022). Big shifts, small steps. Survey of Sustainability Reporting 2022. https://assets.kpmg.com/content/dam/kpmg/xx/pdf/2023/04/big-shifts-small-steps.pdf.

Krawczyńska-Kaczmarek M. (2023). *Finansowanie w formule Sustainability Linked katalizatorem zrównoważonej transformacji w realnej gospodarce*, in: *Zielone finanse w Polsce 2023*, red. L. Kotecki, UN Global Network Poland, Warszawa, https://www.efcongress.com/wp-content/uploads/2023/06/Zielone-finanse-w-PL-2023.pdf.

Krogstrup, S., & Oman, W. (2019). Macroeconomic and financial policies for climate change mitigation: A review of the literature. *IMF Working Papers*, Volume 19/185.

Krueger, P. (2020). The importance of climate risks for institutional investors. *The Review of Financial Studies*, *33*(3), 1067–1111. https://doi.org/10.1093/rfs/hhz137.

Rajesh, K., & Arun, K. (2021). Optimal scheduling of variable speed pumped storage, solar and wind energy system. *Energy Sources, Part A: Recovery, Utilization, and Environmental Effects*. 1–16. https://doi.org/10.1080/15567036.2021.1892243.

Labatt, S., & White, R. R. (2002). *Environmental finance: A guide to environmental risk assessment and financial products*. New York: John Wiley and Sons Ltd.

Lake, D. A., & Baum, M. A. (2001). The invisible hand of democracy: Political control and the provision of public services. *Comparative Political Studies*, *34*(6), 587–621.

Lane, P. R. (2003). Business cycles and macroeconomic policy in emerging market economies. *International Finance*, *6*(1), 89–108.

Lane, P. R., & Tornell, A. (1996). Power, growth, and the voracity effect. *Journal of Economic Growth*, *1*, 213–241.

Leitner, S., & Stehrer, R. (2016). Development of public spending structures in the EU member states: Social investment and its impact on social outcomes. *Working Paper 128*, The Vienna Institute for International Economic Studies, Vienna.

Levine, R. (1997). Financial development and economic growth: Views and agenda. *Journal of Economic Literature, 35*(2), 688–726.
Levine, R. (2005). Finance and growth: Theory and evidence, handbook of economic growth. In A. Philippe & S. Durlauf (Ed.), *Handbook of economic growth* (pp. 865–934). Cambridge: Elsevier.
Li, Y., Gong, M., Zhang, X. Y., & Koh, L. (2018). The impact of environmental, social, and governance disclosure on firm value: The role of CEO power. *The British Accounting Review, 50*(1), 60–75.
Li, Z., Kuo, T. H., Siao-Yun, W., & Vinh, L. T. (2022). Role of green finance, volatility, and risk in promoting the investments in Renewable Energy Resources post-covid-19. *Resources Policy, 76*, 102563.
Liang, H., Saraf, N., Hu, Q., & Xue, Y. (2007). Assimilation of enterprise systems: The effect of institutional pressures and the mediating role of top management. *MIS Quarterly, 31*(1), 59–87. https://doi.org/10.2307/25148781.
Lin, B. & Li, X. (2011). The effect of carbon tax on per capita CO2 emissions. *Energy Policy, 39*(9), 5137–5146.
Liobikiene, G., Matiiuk, Y., & Krikstolaitis, R. (2023). The concern about main crises such as the Covid-19 pandemic, the war in Ukraine, and climate change's impact on energy-saving behavior. *Energy Policy, 180*. https://doi.org/10.1016/j.enpol.2023.113678.
Liobikienė, G., Butkus, M., & Matuzevičitė, K. (2019). The contribution of energy taxes to climate change policy in the European Union (EU). *Resources, 8*(2), 1–23.
Lipski, M. (2021). Wyzwania przedsiębiorstw w zakresie dostępności finansowania w świetle wymogów zrównoważonego rozwoju. *Kwartalnik Nauk o Przedsiębiorstwie, 60*(3), 4–14. https://doi.org/10.33119/KNoP.2021.60.3.1.
Lipski, M. (2024). Working materials regarding the science project KNOP/S24: 1.4. "The quality of management of ESG aspects vs resilience to crisis. Enterprises - financial institutions - local government units", implemented at the Collegium of Business Administration at the SGH Warsaw School of Economics within the subsidy for maintaining and developing research potential in 2022–2024.
Lipski, M., Hościłowicz, P., Rogowski, W., & Gemra, K. (2023). *Czynniki ESG w działalności finansowej i inwestycyjnej przedsiębiorstw – wyniki badań, Zrównoważona transformacja. Stan i uwarunkowania w kontekście ESG*. B. Ocicka & K. Gemra (Eds.). Warsaw: Oficyna Wydawnicza SGH.
Loayza, N. V., Olaberría, E., Rigolini, J., & Christiaensen, L. (2012). Natural disasters and growth: going beyond the averages. *World Development, 40*(7), 1317–1336. https://doi.org/10.1016/j.worlddev.2012.03.002
Lofts, G. (2020). How COVID-19 drives change in financial services sustainability, EY. https://www.ey.com/en_lt/sustainability-financial-services/how-covid-19-drives-change-in-financial-services-sustainability.
Loganathan, N., Shahbaz, M., & Taha, R. (2014). The effect of green taxation and economic growth on environment hazards: The case of Malaysia, MPRA Paper, 56843.
López, R., Galinato, G. I., & Islam, A. (2011). Fiscal spending and the environment: Theory and empirics. *Journal of Environmental Economics and Management, 62*(2), 180–198.
López, F. A., Matilla-García, M., Mur, J., & Marín, M. R. (2011). Four tests of independence in spatiotemporal data. *Papers in Regional Science*, 90, 663–685. https://doi.org/10.1111/j.1435-5957.2010.00335.x
Lopez, R. E., & Palacios, A. (2010). Environmental economics and policy public economics resource /energy economics and policy. Issue Date 2010–10. Publication Type Working or Discussion Paper. DOI and Other Identifiers https://doi.org/10.22004/ag.econ.94795.

López, J., Perez-Rojo, G., Noriega, C., Carretero, I., Velasco, C., Martinez-Huertas, J. A., López-Frutos, P., Galarraga, L. (2020). Psychological well-being among older adults during the COVID-19 outbreak: a comparative study of the young-old and the old-old adults. *International Psychogeriatrics*, *32*(11), 1365–1370. https://doi.org/10.1017/S1041610220000964. Epub 2020 May 22. PMID: 32438934; PMCID: PMC7324658.

Lopez, A. D., Tar, K., Krügel, U., Dange, T., Ros, I. G., Schmidt, M. (2011). Proteasomal degradation of Sfp1 contributes to the repression of ribosome biogenesis during starvation and is mediated by the proteasome activator Blm10. *Molecular Biology of the Cell*, *22*(5), 528–540.

Lu, L., Zheng, H., Chen, M., & Najam, H. (2022). Tackling carbon intensity with green finance in the COVID-19 era: Recommendations for OECD economies. *Climate Change Economics*, *13*(3), 1–22.

Ma, J., Xiong, Z., Waite, T., Ng, W. & Zhao, X. (2011). Enhanced Inactivation of Bacteria with Silver-Modified Mesoporous TiO2 under Weak Ultraviolet: Irradiation. *Microporous and Mesoporous Materials*, *144*, 97–104. https://doi.org/10.1016/j.micromeso.2011.03.040.

Mack, D. L., DaSilva, A. W., Rogers, C., Hedlund, E., Murphy, E. I., Vojdanovski, V., Plomp, J., Wang, W., Nepal, S. K., Holtzheimer, P. E., Wagner, D. D., Jacobson, N. C., Meyer, M. L., Campbell, A. T., & Huckins, J. F. (2021). Mental health and behavior of college students during the COVID-19 pandemic: Longitudinal mobile smartphone and ecological momentary assessment study, part II. *Journal of Medical Internet Research*, *23*(6), e28892. https://doi.org/10.2196/28892. PMID: 33900935; PMCID: PMC8183598.

Maddison, D. J. (2003). The amenity value of the climate: The household production function approach. *Resource and Energy Economics*, *25*(2), 155–175.

Maddison, David & Rehdanz, Katrin, 2011. "The impact of climate on life satisfaction," Ecological Economics, Elsevier, vol. 70(12), pages 2437-2445. Laura Eboli, Gabriella Mazzulla, A methodology for evaluating transit service quality based on subjective and objective measures from the passenger's point of view, Transport Policy, Volume 18, Issue 1, 2011, Pages 172–181, ISSN 0967-070X, https://doi.org/10.1016/j.tranpol.2010.07.007.

Magnani, E. (2000). The environmental Kuznets curve, environmental protection policy and income distribution. *Ecological Economics*, *32*(3), 431–443.

Mahlman, J. D. (1997). Uncertainties in projections of human-caused climate warming. *Science*, *278*, 1416–1417.

Mankiw, N. G. (2006). The macroeconomist as scientist and engineer. *Journal of Economic Perspectives*, *20*(4), 29–46.

Manko, K., & Watkins, T. A. (2022). Microfinance and SDG 7: Financial impact channels for mitigating energy poverty. *Development in Practice*, *32*, 1036–1048. https://doi.org/10.1080/09614524.2020.1863338.

Marin, G., & Vona, F. (2019). Climate policies and skill-biased employment dynamics: Evidence from EU countries. *Journal of Environmental Economics and Management*, *98*. https://doi.org/10.1016/j.jeem.2019.102253.

Massa, M., & Zhang, L. (2011). The spillover effects of hurricane Katrina on corporate bonds and the choice between bank and bond financing. *SSRN Electronic Journal* (July 25, 2011). AFA 2012 Chicago Meetings Paper, Available at SSRN: https://ssrn.com/abstract=1782791 or https://doi.org/10.2139/ssrn.1782791.

Mazzucato, M. (2013). *The entrepreneurial state: Debunking the public vs. private myth in risk and innovation*. London: Anthem.

Mazzucato, M., & Penna, C. (2018). The market creating and shaping role of state investment banks. SPRU Working Paper 2014–2021.

McDaniels, J. (2020). Implications of the COVID-19 pandemic for global sustainable finance. https://unepinquiry.org/publication/implications-of-the-covid-19-pandemic-for-global-sustainable-finance/.

McKibbin, W., Konradt, M., & Weder di Mauro, B. (2021). *Climate policies and monetary policies in the Euro area*. Geneva Graduate Institute.

McKinsey (2020). Addressing climate change in a post-pandemic world. https://www.mckinsey.com/business-functions/sustainability/our-insights/addressing-climate-change-in-a-post-pandemic-world.

McKinsey (2022). How to prepare for a sustainable future along the value chain. https://www.mckinsey.com/industries/consumer-packaged-goods/our-insights/how-to-prepare-for-a-sustainable-future-along-the-value-chain.

Meadows, D., Meadows, D., Randers, J., & William, W. Behrens III (1972). The limits to growth; a report for the club of Rome's project on the predicament of mankind. New York: Universe Books. ISBN 0876631650. Retrieved 26 November 2017.

Mendelsohn, R., & Dinar, A. (1998). The impact of climate change on agriculture and developing countries: Case studies of Indian and Brazil. *Theoretical Economics Letters*, *12*(6), December 30, 2022.

Mendelsohn, R. O., & Neumann, J. E., eds. (1999*). The impact of climate change on the United States economy*. Cambridge: Cambridge University Press.

Mendelsohn, R. O., Schlesinger, M. E., & Williams, L. J. (2000). Comparing impacts across climate models. *Integrated Assessment*, *1*(1), 37–48.

Merton, R. C. (2004). *The design of financial systems: Towards a synthesis of function and structure*. Cambridge: National Bureau of Economic Research.

Metcalf, G. E. (2009). Market-based policy options to control US greenhouse gas emissions. *Journal of Economic Perspectives*, *23*(2), 5–27.

Metcalf, G. E., & Stock, J. H. (2020). Measuring the macroeconomic impact of carbon taxes. *AEA Papers and Proceedings*, *110*, 101–106. https://doi.org/10.1257/pandp.20201081.

Meyer-Ohlendorf, N., & Bart, I. (2020). Climate action regulation 2.0.

Michalski D. (2022). *Finanse zielonej transformacji*. Warszawa: Difin.

Miedziak, R. (2023). Has the COVID-19 pandemic changed the approach to ESG, CSR, sustainable reporting and sustainable development? Evidence from Poland (May 11, 2023). Available at SSRN: https://ssrn.com/abstract=4445006 or https://doi.org/10.2139/ssrn.4445006.

Mikita, M. (2021). Stability of the financial system of the European Union, Studia BAS, No. *3*(67), 87–116. https://doi.org/10.31268/StudiaBAS.2021.28.

Milea, O. M., Pascu, E., & Popa, D. (2015). Quality - Access to Success. Agricultural policy objectives under the Europe 2020 strategy, *16*, 31–34.

Miller, S. & Vela, M. (2013). The Effects of Air Pollution on Educational Outcomes: Evidence from Chile, IDB Working Paper Series, No. IDB-WP-468, Inter-American Development Bank (IDB), Washington, DC.

Millock, K., Nauges, C., & Sterner, T. (2004). Environmental taxes: A comparison of French and Swedish experience from taxes on industrial air pollution. info DICE Report, ifo Institute - Leibniz Institute for Economic Research at the University of Munich, *2*(01).

Missirian, A., & Schlenker, W. (2017). Asylum applications respond to temperature fluctuations. *Science*, *358*(6370), 1610–1614.

Moberg, F., & Galaz, V. (2005). Resilience: Going from conventional to adaptive freshwater management for human and ecosystem compatibility. *Swedish Water House Policy Brief, 3*.

Moles, P., & Terry, N. (1997). *The handbook of international financial terms*. Oxford: Oxford University Press.

Morrison, R. (2021). *Environmental, social and governance theory: Defusing a major threat to shareholder rights, competitive enterprise institute*. Washington. (May 5, 2021). Available at SSRN: https://ssrn.com/abstract=3845709 or https://doi.org/10.2139/ssrn.3845709.

Morley, J. E., Malmstrom, T. K., Miller, D. K. (2012). A simple frailty questionnaire (FRAIL) predicts outcomes in middle aged African Americans. *The Journal of Nutrition, Health and Aging 16*(7), 601–608. https://doi.org/10.1007/s12603-012-0084-2. PMID: 22836700; PMCID: PMC4515112.

Moshiri, S., & Daneshmand, A. (2003). The effectiveness of environmental policy: Does the source of revenue matter? (July 26, 2023). USAEE Working Paper No. 23–594. Available at SSRN: https://ssrn.com/abstract=4521539 or https://doi.org/10.2139/ssrn.4521539.

Moshiri, S. & Daneshmand, A. (2019). How effective is government spending on environmental protection in a developing country? An empirical evidence from Iran. *Journal of Economic Studies*. https://doi.org/10.1108/JES-12-2018-0458.

Nakata, T. & Lamont, A. (2000). Analysis of the impacts of carbon taxes on energy systems in Japan. *Energy Policy*, *29*, 159–166. https://doi.org/10.1016/S0301-4215(00)00104-X.

Nanayakkara, M., & Colombage, S. (2019). Do investors in green bond market pay a premium? Global evidence. *Applied Economics*, *51*, 4425–4437. https://doi.org/10.1080/00036846.2019.1591611.

Naturvårdsverket (2004). Klimatpåverkan från styrmedlen LIP och Klimp. Delrapport i regeringsuppdraget Kontrollstation 2004. Rapport 5382. Augusti 2004. http://www.naturvardsverket. se/Documents/publikationer/620-5382-5.pdf.

Naturvårdsverket (2009). Effekter av investeringsprogrammen LIP och Klimp. Regeringsuppdrag juni 2009. Rapport 5991. Augusti 2009. http://www.naturvardsverket.se/Documents/publikationer/978-91-620-5991-0.pdf.

Naturvårdsverket (2010). Gör arbetet med klimatstrategier någon skillnad? En utvärdering av lokalt klimatstrategiarbete. Klimatinvesteringsprogram. http://www.naturvardsverket.se/sv/Start/Om-Naturvardsverket/Vara-publikationer/ISBN1/6300/978-91-620-6358-0/.

Nerlinger, M., & Utz, S. (2022). The impact of the Russia-Ukraine conflict on the green energy transition – A capital market perspective, Swiss Finance Institute Research Paper Series 22–49. Swiss Finance Institute.

Newberry, B. (2004). The dilemma of ethics in engineering education. *Science and Engineering Ethics*, April, *10*(2), 343–351. https://doi.org/10.1007/s11948-004-0030-8. PMID: 15152860.

Newell, R. G., Jaffe, A. B., & Stavins, R. N. (1999). Energy-efficient technologies and climate change policies: Issues and evidence. Available at SSRN 198829.

Newell, R. G., & Stavins, R. N. (2003). Cost heterogeneity and the potential savings from market-based policies. *Journal of Regulatory Economics*, *23*, 43–59.

Newell, P., Srivastava, S., Naess, L. O., Torres Contreras, G. A., & Price, R. (2021). Toward transformative climate justice: An emerging research agenda. *WIREs Climate Change*, *12*(6), e733, https://doi.org/10.1002/wcc.733.

NGFS (2019). First Comprehensive report. A call for action Climate change as a source of financial risk, Network for Greening the Financial System. https://www.ngfs.net/sites/default/files/medias/documents/ngfs_first_comprehensive_report_-_17042019_0.pdf.

NGFS (2023). https://www.ngfs.net/en/about-us/membership.

Ngo, Q.-T., Tran, H. A., & Thanh, H. T. (2022). The impact of green finance and Covid-19 on economic development: Capital formation and educational expenditure of ASEAN economies. *China Finance Review International*, *12*(2), 261–279. https://doi.org/10.1108/CFRI-05-2021-0087.

Niedziółka, P. (2021). Zielona (r)ewolucja w polskiej bankowości. Finansowanie projektów lądowej energetyki wiatrowej oraz fotowoltaicznej w Polsce z wykorzystaniem metody proojeet finance, Difin, Warszawa.

Nieto, M. J. (2019). Banks, climate risk and financial stability. *Journal of Financial Regulation and Compliance*, *27*(2), 243–262.

Niskanen, A. (1997). Economic profitability of afforestation in Thailand and the Philippines. *Project Appraisal*, *12*(3), 193–203.

Nordhaus, W. D. (1982). How fast should we graze the global commons? *American Economic Review*, *72*(2), 242–246.

Nordhaus, W. D. (1991). To slow or not to slow: The economics of the greenhouse effect. *Economic Journal*, *101*(407), 920–937.

Nordhaus, W. D. (1994a). Expert opinion on climatic change. *American Scientist*, *82*(1), 45–51. http://www.jstor.org/stable/29775100

Nordhaus, W. D. (1994b). *Managing the global commons: The economics of climate change*. Cambridge: The MIT Press.

Nordhaus, W. D. (2007). A review of the Stern review on the economics of climate change. *Journal of Economic Literature*, *45*(3), 686–702.

Nordhaus, W. D., & Boyer, J. G. (1999). Requiem for Kyoto: An economic analysis of the kyoto protocol. *The Energy Journal*, *20*, 93–130. http://www.jstor.org/stable/23296907

Nordhaus, W. D., & Yang, Z. (1996). A regional dynamic general-equilibrium model of alternative climate-change strategies. *American Economic Review*, *86*(4), 741–765.

Nordhaus, William. 2006. "Geography and Macroeconomics: New Data and New Findings." Proceedings of the National Academy of Sciences *103*(10), 3510–17.

Nordisk Kommunikation (2007). Utvärdering av information som styrmedel kopplat till Klimp. Nordisk Kommunikation. http://www.naturvardsverket.se/upload/03_lagar_och_andra_styrmedel/ekonomiska_styrmedel/investeringsprogram/klimp/rapport_information_som_styrmedel.pdf.

Noy, I. (2009). The macroeconomic consequences of disasters. *Journal of Development Economics*, *88*(2), 221–231.

Nurke, M., Hsiang, S., & Miguel, E. (2015). Global non-linear effect of temperature on economic production. *Nature*, *527*, 235–239.

Obiora, S. C., Bamisile, O., Opoku-Mensah, E., & Kofi Frimpong, A. N. (2020). Impact of banking and financial systems on environmental sustainability: An overarching study of developing, emerging, and developed economies. *Sustainability*, *12*. https://doi.org/10.3390/su12198074.

OECD (2008). OECD Green Growth Studies Energy. Acknowledgements (Oecd.Org).

OECD (2015). *OECD Journal: Economic Studies*, 2015(1), OECD Publishing, Paris, https://doi.org/10.1787/eco_studies-v2015-1-en.

OECD (2023). Mechanisms to Prevent carbon lock-in in transition finance, green finance and investment. Paris: OECD Publishing. https://doi.org/10.1787/d5c49358-en.

OECD (2024). Wastewater treatment (indicator). https://doi.org/10.1787/ef27a39d-en (Accessed on 25 May 2024).

OECD, ITF (2019). Transport Connectivity for Regional Integration,Summit 2019 | ITF Summit 2019 (itf-oecd.org).

Ofori, I. K., Gbolonyo, E. Y., & Ojong, N. (2023). Foreign direct investment and inclusive green growth in Africa: Energy efficiency contingencies and thresholds. *Energy Economics*, *106414*(2023). https://doi.org/10.1016/j.eneco.2022.106414

Ordanini A., Miceli L., Pizzetti M., & Parasuraman A. (2011). Crowd-funding: transforming customers into investors through innovative service platforms. *Journal of Service Management*, *22*(4), 443–470.

Pahl-Wostl, C. (2009). A conceptual framework for analysing adaptive capacity and multi-level learning processes in resource governance regimes. *Global Environmental Change*, *19*, 354–365. https://doi.org/10.1016/j.gloenvcha.2009.06.001.

Panagopoulos, Y., & Dimitriou, E. (2020). Large-scale nature-based solution in agriculture for sustainable water management: The Lake Karla case sustainability, *12*(17), 6761. https://doi.org/10.3390/su12176761

Parry, I., & Small, K. (2004). Does Britain or the United States have the right gasoline tax? Resources for the Future Discussion Paper, 02-12 rev.

Pautrel, X. (2008). Reconsidering the impact of the environment on long-run growth when pollution influences health and agents have a finite-lifetime. *Environmental and Resource Economics*, *40*(1), 37–52. https://doi.org/10.1007/s10640-007-9139-y. Available from: https://link.springer.com/article/10.1007/s10640-007-9139-y

Pavlovic, M., Dencic-Mihajlov, K. (2022). CSR reporting during the Covid-19 pandemic: A common way to disclose new social and economic challenges. Proceeding of 3rd International Conference "Eco-nomic and Business Trends Shaping the Future", 154–165. 10.47063/EBTSF.2022.0013.

Pawełek, B. (2020). A comparative analysis of the European Union member states in terms of public spending on environmental protection in 2004–2017. *European Journal of Government and Economics*, *9*(1), 95–114.

Pawełek, B., Baryła, M., & Pociecha, J. (2020). Study of the classification accuracy measures for predicting corporate bankruptcy taking into account changes in the economic environment. *Argumenta Oeconomica*, *1*(44), 5–17.

Pawłowski, A., & Rydzewski, P. (2023). Challenges and opportunities for the energy sector in the face of threats such as climate change and the COVID-19 pandemic—an international perspective. *Energies*, *16*(11), 4454. https://doi.org/10.3390/en16114454.

Pearce, J. A. (1996). A user's guide to basalt discrimination diagrams. In D. A. Wyman (Ed.), *Trace element geochemistry of volcanic rocks: Applications for massive sulphide exploration, geological association of Canada, short course notes* (pp. 79–113), Vol. 12.

Pearce, D. (1998). Environmental Appraisal and Environmental Policy in the European Union, *Environmental & Resource Economics*, *11*(3), 489–501.

Pearce, D. W., Cline, W. R., Achanta, A. N., Fankhauser, S., Pachauri, R. K., Toll, R. S. J., & Vellinga, P. (1996), 'The Social Costs of Climate Change: Greenhouse Damage and the Benefits of Control', in J. P. Bruce, H. Lee and E. F. Haites (Eds.), Climate Change 1995: Economic and Social Dimensions – Contribution of Working Group III to the Second Assessment Report of the Intergovernmental Panel on Climate Change. Cambridge: Cambridge University Press, pp. 179–224.

Pecl, G. T., Araújo, M. B., Bell, J. D., Blanchard, J., Bonebrake, T. C., Chen, I. C., Clark, T. D., Colwell, R. K., Danielsen, F., Evengård, B., & Falconi, L. (2017). Biodiversity redistribution under climate change: Impacts on ecosystems and human well-being. *Science*, *355*(6332). https://doi.org/10.1126/science.aai9214.

Pe'er, G., Bonn, A., Bruelheide, H., Dieker, P., Eisenhauer, N., Feindt, P. H., Hagedorn, G., Hansjürgens, B., Herzon, I., Lomba, Â., & Marquard, E. (2020). Action needed for the EU common agricultural policy to address sustainability challenges. *People and Nature*, *2*(2), 1–12. https://doi.org/10.1002/pan3.1008.

Perry, E. & Karousakis, K. (2020). Enhancing measurability of the post-2020 biodiversity framework by Will Symes, Katia Karousakis, Edward Perry | PPT (slideshare.net). Summary-Record-OECD-workshop-The-Post-2020-Biodiversity-Framework-targets-indicators-and-measurability-implications.pdf.

Pham, L., & Huynh, T. L. D. (2020). How does investor attention influence the green bond market? *Finance Research Letters*, *35*(5). https://doi.org/10.1016/j.frl.2020.101533.

Piedelobo, L., Hernández-López, D., Ballesteros, R., Chakhar, A., Del Pozo, S. González-Aguilera, D., & Moreno, M. A. (2019). Scalable pixel-based crop classification combining Sentinel-2 and Landsat-8 data time series: Case study of the Duero river basin. *Agricultural Systems*, *171*, 36–50. ISSN 0308-521X. https://doi.org/10.1016/j.agsy.2019.01.005.

Pielke, Jr R. A. (2007). *The honest broker: Making sense of science in policy and politics*. Cambridge: Cambridge University Press.

Pigou, A. (1920). *The economics of welfare*. London: Macmillan.

Pindyck, R. S. (2011) Fat tails, thin tails, and climate change policy. *Review of Environmental Economics and Policy*, *5*(2), 258–274.

Pizer, W., & Sexton, S. (2019). The distributional impacts of energy taxes. *Review of Environmental Economics and Policy*, *13*(1), 104–123. https://www.journals.uchicago.edu/doi/10.1093/reep/rey021.

Plambeck, E. L., & Hope, C. W. (1996). PAGE95—an updated valuation of the impacts of global warming. *Energy Policy*, *24*(9), 783–793.

Podedworna – Tarnowska D. (2015). *Private equity/venture capital*, Warszawa: Oficyna Wydawnicza Szkoły Głównej Handlowej w Warszawie.

Polinsky, A. M., & Shavell, S. (2000). The economic theory of public enforcement of law. *Journal of Economic Literature*, *38*(1), 45–76. http://www.jstor.org/stable/2565359.

Popp, A., Jaenisch, N., Witte, O. W., & Frahm, C. (2009). Identification of ischemic regions in a rat model of stroke. *PloS One*, *4*(3), e4764.

Postuła, M. (2015a). *Instrumenty zarządzania finansami publicznymi, Wydawnictwo Naukowe Wydziału Zarządzania Uniwersytetu Warszawskiego*. Warszawa: Wydawnictwo Naukowe Wydziału Zarządzania Uniwersytetu Warszawskiego.

Postuła, M. (2015b). Impact of the Council Directive on Requirements for Budgetary Frameworks of the Member States on the Polish Public Finance System Postuła M.; artykuł [w:] „Management and Business Administration. Central Europe", nr 1(23)/2015

Postuła, M. (2022). *Public financial management in the European Union: Public finance and global crises* (1st ed.). London: Routledge.

Postuła, M., Chmielewski, W., Puczyński, P. & Cieślik, R. (2021). The impact of information and communication technologies (ICT) on energy poverty and unemployment in selected european union countries. *Energies*, *14*, 6110.

Postuła, M., Cieślik, R., Lipski, M. & Chmielewska, A. (2023). Projekty inwestycyjne. Jak nie wpaść w pułapkę (nie)zrównoważonego rozwoju.

Postuła, M., Glinka, B., & Radecka-Moroz, K. (2021). Znaczenie transformacji energetycznej w rozwoju przedsiębiorstw. https://doi.org/10.7172/978-83-235-5538-4.swwz.7.

Postuła, M., & Radecka-Moroz, K. (2021). Fiscal policy instruments in environmental protection. *Environmental Impact Assessment Review*, *84*, 106435. https://doi.org/10.1016/j.eiar.2020.106435.

Puscasu, E. A. (2022). The impact of financial systems on economic growth in European Union member countries. *Proceedings of the International Conference on Business Excellence*, *16*(1), 722–731.

PWC (2021). Droga sektora private equity w kierunku ESG: od zgodności z przepisami do tworzenia wartości. Globalne badanie dotyczące odpowiedzialnego inwestowania w sektorze private equity w 2021r.

PWC (2020). Six key challenges for financial institutions to deal with ESG risks, Compliance and long-term value creation. https://www.pwc.nl/en/insights-and-publications/services-and-industries/financial-sector/six-key-challenges-for-financial-institutions-to-deal-with-ESG-risks.html.

PWC (2023). From threat to opportunity how a tech tipping point is fueling reinvention, resilience and growth. https://www.pwc.com/gx/en/issues/risk-regulation/global-risk-survey.html?WT.mc_id=GMO-CS-NA-FY24-RISK-GRC-T56-CI-XLOS-SUR-GMOCSA00082-EN-OSLI-T1.

PwC (2023a). Managing nature risks: From understanding to action. Available at Managing nature risks: From understanding to action. https://www.pwc.com/gx/en/strategy-and-business/content/sbpwc-2023-04-19-Managing-nature-risks-v2.pdf.

Raddatz, C. (2009). The wrath of God: Macroeconomic costs of natural disasters. *Policy Research Working Paper Series* 5039. The World Bank.

Radulescu, M., Sinisi, C. I., Popescu, C., & Iacob, S. E. (2017). Environmental tax policy in Romania in the context of the EU: Double dividend theory. *Sustainability*, *9*(11), 1–20.

Rahul, R. B., & Anisur, R. (2023). Adaptation to climate change: A study on regional climate change adaptation policy and practice framework. *Journal of Environmental Management*, *336*. https://doi.org/10.1016/j.jenvman.2023.117666.

Rasmussen, L. A., & Conway, H. (2004). Climate and glacier variability in western north America. *Journal of Climate*, *17*, 1804–1815. https://doi.org/10.1175/1520-0442(2004)017<1804:CAGVIW>2.0.CO;2.

Ravetz, J. R. (2006). Post-Normal Science and the complexity of transitions towards sustainability, Ecological Complexity, Volume 3, Issue 4, 2006, Pages 275–284, https://doi.org/10.1016/j.ecocom.2007.02.001

Rehdanz, K. & Maddison, D. (2005). Climate and Happiness. Ecological Economics, *52*, 111–125. http://dx.doi.org/10.1016/j.ecolecon.2004.06.015

Reinhart, C. M., & Rogoff, K. S. (2009). The aftermath of financial crises, American economic review. *American Economic Association*, *99*(2), 466–472.

Riedl, A., & Smeets, P. (2017). Why do investors hold socially responsible mutual funds? *Journal of Finance*, *72*, 2505–2550. https://doi.org/10.1111/jofi.12547.

Roberto Roson & Dominique Van der Mensbrugghe, 2012. "Climate change and economic growth: impacts and interactions," International Journal of Sustainable Economy, Inderscience Enterprises Ltd, vol. 4(3), pp. 270–285.

Rockström, J., Steffen, W., Noone, K., Persson, Å., Chapin, F. S. III, Lambin, E. F., Lenton, T. M., Scheffer, M., Folke, C., Schellnhuber, H. J., & Nykvist, B. (2009). A safe operating space for humanity. *Nature*, *461*, 472–475.

Rokicki, T. (2016). Situation of steel industry in European Union. In Metal 2016: 25th Anniversary International Conference on Metallurgy and Materials. Conference Proceedings. Ostrava: TANGER Ltd., 1981–1986.

Rokicki, T. (2017). Segmentation of the EU countries in terms of the mettalurgical industry, In Metal 2017: 26th Anniversary International Conference on Metallurgy and Materials. Conference Proceedings. Ostrava: TANGER Ltd., 184.

Roson, R., & Sartori, M. (2016). Estimation of Climate Change Damage Functions for 140 Regions in the GTAP 9 Data Base. Journal of Global Economic Analysis, *1*(2), 78–115. https://doi.org/10.21642/JGEA.010202AF

Rousi, E., Selten, F., Rahmstorf, S., & Coumou, D. (2021). Changes in North Atlantic atmospheric circulation in a warmer climate favor winter flooding and summer drought over Europe. *Journal of Climate*, *34*(6), 2277–2295. https://doi.org/10.1175/JCLI-D-20-0311.1.

Russell, J., Rosenthal, D., & Thomson, G. (2010). The international student experience: Three styles of adaptation. *Higher Education*, *60*, 235–249. https://doi.org/10.1007/s10734-009-9297-7.

Russu, C. (2017). Progress and dysfunctionalities in environmental protection in Romania. *Economic Insights – Trends and Challenges*, *6*, 37–44.

Sagar, A. D. and Holdren, J. P. (2002). Assessing the global energy innovation system: some key issues. *Energy Policy*, *30*(6), 465–469.

Sagar, A. D. & van der Zwaan, B. (2006). Technological innovation in the energy sector: R&D, deployment, and learning-by-doing. *Energy Policy*, *34*(17), 2601–2608.

Sahay, R., Cihak, M., N'Diaye, P., Barajas, A., Pena, D. A., Bi, R., Gao, Y., Kyobe, A., Nguyen, L., Saborowski, C., Svirydzenka, K., Yousefi, R. (May 2015). Rethinking Financial Deepening: Stability and Growth in Emerging Markets, IMF Staff Discussion Note SDN/15/08, May 2015, IMF.

Saktiawan, B., Toro, M. J. S., & Saputro, N. (2022). The impact of the Russia-Ukrainian war on green energy financing in Europe, IOP Conference Series: Earth and Environmental Science, Volume 1114, 9th International Conference on Sustainable Agriculture and Environment 24/08/2022 – 25/08/2022 Online. https://doi.org/10.1088/1755-1315/1114/1/012066.

Sanberg, P. R., & Ehrhart, J. A. (2019). Hallmark clinical study of cord blood therapy in adults with ischemic stroke. *Cell Transplantation*, *28*(9–10), 1329–1332. https://doi.org/10.1177/0963689719854354

Sandmo, A. (1976). Optimal taxation: An introduction to the literature. *Journal of Public Economics*, *6*, 37–54. https://doi.org/10.1016/0047-2727(76)90040-2.

Sarvia, F., De Petris, S., & Borgogno Mondino, E. (2021). Multi-scale remote sensing to support insurance policies in agriculture: from mid-term to instantaneous deductions. *GIScience & Remote Sensing*, *57*, 1–15. https://doi.org/10.1080/15481603.2020.1798600.

SBTi (2024). SBTi doubles corporate climate validations in one year as scale up gathers pace, 30 January 2024. https://sciencebasedtargets.org/news/sbti-scale-up-gathers-pace.

Schauer, M. J. (1995). Estimation of the greenhouse gas externality with uncertainty. *Environmental & Resource Economics*, *5*(1), 71–82. https://doi.org/10.1007/BF00691910.

Schneider, B., Godfrey, E. Hayes, S., Huang, M., Nishii, L., Raver, J., & Ziedgert, J. (2003). The human side of strategy. *Organizational Dynamics*, *32*, 122–141. https://doi.org/10.1016/S0090-2616(03)00014-7.

Schoenmaker, D. (2017). Investing for the common good: A sustainable finance framework. Bruegel Essay and Lecture Series. Bruegel. https://www.bruegel.org/sites/default/files/wp_attachments/From-traditional-to-sustainable-finance_ONLINE.pdf.

Schoenmaker, D. & Schramade, W. (2019). *Principles of Sustainable Finance*. Oxford University Press.

Scholtens, B. (2006). Finance as a driver of corporate social responsibility.*Journal of Business Ethics, 68*, 19–33. https://doi.org/10.1007/s10551-006-9037-1 19–33.

Scott, D. L. (2003). *Wall Street Words: An A to Z Guide to Investment Terms for Today's Investor*. Houghton Mifflin Company: Boston.

Sen, A. (1999). *Development as freedom*. New York: Alfred Knopf.

Sen, S., & Vollebergh, H. (2018). The effectiveness of taxing the carbon content of energy consumption. *Journal of Environmental Economics and Management*, *92*, 74–99.

Serafini, G. (2021). Complexity economics and neoclassical economics: A critique. *Chaos and Complexity Letters*, *15*(1), 7–16.

Sewell, W. R. D. & Dales, J. H. (1968). Pollution, property & prices: An essay in policy-making and economics. Toronto: University of Toronto Press, pp. vii, 111. *Canadian Journal of Political Science*. 1969; *2*(3), 386–387. https://doi.org/10.1017/S0008423900025282.

SFDR (2019). Regulation (EU) 2019/2088 of the European Parliament and of the Council of 27 November 2019 on sustainability-related disclosures in the financial services sector.

Shahzad, F., Du, J., Khan, I., Shahbaz, M., Murad, M., & Khan, M. S. S. (2020). Untangling the influence of organizational compatibility on green supply chain management efforts to boost organizational performance through information technology capabilities. *Journal of Cleaner Production*, *266*, 1–13. International Monetary Fund. https://doi.org/10.1016/j.jclepro.2020.122029.

Shih, C., Gwizdalski, A., & Deng, X. (2023). Building a sustainable future: Exploring green finance, regenerative finance, and green financial technology (May 15, 2023). World Scientific Annual Review of Fintech (Forthcoming), Nanyang Business School Research Paper No. 23–18. Available at SSRN: https://ssrn.com/abstract=4449096 or https://doi.org/10.2139/ssrn.4449096.

Shipalana, P., & Chigwenya, C. (2021). The impact of COVID-19 on climate finance and green development. *South African Institute of International Affairs*. Policy Briefing No 233, April 2021. http://www.jstor.org/stable/resrep32593.

Shue, H. (2015). Historical responsibility, harm prohibition, and preservation requirement: Core practical convergence on climate change. *Moral Philosophy and Politics*, *2*(1), 7–31.

Skidmore, M., & Toya, H. (2002). Do natural disasters promote long-run growth? *Economic Inquiry*, *40*, 664–687. https://doi.org/10.1093/ei/40.4.664.

Sleeswijk, A. W., Oers, L. F. C. M. van, Guinée, J. B., Struijs, J., & Hujbregts, M. A. J. (2008). Normalisation in product life cycle assessment: An LCA of the global and European economic systems in the year 2000. *Science of the Total Environment*, *390*, 227–240.

Sobańska-Helman K. & Sieradzan P. (2013). Inwestycje Private Equity/Venture Capital, Wydawnictwo Key Text, Warszawa.

Soukopová, J., & Struk, M. (2011). Methodology for the efficiency evaluation of the municipal environmental protection expenditure. In Joe Turner, A. (Ed.), *International symposium on environmental software systems* (pp. 327–340). Berlin, Heidelberg: Springer.

Spence, A., Poortinga, W., & Pidgeon, N. (2011). The psychological distance of climate change. *Risk Analysis*, *32*(6), 957–972. https://doi.org/10.1111/j.1539-6924.2011.01695.x

Stainer, L. (2006). Performance management and corporate social responsibility: The strategic connection. *Strategic Change*, *15*, 253–264, https://doi.org/10.1002/jsc.761.

Stanners, D. A., & Bourdeau, P. (1995). *Europe's environment: The Dobris assessment*. Bourdeau: Office for Official Publications of the European Communities.

Stern, N. (2007). The economics of climate change - The Stern review. *The American Economic Review*, *98*(2), 1–37.

Stern, N. (2015). Economic development, climate and values: making policy. *Royal Society*, *282*(1812), 20150820. http://doi.org/10.1098/rspb.2015.0820.

Stern, N., & Stiglitz, J. (2021). The social cost of carbon, risk, distribution, market failures: An alternative approach. NBER Working Paper 28472.

Sterner, T. (2007). Fuel taxes: An important instrument for climate policy. *Energy Policy*, *35*(6), 3194–3202. https://www.sciencedirect.com/science/article/abs/pii/S0301421506004113.

Steve, Y. S., Murad, A. B., Gyamfi, B. A., Bekun, F. V., & Uzuner, G. (2022). Renewable energy consumption a panacea for sustainable economic growth: Panel causality analysis for African blocs. *International Journal of Green Energy*, *19*(8), 847–856. https://doi.org/10.1080/15435075.2021.1966793.

Stewart, R. B., Oppenheimer, M., & Rudyk, B. (2013). Building blocks for global climate protection. *Stanford Environmental Law Journal*, *32*(2), 12–43. *NYU Law and Economics Research Paper* No. 12–43. Available at SSRN: https://ssrn.com/abstract=2186541 or https://doi.org/10.2139/ssrn.2186541.

Stolowy, H., & Paugam, L. (2018). The expansion of non-financial reporting: An exploratory study. *Accounting and Business Research*, *48*(5), 525–548. https://doi.org/10.1080/00014788.2018.1470141.

Strambo, C., Nilsson, M., & Månsson, A. (2015). Coherent or inconsistent? Assessing energy security and climate policy interaction within the European Union. *Energy Research & Social Science*, *8*, 1–12.
Stuart, D., Petersen, B., & Gunderson, R. (2022). Shared pretenses for collective inaction: The economic growth imperative, COVID-19, and climate change. *Globalizations*, *19*(3), 408–425. https://doi.org/10.1080/14747731.2021.1943897.
Svirydzenka, K. (2016). Introducing a new broad-based index of financial development. *IMF Working Paper, WP/16/5*.
Szarowska, I. (2011). Relationship between government spending and economic growth in the Czech Republic. *Acta Universitatis Agriculturae et Silviculturae Mendelianae Brunensis 59*, 415–422. https://doi.org/10.11118/actaun201159070415.
Taconet, N., Méjean, A., & Guivarch, C. (2020). Influence of climate change impacts and mitigation costs on inequality between countries. *Climatic Change*, *160*, 15–34. https://doi.org/10.1007/s10584-019-02637-w.
Taghizadeh-Hesary, F., Yoshino, N., & Phoumin, H. (2021). Analyzing the characteristics of green bond markets to facilitate green finance in the post-COVID-19 world. *Sustainability*, *13*(10), 5719. https://doi.org/10.3390/su13105719.
Takakura, J., Fujimori, S., Hanasaki, N. et al. Publisher Correction: Dependence of economic impacts of climate change on anthropogenically directed pathways. Nat. Clim. Chang. 9, 894 (2019). https://doi.org/10.1038/s41558-019-0617-3
Taliento, M., Favino, C., & Netti, A. (2019). Impact of environmental, social, and governance information on economic performance: Evidence of a corporate 'sustainability advantage from Europe'. *Sustainability*, *11*(6), 1738. https://doi.org/10.3390/su11061738.
Talvi, E., & Vegh, C. A. (2005). Tax base variability and procyclical fiscal policy in developing countries. *Journal of Development Economics*, *78*(1), 156–190.
Tamowicz, P. (2007). Business angels. Pomocna dłoń kapitału, Polska Agencja Rozwoju Przedsiębiorczości, Gdańsk.
Tang, D. Y., & Zhang, Y. (2018). Do shareholders benefit from green bonds? *Journal of Corporate Finance*, *61*. https://doi.org/10.1016/j.jcorpfin.2018.12.001.
Tanimoto, K. (2004). Changes in the market society and corporate social responsibility. *Asian Business & Management*, *3*, 151–172. https://doi.org/10.1057/palgrave.abm.9200087.
Taramelli, A., Tornato, A., Magliozzi, M. L., Mariani, S., Valentini, E., Zavagli, M., Costantini, M., Nieke, J., Adams, J., & Rast, M. (2020). An interaction methodology to collect and assess user-driven requirements to define potential opportunities of future hyperspectral imaging sentinel mission. *Remote Sensing*, *12*, 1286. https://doi.org/10.3390/rs12081286.
Tarmuji, I., Maelah, R., & Tarmuji, N. H. (2016). The impact of environmental, social and governance practices (ESG) on economic performance: Evidence from ESG Score. *International Journal of Trade, Economics and Finance*, *7*(3), 67–74.
Tartamella, F., Chillura, A., Pisano, M. F., Cacioppo, A., Licari, S., Caradonna, D., Portaro, S., Calabrò, R. S., Bramanti, P., & Naro, A. (2020). A case report on intensive, robot-assisted rehabilitation program for brainstem radionecrosis. *Medicine*, *99*, e19517. https://doi.org/10.1097/MD.0000000000019517.
Taylor, M. (2008). Beyond technology-push and demand-pull: Lessons from California's solar policy. *Energy Economics*, *30*(6), 2829–2854.
Taylor, M., & Tam, C., & Gielen, D. (2006). *Energy efficiency and CO2 emissions from the global cement industry*. Energy Efficiency and CO_2 Emission Reduction Potentials and Policies in the Cement Industry, IEA, Paris, 4-5 September 2006.

Thompson, S. (2023). *Green and sustainable finance: Principles and practice in banking, investment and insurance*. London: Kogan Page.

Timilsina, G. R. (2018). Where is the carbon tax after thirty years of research? (June 28, 2018). World Bank Policy Research Working Paper No. 8493, Available at SSRN: https://ssrn.com/abstract=3238331.

Tol, R. (1995). 'The damage costs of climate change: Towards more comprehensive estimates. *Environmental and Resource Economics*, *5*, 353–374.

Tol, R. (1999). Spatial and temporal efficiency in climate policy: Applications of FUND. *Environmental and Resource Economics*, *14*(1), 33–49.

Tol, R. (2002a). Estimates of damage costs of climate change. Part I: Benchmark estimates. *Environmental and Resource Economics*, *21*, 47–73. https://doi.org/10.1023/A:1014500930521.

Tol, R. (2002b). Estimates of the damage costs of climate change. Part 2: dynamic estimates. *Environmental and Resource Economics*, *21*, 135–160.

Tol, R. (2014). Correction and update: The economic effects of climate change. *Journal of Economic Perspectives*, *28*(2), 221–226.

Tol, R. (2022). A Meta-analysis of the total economic impact of climate change. *CESifo Working Paper Series* 9919, CESifo.

Tol, R., & Vellinga, P. (1998). Climate change, the enhanced greenhouse effect and the influence of the sun: A statistical analysis. *Theoretical and Applied Climatology*, *61*, 1–7. https://doi.org/10.1007/s007040050046.

Tollefson, J. (2022). Climate change is hitting the planet faster than scientists originally thought. *Nature*, February 28. https://doi.org/10.1038/d41586-022-00585-7. Epub ahead of print. PMID: 35228735.

Tornell, A., & Lane, P. R. (1999). The voracity effect. *American Economic Review*, *89*(1), 22–46.

Tosun, O. K. (11 December 2019). Differences in CEO compensation under large and small institutional ownership. *European Financial Management*. https://doi.org/10.1111/eufm.12252.

Toth, J., & Concini, A. (2019). *The future of the European space sector – How to leverage Europe's technological leadership and boost investments for space ventures – Executive summary*. European Investment Bank. https://data.europa.eu/doi/10.2867/497151.

UN (1987). Brundtland Report. 1987: Brundtland Report (admin.ch).

UN (1995). Supplement to an Agenda for peace: Position paper of the Secretary-General on the occasion of the 50th anniversary of the United Nations. https://digitallibrary.un.org/record/168325.

UN (2023). The Sustainable Development Goals Report. Special edition. 2023, https://unstats.un.org/sdgs/report/2023/The-Sustainable-Development-Goals-Report-2023.pdf.

UN (2014). System of Environmental-Economic Accounting 2012 Central Framework seea_cf_final_en.pdf (un.org).

UN Biodiversity (2024). https://www.un.org/sustainabledevelopment/biodiversity/.

UN Climate Change (2024). https://www.un.org/sustainabledevelopment/climate-change/.

UN Energy (2024). https://www.un.org/sustainabledevelopment/energy/.

Un Environment – World Bank Group Initiative (2017). Roadmap for a Sustainable Financial System. http://documents.worldbank.org/curated/en/903601510548466486/pdf/121283-12-11-2017-15-33-33-RoadmapforaSustainableFinancialSystem.pdf.

UN Health (2024). https://www.un.org/sustainabledevelopment/health/.

UN NEWS (2023). WHO chief declares end to COVID-19 as a global health emergency. https://news.un.org/en/story/2023/05/1136367.

UN Oceans (2024). https://www.un.org/sustainabledevelopment/oceans/.

UNCC (2023). United Nations climate change, annual report 2022. https://unfccc.int/sites/default/files/resource/UNClimateChange_AnnualReport_2022.pdf.

UNCTAD (2023). World investment report 2023, investing in sustainable energy for all, United Nations, Geneva, p. 122. https://unctad.org/system/files/official-document/wir2023_en.pdf.

UNDP (2020). Implications of the COVID-19 pandemic for global sustainable finance: An initial framework for response strategies. https://wedocs.unep.org/handle/20.500.11822/32465.

UNEP FI (2016). Connecting financial system and sustainable development, market leadership paper. http://unepfi.org/wordpress/wp-content/uploads/2016/11/MKT-LEADERSHIP-REPORT-AW-WEB.pdf.

UNFCCC Standing Committee on Finance (2014). Biennial assessment and overview of climate finance flows report. 2014_biennial_assessment_and_overview_of_climate_finance_flows_report_web.pdf (unfccc.int).

United Nations (2015). Transforming our world: The 2030 Agenda for sustainable development. https://unstats.un.org/sdgs/indicators/database/.

United Nations (2023). The sustainable development goals report. Special edition. https://unstats.un.org/sdgs/report/2023/The-Sustainable-Development-Goals-Report-2023.pdf.

Ürge-Vorsatz, D., Herrero, S., Dubash, N. K., & Lecocq, F. (2014). Measuring the co-benefits of climate change mitigation. *Annual Review of Environment and Resources*, *39*, 549–582. Available at SSRN: https://ssrn.com/abstract=2514306 or https://doi.org/10.1146/annurev-environ-031312-125456.

US Country Studies Program (1999). *Climate change mitigation, vulnerability and adaptation in developing and transition countries*. Washington, DC.

Vanino, E., Roper, S., & Becker, B. (2019). Knowledge to money: Assessing the business performance effects of publicly-funded R&D grants. *Research Policy*, *48*(7), 1714–1737, ISSN 0048-7333, https://doi.org/10.1016/j.respol.2019.04.001.

Vehmas, J. (2005). Energy-related taxation as an environmental policy tool--the Finnish experience 1990–2003. *Energy Policy, Elsevier*, *33*(17), 2175–2182. November.

Vehmas, J. (2003). Global trends of linking environmental stress and economic growth. *Turku School of Economics and Busies Administration*, *18*, 55–60.

Vismara S. (2019). Sustainability in equity crowdfunding, Technological Forecasting and Social Change, 141, April 2019, https://doi.org/10.1016/j.techfore.2018.07.014.

Wang, A., Melton, A. E., Soltis, D. E., & Soltis, P. S. (2022). Potential distributional shifts in North America of allelopathic invasive plant species under climate change models. *Plant Diversity*, *44*(1), 11–19.

Wang, Y., & Zhi, Q. (2016). The role of green finance in environmental protection: Two aspects of market mechanism and policies. *Energy Procedia*, *104*, 311–316. https://doi.org/10.1016/j.egypro.2016.12.053.

Webb, M. J., Andrews, T., Bodas-Salcedo, A., Bony, S., Bretherton, C. S., Chadwick, R., Chepfer, H., Douville, H., Good, P., Kay, J. E., Klein, S. A., Marchand, R., Medeiros, B., Siebesma, A. P., Skinner, C. B., Stevens, B., Tselioudis, G., Tsushima, Y., & Watanabe, M. (2017). The cloud feedback model intercomparison project (CFMIP) contribution to CMIP6. *Geoscientific Model Development*, *10*, 359–384. https://doi.org/10.5194/gmd-10-359-2017.

Weitzman, M. L. (2009). On modeling and interpreting the economics of catastrophic climate change. *Review of Economics and Statistics*, *91*(1), 1–19.

Welsch, H., & Ebert, U. (2004). Meaningful environmental indices: A social choice approach. *Journal of Environmental Economics and Management*, *47*(2), 270–283.

West, S., & Williams, R. (2004). Estimates from a consumer demand system: Implications for the incidence of environmental taxes. *Journal of Environmental Economics and Management*, *47*(3), 535–558. https://www.sciencedirect.com/science/article/abs/pii/S0095069603001384.

Weston, P., & Nnadi, M. (2023). Evaluation of strategic and financial variables of corporate sustainability and ESG policies on corporate finance performance. *Journal of Sustainable Finance & Investment*, *13*, 1058–1074.

Wier, M., Birr-Pedersen, K., Klinge Jacobsen, H., & Klok, J. (2005). Are CO2 taxes regressive? Evidence from the Danish experience. *Ecological Economics*, *52*(2), 239–251. https://EconPapers.repec.org/RePEc:eee:ecolec:v:52:y:2005:i:2:p:239-251.

Wigley, T. M. L., & Harvey, L. D. D. (2003). Characterizing and comparing control-run variability of eight coupled AOGCMs and of observations. Part 1: Temperature. *Climate Dynamics*, *21*, 619–646. https://doi.org/10.1007/s00382-003-0357-x

Wilkin, K. M., Holland, V. L., Keil, D., & Schaffner, A. (2013). Mimicking fire for successful chaparral restoration. *Madroño*, *60*(3), 165–172. https://doi.org/10.3120/0024-9637-60.3.165.

Wilkin, K. M., Ackerly, D. D., & Stephens, D. D. (2016). Climate change refugia, fire ecology and management. *Forests*, *7*(4), 77. https://doi.org/10.3390/f7040077.

Wissema, W., & Dellink, R. (2007). AGE analysis of the impact of a carbon energy tax on the Irish economy. *Ecological Economics*, *61*, 671–683.

Woo, J. (2009). Why do more polarized countries run more procyclical fiscal policy? *The Review of Economics and Statistics*, *91*(4), 850–870.

Word bank, (2014) Global Commission on the Economy and Climate, Washington Title (worldbank.org).

World Bank (2019). Reducing income inequality. Making transition work for everyone. http://web.worldbank.org/archive/website00504/WEB/PDF/CHAPTE-2.PDF

Wu, L., Liu, D., & Lin, T. (2023). The impact of climate change on financial stability. *Sustainability*, *15*(15), 11744. https://doi.org/10.3390/su151511744.

Yan, X., & Crookes, R. J. (2009). Life cycle analysis of energy use and greenhouse gas emissions for road transportation fuels in China. *Renewable and Sustainable Energy Reviews*, *13*, 2505–2514. https://doi.org/10.1016/j.rser.2009.06.012

Yohe, G., & Parmesan, C. (2003). A globally coherent fingerprint of climate change impacts across natural systems. *Nature*, *421*(6918), 37–42.

Yohe, Gary & Andronova, Natalia & Schlesinger, Michael. (2004). To Hedge or Not Against an Uncertain Climate Future?. Science (New York, N.Y.). 306. 416–7. 10.1126/science.1101170

Zeng, K. W., Wen, J. Y., Cheng, S. J., Lu, E., & Wang, N. (2014). Critical line identification of complex power system in cascading failure. *Proceedings of the Chinese Society for Electrical Engineering*, *34*, 1103–1111.

Zerbib, O. D. (2019). The effect of pro-environmental preferences on bond prices: Evidence from green bonds. *Journal of Banking and Finance*, *98*, 39–60.

Zhang, Y., Ma, Q., Chen, Y., & Gao, H. (2017). Effects of public hospital reform on inpatient expenditures in rural China. *Health Economics*, *26*(4), 421–430.

Zharfpeykan, R., & Ng, F. (2021). COVID-19 and sustainability reporting: What are the roles of reporting frameworks in a crisis? *Pacific Accounting Review*, *33*(2), 189–198. https://doi.org/10.1108/PAR-09-2020-0169.

Ziemba, M. (2023). Sustainable finance – where we are and how we can go further. *Journal of Finance and Financial Law*, *1*(37), 123–137. https://doi.org/10.18778/2391-6478.1.37.07.

Zioło, Z. (2020). *Finanse zrównoważone, Rozwój*. Ryzyko. Rynek, PWE, Warszawa-Szczecin.

Zioło, M., Spoz, A., Kuklińska-Sadłocha, E. (2021). Zrównoważone rynki finansowe. Perspektywa krajowa i międzynarodowa. Polskie Wydawnictwo Ekonomiczne.

Index

Note: **Bold** page numbers refer to tables and *italic* page numbers refer to figures.